American Christians and the National Interreligious Task Force on Soviet Jewry

American Christians and the National Interreligious Task Force on Soviet Jewry

A Call to Conscience

Fred A. Lazin

LEXINGTON BOOKS
Lanham • Boulder • New York • London

Published by Lexington Books
An imprint of The Rowman & Littlefield Publishing Group, Inc.
4501 Forbes Boulevard, Suite 200, Lanham, Maryland 20706
www.rowman.com

6 Tinworth Street, London SE11 5AL

Copyright © 2019 by The Rowman & Littlefield Publishing Group, Inc.

All rights reserved. No part of this book may be reproduced in any form or by any electronic or mechanical means, including information storage and retrieval systems, without written permission from the publisher, except by a reviewer who may quote passages in a review.

British Library Cataloguing in Publication Information Available

Library of Congress Cataloging-in-Publication Data

ISBN: 978-1-4985-8323-7 (cloth)
ISBN: 978-1-4985-8324-4 (electronic)
ISBN: 978-1-4985-8325-1 (pbk.)

Dedicated to Rachel Dabi Lazin,
whose encouragement, interest, and support made
this scholarly effort possible.

Contents

Acknowledgments ix

1 Introduction 1
2 Vatican II: A Revolution in Catholic Jewish Relations and the Appearance of the "New Nuns" 15
3 Establishing the Task Force 31
4 The Early Years of the Task Force 57
5 The Brussels II Conference 97
6 The Helsinki Accords and Persecuted Christians in the Soviet Union 111
7 International Conferences and the Interreligious Legal Task Force on Human Rights 145
8 Continuity and Change in the Mid-1980s—An Alliance with Evangelical Protestants 171
9 Closing the Task Force 197
10 Conclusion: The Contribution of Sister Ann Gillen and the Task Force to the American Advocacy Movement for Soviet Jewry 219

Appendix 227
List of Abbreviations 229
Bibliography 233
Index 237
About the Author 253

Acknowledgments

After relocating to New York City in the summer of 2008 for my final sabbatical from Ben Gurion University in Israel, I decided to conduct an in-depth study of the role of the American Jewish Committee (AJC) in the Soviet Jewry advocacy movement. In my previous research (Lazin 2005) I had learned of the AJC's important contribution to advocacy efforts on behalf of Soviet Jewry during the 1970s and '80s. Several AJC leaders and professionals held important leadership and staff positions in the National Conference on Soviet Jewry (NCSJ).

AJC officials welcomed my research and gave me access to their in-house library and archives. To my surprise, many of the most interesting materials dealt with the National Interreligious Task Force on Soviet Jewry led by Sister Ann Gillen of the Society of the Holy Child Jesus (SHCJ), which the AJC had co-founded with the National Catholic Council for Interracial Justice (NCCIJ). Around 2012, I decided to focus my research on the Task Force.

AJC librarian, Michelle Anish, helped me locate relevant documents. After the AJC closed the in-house library, the head archivist at AJC, Charlotte Bonelli, and her two assistants, Desiree Guillermo and Cuc Huong Do, assisted my search for relevant documents and provided an hospitable research environment which hosted me for many, many months.

I made several trips to the archives of the Society of the Holy Child Jesus in Rosemont, Pennsylvania. Several sisters religious who worked in the library/archive building helped me with the personal papers of Sister Ann Gillen and documents relating to the Task Force. I have a fond memory of being picked up at the railroad station in Rosemont by Sister Gloria Coleman, aged eighty-five at the time, who drove me to the SHCJ archives. During several visits and phone conversations, she shared recollections of her experiences with Sister Ann in advocacy efforts on behalf of Soviet Jewry. She also related her own story of advocacy for Soviet Jewry.

The archives of the Task Force are located in the Spertus Institute in Chicago. Financial difficulties, however, had closed the archives to the public. With the help of my friend, Peter Friedman (we were graduate students together at the University of Chicago), I received the full cooperation of Kathy Bloch, director of collections at Spertus. She arranged for Joy Kingsolver to assist me. Joy's knowledge of the Task Force files proved invaluable.

The research for this book benefited from my several years as a visiting scholar at the Taub Center for Israel Studies at New York University. The director, Professor Ron Zweig, encouraged me and the Center's administrator Shayne Leslie Figueroa facilitated my scholarly pursuits. The affiliation with NYU also gave me access to Evelyn Ehrlich, a NYU professional research librarian, whose vast knowledge of relevant sources benefited my research efforts. I also profited from conversations about my project with my friend and NYU colleague Professor Hasia Diner.

At the Dorot Jewish Division at the New York Public Library, where I have been doing research since my undergraduate days at UMASS, librarian Eleanor Yadin provided critical assistance. Phil Runkel, an archivist at Marquette University, found relevant papers of Sister Margaret Traxler. At the offices of the Anti-Defamation League (ADL), Rabbi David Sandmel provided important correspondence relating to the Task Force and John Demjanjuk.

I am indebted to each and every person who agreed to be interviewed for this research project. Several provided a great deal of information and insights about Sister Gillen and the Task Force. I owe a special thanks to Professor Thomas Bird, Sister Gloria Coleman, Eugene DuBow, Professor Eugene Fisher, Jerry Goodman, Dr. Kent Hill, Father John Pawlikowski, and Rabbi James Rudin.

A few years ago, Professor Edward Xu of Fudan University in Shanghai, China, invited me to lecture about the Task Force to his graduate course on religion in America. Preparation for the lectures, along with the interaction with his students, helped me to begin to organize the writing up of the research.

I am indebted to Professor Rivka Carmi, president of Ben Gurion University, who approved my access to Ben Gurion University research and travel funds, which enabled me to pursue the research project and the writing of the manuscript. The confidence that she and other colleagues at Ben Gurion University had in my research motivated me to finish the project.

Sima Rabinowitz, a professional writer and editor, assisted me in preparing the book proposal and the manuscript for publication. Most importantly, she served as a sounding board for many of my thoughts during a crucial stage of final revision. Her insights proved invaluable. She also improved the quality of the manuscript.

An anonymous reviewer for Lexington Books provided important insights, suggestions, and encouragement.

My two grandchildren, Carmen Belle Lazin and Arielle S. Regev, provide my inspiration to continue scholarly pursuits. I hope that they will live in a better world than currently exists.

Finally, I owe a special thanks to my wife, Rachel, whose love makes so much possible. Her support, interest, and confidence in me helped me to write this book. It is dedicated to her.

ONE
Introduction

Paradoxically, upon establishment of independence in 1948, Israeli leaders immediately faced an existential threat to the new Jewish State's existence—a population insufficient to ensure both the survival of the State and its Jewish majority. Early in the 1950s, they established a Liaison Bureau (*Lishkat Hakesher*) to promote immigration of the Soviet Union's three million Jews locked up behind Stalin's Iron Curtain, where they lacked religious and cultural freedoms (Buwalda 1997, 35). Initially, the Bureau fostered Jewish identity and culture among Soviet Jews, as well as contact with Israel.[1] A second branch of the Bureau, code-named *Bar*, organized in 1955, tried to influence Western governments to pressure the Soviet Union to allow its Jews to emigrate (Levanon 1999, 73).[2]

Liaison Bureau operatives believed that the American government had the greatest potential to exert leverage with the Soviets and they encouraged American Jewish organizations to influence their government to press the Soviet authorities on the issue.[3] From the start of its efforts in the United States, the Bureau valued the involvement of non-Jews. When Moshe Decter, the Bureau's sole American "agent," drafted a letter to Soviet Premier Nikita Khrushchev asking for an end to discrimination against the Jews, application of the same cultural rights enjoyed by other minorities and family reunification outside the Soviet Union, he had the letter signed by Eleanor Roosevelt, Supreme Court Justice William O. Douglas, former head of the Legal Defense Fund of the National Association for the Advancement of Colored People Thurgood Marshall, and Protestant theologian Reinhold Niebuhr.[4]

By 1970, the Israeli Liaison Bureau argued that the success of American advocacy efforts on behalf of Soviet Jews would not only benefit from but, in fact, required the participation of Christians. The Israelis feared that an exclusively Jewish effort would not convince the American government to act. They encouraged organizations, among them the American Jewish Committee (AJC), to foster greater involvement of Christian Americans in advocacy efforts.

Early in 1971, the Chicago office of the AJC identified a potentially important ally: Sister Margaret Ellen Traxler, executive director of the National Catholic Conference on Interracial Justice (NCCIJ). She had publicly urged American Catholics to protest the convictions of a group of Soviet Jews who, denied the right to emigrate legally, had attempted to hijack a small plane at Smolny airport outside of Leningrad. On learning of her efforts, AJC staff invited Sister Margaret Traxler to lunch.[5] Their initial meeting led to a series of discussions and negotiations and, the following year, to the establishment of the National Interreligious Task Force on Soviet Jewry (NITFSJ, Task Force).[6]

The Task Force sponsors—the NCCIJ and the AJC—were, respectively, an American Catholic lay organization committed to racial justice and an American Jewish organization dedicated to protecting the rights of Jews in the United States and abroad.[7] The timing was right for just such a coalition. The AJC had been involved with the plight of Soviet Jews since the mid-1940s and now faced pressure from Israel's Liaison Bureau to intensify its efforts. Two significant historical events in the Roman Catholic Church paved the way for Christian advocacy on behalf of Soviet Jewry.

The first of these was Vatican II, convened by Pope John XXIII in October 1962. While the Pope's principal concern was Christian unity and "spiritual renewal of the Church," Vatican II also addressed the issue of the Church and the Jews with the broader aim of helping the Church speak "more intelligibly to all faiths" (Feldman 2001, 104).[8] The Pope had met earlier that year with French Jewish sociologist Jules Isaac, author of multiple publications about the Holocaust and the origins of negative Christian attitudes toward the Jews.[9] Isaac argued that Christian teachings provided a fertile environment for the Final Solution and that "Catholics shared the basic assumptions of the Nazis that Jews were fated to suffer punishment" (Connelly 2012, 171–173).[10] The Pope accepted Isaac's proposal that Vatican II address the issue of the Church and anti-Semitism and asked Cardinal Bea, the newly appointed President of Secretariat for Promotion of Christian Unity, to prepare a document on Catholic-Jewish relations for the forthcoming Vatican Council.[11]

On October 28, 1965, Vatican II enacted *Nostra Aetate* (In Our Time), a "Declaration on the Relations of the Church to Non-Christian Religions," by a vote of 2,221 in favor and 88 opposed (Connelly 2012, 1).[12] The fourth section of the document affirmed the bond of Christianity to the Jewish people, Christianity's debt to Judaism, and recognized the legitimacy of the Jewish faith (Rudin 2012, 110 and Tanenbaum 1986, 48).[13] The document absolved the Jews of deicide and rejected all forms of prejudice and anti-Semitism (Feldman 2001, 106; Rudin 2012, 110 and

Sanua 2007, 124).[14] *Nostra Aetate* "made possible a new level of religious tolerance for non-Catholic traditions" and issued an unprecedented call for dialogue without a call to conversion and the need to turn to Christ for salvation (Tanenbaum 1986, 48 and Connelly 2012, 1–3).[15]

Nostra Aetate revolutionized the Church's attitude toward the Jews, marking a "radical break with nineteen hundred years of church history" (Sanua 2007, 127). Most significantly, the declaration had a tremendous impact on Catholic Jewish relations in the United States, while, at the same time, positively influencing Jewish-Protestant and Catholic-Protestant relations and setting the stage for the involvement of Catholic and Protestant clergy in the advocacy movement for Soviet Jewry.[16] Clearly, *Nostra Aetate* put the issue of Jews and anti-Semitism on the agenda of some Catholic clergy, sisters religious, and laypersons.

A second series of events in the Church would prove to be no less important—changes in the life style and working environment of Catholic sisters religious in the United States. Beginning in the 1940s, many orders of sisters underwent a transition from confinement to a narrow Catholic universe (i.e. the "closed" convent and work assignments exclusively in Catholic schools or hospitals) to engagement with the broader American society. In the 1950s, in response to pressure from the National Catholic Education Association (NCEA), Pope Pius XII issued reforms to modernize or eliminate "outdated customs and to improve the educational level of religious in teaching institutions" (Koehlinger 2007, 31–24).[17] Subsequently, Vatican II further loosened restrictive regulations and favored reforms in the activities of sisters religious, which led to more relevant missions (apostolates) (Henold 2008, 10). The ideology of the new nuns in the 1960s immersed sisters directly in "the most urgent problems of society, particularly racial and economic justice" (Koehlinger 2007, 22 and Borromeo, C.S.C. 1967).

During the early 1960s as director of the education department of the NCCIJ, Sister Margaret Traxler fostered apostolate work with African American children in the inner city and encouraged participation in civil rights activities and actions, including the march in Selma, Alabama in 1965.[18] The stage was set for Catholic engagement in interracial and interfaith activism on a wider scale.

THE NATIONAL INTERRELIGIOUS TASK FORCE ON SOVIET JEWRY

This book is about the role of Christian Americans, sisters religious, clergy, and laypersons in the American struggle for Soviet Jewry during the 1970s and 1980s and the transformation of the American advocacy movement for Soviet Jewry from an exclusively Jewish concern to a multi-religious effort. While focusing on the plight of Soviet Jews, the activist

Christians also advocated for persecuted Christians and dissidents with a growing emphasis on human rights. The primary focus of the book is the National Interreligious Task Force on Soviet Jewry (the Task Force) and its executive director, Sister Ann Gillen of the Society of the Holy Child Jesus (SHCJ). A major actor in the movement, the Task Force succeeded in making Soviet Jewry an issue of concern for many non-Jewish Americans, which, ultimately, helped persuade the Congress and the White House to exert pressure on the Soviet Union regarding their treatment of, and policies pertaining to, its Jewish citizens.

This study documents the activities undertaken by the Task Force on behalf of Jews and other persecuted groups in the Soviet Union from its inception in 1972 through its closure by the AJC in May 1988 and considers important questions about the Task Force's efficacy and impact. In what ways did the Task Force influence the general Jewish advocacy movement for Soviet Jewry in the United States and how significant was its effect? Did the Task Force alter the general advocacy effort and in what way? Was the Task Force accepted by mainstream and grass roots Jewish advocacy groups? What was the response of Christian clergy, leaders, and laypersons to the Task Force? Did the Task Force make a difference in the advocacy effort on behalf of Soviet Jewry?

While initially sponsored by the NCCIJ and the AJC, the Catholic Conference abandoned the project within a year or two of its founding and the AJC became its primary sponsor, providing funding, administrative support, and supervision. While it sometimes appeared to be a "front organization" for the AJC, as will be shown in this study, Sister Gillen and the Task Force operated with a significant degree of autonomy.

Although the Task Force founders had hoped to create an extensive and sustained working group of Catholic, Protestant, and Jewish theologians to lead and participate in efforts to fight against the persecution of Jews in the Soviet Union, such a group never materialized.[19] The Task Force remained, instead, a small organization run by Sister Gillen with a few active board members and AJC staff in the Interreligious Affairs Department (IAD) and local offices in different cities, which played supportive roles.

Based and active in Chicago, the Task Force also operated in NYC and Washington, D.C. and conducted activities in communities across the country, as well as in Western Europe, at the Vatican, in Israel, and in the Soviet Union, where Sister Gillen developed personal ties to a number of Jewish and Christian prisoners of conscience.[20] Task Force delegations participated in Security and Cooperation in Europe (CSCE) conferences in Belgrade, Madrid, and elsewhere, which dealt with implementation of the Helsinki Accords; testified before Congressional committees and lobbied officials in the State Department and the White House; and participated in international gatherings of advocacy activists working on behalf of Soviet Jewry. Task Force members participated in annual spring Solidarity Sunday events held around the country, successfully recruiting Christian participants and Christian keynote speakers on occasion.

During the 1970s, the Task Force established local task forces with Catholic, mainline and evangelical Protestants, the Greek Orthodox Church, and Jewish clergy and laypersons in communities throughout the country. Most of these groups remained independent but cooperated with directives from Sister Gillen and collaborated on Task Force programs. Sister Gillen and the Task Force maintained good relations with both major American Jewish umbrella organizations advocating for Soviet Jewry, the National Conference on Soviet Jewry (NCSJ), and the Union of Councils for Soviet Jewry (UCSJ). She spoke many times at NCSJ national meetings and collaborated with them on joint activities. Later, she became more involved with the grass roots UCSJ with which she was officially affiliated; she identified with their activist, non-establishment orientation. The Task Force also collaborated with Community Relations Councils (CRCs) affiliated with local Jewish Federations and with the National Jewish Community Relations Advisory Council (NJCRAC).

While throughout its existence the Task Force and Sister Gillen focused primarily on the plight of Jews in the Soviet Union, they also expressed concern for persecuted Christians and dissidents in the USSR, including Adventists, Evangelicals, and Ukrainian and Lithuanian Catholics. Passage of the Helsinki Accords in 1975, signed by representatives of the United States, the Soviet Union, Canada, and thirty-two European nations, recognized European borders established at the end of World War II and contained a set of human rights, including emigration for family reunification. The Accords enabled foreign individuals and organizations to become involved in what had previously been considered an internal Soviet matter. In effect, the Accords shifted the focus of the struggle for Soviet Jewry more to one of human rights, lending support to the position of the Task Force protesting the persecution of Jews, Christians, and dissidents in the USSR. The Task Force led the way in this universal struggle on behalf of human rights for all religiously persecuted persons in the Soviet Union. It remained active in diverse advocacy efforts on behalf of Soviet Jews, Christians, and what, at the time, were called "captive nations" (the populations of the Baltic countries—Latvia, Lithuania, and Estonia, annexed by the Soviet Union prior to WWII, the countries of Eastern Europe occupied by the Soviets after WWII, and the Ukraine.) [21] AJC closed down the Task Force on May 31, 1988.

SIGNIFICANCE AND THEMATIC CONTENT

This book, the first in-depth examination of the role and influence of American Christians in the advocacy efforts for Soviet Jewry, expands on

Egal Feldman's (1990, 2001) scholarly inquiry into relations between American Jews and Christians. Feldman examined the long history between Jews and Protestants and Jews and Catholics in the United States. His research focuses on the theological issues that divided Judaism, Roman Catholicism, and the various mainline and evangelical Protestant churches in the United States. His second book focuses on how Vatican II revolutionized Catholic theology as it relates to Jews and Judaism and shows how Vatican II resulted in honest dialogue between Jews and Catholics in the United States. In both books, Feldman considers the ways in which the various American Christian faiths have responded to the Holocaust, establishment of Israel in 1948, the subsequent 1967 War, and the reunification of Jerusalem. His focus is on the theological implications of these events for the Christian faiths.

The work here documents how American Christians, Catholics, mainline and evangelical Protestants, and members of the Greek Orthodox Church interacted with American Jews to prevent the annihilation of the cultural and religious identity of Jews in the Soviet Union. This study presents the details, and elucidates the nuances, of the complex interreligious relations and interactions between American Jews and the many groups of Christians in the 1970s and 1980s. It points out the initial dominant role of the Catholics, the active leadership of sisters religious, the ambivalent stand of the mainline Protestant NCC, and the later activism of the Evangelicals.

Most of the studies—of which there are quite a number—about the American advocacy effort for Soviet Jewry barely mention the involvement of Christian Americans (Beckerman 2010, Feingold 2006, Friedman and Chernin 1999, Goldberg 1996 and Orbach 1969). Lazin (2005, 66) includes one endnote referring to Sister Ann Gillen, the Task Force, its sponsors and activities. Spiegel (2008, 295–325) has a chapter on American Christian and Jewish clergy, which provides brief vignettes of Christian activists, including Sisters Gillen and Margaret Traxler. Neither book provides an in-depth presentation on the role and contribution of the Task Force and American Christians in the American Advocacy movement for Soviet Jewry.

It will be argued here that Christian clergy and laypersons played a more significant role in the success of the American advocacy movement for Soviet Jewry than is understood in the existing literature. Most accounts present the Soviet Jewry movement in the United States as a Jewish success story which rescued millions of Jews in contrast to the failure of American Jewry to save European Jews during the Nazi Holocaust (Lazin 1979 and Morse 1968). Rather than being an exclusively American Jewish effort, the advocacy for Soviet Jewry reflected an interreligious effort of Christians and Jews with the latter in the majority and in the lead. In the case study here, two Roman Catholic sisters religious initiated the interreligious effort with the AJC. They were joined by mainline Protestants and much later by the Evangelicals.

Here the author uses a case study—the story of the Task Force from its inception to its closure—to better understand the complexities of the politics of interreligious affairs in the United States during the 1970s and '80s. This study reveals the constructive consequences of Vatican II on the political interaction and cooperation among Catholic, Jewish, mainline and evangelical Protestants, and Greek Orthodox clergy, and laypersons in their efforts to advocate for the liberation of Jews in the Soviet Union; traces the evolution of, and changes over time, of the Task Force; analyzes the motivations of the diverse groups joining the advocacy movement; offers insights into the common cause and shared advocacy efforts of Jews and Evangelicals with regard to the persecution of their co-religionists in the Soviet Union; and, most importantly, evaluates the influence and importance of Christian activist members of the Task Force on the American struggle for Soviet Jewry.

The story of the Task Force begins in Part 1 with the transformation of America prior to, during, and after WWII from a dominant Protestant society to a tri-faith nation (Shultz 2011); the social activism of the NCCIJ, including the 1963 meeting on religion and race where Reverend Martin Luther King Jr. gave the key note address; the new activist role of American Catholic sisters religious; and the enactment of *Nostra Aetate* at Vatican II, which dramatically altered Catholic-Jewish, Catholic-Protestant and Protestant-Jewish relations in the United States.

Part II covers the establishment of the Task Force by the AJC and NCCIJ; the appointment of Sister Gillen as Executive Director and of Kennedy family member and future vice-presidential candidate Sargent Shriver Jr. as Honorary Chair; and the early activities and programs of the Task Force, beginning with the founding Consultation's issuance of a Statement of Conscience, an expression of concern for Soviet Jews and others being persecuted in the Soviet Union. During the initial phases of the Task Force, Sister Gillen spoke about Soviet Jewry in synagogues, churches, parochial schools, Jewish Community Centers (JCCs), and on campuses throughout the country. She and other Task Force members addressed rallies and conferences sponsored by religious organizations, advocacy groups for Soviet Jewry, civil rights groups, and women's organizations, and the Task Force set up local level interreligious task forces in Houston, Seattle, Miami, Louisville, Philadelphia, Chicago, Denver, Tulsa, and Boston, among other cities across the country.

Within two years of its founding, Task Force members were active abroad, as well. Sister Gillen visited the USSR in 1974 where she met with Jewish refuseniks, Christian prisoners of conscience, and supporters of prominent Soviet dissident and human rights activist Andrei Sakharov. She testified before Congress on behalf of victims of Soviet religious persecution and for passage of the Jackson-Vanik Amendment, which denied Most Favored Nation (MFN) status to the Soviet Union because it restricted the emigration of Soviet Jews.

The AJC secured funding for the Task Force and, initially, exerted tight control over its director. Nonetheless, Sister Gillen managed to achieve a degree of independence, which she maintained throughout the life of the Task Force. The AJC's Interreligious Affairs Department (IAD), led by Rabbi Marc Tanenbaum and later by Rabbi A. James (Jim) Rudin, acted both with, and independently of, the Task Force to promote Jewish-Christian relations in the United States and to advocate for Soviet Jewry. Prior to setting up the Task Force, IAD had engaged in efforts to expunge anti-Semitic teachings from Christian textbooks and developed significant ties to mainline and evangelical Protestants, Roman Catholics, and Greek Orthodox churches and clergy. During the 1970s and 80s it expanded its own outreach to evangelical Protestants and forged independent links to prominent Christian leaders, including the Reverend Billy Graham and Catholic Cardinals Terence Cooke of NYC and Joseph L. Bernadin of Chicago. They also cooperated with the National Conference of Catholic Bishops (NCCB), the NCC, and the World Council of Churches (WCC).

Part Two concludes with a discussion of the Second Brussels Conference in 1976 organized by the Israeli Liaison Bureau for advocates of Soviet Jewry. At the Conference, former Israeli Prime Minister Golda Meir publicly praised and physically embraced Sister Gillen, marking a high point in the trajectory of the Task Force and recognizing its significance in the global arena. One AJC official suggested that Sister Gillen had become something of an international Jewish superstar.

Part Three focuses on the consequences of the 1975 Helsinki Accords Final Act for the Soviet Jewry advocacy movement in general and on the Task Force in particular. Signatories recognized the humanitarian aims, including to "facilitate" and "expedite" approval of exit visas to achieve the reunion of families. This was the first time that "human rights were formally recognized in an international agreement as a fundamental principle regulating relations between states" (Buwalda 1997, 116–121).

In the years following the signing of the Accords, Sister Gillen conducted a widely publicized protest on behalf of Soviet Jewry at a UN conference in Copenhagen and continued her extensive speaking engagements and work with local task forces around the country. She lobbied Congress and the State Department, attended AJC meetings and forums, and led implementation of a "co-adoption program" for paired synagogues and churches. A synagogue "adopted" a Christian prisoner of conscience in the USSR, while its partner church "adopted" a Jewish refusenik. During this period, the AJC and the Task Force also expanded their outreach to evangelical Protestants.[22]

Here, the author also covers a controversy that arose regarding advocacy efforts on behalf of persecuted Christians and captive nations in the

USSR. Sister Gillen, Task Force activists, and the AJC's IAD leaders disagreed about whether the Task Force should focus exclusively on Soviet Jewry and how to frame the issues related to the persecution of non-Jews in the USSR. A tenth anniversary conference of the Task Force held in Washington, D.C. in 1982, focused on The Helsinki Accords and balanced concerns about both persecuted Jews and Christians in the Soviet Union.

Part Three concludes with a discussion of the Third Brussels conference in Jerusalem in 1983. Following the political response in Europe to Israel's 1982 invasion of Lebanon, the Presidium and Steering Committee of the World Conference of Soviet Jewry moved the scheduled conference from Europe to Jerusalem. While the conference called for greater Christian participation in the advocacy movement, and heard a keynote address from former Congressman, Jesuit priest and Task Force affiliate, Robert Drinan, SJ, Sister Gillen, and the Task Force played a significantly diminished role in comparison to the Second Brussels conference. In Jerusalem, the program focused almost exclusively on persecuted Jews in the Soviet Union and neglected the plight of Christians and dissidents.

Part Four focuses on the 1980s and the final years of the Task Force. Although Sister Gillen continued her speaking tours throughout the United States, appearing at meetings of the NCSJ, the UCSJ, and testifying before Congress, the Task Force began to stagnate by 1985. The IAD considered rejuvenating the board and sought to enliven its advocacy efforts around religious and cultural persecution in the Soviet Union through a series of public hearings in Los Angeles, Chicago, and Seattle, reflecting the organization's increasing focus on the religious persecution of Christians residing in captive nations. During this period, the Task Force and the AJC launched *Project Lifeline* in which participating newspapers around the country published photos and bios of Jewish and Christian prisoners of conscience in the USSR, urging readers to write to them with letters of support. Sister Gillen worked closely with the representatives of Jewish, Catholic, and Evangelical legal fraternal organizations with whom she established the National Interreligious Legal Task Force on Human Rights (NILTFHR, Legal Task Force). The Legal Task Force filed a writ of *habeas corpus* on behalf of dissident Andrei Sakharov.

Through her work with the Legal Task Force, Sister Ann took up the issue of the alleged falsification of documents by Soviet leaders in their effort to smear enemies of the regime, including both Jewish and Christian (captive nation) activists and their advocates in the United States and Canada. She protested against an agreement between the American Bar Association (ABA) and the Soviet Lawyers Association (SLA) involving the exchange of documents and opposed the prosecution of persons who were alleged to have lied on their citizenship applications by omitting collaboration with the Nazi regime, including the widely publicized case of John Demjanjuk, whom US authorities claimed had been a guard in the Nazi death camp Treblinka (Douglas 2016).[23] In a letter to the Israeli

Ambassador in Washington and in letters to the editor in several Jewish newspapers, Sister Gillen criticized Israel for prosecuting someone based on evidence supplied by the USSR, given the Soviet practice of falsifying charges against Jewish activists including Natan Sharansky.

In 1987, a year before the closure of the Task Force, the largest demonstration organized by advocates of Soviet Jewry was held in Washington, D.C. While it appeared to be a "Jewish" demonstration, led by Jewish leaders, the event had a marked interfaith atmosphere. Two of the religious speakers were Christian and almost all the speakers remarked on the interfaith and interracial makeup of the crowd in attendance. Many of the speakers mentioned the persecution of Christians and dissidents in the Soviet Union. Sister Gillen was not invited to speak, and the Task Force was not mentioned, but the demonstration was evidence of its successful efforts to engage American Christians in the struggle for Soviet Jewry and to broaden the concerns of the American Jewish advocacy movement for Soviet Jewry.

The concluding section of the book describes the factors that led to the shutting down of the Task Force, most notably the Reagan-Gorbachev summits which resulted in open emigration for Soviet Jews and religious and cultural freedom for those that remained in the USSR. There was no further need for an organization dedicated to advocacy for Soviet Jewry; the Task Force was facing considerable financial troubles as the foundation that had underwritten its work since its inception had lost its Wall Street investments; and in the eyes of some in AJC, Sister Gillen, having publicly criticized the Israeli trial of an accused guard at a German death camp, had become a liability. The study summarizes Sister Gillen's post-Task Force activities in the final years of her life, including her work as executive director of the Society of St. Stephens, which supported persecuted Christians in the USSR.

The book concludes with an evaluation of the achievements of the Task Force and assesses its influence in promoting the advocacy effort on behalf of Soviet Jewry in the United States. The author considers the ways in which Sister Gillen succeeded in broadening the base of support for Soviet Jewry and putting the plight of persecuted Christians in the USSR on the public agenda.

METHODOLOGY

This study arises out of the author's earlier research published in 2005, *The Struggle for Soviet Jewry in American Politics: Israel versus the American Jewish Establishment*, which focused on the NCSJ (many of whose members had come from the AJC), the Council of Jewish Federations, and the Israeli Liaison Bureau.[24] The author subsequently began an examination of the archives of the AJC on the subject of Soviet Jewry, which he had not consulted for the earlier work, and discovered a large number of documents and considerable information about the activities of its IAD and their role in establishing and guiding the Task Force.[25]

The author also spent time in the archives of the Society of the Holy Child Jesus (SHCJ), Sister Ann's order, in Rosemont, Pennsylvania, which contain papers pertaining to Sister Ann and the Task Force. He received a limited number documents from Sister Margaret Ellen Traxler SSND papers at Marquette University in Milwaukee. He also visited the Spertus Institute in Chicago which contain the National Interreligious Task Force on Soviet Jewry, Records, 1972–1988. Documents from the archives of the Council of Jewish Federations and Welfare Funds (CJF) and the American Jewish Joint Distribution Committee proved valuable, along with the *AJC Oral History Project on the Soviet Jewry Movement* at the New York Public library.

The author conducted interviews with several members of the Task Force, including Professor Thomas Bird, Queens College of CUNY; Father John Pawlikowski, OSM, PhD, Catholic Theological Union (CTU), Chicago; Professor André LaCocque, Chicago Theological Seminary (CTS); and Sister Gloria Coleman (SHCJ), former chair of the Cardinal's Commission on Human Relations in Philadelphia. He interviewed, as well, former members of the AJC and its IAD, including Rabbi A. James Rudin (national director, IAD); Rabbi Alan Mittleman (IAD staff); Judy Banki (associate national director IAD), Eugene Dubow (director of AJC Midwest office in Chicago and later director of the Community Services Department); and Gerald Strober (IAD staff). Other notable interviewees included Dr. Eugene Fisher, former associate director of the Secretariat for Ecumenical and Interfaith Affairs of the USCCB; Lynn Buzzard, former director of the Christian Legal Society (CLS); Ambassador Ginte Damusis, former director of the Lithuanian Information Center of NY; Dr. Kent Hill, former president, Institutes of Religion and Democracy; Professor Ralph Ruebner, former co-chair of the NILTFHR; and Father Robert George Stephanopolous, former archdiocese director of ecumenical offices of the Greek Orthodox Diocese of America. The broad spectrum of diverse interviews provided an eclectic view of Sister Gillen and the Task Force.

NOTES

1. The Liaison Bureau assigned three Russian-speaking couples to the Israeli Embassy in Moscow (Buwalda 1997, 21, 22). In 1957, it sent a large Israeli delegation to the world youth festival in Moscow (Pinkus 1992, 376). Later, it organized tours of Israeli entertainers. It translated over one hundred and fifty books into Russian including Uris's *Exodus* (Dinstein 1989, 39). According to Pinkus, (1992, 381) Ben Gurion saw the possible Soviet immigration as "feeble in the extreme."

2. The Bureau emphasized that Jews, unlike other peoples and groups, were systematically denied their collective and individual rights guaranteed by the Soviet

Constitution. Their solution to the "Jewish problem" involved giving Jews their constitutional rights and/or letting them emigrate. In contrast advocates for persecuted Christians, dissidents, and captive nations called for regime change. Thus, the Liaison Bureau opposed alliances with advocates for these other causes.

3. By the early 1960s, a Liaison Bureau emissary in the Israeli Consulate in New York City (NYC) coordinated contacts with American Jewish organizations (Jerry Goodman, interview by the author, January 10, 2001). A second emissary at the Israeli Embassy in Washington worked with members of the media, academics, people in the arts, Congress and the American government (see Lazin, 2005, Chapter 2).

4. Decter's Jewish Minorities Research Bureau held a "Conference on the Status of Soviet Jews" at the Carnegie Foundation in NYC on October 21, 1963. Sponsors and or participants included Saul Bellow, Martin Luther King, Senator Herbert Lehman, Arthur Miller, Bishop James Pike, Walter Reuther, Norman Thomas, and Robert Penn Warren (Goodman 1965, 313).

5. Then head of AJC's Midwest office in Chicago, Eugene DuBow (interview by the author, January 14, 2010) recalled that his assistant Judah Graubart had read in the local papers about a nun speaking about Soviet Jewry at a synagogue. In his letter to Sister Traxler, however, Graubart cites a NCCIJ circular reporting on her urging Catholics to protest the treatment of Soviet Jewry (Letter, Judah L. Graubart, AJC to Sister Margaret Ellen Traxler, NCCIJ, May 24, 1971, Spertus papers, box 1, folder 7). In a memo to Rabbi A. James Rudin (May 24, 1971, box 175) Judah Graubart enclosed a NCCIJ newsletter "Interfaith Programming" dealing with Soviet Jewry and Leningrad trials. All archival citations are from the AJC archives unless noted otherwise.

6. After lunch DuBow contacted AJC's Interreligious Affairs Department (IAD) in NYC. Rabbis Marc Tanenbaum, A. James Rudin, and Reverend Gerald Strober of IAD moved the project forward.

7. In the early 1930s, Jesuit John LaFarge founded the first Catholic Interracial Council (CIC) in NYC. Catholic interracialists "stressed the essential spiritual unity of Catholics of all races" (Koehlinger 2007, 50). By the 1950s, there were fifty-one CICs in cities in the Northeast and Midwest. In August 1958, the Chicago CIC hosted a meeting at Loyola University which produced the NCCIJ. It was chartered in 1960 under the directorship of Matthew Ahmann (Stossel 2004, 128). Following pogroms in Russia in 1905, German American Jews established the AJC in 1906 to fight foreign and domestic anti-Semitism (Goldberg 1996, 101; Preston 2012, 205 and Sanders 1988, 235).

8. The Pope sought an *aggiornamento* (updating of the church) (Sanua 2007, 127).

9. Isaac wrote *Jesus and Israel* (1947), *Origins of Anti-Semitism* (1956) and *Teaching of Contempt* (1962).

10. His concept of the "theology of contempt" held that the Jews' failure to recognize Jesus and their killing of Christ led to their suffering as divine retribution (Feldman 2001, 19). In referring to "sources of contempt" in Christian thought, "he meant a latent force, not necessarily visible in acts or words" (Connelly 2012, 172).

11. According to Fisher (1986, 1) Isaac had "occasioned in the Pope's mind the thought that "the council ought to be occupied on the Jewish question and anti-Semitism." Connelly gives Isaac credit for influencing the Pope but not for the Council's change in attitude toward the Jews. Connelly argues that a group of theologians who converted to Catholicism, many from Jewish families, brought about a revolution in the way Catholics viewed Jews and Judaism (see next chapter).
Cardinal Bea, a German Jesuit, also met Isaac on June 13, 1960 (Sanua 2007, 127). Prior to Vatican II, he convened a committee to prepare a draft "Declaration on the Jews" (*De Judaeis*) (Feldman 2001, 106 and Connelly 2012, 192)). According to Eugene Fisher (email message to author, September 5, 2017) *Nostra Aetate* "started out as a statement on the Church's relationship with Jews and Judaism aimed at condemning the deicide, collective guilt charge and . . . recognizing Judaism as a witness to the validity of the Hebrew Scriptures as the word of the One God of Israel, the same God we Christians worship . . . this statement, *De Judaeis* . . . (later expanded) to all the world's great

Introduction 13

religions, with the original statement on the Jews being preserved as no.4 in the widened document, *Nostra Aetate."*

12. "Declaration on the Relation of the Church to Non-Christian Religions *Nostra Aetate* Proclaimed by His Holiness Pope Paul VI on October 28, 1965" http://www.vatican.va/archive/hist_councils/ii_vatican_council/document/vatii-_decl_19651028nostra-aetate_en.html# (Accessed, September 5, 2017).

13. It emphasized that "the Apostles, the Church's main-stay and pillars, as well as most of the early disciples who proclaimed Christ's Gospel to the world, sprang from the Jewish people." Pawlikowski (1986, 169) notes that it referred to St. Paul in Romans 9–11: "It saw the church as grafted onto the tree of salvation whose trunk was Judaism." Church "draws sustenance from the root of that well-cultivated olive tree onto which have been grafted the wild shoots, the Gentiles" (Rudin 2012, 11).

14. It repudiated the idea that all Jews were eternally cursed for the crime of killing Jesus.

15. According to Koehlinger (2007, 43), in emphasizing the unfair persecution of Jews by the Catholic Church, it placed the issue of Catholic anti-Semitism at the forefront of Catholic social thought.

16. It encouraged Catholics to dialogue with Jews and to learn about Jews and Judaism. According to Feldman (1990, 208), it energized Protestants in America to uproot anti-Semitism. American Cardinals Spellman of NYC and Cushing of Boston worked hard for its passage (Rudin 2012, 98ff).
Some Catholic and Protestant clergy and laypersons shared a sense of Christian guilt about the Holocaust (Sister Ann Gillen, Letter to the Editor, September 1989, SHCJ archives). For some of the Task Force activists, advocacy for Soviet Jewry was a second chance, an opportunity to prevent the cultural genocide of the Jews in the Soviet Union. Ironically, some Jewish leaders shared a similar guilt concerning American Jewish inaction during the Holocaust. At the December 6, 1987 rally for Soviet Jewry in Washington, D.C. Rabbi James Rudin (1990) recalled "But the guilt was there, and there was a sense of "God damn it, we're going to do in eighty-seven for Soviet Jews what we . . . should have done . . . earlier" during the Holocaust.

17. While NCEA focused on educational training, other sisters were advocating for moving outside the walls of the convent and Catholic church, schools, and hospitals to agitate for the liberation of others (Koehlinger 2007, 1). The new apostolate focused on the promotion of racial justice in the United States.

18. She participated in the march in Selma. In 1972, she founded the National Coalition of American Nuns (NCAN) which Henold (2008, 1) describes as "Probably the most radical collection of Roman Catholic sisters ever put on a mailing list." Its "Declaration of Independence for Women" demanded "full and equal participation of women in churches," establishment of new democratic church structures without a college of cardinals, and "complete equality of women."

19. At the founding of the Task Force in Chicago in 1972, the Greek Orthodox Church in the United States participated and one of its members served on the executive board. Within a year or two they ceased their involvement in the Task Force.

20. Prisoners of conscience are individuals persecuted for religious beliefs. "Refuseniks" refer to Jewish prisoners of conscience denied the right to emigrate (Snyder 2018, 20). They were also referred to as Prisoners of Zion. According to Loeffler (2018, 194) "in the aftermath of the Six-Day War, Jewish human rights activists coined the nickname "prisoners of Zion" to refer to the endangered Jewish communities of the Arab Middle East and Soviet Europe."

21. Some Ukrainians in the Ukraine and in the Ukrainian Diaspora in the United States and Canada viewed the USSR as Russian occupiers of their homeland.

22. Evangelicals were concerned about both Jews and their own coreligionists in the Soviet Union. In June 22, 1978, a group of seven Seventh Day Adventists took refuge in the US Embassy in Moscow.

23. Sister Gillen objected to evidence being supplied by the Soviet Union and the lack of due process in US citizenship hearings. Demjanjuk was found guilty, stripped

of his citizenship, and ordered deported. He was extradited to Israel where he stood trial accused of being Ivan the Terrible, the infamous guard at the Treblinka Death Camp. The Israeli court found him guilty, but later the Israeli Supreme Court overruled the verdict and ruled that Demjanjuk, was not Ivan the Terrible. Demjanjuk had been a guard at another death camp, Sobibor.

24. The Commercial Press in Beijing, China published a Chinese language edition of the book in 2014.

25. The AJC archives contain an important collection of documents of the Task Force and Sister Ann Gillen.

TWO
Vatican II

A Revolution in Catholic Jewish Relations and the Appearance of the "New Nuns"

Prior to the Second World War, many Americans viewed both Jews and Roman Catholics as newcomers, religiously suspect and questionable citizens who arrived in large numbers in the late nineteenth and twentieth centuries. While American Protestants lived in nearly every region of the country, the majority of the new immigrants lived in cities in the Northeast and Midwest. Unlike their Protestant neighbors, Jews and Roman Catholics retained strong links with their coreligionists abroad. Jews kept ties to fellow believers all over the world and Catholics belonged to a church headed by the Bishop of Rome. Nevertheless, religious beliefs and practices divided American Roman Catholics and Jews. Bitter memories of each other ". . . continued to fester in the free environment of their adopted land" (Feldman 2001, xi–xii, 1). Kevin Schultz (2011, 4) argues that the rise and acceptance of "tri-faith religious tolerance" in the 20th century altered the status of all three religious communities in the United States.[1]

The tri-faith idea began in late nineteenth-century Protestant America with the large influx of Catholic and Jewish immigrants from Eastern and Southern Europe.[2] The initiative came from several prominent Protestant sectors, which sought change. Some left-wing intellectuals and educators challenged the "melting pot" paradigm for absorbing new immigrants. They favored "cultural pluralism," which accepted the need to Americanize immigrants but allowed them to retain some of their own cultural "gifts." A second influence was the Social Gospel Movement led by the Federal Council of Church of Christ, representing mainline Protestant denominations, which lobbied for liberal social causes in American industrial cities in cooperation with the National Catholic Welfare Council and the National Conference of Jewish Charities. By the 1920s these three religious umbrella organizations began joint community chest drives in several American cities.[3]

In 1927, prominent members of the three faiths set up the National Conference of Jews and Christians, which, in 1938, became the National Conference of Christians and Jews (NCCJ).[4] Presbyterian Minister Everett R. Clinchy became President of the Board. In 1934, he argued that the United States was no longer a Protestant nation but a nation of three equal cultural groups. "There could be no Protestant hegemony in America" (Schultz 2011, 16).

Beginning in 1933, the NCCJ began a campaign of tolerance, sending a team of Reverend Clinchy, Rabbi Morris S. Lazaron, and Father John Elliot Ross to visit thirty-eight cities in twenty-one states. They reached fifty-four thousand people in seven weeks. Later, they sent other trios on similar missions. The organization also hosted "Institutes of Human Relations," seminars and local conferences of Catholics, Protestants, and Jews. In 1939 their speakers appeared at ten thousand meetings in two thousand communities in forty-eight states. The trios presented a new image of American unity among Catholics, Protestants, and Jews.

The NCCJ played a key role in shaping the public image of the United States among American soldiers during WWII. Beginning in 1942, the NCCJ sent its clergy trios to American military bases to advocate for an American way of life, which honored and embraced common features of the three faiths "practicing justice and brotherhood." They promulgated the idea that the United States needed religion to survive as a democracy (Schultz 2011, 43–46).[5] NCCJ programs and publications reached over ten million men and women in military service.[6]

The tri-faith credo became the dominant paradigm in post-WWII America. The widespread acceptance of the tri-faith image of America was a national image "that was, for the first time, inclusive of both Catholics and Jews in what only recently had been widely referred to as a 'Protestant country'" (Ibid., 4). As John F. Kennedy proclaimed on television in September 1960, " I believe in an America that is officially neither Catholic, Protestant nor Jewish" (Ibid., 4, 6, 7).

Brown v. Board of Education (1954), related housing discrimination issues in New York and elsewhere, and the lunch counter sit-ins in the South placed the issue of race on the public agenda in the early 1960s. In the summer of 1962, the NCCIJ organized the National Conference on Religion and Race at the Edgewater Hotel in Chicago in January 1963.[7] It marked the centennial of the signing of the Emancipation Proclamation by President Lincoln. Almost seven hundred clergy and others, including Rabbi Abraham Heschel, Sargent Shriver, and Dr. Albert Cardinal Meyer of Chicago attended. In his keynote talk, Reverend Martin Luther King Jr.

touched on the tri-faith America that had positioned Judeo-Christianity "at the center of American moral authority that underscored the importance of individual equality in God's eyes, and thus mandated an end to racial segregation."[8] Ironically, this marked the decline of tri-faith America as other "nonreligious divisions" including race became more significant than those among Protestants, Catholics, and Jews.

In less than ten years the NCCIJ would become a cofounder of the National Interreligious Task Force on Soviet Jewry (NITFSJ). Sargent Shriver would be its honorary chair. And Rabbi Abraham Heschel would be a guiding light in the American Jewish advocacy movement for Soviet Jewry.[9] As importantly, he would play a key role in Vatican II, which opened the door for a revolutionary change in Catholic Jewish relations.

VATICAN II

The Vatican's response to Hitler in the 1930s, and to the subsequent murder of six million Jews in Europe, served as the catalyst for Vatican II's approach to Jewish Catholic relations. In signing the July 22, 1933 Concordat with Hitler, the Papacy agreed to stay out of German politics if Roman Catholics could continue to freely practice their religion (Lewy 1964 and Feldman 2001, 52). This helped legitimize Hitler and gave the Catholic Church freedom to operate within the Third Reich.[10]

During WWII, the Vatican had not condemned the slaughter of the Jews of Europe. For Popes Pius XI and Pius XII, Soviet Communism was the chief enemy of civilization (Feldman 2001, 58). The church's "dread of atheistic Communism dampened Pope Pius XII's zeal to move aggressively to oppose Hitler's war against the Jews."[11]

Following World War II, the French Jewish Sociologist, Jules Isaac, argued that Christianity had provided a fertile environment for the Final Solution. In his series of books, Isaac concluded "the roots of Jew hatred, no matter what form it eventually took, could be traced to Christian teaching" (Feldman 2001, 106). Only this could explain Christian apathy to the killing of Jews, he argued.[12] His works were widely read and influential. In a meeting with Pope John XXIII in June 1960, he accused Church fathers "of laying the foundations of anti-Semitism: The Catholic liturgy and its linguistic anti-Judaism and the Church teachings throughout the ages" (Feldman 2001, 107). He recommended that the Pope appoint a commission within the planned Vatican Council to study the issue of Christian anti-Semitism.[13]

At the Pope's suggestion, Isaac met with Cardinal Bea in June 1960. Three months later, the Pope charged Bea with preparing a declaration dealing with the Jewish people for the Vatican Council (Feldman 2001, 108, 197). This declaration would lead to the document *Nostra Aetate (In Our Time)*, which took almost four years to draft.[14] The document signaled a revolutionary change in the Church's attitude toward Judaism and Jews.

Connelly (2012, 4–5, 298) credits this change to efforts by "converted" Catholic theologians who fought Nazi racial anti-Semitism:

> From the 1840s until 1965, virtually every activist and thinker who worked for Catholic -Jewish reconciliation . . . was born Jewish. *Without converts the Catholic Church would not have found a new language to speak to the Jews after the Holocaust* the revolutionary about-face . . . at Vatican II did not flow .from reflections about the genocide, but rather . . . from struggle among theologians extending from the 1930s to the 1960s: about how to revise centuries of teaching on the crowd's self-deprecation in Mathew 27 ('let his blood be upon us and our children!'), or the place in the Epistle to the Hebrews declaring God's covenant with the Jews obsolete, or the idea flowing from Mathew 28:19 that Christians supposedly had no option but to proselytize Jews . . . scandal of racism was that those expecting security in their new Catholic homes were told that they remained alien, 'in fact,' racially Jewish. In response neophytes argued that nothing in their Jewish origin made them lesser Christians. This is the obvious point of Galatians 3:28. Under Christ people ceased to be Jewish or Greek. Yet racism encouraged converts to delve deeper and to reconsider St. Paul's sustained meditation on the Jewish people contained in his letter to Romans chs. 9–11. There they discovered that Jewish origin made a person a better Christian, because Jews stood 'naturally' closer to faith. . . . People who had freely chosen a new life in faith thus found themselves 'predestined' to convert their new Christian world to a true lost faith; to move discussion about race and antisemitism beyond stale, self-contradictory patterns; to return to original texts and bring the fold back to the original understanding. (Connelly 2012, 10, 63–64)

Pope John XXIII convened the Ecumenical Council (Vatican II) in September 1962.[15] He wanted to bring the Church into the modern world with an *aggiornamento* (updating or a "spiritual renewal of the church") and greater unity in the Christian world (Sanua 2007, 127). He hoped that a modernized church could speak "more intelligibly to all faiths" (Feldman 2001, 105). He appointed German Jesuit Augustin Cardinal Bea president of the Secretariat for Promoting Christian Unity, with responsibilities for drafting and implementing the Council's pronouncements.

A few months before Vatican II, Cardinal Bea convened a committee to prepare a draft of a "Declaration on the Jews" (*De Judaeis*), which eventually became part of Nostra *Aetate*, No. 4 (Feldman 2001,106). [16] Fragile negotiations continued for almost three years.

Rabbi Abraham Heschel of the United States interacted often with Cardinal Bea during the drafting of the "Declaration of the Jews." According to Connelly (2012, 249–251), Cardinal Bea and Rabbi Heschel entered "a sustained conversation" after meeting for the first time in

November 1961.[17] They met again in 1963 when Cardinal Bea visited New York City as the guest of Cardinal Richard Cushing.[18]

The final document was approved on October 28, 1965 by a vote of 2,221 in favor and 188 opposed (http://vatican.ca/archive/hist_councils/ii_vatican_council/documents/vat-ii_decl_19651028_nostra-aetate_en.html, Accessed January 27, 2016).[19] The fourth paragraph of the document treats the subject of the Church and the Jews.[20] It begins :

> ... the Church remembers the bond that spiritually ties the people of the New Covenant to Abraham's stock. Thus, the Church of Christ acknowledges that, according to God's saving design, the beginnings of her faith and her election are found already among the Patriarchs, Moses and the prophets. ... The Church, therefore, cannot forget that she received the revelation of the Old Testament through the people with whom God in His inexpressible mercy concluded the Ancient Covenant. Nor can she forget that she draws sustenance from the root of that well-cultivated olive tree onto which have been grafted the wild shoots, the Gentiles. Indeed, the Church believes that by His cross Christ, Our Peace, reconciled Jews and Gentiles. making both one in Himself (Cf.Eph.2:14–16).[21]
>
> ... She also recalls that the Apostles, the Church's main-stay and pillars, as well as most of the early disciples who proclaimed Christ's Gospel to the world, sprang from the Jewish people. Since the spiritual patrimony common to Christians and Jews is thus so great, this sacred synod wants to foster and recommend that mutual understanding and respect which is the fruit, above all, of biblical and theological studies as well as of fraternal dialogues.[22]
>
> True the Jewish authorities and those who followed their lead pressed for the death of Christ (Cf. John 19:6); what happened in his Passion cannot be charged against all the Jews, without distinction, then alive, nor against the Jews of today.[23] Although the Church is the new people of God, the Jews should not be presented as rejected or accursed by God, as if this followed from the Holy Scriptures.[24] All should see to it, then, that in catechetical work or in the preaching of the word of God they do not teach anything that does not conform to the truth of the Gospel and the spirit of Christ.
>
> Furthermore, in her rejection of every persecution against any man, the Church, mindful of the patrimony she shares with the Jews and moved not by political reasons but by the Gospel's spiritual love, decries hatred, persecutions, displays of anti-Semitism, directed against Jews at any time and by anyone.[25]

"American bishops wasted little time transferring the words of *Nostra Aetate No. 4*, into a meaningful reality..." (Feldman 2001, 120). After 1965, they issued important and widely disseminated guidelines calling for "improved relations" with Jews and Judaism (Fisher 1986, 14–15). In 1967, the United States NCCB established the Secretariat on Catholic Jewish Relations to implement the objectives of *Nostra Aetate No. 4*.[26] The

Secretariat sought to "encourage and assist the various dioceses of the country in their efforts to put into action at all levels of the Church the Council's directions." It urged each diocese to appoint a commission to conduct dialogues, examine its teaching materials, and expunge statements that distorted Judaism. The Secretariat called for cooperation in the area of social action and for scholarly investigation of those issues which had created past distortions about Jews and the religious heritage shared by Catholics and Jews (Feldman 2001, 123).[27]

The first big challenge to a new era in Catholic (and Christian) Jewish relations came with the Six Day War in 1967. The response of many American Catholic (and mainline Protestant) clergy disillusioned many American Jews who felt that American Christians did not understand the meaning and importance of the State of Israel to American Jewry.[28]

Sanua (2007, 140) argues that many interfaith activities came to a stop as Jews had expected that "newfound Christian allies would come to their aid with enthusiastic declarations and offers of support while Arab forces armed with Soviet weapons were massing on the borders of Israel and threatening . . . to annihilate Jewish population of the state of Israel." When the AJC and others asked for statements or petitions on behalf of Israel, key Christian bodies including the NCCB, the NCC, and the WCC "were ambivalent, silent, or blatantly anti-Israel during and after the struggle" (Sanua, 146–147). While some Jewish leaders and theologians sought to end the dialogue, many—including Rabbi Marc Tanenbaum of the AJC—preferred to continue to engage in dialogue (Fisher 1986, 29).

In October 1974, Pope Paul VI appointed the Vatican Commission for Religious Relations with the Jews, headed by Johannes Cardinal Willebrand. The Commission issued "Guidelines and Suggestions for Implementing the Conciliar Declaration *Nostra Aetate No. 4.*" The eight-page document was more pragmatic and less theological than previous documents. Its purpose was to help facilitate local church efforts to reform their traditional relationships with Jews and to understand Judaism. It condemned anti-Semitism, urged more dialogue with Jews, and banned the use of efforts to convert them. It sought to reverse traditional teaching embedded in the liturgy and stressed, instead, "the existing links between the Christian liturgy and the Jewish" opposing the idea of displacement of Old Israel with the new (Feldman 2001, 112). These guidelines led to revision of the US NCCB guidelines, which, as a result, recognized the importance of the State of Israel. "Together, all these guidelines described a genuine desire on the part of American Catholic leadership to follow the spirit evinced by *Nostra Aetate, No. 4* and to implement its suggestions" (Feldman 2001,124).

SISTERS RELIGIOUS

Major changes within the community of sisters religious in the United States following WWII and Vatican II in 1965 created the fertile conditions for the formation of the NITFSJ. Without these changes it is unlikely that Sister Margaret Traxler would have helped initiate the Interfaith Task Force for Soviet Jewry, nor would Sister Ann Gillen have become its director.

The confinement of American sisters religious was a twentieth-century phenomenon, turning efforts inward away from the outside world and significantly restricting the apostolate of American women religious between the World Wars (Koehlinger 2007, 6).[29] It created a "closed society" of convents and confined many sisters to work in Catholic schools and hospitals.[30] Beginning in the 1940s, several orders raised the issue of the professional training of sisters who worked as teachers (Koehlinger 2007, 30). The National Catholic Education Association (NCEA) led the way by addressing the pervasive educational deficiencies among young sisters.[31] Remarks at a 1952 NCEA panel about the need for sisters to create "a more coherent and consistent plan for educating and training young sisters" led to grassroots effort known as Sister Formation Conferences (SFC) in 1954, which combined previously separate religious and academic educational components into a unified training program under the rubric "formation" (Koehlinger 2007, 31). Prior to Vatican II, the SFC had changed the rules about anachronistic dress, desire for a new apostolate, and ways to modernize sisterhood. Its aim was to respond to the unique desires and capacities of each individual and her vital engagement with the world, rather than obedience to rules and authority.[32] The SFC stressed intellectual development, theological competence, and preparation for apostolic works.

The post-WWII period also saw a change in the demographics of new novices in the United States. They were better educated, more of them came from the middle class, and they were more familiar with the non-Catholic world than their predecessors. For many sisters religious, their education took a quantum leap forward. Many more thought of themselves as competent professionals and not merely as nameless servants of the church (Koehlinger 2007, 32–34).

In the 1950s, Pope Pius XII encouraged reforms to make sisters more effective in their public works. He asked sisters "to consider modernizing or eliminating outdated customs and to improve the educational level of religious in teaching institutions" (Ibid., 27). Between 1950 and 1952, he called on Rome religious superiors for a series of international congresses to "adapt their institutes to the demands of modern society and to eliminate unnecessary restrictive regulations."[33]

These international congresses brought together Mother Superiors from diverse chapters and introduced "a novel ethos of unity and collaboration into the reform process, undermining the dominant culture of isolation and competition that existed between religious communities in first half of 20th century" (Ibid.). They also set in motion a process of rapid "institutional propagation in the United states, creating specialized organizations and conferences for women religious" (Ibid.).[34]

Taken together, the reforms of Pius XII and American organizations of sisters religious prior to Vatican II produced two separate but related shifts. "First, *aggiornamento* signaled a decisive end to the ethos of enclosure that had shaped religious life since the end of WWI" (Ibid., 35). Second, the SFC had begun to reinvigorate the apostolate and "... paved the way for the primary focus of the apostolate to be relocated in the vocation and conscience of the individual sister rather than in the charisma or corporate works of her religious congregation" (Ibid, 36).

By 1962, sisters religious in the United States counted among their members a group of sisters prepared to respond to the reforms of Vatican II. In the early 1960s, there was attention drawn to their shorter dresses; nuns had marched in the civil rights protest in Selma; worked in inner cities; and written theology. Henold (2008, 9) argues that the Catholic Church served as a catalyst "for both provoking and inspiring Catholic feminism in the early sixties through Second Vatican Council." There Pope John XXIII endorsed the goal of *"aggiornamento,"* which was to open the window of the Church to the modern world.[35]

The Vatican Council loosened the most restrictive regulations on sisters, who could now experiment with new "configurations of mission, community and lifestyle" (Koehlinger 2007,10).[36] It provided them with "outward-oriented theology that justified and encouraged direct engagement with social problems." Vatican II and subsequent guidelines justified a "more intense or more effective apostolic engagement with the world beyond convent walls and Catholic parish schools" (Koehlinger 2007, 10).

Vatican II affirmed ecumenism and made "possible a new level of religious tolerance for non-Catholic traditions," including Judaism. The reforms also placed the issue of Catholic anti-Semitism at the forefront of Catholic social thought, provoking conversation about ethnic and racial prejudice generally"(Koehlinger 2008, 42–43).[37]

A small number of Catholic lay persons and clergy had favored racial integration as early as the 1930s when Jesuit John LaFarge founded the first Catholic Interracial Council in NYC. He stressed "the essential spiritual unity of Catholics of all races" (Koehlinger 2007, 51).[38] Established in Chicago in 1958 to unite all local councils, the NCCIJ convened the January 1963 National Conference on Religion and Race to promote "interracial and interreligious understanding." Martin Luther King Jr. urged the assembled clerics "to assume more visible leadership on issues of race." The conference brought concern for racial justice among Catholics previously confined to a loyal but small group "of lay interracialists and practiced by a limited number of religious congregations . . . into the public spotlight" (Koehlinger 2007, 53–54).[39]

As many American Catholics moved to suburbia after WWII, some sisters preferred to stay in urban areas and work with the poorer, racially mixed population, many of whom were non-Catholics. The civil rights movement of the 1960s provided sisters with racial focus for the Vatican Council's mandate to "promote human justice."[40] The NCCIJ became actively involved in the African American community. Its newly founded Department of Educational Services (DES) in 1965 (Koehlinger 2007, 79–80) sought to increase awareness of racial justice issues among Catholics. It pushed for "dramatic revision of the apostolate. . ." including educational projects in African American communities and educational institutions and conducted outreach to women religious. Sister Margaret Traxler joined DES in February 1965 and became its director that summer.[41]

"As DES director, Margaret Traxler seemed to attract media attention, and her propensity to say outrageous things meant that she was often quoted in print" (Koehlinger 2007, 81). She directed pilot projects to engage sisters in the civil rights movement, many of which were funded by the "War on Poverty."[42] Many of the federally funded racially focused apostolates among sisters were outside of traditional congregational works in Catholic institutions (Koehlinger 2007, 57). Sister Traxler followed closely both the American racial crisis and the institution of religious life for women and kept in contact with the Church, bishops and government, and civil rights leaders, as she sought opportunities to involve sisters religious in non-Catholic spheres (Koehlinger 2007, 82).

By 1972, however, DES "had lost much of its momentum toward racial justice." The rise of the Black Power movement contributed to this shift by opposing white engagement with African American social problems (Koehlinger 2007, 56). DES switched its focus "away from racial injustice in American society and toward gendered oppression within the Church and by extension, away from African Americans and back toward sisters themselves" (Koehlinger 2007,121).

Among Sister Traxler's many concerns was the persecution of Soviet Jewry. She sometimes spoke publicly about the subject and she urged members of the NCCIJ to advocate for Soviet Jewry. After being approached by the AJC, she entered into negotiations with them to establish the Interreligious Task Force on Soviet Jewry. She enlisted Sargent Shriver to serve as honorary chair of its Steering Committee. She found a director for the Task Force, Sister Ann Gillen (Eugene DuBow, interview by the author, NYC, January 14, 2010). Her commitment to advocacy for Soviet Jewry, however, remained secondary to her continued interest in furthering the needs and standing of sisters religious. While continuing to support Sister Gillen and the Task Force her heart remained with sisters religious.

During 1969–1970, Sister Traxler had co-founded National Coalition of American Nuns (NCAN) representing 1,800 sisters religious, "probably the most radical collection of Roman Catholic sisters ever put on a mailing list."[43] The NCAN issued a "Declaration of Independence for Women" and demanded "full and equal participation of women in churches," the establishment of a new democratic church structures, abolishment of the College of Cardinals, and complete equality of women (Henold 2008,1–3).[44] For Sister Traxler "Like the faithful women of the Gospel, Sisters must follow Christ into the world ministering to His needs in the person of the poor, the sick, the persecuted" (Henold 2008, 90–91). Unlike radical feminists NCAN "took for granted that faith itself, rooted in the Gospels, was a liberating message that could be separated from the church's sexism" (Ibid.). In Sister Traxler's words "Another name for God is Justice."

NCAN became involved in a broad range of social justice issues, including the anti-war movement, the rights of workers, political prisoners, the legalization of prostitution, fair housing legislation, and the plight of Soviet Jews. NCAN was the first Catholic feminist organization to take a public stand in favor of a woman's "right to choose" (Henold 2008, 221–23).[45]

NCAN also worked for the ordination of women.[46] When the NCCB upheld the church's prohibition on the ordination of women in 1974, Sister Gillen, representing NCAN, accused them of blind adherence to "the male perspective called tradition, which NCAN calls 'the male monologue,' dampened the hierarchy's desire for justice and warped its understanding of Christ" (Henold 2008, 92).

Feminism was important to Sisters Traxler and Gillen, as well as to many other sisters involved in the Interreligious Task Force and it influenced their work. It is interesting to consider "A Passover Seder for Women," (April 1979, box 175) which Ann Gillen prepared around 1979. She described it as brief document ". . . because women are still struggling to pass over to freedom. . . . We eat matzos . . . to recall all prisoners who today eat the bread of affliction, especially Jews and Christians in the USSR and in Eastern Europe, ours sisters Mijole Sadunaite, Maria Slepak, Ida Nudel and so many others."[47] She made reference to the four questions of the Seder, which are traditionally asked by the youngest male child: "we see, sadly, that even freedom events can become routines which oppress others, Daughters have been silenced, rendered subordinate and valued as inferior as a result of the cult of the first-born, the cult of the male which debases religion today." She continued: "Why do males only recline . . . while women continue to slave in kitchens across the whole world? Why do we eat bitter herbs tonight? Let us feed our brothers bitter herbs until they can taste the sorrow which is alienating women from the family" (Ibid.).

As with their engagement in issues of racial discrimination, nuns who protested religious discrimination, as well as their patriarchal views of women, attracted publicity and made headlines. It may be, however, that on all of these issues their contributions were mainly symbolic. Jerry Goodman (interview by author, NYC, August 16, 2011) former director of the National Conference of Soviet Jewry (NCSJ), argued that the influence of the Task Force was symbolic. "Non-Jews got more publicity than Jews when advocating for Soviet Jewry." He mentioned that a nun (Sister Ann Gillen), after being strip searched by Soviet police, told her story in the White House (see chapter 7). It will be argued here that Sister Ann Gillen, other sisters religious, and the Task Force significantly influenced the advocacy efforts for Soviet Jewry in the United States.

NOTES

1. Andrew Preston presents an alternative narrative (2012, 199–205, 321–22, 332–35, 382, 420) in his discussion of the development of civil religion and the construction of a "Judeo-Christian" national identity in the United States.

2. The rise of the Klu Klux Klan and anti-Semitism in the 1920s and 1930s also fostered its influence. According to Preston (2012, 199–201) "Anti-Semitism . . . by the late nineteenth century . . . had infected "practically every stratum in society."

3. In 1908, the Protestant Religious Education Association, along with a small number of Jews and a smaller number of Catholics, discussed a strategy to combat secular society. In 1914 representatives of all three religious groups joined the Church Peace Union (later the Carnegie Council) to protest America's entry into WWI and to abolish war (Schultz 2011, 28).

4. Representatives of the Federal Council, the Central Conference of American Rabbis (CCAR), the Union of American Hebrew Congregations (UAHC), and the Archdiocese of New York supported this effort. In 1950, the Federal Council of Churches became the National Council of Churches of Christ (NCC).

5. Writing about Roosevelt's foreign policy during World War II, Preston (2012, 321–22) argues that, ". . . religion became one of the dominant ideological themes . . . drawing upon . . . 150 years of American political thought." He applied it in a new way which "embraced what had essentially been Protestant ideas . . . but included America's other main religions, Catholicism and Judaism, as believers in them." Roosevelt prioritized "faith itself, as opposed to Protestantism or even Christianity, as the essence of American democracy."

6. While some requested that all races hear the trios together, the NCCJ settled for "whenever possible." They never sent African American clergy as part of a trio to military bases (Schultz, 2011, 57). Clinchy favored keeping the cause focused exclusively on religion. He opposed those in NCCJ who favored broadening the mission to cover race (Ibid., 52–54). In the 1930s, the NCCJ introduced brotherhood week. After the war, it was rebranded American Brotherhood Week and it became a project of the Ad Council which conducted a six-year national campaign dubbed "United America" (Ibid., 69). The Ad Council rejected efforts by National Association for the Advancement of Colored People (NAACP), Council for Democracy and the AJC to have the radio ads also focus on race issues (Ibid., 72).

7. Mathew "Mat" Ahmann, head of the NCCIJ, initiated the conference. Other co-sponsors were Rabbi Philip Hiatt of the Synagogue Council of America, Reverend. J. Oscar Lee of NCC, and the National Catholic Welfare Conference.

8. Schultz writes (2011, 179–80) that the tri-faith culture helped "make possible the civil rights movement of the 1960s." Preston writes (2012, 490): "in the United States,

Judeo-Christian appeals to tolerance had arisen out of a need to distinguish Americanism from anti-Semitism, fascism, and Nazism. But in the context of the Cold War, religious tolerance was broadened to include racial tolerance as well." He also notes the keynote (2012, 491) address of the renowned African American preacher Benjamin E. Mays, a mentor of Martin Luther King, at the 1954 World Council of Churches (WCC) assembly in Evanston, Illinois. Mays "called for all churches, white and black to live up to the demands of their Christian witness, unite as one, and dismantle racism everywhere in the world-including America."

9. According to Rabbi Rudin (interview by the author, New York City [NYC], July 30, 2015) Rabbi Marc Tannenbaum of AJC's IAD participated in the conference at the Edgewater Hotel.

10. Pius XI's anti-Nazi encyclical of 1937 *Mit Brennender Sorge* ("with burning concern") denounced Nazi racial laws and Germany's failure to live up "to Vatican agreement . . . but did not mention Nazi anti-Semitism or Nazi atrocities committed against Jews." Feldman (2001, 52) argues that this implied that if Hitler had kept the agreement and allowed the Church to exist freely that the plight of German Jews would have been ignored by the Church.

11. Feldman (2001, 91) quoting Robert Wistrich "His silence in the face of mass extermination of Jews which took place at his very doorstep was deafening." Wistrich argues that the Pope hoped for German victory as late as 1943. While Roman Catholics would have a place in Nazi Europe they would have none if the Soviet Union won the war (Ibid. 2001, 92). Some Roman Catholics and Jews have claimed that Pius XII saved hundreds or thousands of Jews. Citing Drinan in 1980, Feldman (2001, 89) argues that the Catholic Church ". . . failed in any significant way to provide political or moral leadership to combat the anti-Semitic designs of Hitler's Germany." Drinan argued earlier that Christianity "allowed the Nazi philosophy to grow in its midst" (Feldman 2001, 185). According to Fisher (1986, 13) in the Holocaust hundreds of thousands of baptized Christians committed murderous acts against Jews (kin people of Jesus) and the Church was mainly silent.

12. His 1947 book *Jesus and Israel* documented misrepresentations about Judaism in interpretations of early Christian scriptures. Edward Flannery argued that this was the most potent "exposure of Christian anti-Judaism written by Christian or Jew" (Feldman 2001, 106–07). His 1956 book *Origins of Anti-Semitism* argued that Christianity made pagan anti Judaism more virulent than it had been in classical times. In 1962 he wrote *The Teaching of Contempt*, which he hoped would help to end anti-Semitism. His use of the term "roots of contempt" meant "a latent force, not necessarily visible in acts or words" (Connelly 2012, 172).

13. Pope John XXIII was elected Pope in 1958. As Angelo Cardinal Roncalli in World War II he served as Vatican diplomatic envoy in Bulgaria, Turkey, and France and as Patriarch of Venice. He helped rescue thousands of Jews (Feldman 2001, 105 and Sanua 2007, 127). In 1959, he ordered the removal of the phrase "unbelieving Jews" from Good Friday services. He later deleted other passages regarded as offensive to Jews including the call for conversion of "the perfidious Jews" during Good Friday services (Sanua 2007, 127).
According to Eugene Fisher (1986, 1–2), in the original meeting between the Pope and Isaac "had occasioned in the Pope's mind the thought that 'the Council ought to be occupied with the Jewish question and anti-Semitism.'"

14. This was complicated by the death of Pope John XXIII in 1963 and succession of Pope Paul VI who was far less committed to change and more likely to accede to international pressure to squash the document (Sanua 2007, 128).

15. He only attended the first meetings before his death. "But it was John's inspiring leadership, brief as it was, that gave the council a sense of purpose and direction" (Sanua 2007, 127).

16. See n.11 in chapter one. *Nostra Aetate 4* is a declaration on the relations of the Church to non-Christian religions including Buddhism and Islam but mostly refers to the Jews.

17. At the first meeting Heschel prepared an AJC sponsored memo for Bea's Secretariat urging the Vatican declaration to reject deicide and recognize "Jews as Jews" (Connelly 2012, 250). According to Feldman (2001, 113) Heschel was the most influential American Jew in Rome during Vatican II. Isaac also consulted with Bea and the Council. Long before Vatican II the AJC worked with Catholic Church authorities to remove anti-Semitic content from Catholic teaching materials (Ibid., 85, 107; Fisher 1986, 125–34; and Bishop 1974). The AJC lobbied a WCC 1961 New Delhi Conference declaration which stated that anti-Semitism is a sin "against God and Man" and that all humanity bore responsibility for death of Christ not just one people (Sanua 2007, 126).

18. The AJC hosted a dinner for Cardinal Bea at the Plaza Hotel. Rabbi Heschel chaired an unpublicized meeting at AJC headquarters (March 21, 1963) with Cardinal Bea and Rabbi Louis Finkelstein, Chancellor of Jewish Theological Seminary; Rabbi Emmanuel Rackman, former president of Rabbinical Council of America; Rabbi Joseph Lookstein, president of Bar Ilan University and Rabbi Albert Minda, president of CCAR. Rabbi Joseph B. Soloveitchik of Yeshiva University who had read and commented on AJC's research memos to Vatican II planned to attend but at the last minute his wife took sick. Bea pledge support for a declaration denouncing anti-Semitism and that Jews were guilty of deicide (Sanua 2007, 127, 128). In May 1963, an AJC delegation had an audience with Pope Paul VI. He gave them "a grudging endorsement of the idea that Jews should not be held guilty of deicide." The AJC obtained a State Department promise that President Kennedy would make AJC views known to the United States Ambassador to Italy. An AJC group toured Latin America, papal endorsement in hand, "to line up support for the declaration from Catholic leaders who would shortly be travelling to Rome for the next session of the Council" (Sanua 2007, 131).

19. "Declaration on the Relation of the Church to Non-Christian Religions: Nostra Aetate. Proclaimed by his Holiness Pope Paul VI on October 28, 1965." It begins: "In our time, when day by day mankind is being drawn closer together, and the ties between different peoples are becoming stronger, the Church examines more closely her relationship to non-Christian religions. In her task of promoting unity and love among men, indeed among nations, she considers above all in this declaration what men have in common and what draws them to fellowship." Paragraph three addresses the Moslems: "The Church regards with esteem also the Moslems."

20. Several compromises characterized the document. For example, there is no mention of the Holocaust nor of the significance of State of Israel and the word "deicide" does not appear. But it was an important beginning "of a genuine revolution" in Catholic Jewish relations (Feldman 2001, 116, 117). "The Council's work altered, perhaps irrevocably, the relationship of Christians and Jews" (Ibid. 104). The declaration acknowledged the Jewish roots of church, repudiated age-old idea that all Jews were eternally cursed for the crime of having killed Jesus, "stated that hatred of Jews should have no place in Church teachings, and called for fraternal Christian-Jewish dialogue" (Sanua 2007, 124). Connelly (2012, 3–4) notes that the document does not say that "church must conduct a mission to the Jews, or that the Jews must turn to Christ."

Vatican II also enacted *Sacrosactum Concilium* on reform of liturgy "repudiating" and "deploring" all "hatred, persecutions and displays of anti-Semitism directed against the Jews at any time and from any source" (Fisher 1986, 135 and Sanua (2007, 133–34).

21. According to Reverend John T. Pawlikowski (Fisher 1986, 169), *Nostra Aetate* stresses Christianity's profound debt to Judaism picking up from St.Paul in Romans 9–11 "It saw the church as grafted onto the tree of salvation whose trunk was Judaism." It implies continuing life for Judaism from a Christian theological perspective "for if the trunk has died the branches can hardly stay healthy."

22. Until now Church had frowned on biblical and theological discussions with Jews (Feldman 2001, 109).

23. It erased "the ancient accusation of Jewish collective guilt for the Christian Savior's execution . . . a principle root for centuries of anti-Semitism" (Ibid.).

24. Thus, New Israel has not displaced Old Israel in the eyes of God (Ibid. 110).

25. Paragraph 5 ends: "The Church reproves, as foreign to the mind of Christ, any discrimination against men or harassment of them because of their race, color, condition of life, or religion. On the contrary, following in the footsteps of the holy Apostles Peter and Paul, this sacred synod ardently implores the Christian faithful to 'maintain good fellowship among the nations' (1 Peter 2:12), and, if possible, to live for their part in peace with all men, so that they may truly be sons of the Father who is in heaven"(CF. Matt. 5:45).

26. Its "Guidelines for Catholic-Jewish Relations" urged Catholics to reappraise their attitude toward Jews, and to have "fraternal encounters" with them, and to learn about Judaism via dialogue (Feldman 2001, 122, and Fisher 1986, 15). Father Edward H. Flannery served as executive secretary of the Secretariat. He was succeeded by Eugene J. Fisher (Ibid., 15, 53). In dialogues with Jews, Flannery urged Catholics to adopt the agenda of American Jews who wanted to discuss Holocaust, anti-Semitism and the State of Israel (Feldman 2001, 130).

27. The Archdiocese of NYC was the first to comply in 1969 when it issued "Guidelines for the Advancement of Catholic Jewish relations in the Archdiocese of NY." Writing in 1986, Rudin argued that most American Catholic textbooks in parochial schools were purged of anti-Jewish material and anti-Semitic prayers were being removed from church liturgy (Fisher 1986:15). The American Church was aided by the scholarly writings on Jewish Catholic Relations of Msgr. John Oesterreicher, Father John Pawlikowski, Father Ronal Modras, and Dr. Leonard Swidler and by the proliferation of diocesan regional and national Jewish Christian workshops, studies of Catholic text books, and studies on reforming liturgy (Fisher 1986:24). In January 1967, Rabbi Marc Tanenbaum reported on eighty-one AJC projects involving twenty-three interreligious institutes for laymen in twenty-one cities, eight teacher and clergy training projects in seven cities, and thirteen Catholic Jewish institutes at seminaries in twelve cities, and five textbook reform projects (Sanua 2007:136). The AJC program in seminary education brought together faculty and students from Christian seminaries with Jewish scholars and rabbinical students for conferences and dialogues (Fisher 1986: 132, and Eugene Fisher's *Seminary Education and Christian Jewish Relations: A Curriculum and Resource Handbook*, published by the Washington D.C. National Catholic Education Association, 1983).

28. In describing American Jewry after the 1967 War, Preston writes (2012, 560) "For American Jews, the impact was momentous. . . . If the war began as potentially another holocaust, it ended with a new dawn of Jewish perseverance. Among American Jews, support for Israel now became the identifier of both their Judaism and their Jewishness."

29. Prior to 1918, they were "able to organize community life in ways that supported vigorous apostolic activities" (Koehlinger 2007, 25). The papal bull *Conditae a Christo* of 1900 required sisters to adhere to restrictions of partial cloister that severely limited their contact with world beyond the convent. Canon Law in 1918 codified these restrictions as the norm for active congregations fostering a "cloister mentality" (Ibid., 6). According to Henold (2008, 7–8) Canon Law "properly refers only to contemplative, or cloistered women" as "nuns." For those that are active ("non-contemplatives") or "active" ministries the term is either "women religious" or "sister."

30. Koehlinger (2007, 25–26) argues that limitations from canon law "conflicted with the fulfillment and sense of purpose they experienced through active ministry." Code of Canon Law frame consecration and apostolate as unequal components of the religious state and define sisters' identities primarily in terms of convent centered prayer (Ibid., 24–25).

31. Beginning in1952, the NCEA held meetings to integrate American and papal reform proposals into a significant movement of collective self-improvement. Sisters who proposed major changes to dominant norms of Canon Law embedded in religious rules could claim papal approbation for their activities.

32. Both the SFC and the Conference of Major Superiors of Women focused on *aggiornamento* (i.e. *bringing up to date religious institutions*). SFC issued a newsletter and held annual conferences and summer programs. The Vatican supported these efforts.

33. He was careful to maintain traditional norms of religious authority. He did not foresee the effects these modest reforms would have on women religious in the United States.

34. In 1956 the Pope initiated the Conference of Major Superiors of Women which then negotiated with the American hierarchy and Vatican for more autonomy and reform in the work of women religious (Koehlinger 2007, 21, 65).

35. Henold (2008, 21) argues that Vatican II, more than the writings of Betty Friedan, provoked, inspired, and served as a catalyst for feminist consciousness in the early 1960s among many Catholic feminists and sisters religious. Ironically, while the Vatican II aggiornamento energized women with the idea that it was a vehicle for change, it also showed them that they were second class citizens in the church. They had been excluded from Vatican II, although twenty-three women were admitted as auditors for the third session (Ibid., 46). One area of change at Vatican II was liturgical (Ibid., 141–42). In the early 1970s a feminist liturgical movement emerged via "new nuns" and women of the Grail. After 1975, one of feminist liturgy's most important functions was "to validate women's call to ordained ministry" (Ibid., 155–56).

36. *Perfectae Caritatis*, a Vatican II document on religious life called for substantial revision to rules and priorities of religious orders (Koehlinger 2007, 42–43). Issued on October 28, 1965, it challenged religious congregations "to adapt themselves to the circumstance of the modern world." It urged superiors to educate sisters about the state of the world and to provide adequate knowledge of social conditions. By 1965 most facets of religious life (dress, religious observance, enclosure living arrangements, and financial maintenance of sisters) were in flux in the United States and open to negotiation between sisters and their congregations (Ibid., 37). The document shifted focus from the order to the individual; religious "inner renewal" took precedence over just following rules (Ibid., 48).

37. After Vatican II, the Church released on December 7, 1965 *Gaudium et Spes* a Pastoral Constitution of the Church in the Modern World. It called on the Church to champion dignity of the human vocation, restore hope to those that despaired. It affirmed as "universal and inviolable" certain human entitlements such as food, clothing, shelter, and freedom of conscience and advocated for more humane and just living conditions. Sisters who favored civil rights often cited *Gaudium* arguing that the Church called them to "create and deepen relationships with African Americans" (Koehlinger 2007, 47). At a SFC workshop in the summer of 1963 at Marquette University, Rabbi Marc Tanenbaum of the AJC urged to free the Church of prejudice in texts and teaching. He spoke to other sisters on the same subject at an additional fifteen colleges. The sisters growing awareness of Catholic anti-Semitism and a subtle shift toward devotional ethics of "compassionate solidarity" with the suffering poor created the context for sisters to "integrate human-rights concepts into their understanding of apostolic work" (Ibid., 44–45).

38. Schroth (2011, 52) writes "LaFarge . . . had become a Jesuit after having been ordained a diocesan priest while studying in Europe, had as a result of working in the black parishes of Maryland become an advocate for racial understanding and an editor at *America*." See Connelly's discussion of contact between LaFarge and Pius XI. LaFarge had written a book *Interracial Justice*. At the request of the Pope, he prepared an encyclical on the race question which was never issued (Connelly 2012, 50–51. According to Connelly (2012, 99–100) LaFarge's writings suggested in 1939 that Catholics shun Jews. Also see Passelecq and Suchecky's (C1997) book *The Hidden Enclyclical of Pius XI*.

39. Sister Traxler later commented that the conference "brought to light that "there was a relationship between religion and prejudice, a reality that at the time seems clear but at the time was not always acknowledged" (Koehlinger 2007, 53). The NCCIJ participated in the 1963 March on Washington.

40. The 1963 March on Washington and Civil Rights movement exposed the depth of racism in the entire country. Many sisters sought apostolic works that promoted racial justice by administering to African Americans (Koehlinger 2007, 56).

41. She transformed " the DES into the central nervous system of the racial apostolate." She was "well-traveled, well-connected, and politically savvy" and "Energetic, ambitious and a gifted writer" (Koehlinger 2007, 81, and Henold 2008, 89–91). She was born in Henderson, Minnesota in 1924. She entered the novitiate of the School Sisters of Notre Dame in 1942. She earned an MA from the University of Notre Dame. She then devoted herself to interracial justice and to women's rights. She marched in her habit with Martin Luther King in Selma in 1965 (Henold 2008, 90). She taught in Catholic schools and colleges for seventeen years. She also became a radical feminist deeply committed to the Catholic religion. She believed that Christ was a feminist who treated "women with far more concern than the National Conference of Bishops" (Ibid., 92).

42. Sargent Shriver, head of the Office of Economic Opportunity (OEO), was "a devout Catholic" and a co-founder of NCCIJ (Koehlinger 2007, 56, 57). Many nuns and diocese via the NCCIJ's DES applied for and received OEO funding to work with programs that "addressed racialized poverty."

43. Sister Gillen, while director of the Task Force, also served on the board of NCAN. Her *NYT* obituary (www.nytimes.com/1995/02/02/obituaries/sister-ann-gillen-rights-leader-76.html) lists her as having been executive director of NCAN in the 1970s. Rabbi Jim Rudin disputes this (email to the author, October 19, 2016).

44. The NCAN newsletter *Trans-Sister,* founded in the late 1960s by Audrey Kopp and Mary Peter Traxler (later Margaret Ellen Traxler, when she reverted to her birth name), who worked for NCCIJ. In 1969, eighty-nine subscribers met for "Sisters Survival Seminar" and the NCAN was born, and within one year, had one thousand members. Its eighteen hundred members in the early 1970s constituted approximately 2 percent of sisters religious (Henold 2008, 89–91).

45. Even in 1982, when this statement was issued, it began "while we continue to oppose abortion, in principle, and in practice. . ." In 1975, Sister Traxler wrote to Betty Ford congratulating her on her handling of the abortion issue on *Sixty Minutes*. Ford spoke against the Hyde Amendment that would revoke federal funding for abortions for poor women. Sister Traxler referred to Hyde as a "fat ass" and sent him a copy. In November 1977, Sister Traxler stated, "I am pro-life, but I respect each person's conscience. . .". Henold (2008, 221) comments, "In other words she was pro-choice." By the mid-1970s Catholic feminists lobbied for the Equal Rights Amendment (ERA) and developed more ecumenical ties to other religious feminists.

46. In January 1977, the Vatican's Congress for the Doctrine of Faith (CDF) released the "Declaration on the Question of the Admission of women to the Ministerial priesthood" (Henold 2008, 189–190) which upheld the "refusal to ordain women. It argued that "an ordained priest must bear a 'natural resemblance' to Christ to fulfill the priestly function."

47. Maria and Vladimir Slepak were long-time Jewish refuseniks, and Ida Nudel was a Jewish refusenik sentenced to internal exile in Siberia. Nijole Sadunaite was a persecuted Lithuanian Catholic nun. Their contact with Sister Gillen and the Task Force is described in later chapters.

THREE
Establishing the Task Force

The American Jewish Committee's concern with the plight of Soviet Jewry began during the early years of the Cold War. The AJC feared the cultural annihilation of Europe's largest remaining Jewish community (Lazin 2005, 23–4). The Committee cooperated with Israel's Liaison Bureau to bring the plight of Soviet Jewry to the wider American public in hopes of pressuring their government to protest anti-Jewish policies in the Soviet Union.[1] In 1954, the AJC President Irving Engel testified before a House Committee on Communist Aggression, which resulted in a Congressional Report critical of the treatment of Jews under Communism. In 1959, a high-level AJC delegation met with Soviet Deputy Premier, Anastas Mikoyan, in NYC (AJC Executive Board Meeting, November 1, 1963, box 469). AJC's Paris office assisted Liaison Bureau efforts to influence public opinion on Soviet Jewry in Europe. It funded activities of the World Union of Jewish Students publicizing the plight of Soviet Jewry in Western Europe and Great Britain and a French publication on Soviet Jews (Memo, Zechariah Shuster to Simon Segal, November 21, 1967, Bert Gold box 37).[2]

In the early 1960s, AJC leaders called for the participation of Christians in advocacy efforts for Soviet Jewry. They argued that the issue of Soviet Jewry should not be presented as "an issue that is of particular interest to Jews and Jews only" (AJC Executive Board Meeting, November 18, 1963). On December 7, 1962, the AJC recruited forty-six American clergy and lay leaders (Jewish and Christian) to sign a public cable to Premier Khrushchev asking for easing of repressive measures against Soviet Jews and granting of equality for Jews with other nationalities and religions.[3]

While the AJC policy of involving Christians reflected its traditional advocacy approach, it also coincided with Israeli Liaison Bureau efforts to recruit non-Jews in the American and European advocacy efforts on behalf of Soviet Jewry. In 1963, Moshe Decter, the sole American agent of the Liaison Bureau in the United States, organized the Conference on the Status of Soviet Jews. He recruited Martin Luther King Jr., Herbert H. Lehman, Bishop James A. Pike, and Norman Thomas to be founders. The organization brought together intellectuals, writers, and artists, many of them non-Jews, to protest the discrimination against Soviet Jews. In March 1970, one hundred and seventy American artists, educators, and writers issued a "declaration of solidarity with Soviet Jews" and 1,300 faculty from one hundred campuses signed a document stating: "We—Jews and non-Jews—declare our solidarity with Soviet Jews. We say to the Soviet Government: For those who wish to live as Jews in the USSR, let them enjoy the full range of rights to which they are entitled. And those many who wish to leave for Israel or elsewhere, to unite families and achieve personal fulfillment, we say—Let them go!" (Press release, American Jewish Conference on Soviet Jewry, March 28, 1970, Bert Gold box 193).[4]

By the late 1960s, individual Christians and clergy in the United States protested the Soviet government's treatment of its Jewish citizens. Most of the protestors charged discrimination and voiced concern about cultural genocide.[5] In December of 1970, Andrew Young of the Southern Christian Leadership Conference (SCLC), issued a statement "supporting the rights of Soviet Jews." He called upon Christians everywhere "to join in an expression of support of the Jewish people living in Russia" who were being denied religious freedom by a government intent on destroying a rich "Jewish cultural heritage" (Letter, Rabbi A. James Rudin to Reverend Andrew Young, December 18, 1970, Bert Gold box 193).[6]

Following the assassination of Martin Luther King Jr. and racial unrest in 1968, John Steinbruck, a Lutheran pastor in Easton, Pennsylvania, contacted the local rabbi and a Catholic priest to "advocate for the at-risk population of Easton. . . . Shortly thereafter the organization took up . . . the persecution of Soviet Jewry" (www.projecteaston.org/pages/history.htm, accessed December 22, 2013, and John Steinbruck, telephone interview by author, December 2013). In December 1971, as senior pastor at the Luther Place Memorial Church in Washington, D.C., he urged other clergy to join him in the daily silent vigil for Soviet Jewry opposite the Soviet Embassy. He wanted a Christian presence at the vigil (Letter, John Steinbruck to Dr. John E. Howell, First Baptist Church, December 23, 1970, box 211, folder 8).[7] Later, he would actively participate in the National Interreligious Task Force and lobby his national Lutheran church organizational leaders to advocate for Soviet Jews.[8]

Steinbruck was not alone. Christian churches and clergy throughout the country were protesting the plight of Soviet Jews by the early 1970s. Following the December 1970 sentences at the Leningrad trials, the AJC noted "The Christian religious press was even more urgent than the general press in its appeals on behalf of the condemned Jews and in its expression of sympathy for Soviet Jews" (AJC Press Release, March 24, 1971, Bert Gold box 193).[9] Rabbi Jim Rudin reported on telegrams and petitions signed by grassroots Christian groups focusing on Soviet anti-Semitism and on the right of Jews to emigrate (Memo, Rabbi A. James Rudin to Rabbi Marc Tanenbaum, "Analysis of Christian Reaction to Leningrad Trials," February 19, 1971, Bert Gold box 193).[10] Bishop Iakovos of the Greek Orthodox Church of North America focused on the human rights issue. Eugene Carson Blake of the WCC compared the situation of Soviet Jews to Blacks in South Africa and to the Basques in Spain. Protesting American evangelical Protestants on both the national and local levels focused on anti-Semitism and emigration issues. Angela Davis in a *Commonweal* editorial on January 7, 1971, compared her case to the Leningrad trials. An interfaith group in Minneapolis compared the situation of Jews in the USSR to that of prisoners of war in Vietnam, while the *Christian Century* recalled American draft resisters.

In March 1971, the House of Delegates of the National Federation of Priests Councils meeting in Baltimore Maryland adopted a resolution condemning "Anti-Semitism in the Soviet Union" (Sister Ann Gillen, Report of NITF Secretariat, April 2, 1974, box 176). The priests called for an end to persecution and for religious and cultural freedom and the right to emigrate for those who wanted to leave.

In May of 1971, Rivka Aleksandrovich addressed the General Assembly of the United Presbyterian Church in Rochester, New York. She made an appeal for her daughter Ruth on trial in Riga and not allowed to leave the USSR. The Church's standing committee on "church and society" called upon the 183rd General Assembly to "denounce the unjust confinement and the forthcoming trials of those Soviet citizens of the Jewish faith who are being denied their right to self-determination and their right to emigrate." The General Assembly appealed to President Nixon to intercede with Soviet authorities.[11]

Shortly thereafter, Rabbi Marc Tanenbaum, head of AJC's IAD, arranged for Rivka Aleksandrovich to meet the Reverend Billy Graham in Chicago. Reverend Graham then issued the following telegram to President Nixon:

> I am deeply concerned and disturbed about the plight of Soviet Jews. Some . . . imprisoned. . . . Apparently, their only crime is that they are Jewish. I am asking Christians everywhere to join in prayer on their behalf. Especially . . . pray for Ruth Aleksandrovich, one of the youngest political prisoners in the world who has been imprisoned and held incommunicado in Riga for nine months.[12]

From coast to coast, church groups and clergy supported the cause of Soviet Jewry. In response to a mailing about Soviet Jewry from the AJC Washington office to opinion influencers throughout the United States, hundreds of Christian leaders issued statements on the subject and participated in interfaith meetings and rallies for Soviet Jewry (Report of the AJC Interreligious Affairs Commission delivered by Mr. Norman Rabb before the NEC, "Report on Interreligious priorities" October 29, 1971, box 174). In May 1971 in Minneapolis, the local archbishop and president of the local Council of Churches endorsed a resolution calling for recognition of the right of Soviet Jews to emigrate to Israel and for those remaining to live in accord with their Jewish cultural and religious heritage and to raise their children in accordance with their beliefs (Letter, Rabbi Max A. Shapiro to Rabbi Marc Tanenbaum, May 27, 1971, box 210, folder 5).[13] Similarly, in Boston the Archdiocese Commission on Catholic Jewish Relations and nearly four hundred other concerned persons protested the "suppression of . . . {Jews in the USSR} . . . to live in accordance with their cultural and religious heritage." In August 1971, delegates from eighty-seven countries representing forty million people on the executive committee at the 12th World Methodist Council in Denver voted unanimously "against the suppression of Jewish culture and religious traditions and restrictions on the proper rights of Jews who emigrate to other lands" ("Resolution on Human Rights in the Soviet Union," August 25, 1971, box 210, folder 5; and Rabbi Rudin, "Christian Churches support Soviet Jews," box 210, folder 5). In October 1971, the Christian Church (Disciples of Christ) issued a strong statement at their biennial General Assembly in Louisville urging the Soviets to allow Jews to live in "accord with their cultural and religious heritage and . . . to allow free emigration to Israel and elsewhere."[14]

While most of these protests focused exclusively on Soviet Jews, some also addressed the persecution of Christians in the Soviet Union. The Second National Conference of Southern Baptists and Jewish Scholars expressed its concern "over the denial of fundamental human rights of Baptists, other Christians and Jewish persons in the Soviet Union" (*Congressional Record*, August 4, 1971, box 210, folder 5). Ruth Rohlfs, president of the Baptist Convention, also expressed concern for the repressive "treatment reportedly accorded to Jews and other religious minorities in the Soviet Union" (Rabbi Rudin, "Christian Churches . . ."). The Lutheran Council of America linked the problem of Soviet Jews with the "problem of evangelical Christians behind the Iron Curtain" ("Statement of Oppression Issued by Norway Bishops from Erik W. Modean of News Bureau of Lutheran Council in USA," December 7, 1971, box 210, folder 5; and Memo, Brant Coopersmith to Rabbi Tanenbaum, December 20, 1971, box 210, folder 5). The National Association of Evangelicals (NAE) declared that "no human right is superior to that of worshipping according to the dictates of one's conscience" and cited the plight of Soviet Jews "and all other deprived religious groups and nationalities" in the Soviet Union (Religious News Service (RNS) "NAE Upholds Religious Freedom," April 17, 1972, box 210, folder 2).[15]

In discussing religious persecution in the Soviet Union, Rabbis Tanenbaum and Rudin of the IAD consistently mentioned Christians and Jews. Others in the AJC, however, and in other mainstream Jewish organizations, either opposed the inclusion of Christians or remained ambivalent. The Israeli Liaison Bureau, while encouraging participation of Christians in the advocacy efforts for Soviet Jewry, urged that the advocates focus only on Soviet Jews and not get involved with other persecuted religious, ethnic, national, and human rights groups (see above, chapter one, n.22). The Liaison Bureau argued that its advocacy for Soviet Jews wanted to obtain rights for Jews to practice their religion and culture as guaranteed in the Soviet Constitution. If this could not be achieved, they favored emigration and resettlement in Israel. They were not calling for regime change. They believed that the dissidents, and certain ethnic and national minority groups, favored regime change and, therefore, represented a serious threat to the Soviet authorities. Concern for persecuted Christians in the Soviet Union would remain a contentious issue for many Jewish organizations active in the advocacy movement for Soviet Jewry.

In early 1972, Father Casimir Pugevicius, an activist American Catholic priest who championed Lithuanian religious rights, wrote to Rabbi Tanenbaum after hearing him speak at a meeting sponsored by the National Catholic Office for Radio and Television. He referred to a recent letter to the editor written by Rabbi Tanenbaum regarding the cause of the human rights of the three million Jews in the Soviet Union and other religious communities. "Yours is the first public statement I have seen from a Jewish source which acknowledges that religious groups other than the Jewish have also suffered from the Soviet Regime. I think it is most important that we make common cause in this matter" (Letter, Rev. Casimir Pugevicius to Rabbi Marc Tanenbaum, January 6, 1972, box 210, folder 4). Father Pugevicius would participate in many Task Force activities.

In the summer of 1970, a member of AJC's Foreign Affairs Department (FAD) proposed the establishment a national or international committee of non-Jews to advocate for Soviet Jews. It would be modeled on the AJC's Committee of Concern (for Jews in Arab Countries). The Liaison Bureau representative in New York City, Yehoshua Pratt, "liked the idea." and Bert Gold, AJC's executive vice-president agreed, in principle, that the AJC should undertake the assignment (Memo, Jerry Goodman to Simon Segal, "re Soviet Jews, July 30, 1970," Bert Gold box 193).[16] In late 1970, the head of AJC's Paris office discussed with a senior Liaison Bureau official a proposed international conference to be held in Brussels. The AJC official favored inviting non-Jewish guests and speakers or holding a Jewish conference first to be followed by a much wider "non-Jewish" conference (Memo, Abraham Karlikow, AJC Paris, to FAD, December 31, 1970 {strictly confidential}, Bertram Gold box 193).[17]

In February 1971, AJC's IAD discussed a possible one-day Christian Conference on Soviet Jewry to be held in either NYC or in Washington, D.C. (Memo, Rabbi A. James Rudin to Rabbi Marc Tanenbaum, February 18, 1971, IAD box 212, folder 7).[18] They hoped for "an air of emergency" to attract many Christian leaders.[19] Possible speakers included Coretta Scott King, Ethel Kennedy, and unnamed Soviet Jews and Christians. A "service of hope" would be conducted by the participants. Finally, they proposed that a "document or statement should come out of such a conference signed by all the participants" to be used later ". . . as a working document by all Christian groups . . ." and distributed to Christian communities worldwide. Rabbi Rudin proposed a date near Passover and Easter—"The Exodus theme of course is obvious." A few months later, an AJC task force on "the World of the 70s" called on the AJC to create a broad-based interfaith group to protect Jewish rights in the Soviet Union (Minutes, AJC Task Force Meeting, June 30, 1971, box 85).

By early 1971, the AJC had the idea for an interreligious advocacy group for Soviet Jewry. In August, a member of the Chicago AJC staff wrote to Rabbi Rudin requesting a proposal for such an organization. He explained that he was being pressured by Sister Margaret Traxler, the head of the NCCIJ.[20]

By September, the AJC and the Catholic Conference headed by Sister Traxler had agreed tentatively on such an endeavor.[21] They proposed a conference of fifteen to twenty leading Catholic and Protestant theologians to be held on October 13, 1971 and hoped to form an advisory panel to generate a far-reaching Christian programmatic effort on behalf of Soviet Jews. They envisioned a national Christian consultation (conference) and possible ongoing functioning organization (Memo, Thomas Van Straaten, to members of the Interreligious Affairs Committee of AJC Chicago chapter, October 1, 1971, box 175). Sister Traxler, Rabbi Marc Tanenbaum, and Professor André LaCocque would be the co-conveners. Judah Graubart, of AJC Chicago's office, noted that, while the principal concern was rights for Soviet Jews "who have been the most visible of the oppressed minorities we are not thinking exclusively in terms of Jews alone. For we believe that in the long run behind the particularistic Jewish questions lies the universal question of the denial of human rights to many other Soviet minorities."[22]

At the national AJC office in NYC, the IAD took responsibility for the project. It assigned Reverend Gerald Strober to work with Sister Traxler, André LaCocque, and others in Chicago.[23] The Chicago AJC provided logistical support. The NCCIJ, CTS, and AJC convened the conference on October 13, 1971, which focused on Jews and other persecuted groups in the USSR (Memo, Eugene DuBow to David Geller re "Interfaith Task Force on Soviet Jewry," box 175).[24]

Dr. Thomas Campbell, president of CTS, welcomed the participants. André LaCocque spoke about anti-Semitism in the present-day USSR.[25]

He emphasized that it had become a tradition for CTS to express its concern for Judaism and the Jewish people. For us, he told the participants, "Israel is the corner-stone of ecumenism. If we argue that the hurt of our fellow man cannot leave us indifferent then, it is all the truer that the plight of the Jews qua Jews constitutes for us *the* issue par excellence on which our faith, our hope, and our love stand or fall." Not because of Auschwitz, "but on the ground of the Truth, theologically acknowledged and maintained. . . . By this, we mean that God has committed Himself with man; specifically, for man is always specific and 'God is specific—with the Jew.' He suggested that Jews had not accepted the legitimacy of Hitler and now should not accept the legitimacy of the Soviet Union (Welcome address by André LaCocque, October 13, 1971, box 210, folder 5).[26]

Mikhail Zand, an Israeli academic and former Prisoner of Zion, talked about the difficulties of being Jewish in the Soviet Union. It had become almost impossible "to practice his religion . . . or to enjoy his culture without fear of arrest and imprisonment." For a growing number, the solution was to emigrate to Israel. Zand emphasized that Christian voices in the United States were important and had the capacity to influence the Soviet authorities (Memos, Judah Graubart, "Report on October 13 Meeting," October 18, 1971 and Eugene DuBow to David Geller, "Interfaith Task Force," October 18, 1971, box 175).

Later in the day, Reverend Gerald Strober in an "Interfaith Response" talked of the importance of engaging the media and the need for a newsletter. Sister Traxler gave the closing remarks. At the end, all present "unanimously agreed to form an Interreligious Task Force on Soviet Jewry with Traxler and LaCocque as co-chairs and Graubart as Secretary." They hoped to hold a Consultation in March 1972 (Memo, Graubart to Father Flannery, October 22, 1971, box 175).

The Initiative remained with the AJC in NYC.[27] David Geller, coordinator of AJC's activities on Soviet Jewry, would advise and assist AJC Chicago and the Task Force members. He coordinated his efforts with the IAD. Task Force members met with Strober and Geller on November 12 at NCCIJ's offices to discuss plans for the March Consultation (Memo, Margaret Traxler and André LaCocque to Members of NITFSJ, re "Planning meeting for National Interreligious Consultation on Soviet Jewry [NICSJ]," October 25, 1971, box 175).[28] Participants learned that Sargent Shriver and Coretta Scott King would be the honorary co-chairs. Sister Traxler and Professor LaCocque were to serve as working co-chairs (Minutes of NITFSJ, November 12, 1971, box 175; and Memo, Graubart to Geller, re "Task Force," December 19, 1971, box 175).[29] A letter signed by all four would invite people to the March Consultation. The group wanted "to keep at a minimum" Jewish participants (Memo, Judah Graubart to Samuel Katz at the ACJ in NYC, November 29, 1971, box 175).[30] Two weeks later, Strober urged the compilation of a list of honorary sponsors for the Task Force from the religious community, politics, business, professions, labor, and the arts. Sargent Shriver and Coretta Scott King would invite them to serve (Memo, Gerald Strober to Rabbi Marc Tanenbaum, November 23, 1971, box 175).[31]

Later that month, Coretta Scott King declined the invitation to be honorary co-chair of the National Interreligious Consultation on Soviet Jewry (Memo, Eugene DuBow to Samuel Katz, "NITFSJ," December 1, 1971, box 175). Due to the need to spend her time urgently fundraising for the Martin Luther King, Jr. Memorial Center in Atlanta, she had to restrict the use of her name "in conjunction with additional fund raising." She emphasized her commitment to Soviet Jewry: "Although I cannot grant permission for the use of my name, I feel that I should say, on numerous occasions, I have made statements (and signed other statements) condemning Soviet discrimination against Jews. I am sure that my position on the matter is well known" (Letter, Coretta Scott King to Sister Margaret Traxler, December 6, 1971, box 175).

The Consultation would be co-hosted by the CTS and CTU and held at the CTS. Eugene DuBow, director of Chicago (Midwest) AJC again reiterated ". . . the . . . consensus that AJC's visibility should be kept to an absolute minimum, while that of the Christians involved should be emphasized as much as possible (Memo, DuBow to Katz, December 1, 1971).[32]

By mid-December, Rabbi Marc Tanenbaum joined Sister Traxler and Professor LaCocque as a co-chair of the Consultation (Memo, Gerald Strober to Hyman Bookbinder, December 14, 1971 and Memo, Gerald Strober to David Geller, December 12, 1971).[33] Prior to the Consultation, Reverend Robert G. Stephanopoulos, Director of Inter-church Affairs of the Greek Orthodox Archdiocese of North and South America, became the fourth co-chair of the NICSJ (Press Release, March 8, 1972, box 174).[34] A January memo clarified AJC's view of the proposed Task Force, explaining that it would serve as the national organization through which concerned Christians may act on behalf of the Soviet Jewish community. The Task Force would develop and implement interreligious programs at local and national levels and would be involved in consultations, publications, a new monthly periodical, and high-level interreligious missions to the USSR, with local level activities at churches and universities in the United States. The memo emphasized AJC's continuing efforts to "mobilize non-Jewish public opinion to bring effective pressures on the Soviet Union to change" policies that deprive Jews of the right to "their own cultural and religious life and violating their human right of freedom to emigrate." It viewed the forthcoming Consultation involving Catholic, Protestant, and Jewish spokespeople "as the interfaith equivalent of the 1972 Brussels Conference on Soviet Jewry" (AJC memo, January 21, 1972, box 175).[35]

The memo also referred to a separate or more specialized "task force" consisting mostly of Christian theologians (Ibid.).[36] The initiators of the Consultation may have intended this group to become a permanent institution, which would set policy for the larger Task Force. In time, and with the later establishment of a permanent secretariat, this body would cease to function. In many ways the Task Force became on organization of one run by Sister Ann Gillen.

THE CONSULTATION

The Consultation began on March 19, 1972 at the Center for Continuing Education on the campus of the University of Chicago.[37] At the opening dinner, Reverend Daniel Barrett, interim executive director, Church Federation of Greater Chicago; Reverend Edward Egan, co-chancellor of the Archdiocese of Chicago; and Rabbi Moses Mescheloff, president of the Chicago Board of Rabbis, gave greetings.[38] In the first keynote address, Rita Hauser, the United States Representative to the UN Human Rights Commission, announced that the administration would continue to aid Soviet Jews by "pressing the Soviet government to let emigrate all those Jews who seek to leave . . . (and by) resisting every attempt on the part of the Soviets to argue that the treatment of Soviet Jews is of concern only to the Soviets." She said that "the denial of basic rights violates the charter of the UN" and that "Jews are subjected to a greater degree of cultural deprivation and state control than most other Soviet minorities." She hoped that the "horrors set upon the Jews of Europe but forty years ago would be remembered in spurring this nation on to greater and continued efforts to help the emigration of Jews wanting to leave the Soviet Union" ("More Aid Urged for Russian Jews" *Chicago Tribune*, March 20, 1972, box 176; and NICSJ Press Release, March 19, 1972, and WINS Commentary of Rabbi Marc Tanenbaum, box 175).

In the second keynote, Charles Evers, mayor of Fayette, Mississippi, and older brother of slain civil rights activist Medgar Evers, urged President Nixon to tell the Soviets on his upcoming visit to "let the Jewish people go." He added: "I am proud to be a part of ending this oppression. I am also here because as one who remembers the Jewish participation in the Mississippi civil rights struggle, I do not forget those who helped me" ("Report on National Interreligious Consultation on Soviet Jewry," March 19, 20, 1972, box 302, folder 4; and "Press Release," March 21, 1972, box 95).[39] In the final keynote speech, Shlomo Shoham, a Soviet Jewish émigré, emphasized the importance of Christian voices speaking out in favor of Soviet Jews ("Report on . . .," March 19, 20, 1972, box 302, folder 4).[40]

The following day began with an information and planning session chaired by NCCIJ Board Chair Walter T. Hubbard Sr., with Professor

Thomas Bird of the City University of New York (CUNY); Bernard Gwertzman, Diplomatic correspondent of the *NYT;* and Richard Maas, chair of NCSJ (and former AJC President).[41] At lunch, chaired by Professor André LaCocque, Representative Robert Drinan (D-MA), a Jesuit priest, urged President Nixon to champion the cause of Soviet Jewry. He charged Stalin with "a frontal assault on every aspect of Jewish culture. . . . What Stalin commenced Khrushchev finished. In short the Soviet government during the years 1939 to 1967 carried out the destruction of Jewish cultural life." After 1967, he argued, Soviet anti-Semitism became synonymous with anti-Zionism. He credited foreign protests with influencing the Soviet decision to commute sentences of the alleged Leningrad hijackers and for a more liberal emigration policy. He argued that any large-scale future emigration would depend "upon the continuing pressure of world opinion on Moscow as well as the quality of the absorption and adjustment of Russian immigrants in Israel." He credited the proposed Koch bill (Soviet Jews Relief Act of 1971), which would create thirty thousand non-quota visas for Soviet Jews, with pressuring both American and Soviet officials, and which had, in turn, led the Soviets to ease visa regulations allowing some forty thousand Jews to leave for Israel ("Drinan's Address," March 20, 1972, box 175).[42]

Representative Drinan spoke about how Israel's emerging problems presented new challenges to Christians. Christians in Europe and in the United States had not provided enough assistance in past generations, he said—"hardly an encouraging demonstration of the solidarity which should exist between all of those who worship the God of Abraham, Isaac and Jacob." As President Nixon prepared to visit the Soviet Union, advocates for Soviet Jewry, he urged, should remind him that the UN's Universal Declaration of Human Rights, subscribed to by the USSR in December 1948, contained "a very clear assertion of the right of every person in the world to emigrate to the country of his choice"; that oppression of Jewish cultural institutions by Soviet officials clearly was contrary to Articles 124 and 125 of the Soviet Constitution, and that the people and government of the United States would continue to arouse world opinion unless the Soviet Union guaranteed "categorically and openly the religious and cultural freedom of the Jewish people who reside in the USSR." He announced that he had accepted the invitation of the NICSJ to visit Israel to evaluate the situation and subsequently report to interested individuals in United States. He would speak with Soviet Jews there "as a consultant to the Task Force" ("Report on . . . ," March 19, 20, 1972, box 302, folder 4).[43]

He closed his remarks by saying: "I have the hope that American Christians will be aroused at the injustices being inflicted on persons of the Jewish faith in Russia. He quoted the Protestant Theologian Reinhold Niebuhr "Who told us that no one can be a good Christian until first he is a good Jew" (*Congressional Record [CR]*, vol. 118, March 27, 1972, no. 47

HR "Consultation on Soviet Jewry," Hon Robert F. Drinan, p. E3092-D3093, March 27, 1972, box 176).

A series of afternoon workshops followed on how Christians and Jews could mobilize their constituencies more effectively in support of Soviet Jewry ("Report on. . . ," March 19, 20, 1972, box 302, folder 4).[44] Sister Traxler chaired a concluding plenary session where participants decided to organize an interreligious delegation to meet with, and urge President Nixon, to intercede on behalf of Soviet Jews during his forthcoming May visit to the Soviet Union. They also voted to organize an interreligious delegation to visit the USSR to meet with prisoners of conscience. They hoped to hold local and regional consultations and a national consultation within a year.[45]

Prior to the closing event, participants held a torchlight procession through Chicago (Memo, Rabbi Tanenbaum to Bertram Gold, "NICSJ," April 12, 1972). An Interreligious Assembly in the auditorium of the Holy Name Cathedral followed (Letter, Rabbi Mordecai Simon to Rabbi A. James Rudin, February 7, 1972).[46] Rabbi Ernst Lorge of CCAR chaired the evening program. Speakers included The Most Reverend Fulton J. Sheen; Rabbi Marc Tanenbaum; Dr. Cynthia C. Wedel, President of the NCC; Reverend Dr. W. L. Wilson, Chair of the National Committee of Black Churchmen; and Dean Emanuel Vergis, representing Archbishop Iakovos of the Greek Orthodox Church (" Report on . . . ," March 19, 20, 1972, box 302, folder 4).[47]

At the end of the assembly, the seven hundred attendees rose and accepted the "Statement of Conscience," which called on the "conscience of mankind to make known its profound concern about the continued denial of the free exercise of religion, the violation of the right to emigrate, and other human rights of the three million Jewish people of the Soviet Union and of other deprived groups and nationalities" (Memo, Rabbi Marc Tanenbaum to Bertram Gold, April 12, 1972, box 174).[48]

The Statement expressed the view that discrimination against the Jews of the Soviet Union gave everyone reason to believe that "under the pretext of being anti-Zionist, it is the very contribution of the Jews to humanity which is under attack . . . the Jewish testimony in the world that man's identity and freedom are not granted primarily by any state or constitution but are found in the nature of man himself. That is why each human being is threatened in his fundamental right to freedom of conscience when the Jews are persecuted" ("The Statement of Conscience of the NICSJ," box 210 folder 2).[49]

The statement urged continuation of the struggle for the freedom of Soviet Jews, "all Christians and intellectuals . . ." and then appealed to President Nixon to convey in "clear and forthright terms to Soviet authorities" when in Moscow, that the American people "Christians and Jews, black and white, liberal and conservative" believe "that these discriminations and denials of Soviet Jewry and others be stopped now and that fundamental human rights be granted—now."[50] While the Statement of Conscience of the Interreligious Consultation focused on the plight of Soviet Jewry, it referred frequently to the plight of other persecuted religious groups in the Soviet Union.[51]

In the absence of a full-time director, following the Consultation, both the AJC and Sister Traxler of the NCCIJ carried on the work of the Task Force.[52] Sister Traxler pledged NCCIJ's "effort to wholehearted support of our NITFSJ. My deepest heart is in it and I will not be turned around" (Letter, Sister Margaret Traxler to Rabbi Marc Tanenbaum, March 24, 1972, box 174).[53]

On a Sunday in late spring every year, the NCSJ and other advocacy groups for Soviet Jewry held Solidarity Day events. The NCSJ cooperated with the Greater New York Conference on Soviet Jewry (GNYCSJ) to hold a national demonstration in NYC. Prior to the April 30, 1972 event, the GNCSJ asked Rabbi Marc Tanenbaum to help "involve the Christian community as much as possible in a visible way" (Letter, Malcolm Hoenlein, Director of GNCSJ, to Marc Tanenbaum, April 10, 1972, box 210, folder 2).[54] In recruiting Christians for Solidarity Sunday, the AJC operated independently while cooperating with Sister Traxler and other Task Force activists.[55]

At the same time, the four co-chairs of the Task Force issued a joint letter calling on clergy to participate in the April 30 Solidarity Day events. They suggested offering special services in churches and synagogues during the weekend of April 29. They also included a sample petition urging President Nixon to protest the treatment of Jews in the USSR during his forthcoming visit to Moscow (Form letter of Traxler, LaCocque, Stephanapolous and Tanenbaum, April 10, 1972, box 210, folder 2). Sister Traxler also wrote letters on her own, as well as one in the name of the Task Force.[56]

Christian clergy from around the country responded to the separate appeals of the Task Force, the AJC, and other bodies (Memo, Rabbi Tanenbaum to Mort Yarmon, April 24, 1972, box 210, folder 2; and RNS, "Solidarity with Soviet Jewry Pledged by Christian leaders," April 24, 1972, box 175).[57] In August 1972, the Task Force co-chairs issued a memo to Consultation participants regarding Soviet exit fees, which required émigrés to repay the Soviet Union for their higher education (August 25, 1972, box 2010, folder 4; and NCSJ document on October 20, 1972).[58] The fees were beyond the means of the average Jewish émigré. The education tax influenced Senator Henry Jackson's (D-WA) decision to introduce his amendment to the Trade Bill, denying Most Favored Nation status (MFN) to the Soviet Union until it allowed Jews to emigrate freely.[59] Recipients were urged to send letters and telegrams to local newspapers, the White House, and the secretary of state "urging their intercession" and to send letters to Soviet authorities in Washington, D.C., and to Kurt Waldheim at the UN (August 25, 1972).[60]

SETTING UP THE TASK FORCE

Arguably one of the most important components of the Consultation was authorization to set up a permanent interreligious secretariat on Soviet Jewry. At the time, the AJC issued a job description for the position of director for a Christian Secretariat for Soviet Jewry, which later became the position of executive director of the NITFSJ (NICSJ "Recommendations," n.d., box 174; and "Job Description of Position: Director of Christian Secretariat for Soviet Jewry, n.d., box 177). The proposed Task Force would establish relationships with major Christian and Jewish organizations and officials; organize a network of people in communities around the United States; and undertake programming with national men's and women's organizations.[61] The Consultation urged the AJC, in cooperation with Christian leaders, to help convene interreligious bodies in other cities and to make better use of existing local interreligious committees. The new organization would establish contact with the Student Struggle for Soviet Jewry (SSSJ).[62] The Consultation also urged outreach to African Americans.[63]

The goal was to make Soviet Jewry a priority concern in local, regional, and national councils of churches and to encourage them to participate in Solidarity Day observances. The new Secretariat was expected to communicate with Christian and Jewish groups overseas, including the Vatican, the WCC, the World Baptist Alliance, and the World Presbyterian Alliance, as well as with Amnesty International, and the UN Commission on Human Rights, among others.[64]

The job description for the position of Executive Director included disseminating information about Soviet Jewry to Christians in the United States who were "painfully unaware of the oppression of Soviet Jews." The Consultation proposed preparation of an information data sheet on the state of religion in Russia, emphasizing the distinctive nature of the problems faced by Soviet Jews. They urged the distribution of petitions of Jewish groups among Christian bodies. They proposed setting up a hotline and urged Christians to write articles in denominational and local publications. The new Task Force would send press releases on a regular basis to denominational publications. They proposed publication of a newsletter on Soviet Jewry. Finally, they proposed introduction of the issue of Soviet Jewry in national and local religious radio and television programs, the use of interfaith media, and a bumper sticker campaign.

Sister Gillen attended the Consultation and led one of the workshops. A Catholic nun living and working in Houston, she had been very active in interfaith work and in the Soviet Jewry movement. At the Consultation, she met with Rabbi Tanenbaum and Sister Traxler about the position of executive director of the proposed Task Force. The hiring process took several months (Memo, Sister Ann Gillen to Rabbi Marc Tanenbaum, March 22, 1972, box 174).

SISTER ANN GILLEN

Sister Ann Gillen, who would become the executive director of the Task Force, was born in Texas City, Texas, in 1918 and attended parochial schools in Houston.[65] She received a scholarship to study at Rosemont College near Philadelphia (1936-1940), which was operated by the Society of the Holy Child Jesus (SHCJ). She majored in English, with a minor in history. In 1943, she ". . . took vows of poverty, chastity and obedience for a five-year trial period, at the end of which . . . [she] . . . decided to renew . . . vows for life . . . these vows may seem severely limiting, but actually their essential purpose is to liberate the person for the widest time of human service."[66] For seventeen years, she taught religion, history, and English at SHCJ high schools and earned a master's degree in American History from Villanova University. In 1957, she began three years of graduate study in theology at the Regina Mundi Pontifical Institute in Rome. On her return to the United States, she taught in California and then in Pennsylvania at Rosemont College. In 1969, she enrolled as a PhD student at Dropsie College in Philadelphia, where she studied comparative religion under Theodor Gaster, Jewish history with Solomon Grayzel, and history of the interpretation of biblical literature under Moshe Goshen-Gottstein.

Sister Gillen became convinced early on that "Christians must know the Jewish people, must learn something of their tradition and spirit if only to understand more fully the many meanings of biblical literature and the literal sense that was originally intended." Her studies at Dropsie broadened her perspective on the unhappy relations of Christians and Jews, who were trapped in a majority-minority relationship. Later, she spent two months studying and touring in the Holy Land. She decided that her future apostolate work would entail a broad type of education with special emphasis on Jewish-Christian concerns.

In 1971, she went to Houston, Texas, to direct "Project Awareness," in cooperation with the Anti-Defamation League (ADL), NCCJ, and the Catholic Commission on Ecumenism and Interreligious Affairs.[67] She also participated in an ecumenical committee, which surveyed how Christian religious educational texts treated the subject of Jews and Judaism. In her second year in Houston as a program associate of NCCJ, she worked with an interfaith committee to aid Bangladesh and ran a "Building a Better City" workshop. Other projects included the annual Christian Day of Atonement ceremony at Rothko Chapel and setting up groups of Christians who were concerned about Israel and Soviet Jewry. Following a summer seminar series at St. Thomas University, she worked to bridge the knowledge gap in Jewish-Christian dialogue. This brought her into contact with the local Houston AJC, the Jewish Community Council, and Church Women United of the YWCA. In early 1972, she served on the executive committee of the NCAN, headed by Sister Traxler.[68]

In a speech she gave in May 1972, Sister Gillen talked about how, during the Holocaust and Six-Day War, "many Christians have indeed been silent and inactive, if not actually opposed to the concerns of Jews and Judaism" (Ann Gillen, "The Interfaith Commitment," May 17, 1972, box 210, folder 2). In recent years, she argued, the two communities had come closer together in "a serious attempt to reopen the doors of dialogue, to collaborate in areas of common concern." Some Christians, she said "admitted that the concern of one community is *their* concern; what hurts or threatens the Jew also hurts and threatens the Christians. . . . We recognize our common brotherhood and *sisterhood*, our common humanity." She closed her remarks by saying, "I intend to dedicate my efforts to this goal that by the year 2000 there will be an end to the vicious thing called anti-Semitism. I believe that we are called to express the truth together and that in this truth and in our collaboration to know and share the truth, we will together redeem the times."[69]

By mid-May 1972, Rabbi Tanenbaum wanted to hire Sister Gillen to head the NITFSJ. She said that she was impressed with his vision and believed that their "collaboration might one day become a Secretariat for Human Rights" (Letter, Sister Ann Gillen to Rabbi Marc Tanenbaum, May 17, 1972, box 210, folder 2).[70] Two weeks later, he wrote her after speaking with Sister Traxler: "We are talking about some future plans in which I hope we can involve your professional skills and talents." As soon as he could share definitive plans, he or Sister Traxler would call her (Letter, Rabbi Marc Tanenbaum to Sister Ann Gillen, June 8, 1972, box 174).[71]

Rabbi Tanenbaum wanted to secure outside funding before hiring Sister Gillen. In early September, he approached the Martin Tananbaum Foundation. He explained that the AJC had set up the NITFSJ, which had attracted many prestigious people from all walks of life committed "to the human rights of Soviet Jews and others . . . an interfaith body, one of its kind in the United States . . . [that can play] . . . a crucial role in the present effort to influence the Soviet government to change its policies" (Letter, Rabbi Marc Tanenbaum to Mrs. Maurice Goldstick [board member of Tananbaum Foundation], September 7, 1972, box 177). The lack of funding, he said, would prevent transformation of the NITFSJ "into an effective agency," which could build critical support for Soviet Jewry in this crucial hour. He told the Foundation: "a very competent Catholic nun, Sister Ann Gillen of Houston, Texas, has volunteered her services to serve as executive secretary provided that we can meet some of her basic salary, travel and administrative needs." He indicated that approximately $20,000–25,000 for the following year would be needed.[72] The Tananbaum foundation provided an initial donation of $10, 000 for the first year (Letter, Rabbi Marc Tanenbaum to Mr. Arnold S. Alperstein, October 12, 1972, box 177). The AJC decided to proceed with hiring a full-time director for the Task Force.

At about this time, the Chicago Midwest Office of the AJC lobbied to have the NITFSJ to remain within the offices of the NCCIJ in Chicago. Eugene DuBow explained that it would be beneficial for everyone for the mailing address to remain the same and suggested that a certain amount of time be put in at her office to create "some semblance of activity emanating from there." He said that the Task Force newsletter would be published in the AJC offices in Chicago (Memo, Eugene DuBow to Mr. Gerald Strober, NITFSJ October 5 Meeting, September 11, 1972, box 177).[73]

The AJC hired Sister Ann Gillen as the full-time director of the NITFSJ in early October 1972. She arrived in Chicago on October 19, 1972 and began working in an office at the NCCIJ. She referred to her office as the Secretariat for Soviet Jewry (Letter, Sister Ann Gillen to Rabbi Marc Tanenbaum, October 23, 1972, box 177).[74] The AJC issued a press release ("Nun to direct activities for Soviet Jewry," November 20, 1972, box 176) announcing her appointment. The same day, Sister Traxler, Professor LaCocque, and Rabbi Tanenbaum held a press conference in Chicago to introduce her (Memo, Eugene DuBow to Rabbi Tanenbaum, November 20, 1972, box 177).[75] The proposed budget for the Task Force for the period from October 1972 through December 1973 was $47,000 (Proposed Budget of NITFSJ, October 1972–December 1973, n.d., box 177).

From the start, AJC controlled the Task Force. Its Interreligious Affairs Department (IAD) had ". . . the final responsibility for maintaining AJC relationships and joint activities with the Task Force. This department makes the ultimate decisions regarding AJC participation in policies and programs to be conducted by the Task Force" (Memos, Will Katz to Eugene DuBow, April 13, 1972, box 74; and November 15, 1972, box 177).[76] However, David Geller of AJC's Foreign Affairs Department (FAD) and the AJC staff person in charge of Soviet Jewry issues, served as the AJC's coordinator of the Task Force. Since the IAD was located in New York City, for the sake of convenience the Chicago AJC would "serve as a liaison for facilitating communication between the Task Force and the national IAD." The Chicago AJC office also provided technical assistance and support (Memo, Will Katz to Eugene DuBow, "The NITFSJ Chicago Office," November 15, 1972, box 177).[77] Having the Task Force located within the NCCIJ, and directed by a Catholic nun, enhanced its image as an organization of American Christians fighting for Soviet Jewry and also reduced the appearance of the AJC as being in control. Nonetheless, Sister Gillen was strictly supervised by the AJC and dependent on them for funding, information, and guidance.

NOTES

1. In the early 1950s in cooperation with the Israeli government, AJC arranged for the publication of Solomon Schwartz's Jews *of Eastern Europe and The Jews of the Soviet Union* by Syracuse University Press (AJC Executive Board Meeting, Foreign Affairs Committee (FAC), November 1, 1963, box 469; and Lazin 2005, 59 n42).

2. It also funded a Liaison Bureau project which brought cultural and other "materials" into the Soviet Union.

3. In 1963, the AJC got prominent scholars and clergy to sign a petition to Khrushchev urging repeal of decrees on economic offenses which resulted in mounting death penalties meted out to Soviet Jews (Jerry Goodman speech, "In Defense of Soviet Jewry: The AJC Role," October 31, 1969, Bertram Gold box 37; and AJC Executive Board Meeting, November 18, 1963). The AJC may have been following "suggestions" or "requests" from the Israeli Liaison Bureau. At a minimum, it coordinated its Soviet Jewry activities with the Liaison Bureau.

4. Later in December 1970, fourteen leading American intellectuals including Saul Bellow, Noam Chomsky, Henry Steele Commager, Father Theodore M. Hesburgh, Dwight Macdonald, Bayard Rustin, and Robert Penn Warren assailed the trial of eight Jews in Leningrad. William O. Douglas, Merle Fainsod, A. Philip Randolph, Walter Reuther, Bayard Rustin, and Robert Penn Warren sponsored a June 22, 1971 public hearing on Soviet Jewry in New York City (AJC Press release, December 23, 1970, Bertram Gold box 193; and Letter, Moshe Decter to Philip Hoffman of AJC, June 8, 1972, Bertram Gold box 193).

5. For example, in August 1970 in Denver, thirty-three people conducted a three-day fast in support of mistreated Leningrad Jews. They included a Catholic nun, nine members of a Protestant fundamentalist group, and twenty-three Jewish students and faculty (AJC Press release, August 11, 1970, Bertram Gold box 193).

6. On syndicated radio, Rabbi Rudin cited an editorial in the *Cincinnati Herald* calling for African Americans to join with the Jewish community in condemning the current Soviet policy of anti-Semitism because they have a stake in the struggle of Russian Jews to gain their human rights (AJC Press release, February 19, 1971, Bertram Gold box 193).

7. In February 1971, he organized two busloads of youth and pastors from five Lutheran churches in Hazelton, PA to join the silent vigil (Letter, Brant Coopersmith to Jerry Goodman, February 2, 1971, box 211 folder 8).

8. Washington, D.C. AJC Director Brant Coopersmith wrote Gerald Strober (re: "More on John Steinbruck," box 211, folder 8) that Steinbruck had placed this subject on the agenda of the Inter Lutheran Council in Washington, D.C. When a Lutheran publication reported that Deputy Secretary of State Richard T. Davies had stated that Soviet Jews were not living in terror, Steinbruck convinced Davies to write to the publication with a copy of his entire testimony which stated that Soviet Jews were living in fear (Memo, Brant Coppersmith to David Geller, December 22, 1971, box 211, folder 8).

9. A group of sixteen refuseniks (fourteen of them were Jewish) planned to hijack a plane at the Smolny Airport near Leningrad on June 15, 1970. They were all arrested and tried in December 1970. One of the participants was Sylva Zalmanson who received a ten-year sentence. Her husband, Edward Kuznetsov, received a death sentence which was later commuted (Beckerman 2010, 178–96 and Lazin 2005, 34).

10. Some protests focused on capital punishment and the sentencing to death of two of the alleged Leningrad hijackers. This was evident in appeals in 1969 and the early 1970s by the Pope Paul VI, Cynthia Wedel, President of the NCC; the Roman Catholic Bishop of Toronto, and the leadership of the United Presbyterian Church of the United States.

11. The IAD arranged for her to address national conferences of Methodists, American Baptists, Episcopalians, United Church of Christ, and Presbyterians (Report of the AJC Interreligious Affairs Commission . . . Session of National Executive Coun-

cil [NEC] "Report on Interreligious Priorities," October 29, 1971, box 174). Sixteen American Christian leaders sent telegrams to President Nixon urging him to "intercede with . . . Soviet Union . . . to secure the release and the restoration of full religious and civil rights of those Jewish citizens currently on trial" (Rabbi A. James Rudin, "Christian Churches support Soviet Jews," December 5, 1971, box 210, folder 5). The Presbyterian General Assembly also requested that the WCC "to raise this concern with our fellow Christians within the Soviet Union and ask them to furnish full information on this matter to all member churches" (Human rights of Soviet Jewry resolution introduced to 183 General Assembly of United Presbyterian Church in USA, May 24, 1971, Rochester NY, box 193).

12. The Reverend Dr. Eugene Carson Blake of WCC in Geneva had also taken a personal interest in Aleksandrovich's plight (Letter, Rabbi Marc Tanenbaum to Dr. Eugene Carson Blake, July 6, 1971, box 210, folder 5).

13. In a radio broadcast, Rabbi Rudin referred to Martin Luther King Jr.'s support for Soviet Jewry and to a statement in the *New York Times* (*NYT*) for the right of Soviet Jews to leave for Israel signed by Coretta Scott King, Roy Innis, and Roy Wilkins (AJC press release, May 28, 1971, Bertram Gold box 193).

14. Rudin, "Christian Churches . . ." (box 210, folder 5). In November 1971 for example, St. John the Divine Cathedral in NYC dedicated the Evensong service to Soviet Jewry (Letter, Rabbi Rudin to Dr. Peter Day, November 8, 1971, box 210, folder 5).

15. Similarly, in supporting the National Solidarity Day for Soviet Jews, Reverend Joseph L. Bernadin stated that it would draw American Christians and Jews closer together "in the knowledge that Soviet restriction of religious and civil liberties extends not only to Jews but to Christians as well." He cited a petition by seventeen thousand Lithuanian Catholics on suppression of their religion ("Statement of Most Rev Joseph L. Bernadin," NCCB, April 21, 1972, box 210 folder 2; and RNS, "Solidarity with Soviet Jewry pledged by Christian Leaders," April 24, 1972, box 175). Finally, the Most Reverend Anthony Bosco (Letter to Reverend . . . , April 27, 1972, box 210, folder 4), the auxiliary bishop of Pittsburgh, in supporting Solidarity Sunday added a prayer "that Lithuanian Catholics behind the Iron Curtain be granted freedom to profess their faith in Jesus Christ without harassment or difficulty."

16. The use of the word "assignment" might indicate that the Liaison Bureau initiated the idea (Memo, Jerry Goodman to Simon Segal, "Soviet Jews, August 3, 1970," Bertram Gold box 193). The purpose of the committee could have been to free Jewish prisoners (December 2, 1970, Memo, Jerry Goodman to Moshe Decter re: "National Committee to Free Jewish prisoners," December 2, 1970, Bert Gold box 193). At its meeting in Houston Texas (December 4–6, 1970) AJC's NEC adopted a "Statement on Soviet Jewry" (Bert Gold box 193) ". . . help to create national and international alliances of men and women of all faiths and ethnic backgrounds to uphold the rights of Soviet Jews to freedom and security."

17. Later a press release for the first Brussels Conference made no mention of the participation of non-Jews (Memo, Abraham Karlikow to Jerry Goodman, January 14, 1971, box 195). In an earlier memo announcing the Brussels Conference (February 23–24, 1971) it was hoped that some Nobel prize winners would attend along with a "sprinkling of eminent non-Jewish personalities" (Memo, Abe Bayer to Mr. Abraham J. Marks, June 17, 1970, box 195) and (Lazin 2005:35ff).

18. Rabbi Rudin suggested holding it at either the Union Theological Seminary, St. Patrick's Cathedral, or the Cathedral of St John. In D.C., he proposed either the Washington National Cathedral or Catholic University.

19. Rabbi Rudin preferred "an emotional religious reaction to a crisis."

20. He wrote "We have a magnificent opportunity with Sister Margaret and I hate to lose it." The NCCIJ dealt with Soviet Jewry and the Leningrad trials in its newsletters (Memo, Judah Graubart to Rabbi A. James Rudin, "Religious Interfaith programming," May 24, 1971, box 175; and Memo, Judah Graubart to Rabbi A. James Rudin, re: "Christian Conference on Soviet Jewry," August 9, 1971, box 210, folder 5). Eugene

DuBow, head of the AJC office in Chicago, invited her to lunch. After talking with her about joint action he contacted Gerald Strober of the IAD (Eugene DuBow, interview by author, NYC, January 14, 2010). DuBow referred to Sister Traxler as "Mighty Trax."

21. The AJC also discussed the idea with André LaCocque (telephone interview by author, December 17, 2013), a professor of theology at Chicago Theological Seminary (CTS). He mentioned that the AJC had approached him and Sister Traxler; he discounted the idea that the initiative came from Sister Traxler. LaCocque had previously checked the contents of Christian text books for the AJC (Letter, Judah Graubart to André LaCocque, September 7, 1971, box 210, folder 5; also see Letter, Rita Hauser to Rabbi Marc Tanenbaum, November 16, 1973, box 177).

22. Graubart noted that we "are attempting to maintain as minimal a profile as possible in order to keep the Christian visibility at a maximum." He urged minimum publicity at this stage because he did not want the Christians to think that they were being exploited (Memo, Judah Graubart to Mr. Joel J. Sprayregen, box 210, folder 5).

23. Strober, born to Jewish parents, converted to Christianity at age eighteen. He joined a Baptist congregation. In the mid-1960s he changed his denominational affiliation to Presbyterian. In 1968 he became a consultant to the IAD where he worked through 1974. He returned to the Jewish faith around 1974 (Strober 1974: 283–85).

24. According to LaCocque (telephone interview by author, November 27, 2013), CTS hosted but did not co-sponsor the conference. Attendees included Dr. Thomas Campbell, president of CTS; Eugene DuBow, regional director of the AJC; Father Edward Flannery, Secretariat for Catholic Jewish Relations, Seton Hall University; Monsignor John Gorman, Mundelein College; Judah Graubart, assistant area director of the AJC; Sister Adrian Marie Hofstetter, chair, Sisters Uniting of Memphis TN; Dr. André LaCocque, CTS; Richard Levin, chair AJC Chicago; Dr. Clyde Manschreck, CTS; Sister Suzanne Noffke, president Siena Center, Racine, WI; Father John Pawlikowski, dean of students Catholic Theological Union (CTU); Dr. Joseph Sittler, University of Chicago School of Divinity (UCSD); Reverend Gerald Strober IAD; Sister Margaret Traxler, NCCIJ; and Dr. Mikhail Zand, Bar Ilan University.

25. Born in Belgium in 1927, he grew up in Liege during the German occupation. His parents helped hide a family of Jewish refugees from Austria. As a youth he was puzzled by the hatred and persecution of Jews. He studied theology at Strasbourg and Montpelier France where he earned a PhD. He later studied and spent a sabbatical year in Israel. In 1969 he joined the faculty at CTS as a Professor of Old Testament (André LaCocque, telephone interviews by the author, November 27, 2013 and December 17, 2013.) Another active member of the Task Force (telephone interview by the author, August 5, 2011) commented that LaCocque had no ties to Protestant institutions and was more French than American).

26. He referred to the Prague Spring and the Spring of United States Youth as "spiritually "Jewish" revolutions ("impossible without Moses, the prophets, Jesus, the Baal Shem Tov. . . . They demonstrate the defeat of tanks and airplanes by the Word and the Spirit. They proclaim the truth of these words of a German popular song adopted by the martyrs of the concentration camps: *Die Gedanken sind Frei*").

27. Again, the AJC Chicago asked: "Where do we go from here? Sister Traxler and Dr. LaCocque are waiting to hear from us?" (Memo, Eugene DuBow to David Geller, re: "Interfaith Task Force . . . ," October 18, 1971, box 175). Strober wrote that ". . . we . . . see the consultation as a major event . . . demanding a major keynote speaker." He suggested Rivka Aleksandrovich. David Geller would present a proposed program along with logistic suggestions (Memo, Gerald Strober to Rabbi Marc Tanenbaum, October 19, 1972, box 175).

28. On a visit to Washington, D.C., Graubart met Representative Robert Drinan (D-MA) who told him that he was "extremely concerned with the plight of Soviet Jews and intimated his interest in attending our March consultation" (Memo, Judah Graubart to Eugene DuBow re: "Soviet Jewry petition drive," October 25, 1971, Bertram Gold box 193). Graubart also met with Jerry Goodman of the NCSJ and Yehoshua Pratt of the Liaison Bureau. In early November 1971, he wrote David Geller (Memo,

November 8, 1971, box 175) that Sister Traxler was also thinking in terms of an ongoing secretariat "a thought which, . . . , is very similar to ours." He also told Geller about a planned meeting with Myron Kuropas of the local Ukrainian National Alliance. He hoped to cooperate with the Alliance but only if they were not anti-Soviet. Early efforts by AJC and Task Force to reach out to non-Jews advocating for their co-religionists in the Soviet bloc were not overly successful.

29. DuBow, Geller, Strober, and Graubart from AJC along with LaCocque, Pawlikowski, Traxler, and Sister Joyce Williams, director of educational services at the NCCIJ participated. Strober presented a tentative program. "Shriver has indicated that he does not wish to speak even if he can attend." They suggested the names of Cardinal Cody, the Reverend Billy Graham, and Rabbi Tanenbaum as possible speakers for the final ceremony. Pawlikowski would speak with Cardinal Cody and Strober would contact Rabbi Tanenbaum and Reverend Graham.

30. They also discussed the participation of Elmer Winter (AJC), Elie Wiesel, Dick Levin (AJC chapter chair), and Rabbi Abraham Heschel. They decided to invite Representative Drinan and the entertainer and American Jewish Congress activist Theodore Bikel. They hoped to attract one hundred to one-hundred-and-fifty key people from the religious communities. Participants would cover their own travel expenses with lodging and meals provided by special funding raised by the Chicago AJC and Sister Traxler.

31. Later, DuBow noted that the IAD planned to send out a mailgram signed by Shriver to approximately one-hundred-and-thirty people of national prominence asking them to serve as honorary co-sponsors. Once a minimum number agreed, their names would be added to Task Force letterhead and an invitation to Christians would be sent on Task Force letterhead (Also, Memo, Strober to Graubart, December 2, 1971, box 175 includes a list of potential sponsors). He asked Graubart to check with Sister Traxler and Pawlikowski for additional names. Gerald Strober and David Geller asked all regional directors of the AJC to provide names of ten non-Jews active in the struggle for Soviet Jewry who should be invited to the Consultation. The AJC would cover expenses for their hotels and meals, but not their travel (Memo, Gerald Strober and David Geller to Area Directors and Executive Assistants, re: "NICSJ," January 12, 1972, box 175).

32. He asked Katz to speak to AJC's Executive VP Bertram Gold about restricting Jewish participation.

33. Strober hoped to invite as key note speakers Senators Edward Brooke (R-MA) and Hugh Scott (R-PA), Dr. Henry Kissinger, and former US ambassadors to the Soviet Union, Charles Bohlen or Llewellyn Thompson. Shriver invited Senator Brooke (Telegram, Sargent Shriver to Senator Brooke, December 17, 1971, box 175). Shriver also contacted Cardinal Cody about using the Holy Name Cathedral for a service at the Consultation. The AJC in Washington contacted Charles Bohlen, and Strober was in touch with Professor Tom Bird. Hyman Bookbinder, the AJC's Washington representative, discussed the Consultation with Leonard Garment of the White House (Memo, Bookbinder to Leonard Garment, December 17, 1971, box 175) Bookbinder wrote "I'm sure I need not point out to you the need to make it clear to the world, and especially to Soviet authorities, that the cause of Soviet Jewry does not concern the American Jewish community alone. The forthcoming Consultation can make a powerful contribution to this end." In early January, AJC public relations head Morton Yarmon confirmed the participation of *NYT* reporter Bernard Gwertzman. In a letter to Gwertzman (January 7, 1972) Yarmon emphasized "you are in no way expected to take an advocacy stand." The AJC provided a $300 honorarium. Gwertzman had previously served as *NYT* Moscow Bureau Chief from 1969–1971 (http://www.cfr.org/experts/history-and-theory-of-international-relations-iran-iraq/bernard-gwertzman/b3348/bio , Accessed December 26, 2013).

34. Professor Bird (interview by the author, NYC, February 11, 2011) recruited Stephanopoulos. The affiliation of the Greek Orthodox Church with the Task Force would not last very long. An AJC news release in February (February 17, 1972, box

175) announced that the planned Consultation would "help obtain full human rights for Jews and other deprived groups in the Soviet Union." Reverend Edward M. Egan told Rabbi Tanenbaum (box 175) that Cardinal Cody would be in Rome during the consultation. DuBow suggested to David Geller (Memo, "program for NICSJ Monday evening interreligious assembly," February 28, 1972, box 175) that they invite an interracial (white and African-American) choir from Evanston and a UAHC Soviet Jewry caravan (troupe).

35. The First Brussels Conference in February 1971 brought together over six hundred mostly Jewish advocates for Soviet Jewry from thirty-eight countries (Orbach 179, 60 and Lazin 2005, 35). The proposed Task Force annual budget required at least $50,000.

36. This group included Dr. Jerome Brauer, UCSD; Dr. Thomas Campbell, president, CTS; Father Edward Flannery, Seton Hall University; Monsignor John Gorman, Mundelein College; Sister Adrian Marie Hofstetter, Sisters Uniting; Dr. André LaCocque, CTS; Richard H. Levin, chair, Chicago AJC; Dr. Clyde Manschreck, CTS; Sister Susan Noffke, Siena Center; Father John Pawlikowski, CTU; Dr. Coert Rylaarsdam, UCSD; Dr. Joseph Sittler, UCSD: Reverend Gerald Strober, IAD; and Sister Margaret Traxler. A revised list on the program for the Consultation omitted Dr. Thomas Campbell, Dr. André LaCocque, and Sister Margaret Traxler. It also added Eugene DuBow, Judah Graubart, Rabbi A. James Rudin, and AJC President Elmer Winter.

37. About 125 persons registered, including twenty-eight Catholic nuns, fifteen representatives of Catholic organizations, eight Rabbis, thirteen representatives of Jewish organizations, twenty-one representatives of Protestant organizations and seminaries, and eighteen Protestant clergy.

The program listed R. Sargent Shriver as honorary chair. The list of honorary sponsors included Ralph D. Abernathy, Hon. Herman Badillo (D NY), Leonard Bernstein, Hon. Julian Bond (D-GA), Hon. Edward Brooke (R-MA), William F. Buckley Jr., Miss Dorothy Day, Charles Evers, Hon. Gerald Ford (R-MI), Arthur Godfrey, Hon. Arthur Goldberg, Hon. John A. Gronouski, Gen Alfred Gruenther, Hon. Fred Harris (D-OK), Mrs. La Donna Harris, Hon. Philip Hart (D-MI), W. Randolph Hearst Jr., Rev. Theodore Hesburgh, Rabbi Abraham Heschel, Rt. Rev. John Hines, Hon. Harold Hughes (D-IA), His Eminence Iakovos, Hon. Daniel Inouye (D-HI), Mahalia Jackson, Dr. Clark Kerr, Tom Landry, Willie Mays, Hans J. Morgenthau, Hon Wayne Morse (D-OR), Hon. Richard Ogilvie (R-IL), Hon. Charles Percy (R IL), A. Philip Randolph, Jackie Robinson, Bayard Rustin, Hon. Hugh Scott (R-PA), Hon. Adlai Stevenson III (D-IL), Ed Sullivan, Theodor White, and Roy Wilkins. The AJC (national and Midwest offices) coordinated the event with the media (Memo, Lillian Block to Rabbi Marc Tanenbaum, March 8, 1972, box 175; and Memo, Natalie Flatow (AJC NY) to Sheryl Leonard (AJC Chicago) re: "media contacts-NICSJ," March 16, 1972, box 175). Media representatives came from the *Chicago Sun Times*, NYT, *Jewish Post and Opinion*, *The New World*, *Together Magazine*, the *National Catholic Reporter*, the Associated Church Press, and Radio Liberty. Lillian Block of the RNS expressed interest in a Consultation story. The National Catholic News Service sent Jack Bacon to cover the event and expressed interest in publishing texts of the speeches. The Jewish Telegraphic Agency (JTA) asked Gerry Strober to call in with news. Mayo Mohs, religion editor of *Time* magazine expressed interest. Raphael Rothstein, a stringer from *Haaretz*, and Guenter Lawrence of *The Jewish Chronicle (London)* were interested (ibid). Radio Liberty broadcast two reports on the conference to listeners in the Soviet Union (Letter, James Critchlow, Radio Liberty to Rabbi Tanenbaum, March 21, 1972, box 174).

38. Despite the important symbolic role Shriver played in sending out invitations and allowing his name to be identified with the entire interfaith effort, he did "not show up" (Memo, Eugene DuBow to Bernice Newman, box 176).

39. Previously, Rabbi Tanenbaum wrote him (January 18, 1972, box 175) "Your presence will mean a great deal to all of us both symbolically and substantively for it will strengthen the conviction of this nation that the human rights of the three million Jews of the Soviet Union are interdependent with human rights of black people and all

others who suffer from oppression and discrimination." The AJC provided a $250 honorarium and covered his expenses.

40. The Liaison Bureau arranged for him to speak (Memo, David Geller to Bert Gold, January 20, 1972, box 175).

41. Hubbard would later serve alternatively as president and executive director of the National Office of Black Catholics (Yockey 2007).

42. He argued that the bill also influenced Attorney General John Mitchell and the State Department in early October to extend to Soviet Jews privileges extended in the past to refugees from Hungary in 1956, from Czechoslovakia in 1968, and from Cuba since the rise of Castro. Representative Drinan had also served as dean of Boston College Law School (see Schroth 2011).

43. He visited Israel in May 1972 as a member of Congress and as a representative of the Task Force (Robert Drinan, "Statement," May 30, 1972, box 174). He pledged to alert Christians in the United States to the new crisis that had arisen in Russia and in Israel due to the exodus of Soviet Jews. Over forty thousand would arrive in Israel between July 1, 1972 and July 1, 1973. This marked a change in Soviet policy which had previously not allowed anyone to leave. The change, he argued, was due to "pressure by public opinion on Russia mounted by Americans and particularly by non-Jewish Americans." Most importantly, Christians in the United States and elsewhere "must not be silent on the occasion of this new crisis in world Jewry. No one can deny that too many Christians were silent during the Holocaust. The shame of Christian inactivity during that period must not be renewed." Finally, he hoped that Christians around the world would sponsor a second Brussels conference with Catholic, Protestant, and Orthodox leaders from every nation.

44. Thomas H. Gibbons (US Department of Labor); Sister Ann Gillen, Houston, Director of Project Awareness and a Program Associate of the Houston Chapter of NCCJ; Reverend David Hunter, Deputy General Secretary of NCC; and Richard Levin, chair of the Chicago chapter of the AJC, led the workshops.

45. They hoped to introduce human rights issues into the presidential debates of 1972. They urged Christians and Jews to demonstrate on National Solidarity Day on April 30. "Delegates declare that a Christian witness is essential to making an impact on Soviet authorities." This would also have a constructive impact on other minorities in the Soviet Union, including Lithuanian Catholics, dissident Baptists, and Jehovah Witnesses. They urged Methodist Bishops to communicate the general theme of the Consultation to the USSR. They asked Consultation participants to phone individual Jewish contacts in the Soviet Union and to set up local interreligious committees. They called on church groups to organize visits to the Soviet Union. In a similar national interreligious conference for the following year, they hoped to organize an interreligious coalition on human rights. They planned to debrief young people on relevant issues before going to the USSR. They called on the Voice of America (VOA) to introduce Yiddish broadcasts. Finally, they hoped to publicize this cause to Ukrainians in the United States and Canada in light of the elevated attention on anti-Semitism in both the United States and the Soviet Union.

46. Sponsors included the Task Force, the Chicago Conference on Religion and Race, the Chicago Board of Rabbis, and the Catholic Archdiocese and Church Federation of Greater Chicago.

47. Bishop Sheen explained that every person has two of three critical moments in his or her life when he or she can save their soul. For President Nixon, one such moment would be his forthcoming trip to Moscow. "May the God of love inspire our President to plead for all persecuted people in Russia even as we raise our voices against the persecution of the Russian Jews and other religious groups" (Press Release, NICSJ, March 21, 1972, box 195). Rabbi Marc Tanenbaum encouraged Nixon to put the issue of Soviet Jews on his Moscow agenda. Dr. W. L. Wilson said it was fitting for "a member of America's largest minority" to voice concern for the plight of Jews in the Soviet Union." Dr. Cynthia C. Wedel, stated that Protestants should have a special feeling for the persecution of Soviet Jews. "We must remember our Jewish forefathers.

The Lord we serve lived and died a Jew. We can never see a Jew suffer without saying 'this is our brother." Preston (2012, 335) makes reference to Bishop Sheen's "Catholic Hour" on the radio in 1943. Sheen presented WWII as a "theological struggle" that pitted the forces of democracy and faith against "the totalitarian world view which is anti-Christian, anti-Semitic and anti-human." He argued that the "Christian view includes . . . Jews who historically are the roots of the Christian tradition and who religiously are one with the Christian in the adoration of God and the acceptance of the moral law as the reflection of the eternal reason of God."

48. A press release by the NICSJ claimed this was the largest national interreligious assembly ever held for the cause of Soviet Jewry. The Consultation intended to distribute copies of the Statement of Conscience to Christian leaders and authorities in the Soviet Union, at the UN, the United States government, both major political parties, and to the Communist parties outside the Soviet Union (Report on . . . ," March 19, 20, 1972, box 302 folder 4). They also expected it to be featured in observance of "Solidarity Day," held by advocates for Soviet Jewry on April 30, 1972.

49. Aware of their own failures regarding racism, they could not "remain silent as long as the Soviet Union continues to hamper or strangle the spiritual and cultural life of the Jewish people through extreme and special acts of discrimination." The document urged the Soviets to grant religious rights to Russian Jewry including the publishing of religious books, the training of Rabbis and to establish ties with overseas Jewish groups. "Let them live as Jews or let them leave to be Jews."
They protested the continued imprisonment of Jewish and non-Jewish prisoners of conscience and the confinement of some to mental hospitals. They also protested Soviet anti-Semitic and anti-Zionist propaganda which violated the UN Declaration for Human Rights and fostered incitement, hate, and violence.

50. It hoped to relax tensions between the United States and the Soviet Union noting that the best way for Soviets to show a commitment to peace and justice was to grant justice and freedom to Jews and other deprived "religious groups and nationalities." See below the testimony of Sister Margaret Traxler on April 10, 1974, which added the following to the Statement of Conscience: "Thou shalt not stand idly by while the blood of my brother cries out to thee from the earth" and "Let Justice roll down as the waters, and righteousness as a might stream." The Consultation hoped to have a delegation present the Statement of Conscience to the President before his May trip to the Soviet Union. They hoped to seek the advice of Appeals to Conscience Foundation and NCSJ ("Report on . . ." March 19, 20, 1972, box 302, folder 4). Rabbi Tanenbaum consulted with Max Fisher about a possible meeting with President Nixon (Letter, March 23, 1972, box 174). He shared with Fisher a copy of a telegram he wanted to send Nixon (March 24, 1972, box 175) which asked the President to respond to Sister Traxler NCCIJ in Chicago. Signing were the Reverend Dr. Arnold Olson, President, Evangelical Free Church of America; Rabbi Tanenbaum; Dr. Cynthia Wedel; and Reverend Dr. M. L. Wilson. Rabbi Tanenbaum also contacted the Reverend Billy Graham on this matter. The Task Force/AJC received no response to the telegram and no Task Force delegation met with President Nixon prior to his trip to Moscow (Letter, Marc Tanenbaum to Max Fisher, April 4, 1972, box 174). A press Release of American Baptist News Service, April 24, 1972, box 176, reported: "Three Baptist Presidents Urge Nixon to Intercede on Behalf of Russian Jews;' a Memo, David Geller to Seymour Lachman, April 24, 1972; Press conference, NCSJ meeting of April 23, 1972, Bertram Gold box 193); and a Memo, Milt Heller to Murray Shapiro, April 24, 1972, box 201, folder 2). Rabbi Tanenbaum also gave high priority to an interreligious delegation to the USSR. He hoped that Sister Traxler and Father Drinan would participate (Letter, Rabbi Tanenbaum to Margaret Traxler, March 23, 1972, box 174). This note, and others at the time, suggest that the AJC was in charge.

51. In a letter to the editor of the *Chicago Daily News*, cleared by Gerald Strober, (April 21, 1972, box 210, folder 2) Sister Traxler and Dr. LaCocque wrote "In considering the plight of the Jewish minority, we would do well to remember that their struggle is not merely that of a single people yearning for their inalienable rights. It is rather

the personification of a deeply rooted movement within the USSR, a movement broadened by the protests of many Christian and intellectual dissidents, who likewise desire the same human rights which their Jewish brethren are demanding."

52. Negotiations with Sister Gillen to become executive director went on for months after the Consultation.

53. She noted that the NCCIJ Board would select a committee to visit the Apostolic Delegate in D.C. to discuss possible communication with Rome. She hoped to ask Shriver "to sign a letter to the Vatican asking for intervention in behalf of Soviet Jews."

54. He also wanted the Cardinal and other Christian leaders to sign a petition to urge Nixon to act "... on behalf of Soviet Jewry during his visit to Moscow."

55. In the IAD, Rabbi Rudin coordinated with national Christian bodies, and Gerry Strober organized local churches (Letter, Rabbi A. James Rudin to Bishop James Armstrong, United Methodist Conference Center, GA, April 11, 1972, box 210, folder 2). He wrote a similar letter to Reverend William Harter of the United Presbyterian Church (box 210, folder 2).

56. For example, she asked Oral Roberts (Letter, April 12, 1972, box 210, folder 2) "to support Solidarity Day by issuing a statement which would indicate your interest and backing of the Solidarity Day purpose." She signed as co-chair of the Task Force and chair of NCAN. At the main Solidarity day event in Chicago, Sister Traxler spoke along with Rabbi Irving Greenberg and Irena Markish (Memo, Judah Graubart to David Geller, May 3, 1972, box 210, folder 2). Reverend Pawlikowski of the Task Force addressed the Solidarity Day rally at Sinnissippi Park in Rockford, IL. He also testified before the Illinois Senate on a resolution urging President Nixon to raise the issue of Soviet Jewry during his forthcoming visit, "Talk by Pawlikowski at rally ...." April 30, 1972, box 210, folder 4).

57. The RNS piece noted Christian support at many of one hundred separate rallies sponsored by the NCSJ. AJC files have notes about solidarity Sunday from Christian federations and churches in Texas; the Catholic archdioceses of Louisville, Atlanta, Pittsburgh and Long Island; the Texas Conference of Churches the three largest Lutheran denominations in the United States; the United Presbyterian Church Council; the Council of Churches of Washington D.C.; the NCCB, and others.

58. The NCSJ document included a fact sheet from the NCSJ and a reprinted article from the *NYT* describing the new Soviet exit tax.

59. The Jackson-Vanik Amendment denied MFN to any nation denying its citizens the right to emigrate (Lazin 2005, 45–51).

60. A memo from the four chairpersons of the Task Force of September 25, 1972 on emigrant tax (box 174) contained statements from the Leadership Conference of Women Religious and the National Assembly in Seattle (September 9, 1972) on the protest to President Nixon; the statement of Walter Hubbard, chair, NCCIJ; and the statement of Sister Traxler (NCAN).

61. It should cooperate with interreligious women's programs with Church Women United, WICS (Chicago), Jewish women's groups, and the National committee of Negro Women.

62. The SSSJ was set up by Yakov Birnbaum and was intended as a mass grassroots organization led by student activists (Snyder 2018, 27 and Lazin 2005, 16, n.24).

63. It noted that eleven African American leaders along with César Chavez and the Hon. Representative Herman Badillo (D-NY) had become Honorary Sponsors of the Task Force.

64. The recommendations urged Catholics who had attended the Consultation to communicate to all levels of the Church a "sense of special urgency to relieve oppression of Soviet Jews." They hoped to contact Apostolic Nuncio, Vatican officials, Cardinal Krol, and others in the Catholic hierarchy in the United States.

65. The following is from Sister Gillen, Society of the Holy Child Jesus (SHCJ), supplied by Sister Gloria Coleman, email to the author, November 3, 2016.

66. She was given the name Sister Mary Simon (Letter, Dorothy Cropper, archivist SHCJ to Norma, n.d., SHCJ archives, box 1, folder 1). All cited documents from the SHCJ archives are from the Sister Ann Gillen papers.

67. The project invited Jewish women to come to Catholic schools and talk about Jewish holidays.

68. NCAN brought together quarterly representatives of six national sisters groups to collaborate. One of these groups, the National Assembly of Women Religious (NAWR) responded positively to Sister Ann's proposals at the 1971 Minneapolis meeting to support the national day of solidarity for Soviet Jewry and to collaborate with the AJC and the ADL (Copy of motion introduced by Sister Ann Gillen, NCAN rep at NAWR in Minneapolis, April 30, 1972).

She was also active in the Citizens Conference on ending the War in Vietnam and represented NCAN in a Citizens Inquiry group on Ireland. In 1971–1972, she participated in two workshops in Washington D.C. under The Network, a group of sisters religious. She served as a member of the board of Common Cause.

69. Sister Ann Gillen, "The Interfaith commitment." The Necrology (church obituary) for Sister Ann Gillen prepared by the SHCJ reads: "Certainly, the publication of Vatican Council II document *Nostra Aetate* fired in her determination to do what she could to help the cause of the Jewish people, especially those of the Soviet Union" (SHCJ archive).

70. She joked with Rabbi Tanenbaum that she would work for nothing. "However, I also hope to help educate sisters in an awareness that professional pay standards exist, for many fear to embark on new career ventures, and institutions are loathe to release sisters for new works through financial insecurity, in part." She added that she hoped "that my congregation might let me use whatever is beyond my personal needs to assist others who are interested in Jewish Christian dialogue but unable to participate through lack of education." She estimated that the Task Force would need about $31, 500 which included her salary of $15,000. She also thought that her salary might "allow the option of our later including Sr. Regina of Jesus as part time . . . if she is available."

71. In a letter to Sister Traxler (June 9, 1972, box 174), Rabbi Tanenbaum wrote that the AJC would join with the NCCIJ in sponsoring the tenth anniversary observance of the National Conference on Religion and Race.

72. Mr. Irving M Engel of the AJC wrote Walter Mendelsohn of the Edmond de Rothschild Foundation about funding the proposed task force budget of $55, 000 for the first year (box 175). The Foundation gave AJC $1000 for the Consultation (Letter, Boris H. Bergreen AJC to Mr. George Shapiro, July 9, 1972, box 172).

73. "Naturally, anything we do would first have to be okayed by the IAD. In fact, it would probably be a good procedure for us to clear everything with IAD before we even submit it to Sr. Traxler, Prof LaCocque and the Greek Orthodox co-chair in NY." The original job description for Director of the Task Force stated that the NCCIJ would provide free office space and secretarial assistance to the Task Force. This may have been a factor in having it remain in Chicago.

At the time, the Chicago AJC received mailings from the NCSJ and "turned them around" or adjusted them for American Christians and then resent them from the NITFSJ. They were the first Task Force mailing in months. DuBow offered the services of Judah Graubart to assist the Task Force until it was funded.

74. She asked Rabbi Tanenbaum for his thoughts on the project name: Soviet Jewry Secretariat or Christian Secretariat for Soviet Jewry. She said that she could get by on a salary of $500 per month which would leave her $4,000 from the Tananbaum grant for projects. She wrote that Sister Traxler announced to the major superiors of groups of sisters religious that a permanent Secretariat on Soviet Jewry, a Christian Jewish Voice of Conscience, had been established.

75. In a memo to Rabbi Marc Tanenbaum ("The Task First Edition," November 30, 1972) Isaiah Terman wrote that, at the last minute, Father Robert Stephanopoulos was unable to attend the November 20 press conference.

76. Since the Task Force was a national organization, AJC's IAD supervised. Katz wrote ". . . the major responsibility of your (Chicago) office in this regard has been completed—so now it's back to your local concerns with Soviet Jewry and other matters." The regional office would supply technical assistance if requested. Graubart (in memo to Rabbi Tanenbaum, "NITFSJ," November 1, 1972, box 177) also suggested that Ann meet with AJC staff in Philadelphia and Milwaukee during scheduled visits. In a response, Will Katz of the AJC in New York (Memo to DuBow, cc: Graubart and Tanenbaum, November 8, 1972, box 177) wrote "no one should be contacted until Marc meets with Sister Gillen. After that, appropriate field staff will hear from Marc or myself."

77. Katz wrote that the Chicago office would serve as a channel for communication between the Task Force and IAD but at times when they communicate directly your office will not be involved . . . "responsibility for implementing any such suggestions belongs only with IAD." Initially Gerald Strober of IAD supervised. When he left the AJC in 1974, Rabbi Rudin took over.

FOUR

The Early Years of the Task Force

The AJC and the NCCIJ together established the Task Force in 1972. During the first year, the NCCIJ provided office space and some secretarial and office support. Shortly thereafter, it ceased its involvement and ended its support.[1] The AJC became the sole sponsor, provided most of the budget, and exerted considerable influence, if not control, over the Task Force and its director (AJC Report " . . . activities on behalf of Soviet Jewry," January 6, 1975, box 209, folder 3). The Task Force "cooperated" extensively with the AJC on the national and local levels (Sister Ann Gillen "The NITFSJ: A report 1972–1974," May 1974; Sr Margaret Ellen Traxler Papers, MET, series 5, box 7, folders 2–4).[2]

FINANCES AND SUPERVISION

In November 1972, the AJC secured a grant for the Task Force from the New York-based Martin A. Tananbaum Foundation ("Report to the Plenum of NEC of AJC from IAC, December 2, 1973, box 174; and "IAC Background Memo, AJC NEC meeting, December 1–3, 1973, Hollywood FL, box 174).[3] The Foundation renewed the grant each year until 1988 when the foundation ceased operations. The AJC absorbed most Task Force expenses not covered by the Tananbaum grant.[4]

The AJC hired Sister Gillen as director of the Task Force but did not consider her an AJC employee (Memo, Rabbi Marc Tanenbaum to Eleanor Katz, December 29, 1972, box 195). The AJC drafted an initial budget, which, in addition to her salary of six thousand dollars, allowed for approximately four thousand dollars for travel, administration, publications, and other program needs.[5] In March 1973, Eugene DuBow, the AJC Midwest (Chicago) Director urged (Memo to Rita Blume, March 7, 1973) that Sister Gillen's salary be increased, along with additional funding for a secretary, administrative costs, office rent, increased programming, and travel. He warned: "At this point the operation is hamstrung by a severe limitation of funds and of course it could be greatly expanded and improved if we were to get a larger grant."[6]

In a grant request for $15,000 dollars for 1974, Rabbi Tanenbaum (Letter to David T. Goldstick, February 8, 1974) emphasized the need to hire a full-time secretary to help manage the workload and to free Sister Gillen for the important task of "organizing various communities."[7] The Yom Kippur War, and resulting financial burdens on Israel and various Jewish organizations in the United States, threatened the AJC's financial support of the Task Force (Memo, Strober to Neil Sandberg, January 14, 1974, box 176). Strober approached AJC regional office heads about funding the Task Force. Without additional funding Strober warned them, the Task Force would go out of business by the summer.[8]

In April 1974, the Tananbaum Foundation gave the AJC a grant of $15,000 for the Task Force. The following year, the Tanenbaum Foundation awarded the AJC $17,500 (Draft letter, Rabbi Marc Tanenbaum to David Goldstick, C 1976).[9] In the application Rabbi Tanenbaum wrote about Sister Gillen: "We are told she has become an international force in the Soviet Jewry freedom fight and for this, you and your fellow Trustees should feel a rewarding sense of gratification for without your support, Ann's work could not have been continued."

Initially the Chicago Midwest AJC office supervised Sister Gillen. The assistant director, Judah Graubart, took charge of her orientation and training. He remarked in a letter to Rabbi Tanenbaum (October 31, 1972, box 177) that she was a flexible person who wanted both to learn and to do a good job. He agreed with her that she needed a lot of guidance, and he expected her to learn quickly.[10]

In October 1973, the IAD assigned Gerald Strober to supervise Sister Gillen and the Task Force (Memo, Strober to Rabbi Tanenbaum, October 2, 1973).[11] Strober saw his role as raising money, adding sponsors, and supervising Sister Gillen. He also wanted to help establish the proposed smaller task force of twenty to thirty Christian theologians who would advise the AJC and the Task Force on involvement of Christians in the advocacy for Soviet Jewry. He proposed a three-month trial period during which he wanted to put the Task Force into "viable condition." He hoped that satisfactory arrangements could be worked out so that "she would understand her role and the fact that she would be directly under my administrative supervision. If this is not possible and if in the three-month period she does not shape-up, I believe we must begin the search for a qualified permanent director" (Memo, Gerald Strober to Rabbi Marc Tanenbaum, October 2, 1973, box 212).

These remarks suggest that some tension existed between the AJC and Sister Gillen during her first year of employment (Memo, Jerry Strober to Rabbi Marc Tanenbaum, November 19, 1973, box 212, folder 4).[12] He had second thoughts about dropping her completely as of December 31 "from a public relations point of view" (Memo, Strober to Rabbi Tanenbaum, November 19, 1973). He recommended strengthening the Task Force and working "out a new relationship for Sister Gillen." He urged the AJC to make it clear to her that administrative responsibility for the Task Force was "being shifted to New York." He warned that if she would not go along with the change in her situation, then he would have to work out "a satisfactory termination based on our previous commitments to her" (Ibid.).

In less than a month, Sister Gillen's standing and position improved under Strober's leadership. She wrote to him (Memo, December 3, 1973) praising his comments at the NCCIJ Board as being on the mark and for being diplomatic. She asked him "Where do we go from here, Gerry? Can you straighten this out with New York or should I write? I want to start with the Sister secretary as soon as possible."[13] In mid-December, Rabbi Tanenbaum authorized a salary increase for Sister Gillen (Memo, Rabbi Tanenbaum to Phil Shamis, December18 1973, box 176).[14] She still sought Strober's approval (Memo, Ann Gillen to Gerald Strober, February 1, 1974).[15] At the same time, she sometimes operated independently (Letter, Sheila Woods (NCSJ) to Gerald Strober, February 12, 1974, box 168).[16] By late Spring 1974, she was more secure in her position and was about to leave on a trip to Europe, the USSR, and Israel.[17] Through 1976 and 1977 the AJC's supervision remained tight and broad in scope. As Sister Gillen gained experience and momentum, she exercised greater independence. By the 1980s, she was more influential and more independent from the AJC.

TASK FORCE PROGRAMS AND ANN'S SPEAKING ENGAGEMENTS

In October 1972, Sister Gillen discussed her plans for the Task Force with the AJC's Chicago staff (Memo, Judah Graubart to Rabbi Marc Tanenbaum, re: "NITFSJ," November 1, 1972, box 177).[18] She wanted to hold two regional conferences between January and April of the following year. The first would be in Houston, where she had worked and had contacts in the Jewish and Christian communities. She also wanted to engage with communities on the West Coast (Ibid.).[19] In addition, she wanted to hold a second national Interreligious Consultation in April in Washington, D.C. at Reverend John Steinbruck's church.

The AJC suggested that she address national conventions of Christian clergy (Memo, Sister Ann Gillen to Rabbi Marc Tanenbaum, May 23, 1974, box 176).[20] She took advantage of her previous contacts with sisters religious and Catholic clergy (Letters, Ann Gillen to Rev Robert J. Bueter of *National Jesuit News*, Chicago, December 4, 1973 and January 31,

1974).²¹ Early on, she contacted other nuns about the plight of Soviet Jewry (Letter, Ann Gillen to Sister Ethel Kennedy, November 30, 1972, box 177). She addressed the Leadership Conference of Women Religious (LCWR) in early February 1973, calling on Christians to help relieve the suffering of Jews in USSR (RNS Press Release "Sisters Urge help for Soviet Jews...," February 1, 1973, box 176). And she led a workshop at the LCWR Assembly in August 1973 in Washington, D.C. (n.d. "Supplementary report..., March 30, 1976, and Letter, Sister Ann Gillen to Mary Danile Turner, SN, Exec. Dir. of LCWR, March 30 1976, box 175); (Henold 2008, 97, 101–103, 201, and 229).²²

Sister Gillen urged William Brown F. S. C. of the National Assembly of Religious Brothers (Letter, June 20, 1973) to create a place among future works of the Brothers for Jewish Christian Dialogue for concerns like the Task Force. She also held an initial meeting with representatives of the Catholic Archdiocese of Boston about a future conference (Letter, Rabbi Marc Tanenbaum to David T. Goldstick Esq., February 8, 1974). In the fall of 1973, Sister Gillen invited sisters religious to participate in a Human Rights Day program sponsored by Jewish Temple sisterhoods in all major American cities on December 10 ("News about the National ITFSJ," n.d., box 176).

In December 1973, Sister Gillen organized a Sisterhood of Conscience for Sylva Zalmanson, enlisting the support of national Jewish and Christian women's organizations. Her efforts on behalf of Zalmanson exemplified her energy, commitment, and mode of operations (Form Letter, Sister Ann Gillen to NITFSJ, n.d.).²³ Zalmanson was freed in August 1974 after serving four years for the Leningrad hijacking (*The Task*, volume 2, number 2, November 1974, box 210, folder 3). In the fall of 1975, Zalmanson conducted a hunger strike at the UN to help free her husband. The New York Women's Coalition on Soviet Jewry organized the event ("Highlights of Sylva Zalmanson's fast for freedom," n.d., box 176). At the demonstration near the Isaiah Wall at the UN, Sister Gillen spoke and Rabbi Shlomo Carlebach sang (NCSJ press release, September 29, 1975, box 176); Ann Gillen, "Letter to Friends of Sylva Zalmanson," September 30, 1975, box 176; and RNS, "Escapee protests Husband's internment: Interreligious Task Force backs "fast" of Jewish woman at UN," October 2, 1975, box 176).²⁴

In writing fellow sisters across the country about her contact with Sylva Zalmanson, Sister Gillen referred to the new Vatican guidelines on Catholic Jewish relations urging them to respond in areas of education, liturgy or prayer, and to cooperate in "areas of common social concern." She invited the sisters to adopt Sylva Zalmanson as a "sister." "In her fasting when she will become weak; in our cooperation we could strengthen her cause and make it successful" (Letter, Ann Gillen to Sisters Uniting, October 1, 1975, box 209, folder 3). The NITFSJ, along with the AJC in Chicago, held a special interfaith prayer service for Zalmanson at Chicago's Civil Plaza. A twenty-hour vigil and fast at the site by sympathizers followed (NITFSJ press release issued by John Reich and Sister Ann Gillen, October 7, 1975, box 175).[25]

Sister Gillen developed several other major programs. One, named *Children of the Otkazniki* (refuseniks), established ties between American children with Soviet children whose parents were denied exit visas (NITFSJ "Report on Activities" February 1974 and Letter, Rabbi Marc Tanenbaum to Ms. Goldstick, February 8, 1974). Other programs included the Friends of Federovs, the Pen Pal program, The Mother's Day Project, Fast for Freedom in Chicago, Adopt a Scientist, and the Committee of Correspondence for Human Rights.[26]

The Task Force redistributed materials on Soviet Jews issued by Jewish groups intended specifically for Christian groups and individuals. In 1974, Sister Gillen sent Brother Olsen of the National Catholic Education Association (NCEA) Prisoner of Conscience medallions and Pen Pal Packets to share with key people (Letter, Sister Gillen to Brother John D. Olsen, Exec. Sec., Secondary School Department, NCEA, DC, 1974, box 176).[27] The Task Force also worked with Jewish groups, collaborating, for example, with the Greater New York Board of Jewish Education and the Greater New York Conference on Soviet Jewry (GNYCSJ) on "Operation Write On!" (Memo, Gerald Strober to Rabbi Marc Tanenbaum, April 11, 1974, box 10, folder 3); and Memo, Eugene DuBow to Strober and Geller, March 5, 1974, box 176).[28]

Sister Gillen and the Task Force adopted NCSJ's "Operation Redemption" program involving prisoners of conscience (Letter, Gerald Strober to Sheila Woods at NCSJ, January 7, 1974, box 168; and Letter, Sheila Woods to Gerald Strober, February 12, 1974, box 168). Sister Gillen co-signed an appeal with the head of NCSJ for a Prisoner of Conscience, German Chernyak, of Leningrad to cease his hunger strike on Yom Kippur (Letter, Sheila Woods to James Rudin, September 23, 1974, box 168).[29] She and the Task Force initiated "Project Co-Adoption" which involved the cooperation of churches and synagogues. Church members "adopted" Jewish prisoners; synagogue members adopted Christian prisoners, including Baptist George Vins and Yuri Federov.[30] She hoped that churches and synagogues in the same neighborhood might have joint meetings and work together to build co-adoption bridges in an effort "to promote mutual respect and reconciliation among ourselves" (Ann Gillen, "NITFSJ, A Report 1972–74 . . . ").

Much of Sister Gillen's outreach and educational work involved speaking and demonstrating. She addressed the Assembly of the Texas Conference of Churches on February 19, 1973 in Austin "Concerning the Plight of Soviet Jewry." She emphasized that Soviet Jews were "much more severely repressed in their civil rights and the practice of their religion than members of other faiths within the Soviet Union" (NITFSJ,

"Outline of activities from October to March 1973" in MET, series 5, box 7, folder 2–4).[31]

A month later, Sister Traxler joined Sister Gillen in a protest at the World Trade Conference in Chicago, where Soviet Deputy Trade Minister V. S. Akhimov held a press conference. The Sisters, along with Rabbi Eric Friedland of the Jewish United Fund of Chicago, held a follow-up press conference in which they emphasized the plight of Soviet Jewry and the proposed Jackson-Vanik Amendment to deny the Soviet Union Most Favored Nation (MFN) status. The three then "crashed" an official luncheon in order to gain access to the Soviet Deputy Minister. The *Chicago Sun Times* published a picture of Sister Traxler attempting to confront him at the event (Memo, Judah Graubart to David Geller, March 8, 1973 with "Protest at Trade Conference," *Chicago Sun Times*, March 8, 1973). Several follow-up articles on Soviet policies toward Jews appeared in the local press.

Sister Gillen spoke often at synagogues, churches, and conferences of both Christian and Jewish groups (Letters, Dr. Richard L. Firster, director of Judeo-Christian Relations, American Baptist Churches of PA and DE to Sister Ann Gillen, April 4, 1974 and Sister Ann Gillen to Mr. Alex Holstein, Syracuse, September 14, 1974, box 176; and Letter, Sister Ann Gillen to Rev. Brian Hehir, ND C1976, box 175). Her routine and schedule were rigorous and intense. In mid-June 1975, she spoke in Wilmington, Delaware, before the local Jewish Community Relations Council (JCRC) (Letter, Abraham Bayer, NJCRAC, to Ann Gillen, June 20, 1975, box 176). A few days later, she spoke at Messiah College in Philadelphia (Letter, Rabbi A. James Rudin to Dr. Ronald Sider, Dean, Messiah College, June 23, 1975, box 176).[32] The following month she appeared at events in Wilmington and in Chicago, spent the next week in Houston speaking and meeting, worked in Chicago a few days later, and then attended a Common Cause meeting in Washington, D.C. She returned to Chicago on September 22 for a Task Force meeting. She spent the week of September 23–30 in NYC and from October 28–30, 1975, she participated in a national workshop on Christian Jewish relations in Memphis ("Schedule of Sr. Ann Gillen, n.d., box 176). In almost every city she visited, the RNS, the Jewish press, and general media publicized her local and national activities (Letter, Rabbi James Rudin to Dr. Arnold T. Olson, president Evangelical Free Church of America, October 23, 1975. "USSR Harassment of Jews Accelerates, A nun Reports." Press release, RNS, November 25, 1975).[33]

She also focused on women's groups. In December 1975, she spoke at the St. Louis Women's Plea for Soviet Jews (*Missouri Jewish Post and Opinion*, December 5, 1975, box 175; and Letter, Rabbi Stiffman to Sister Ann Gillen, January 13, 1976, box 175). In December 1975, in Toledo, Ohio, she gave a talk and helped set up a "women's committee for Soviet Jewry" (Letter, Alex Greenblatt to Sister Ann Gillen, January 21, 1976, box 175).

Sister Gillen and the Task Force cooperated with the NCSJ and with the Union of Councils (Supplementary Report—March to June 1973; Letter Jay E. Brett of AJC Buffalo Niagara Frontier Chapter to Ann Gillen with clipping from *Buffalo Evening News* of April 5, 1973, April 11, 1973).[34]

Other regular speakers for the Task Force included Sister Traxler and Rabbi Rudin. In December 1975, Sister Traxler gave the keynote address at the Women's Plea for Human Rights for Soviet Jews in Detroit. She told her audience that she had been moved by a visit in high school to Dachau after which she vowed to bring Christians to an awareness "of what we have done in our history to Jews." She noted that in 1975 the Soviet dissident Andre Sakharov said, "that only Christians in America can liberate the Jews in Russia" (Jewish Community Council of Metropolitan Detroit, December 10, 1975, box 175; and Catherine Haven "Nun Seeks Commitment from US Christians to assist Soviet Jewry" in *Michigan Catholic*, December 17, 1975, MET, series 5, box 6, folder 2–4).[35]

Sister Gillen also undertook regional speaking tours. For example, she traveled to the West Coast in March 1974 to meet with Jewish, Christian, and interfaith groups in Los Angeles, San Francisco, Seattle, and Spokane (Letter, Sister Ann Gillen to Bishop Leo T. Maher, January 16, 1973).[36] Radio and television news programs and local newspapers covered many of her activities.[37] She worked hard to establish interfaith cooperation focusing on Soviet Jewry, while not neglecting the persecution of Christians and others in the Soviet Union (Spring Report of the NITF Secretariat . . . , April 2, 1974, box 176).[38] In Los Angeles, she met with AJC staff and with Zev Yaroslavsky of the UCSJ and the JCRC people. She conducted a press conference at the AJC with Dorothy Townsend of the *Los Angeles Times* and Is Lechtman of *B'nai B'rith Messenger*. She participated in a radio interview, spoke at a synagogue, and had lunch with the San Fernando Interfaith Council (Letter, Murray Tenenbaum to Sister Ann Gillen, April 3, 1974, box 176).[39]

In San Francisco, she led a workshop at the National Federation of Priests Councils (Letter, Ann Gillen to Mr. Ernest Weiner, AJC, San Francisco, April 8, 1974, box 176).[40] She also had an interview with *The Catholic Monitor* for educational television, where she talked about Soviet Jewry and the Children of the Otkazniki program. She had an interview with the *San Francisco Chronicle and Examiner*. She also met with temple sisterhood groups regarding the Sisterhood of Conscience and Pen Pal Programs. In Seattle, she met with staff of the AJC, had lunch with Seattle's Interreligious Committee, and participated in an interview with the local *Jewish Transcript*. She also met with sisters religious and African American clergy. She spoke at the University of Seattle and had an interview with the *Seattle Times*. In Spokane, she was interviewed by the *Spokane Daily Chronicle* and had lunch with a group interested in setting up an interfaith group for Soviet Jewry. She spoke at a Jewish temple and met the chancellor of the Roman Catholic diocese of Spokane and the assistant superintendent of Catholic schools regarding the Pen Pal Program.[41]

RELATIONS WITH THE ISRAELI LIAISON BUREAU

The Task Force also maintained ties with the Israeli Liaison Bureau. The NITFSJ followed knowingly, or unknowingly, the wishes of the Bureau. The Liaison Bureau was a clandestine operation focused on Soviet Jewry in the office of the Israeli prime minister (Lazin 2005). In the United States one of its agents served as a member of the Israeli Consulate in New York City and at the UN. He/she dealt with relations with American Jewish organizations, advocacy for Soviet Jewry, and the media.

Early on, the NITFSJ became interested in the subject of both Jewish and non-Jewish prisoners of conscience (See above, chapter 1, n.20). December 1972 marked the fiftieth anniversary of the Soviet Union. On past anniversaries Soviet officials gave amnesty and freedom to certain criminals, excluding political prisoners. The Liaison Bureau mounted a worldwide campaign to pressure the Soviet Union to release, and grant amnesty, to "those Jews who have been arrested in conjunction with trials arising out of their desire to go to Israel . . . ," on the fiftieth anniversary (Memo, Abraham Karlikow to David Geller, November 16, 1972, Bertram Gold box 193).[42]

The AJC joined this effort. Its coordinator for Soviet Jewry, David Geller, suggested mounting a worldwide effort timed for the final two weeks of December. Rabbi Tanenbaum met with Sister Gillen in Chicago to develop a program around the theme of amnesty, which might include statements from prominent Christian theologians and leaders (Letter, David Geller to Abraham Karlikow, Jacobo Kovadloff, Sergio Nudelstejer, Bernard Resnikoff, and Zachariah Shuster re: "Amnesty for Jewish prisoners in USSR," November 17, 1972, Bertram Gold box 193).[43] He wanted to create an advertisement with signatures of Christian dignitaries from around the world (Memo, David Geller to Rabbi Tanenbaum, November 28, 1972, box 177).[44]

As part of a coordinated effort by the Liaison Bureau to gain amnesty for thirty-nine Jewish prisoners of conscience on the 50th anniversary of the Soviet Union, Sister Gillen urged Task Force affiliates (Memo, n.d., box 210; and NITFSJ "Information Alert," November 1, 1972, box 177) to send cables and letters to Soviet leaders and President Nixon, hold rallies and meetings at the local level, and appeal to the local media. She cosponsored a demonstration on December 12, 1972 at Prudential Plaza in Chicago marking "freedom month" for Soviet Prisoners of Conscience.[45]

In working for amnesty for prisoners of conscience on the fiftieth anniversary of the Soviet Revolution, the Task Force participated in a general campaign initiated by the Israeli Liaison Bureau. Sister Gillen may or may not have been aware of the role of the Liaison Bureau in these efforts. In another instance, there seems to have been more direct cooperation between the Task Force, the IAD, and the Liaison Bureau.

In October 1975, Rabbi James Rudin wrote Sister Gillen (Memo, October 3, 1975, box 176) that he and Rabbi Tannenbaum would appreciate her "sending the enclosed letter to Mr. Levine in California and mailing it directly to him from Chicago." The letter, prepared by IAD and signed by Sister Gillen on NITFSJ stationery and dated September 30, 1975, was addressed to Mr. Melvin Levine of Beverly Hills. The letter requested that he undertake a "fact finding mission to the Soviet Union." She informed him that several prominent national government and public affairs personalities were interested in joining the mission, including Mr. Maxwell Greenberg, a prominent lawyer active in the Los Angeles Jewish community. She requested that he ask Senator Alan Cranston (D-CA) to serve as chair and to join the mission. The Task Force was prepared to pay the expenses for Senator Cranston, Mr. Greenberg, and Mr. Levine. As instructed, she sent a copy of the letter to the Honorable I. Rager at the Israeli Consulate, the Liaison Bureau agent in New York City.[46] Mr. Levine responded to Sister Gillen (Letter, October 23, 1976, box 176) that he was flattered and would be delighted to explore the proposed plan. He reported that Max Greenberg was also willing to participate. He intended to contact Senator Cranston's office and would get back to her.[47]

THE SECOND NITFSJ CONSULTATION

In April 1973, the Task Force sent out 1,300 invitations signed by Sargent Shriver for the Second National Interreligious Consultation on Soviet Jewry scheduled for May 14 and 15 in Washington, D.C. (Letters, Gerald Strober to Sister Ann Gillen, January 1, 1973, box 176; Rev. John Steinbruck to Sister Ann Gillen, January 4, 1973; box 211, folder 8; and Sister Ann Gillen to Rev. John Steinbruck, January 24, 1973, box 176).[48] Only forty-five people, including the speakers, attended (NICSJ, DC Registration List, May 14, 15, 1973, box 174). Sargent Shriver welcomed the participants at the opening session (Letter, Sister Ann Gillen to Sargent Shriver, May 18, 1973).[49] Sister Gillen then gave a progress report on the Task Force. In the afternoon, Professor Elihu Bergman of the Harvard Center for Population Studies gave a briefing, followed by a talk by deputy assistant secretary of state for European Affairs, John Armitage, at the State Department. In the evening, participants held an interfaith vigil at Reverend John Steinbruck's Luther Place Memorial Church followed by a candlelight procession to the site of the silent vigil opposite the Soviet Embassy.[50] The Consultation met the next morning at the A. M. E Church. Lunch took place on Capitol Hill, followed by visits with Congressional Representatives, including Senator Henry Jackson (D-WA) and Congressman Charles Vanik (D-OH).[51] Jerry Goodman of the NCSJ conducted a closing debriefing session. In statement issued after the conference, the NITFSJ announced that the struggle would continue "until every Soviet Jew can either live as a Jew or leave for nation of his choice" (NITFSJ, Press Release, May 15, 1973, box 174).[52]

While many in the AJC thought that the Consultation had attracted too few participants, its Washington lobbyist praised the event: "And while the actual attendance at the meeting was somewhat of a disappointment, it was a great success in terms of its impact where it counts and on the follow up it will undoubtedly encourage" (Letter, Hyman Bookbinder to Sister Ann Gillen, May 24, 1973).[53]

LOCAL INTERRELIGIOUS TASK FORCES

From the start, the NITFSJ hoped to establish local level task forces.[54] Some were set up with ease, others took years to establish, and some efforts failed.[55] While cooperating with the NITFSJ, most remained independent of it.

Sister Gillen's first efforts to set up a local/regional interreligious task force took place in Houston, Texas, where she had previously lived and worked. The NITFSJ scheduled a regional interreligious consultation on Soviet Jewry in Houston for February 28, 1973 (Memo, David Geller to Seymour Lachman, January 22, 1973, box 176).[56] The turnout was disappointing (Letter, John Wildenthal to friends, February 6, 1973; and Memo, Sister Ann Gillen to David Geller, March 5, 1973). But Sister Gillen felt that they had reached a good group of "leaders and movers" (Letter, Sister Ann Gillen to John Wildenthal, May 24, 1973).[57] In September, John Wildenthal's Houston Committee of the NITFSJ sent out several telegrams urging support of the Jackson-Vanik amendment. Sister Gillen spoke again for the local task force in January 1974 (Letter, Sister Ann Gillen to John Wildenthal, January 21. 1974, box 176).[58] The Houston Committee of the NITFSJ organized the Second Annual Interfaith Prayer Meeting for the Freedom of Soviet Jews on June 7, 1974 on the steps of City Hall. The JCC of Metropolitan Houston co-sponsored the event (Press release, JCC of Metropolitan Houston, June 5, 1974).

Washington, D.C. became a center of widespread interfaith activity on behalf of Soviet Jewry. The Task Force held many events in the city involving local Christian clergy and lay people. The Reverend John Steinbruck, Pastor of Luther Place Memorial Church, played a key role.[59] In asking him to join the NITFSJ, Sister Gillen noted (Letter, April 5, 1974) the failed effort to establish a Washington Task Force, but commented that "John Steinbruck is a Task Force in himself."[60]

Reverend Steinbruck organized a 1974 Easter Sunday procession for Soviet Jewry, which included a Passover Seder on Palm Sunday sponsored by the Downtown Cluster of Congregations in Washington, D.C. (Memo, Brant Coopersmith to Rabbi Marc Tanenbaum, April 5, 1974, box 210, folder 3).[61] Other clergy included the African American church leaders Reverend Dr. Robert T. Pruitt, pastor of the Metropolitan AME Church, and Mrs. Elois Jones, president of the Downtown Cluster of Congregations and member of the Asbury Methodist Church. Dr. Pruitt was heckled at church and called "Uncle Tom" by some young African American men saying, "what about the rights of people in South Africa?" This was the only incident that marred "what turned out to be an inspiring and impressive occasion" (Ibid.). Later in a note to Sister Gillen (April 15, 1974), Reverend Steinbruck expressed disappointment that no Catholic clergy participated.

Sister Gillen had various degrees of success in establishing local task forces in Milwaukee, Baltimore, Louisville, Philadelphia, Boston, and Miami. In Milwaukee and Baltimore, she led the initiative (Letter, Sister Gillen to Norman Sider, JCRC Indianapolis, December 17, 1973; and Ann Gillen, "Spring report . . .," April 2, 1974, box 176).[62] In December 1972, she headed a panel of experts in Milwaukee at a public hearing on the denial of rights to Soviet Jews, which was sponsored by the Milwaukee Leadership Conference of Jewish Women's Organizations at the student union at the University of Wisconsin. She spoke about Soviet Jewish prisoners of conscience (Memo, Eugene DuBow to Mrs. Sylvia Weber, November 3, 1972, box 177; Letter, Sister Ann Gillen to Mrs. Herman Tuchman, November 20, 1972, box 177; and Letter, Eugene DuBow to Mrs. Sylvia Weber, March 12, 1972).[63] In May following a talk at Hadassah in Milwaukee, Sister Gillen wrote to a nun there about the need to involve more Christians in Jewish and human rights causes. She suggested setting up a Milwaukee task force (Letter, Sister Ann Gillen to Sister Maureen Hopkins SDS Milwaukee, May 19, 1973).

In late December 1973, Sister Gillen spoke at a meeting organized by the Baltimore Committee for Soviet Jewry. She hoped her hosts would develop an interfaith committee for Soviet Jewry (Letter, Ann Gillen to Sol Goldstein, January 8, 1974, box 176). She returned on January 22 with Gerald Strober to meet with local AJC staff and Christians about a regional Task Force meeting in April (Memo, Gerald Strober to Rabbi Tanenbaum, January 14, 1974, box 212, folder 3). The Baltimore Committee on Soviet Jewry held a one-day conference on "Détente and Human Rights" at the College of Notre Dame in Baltimore on April 30th (Letter, Lois Rosenfield to Dr. Thomas Bird, February 22, 1974; and Memo, Sol Goldstein to Baltimore Interfaith Committee on Human Rights, March 4, 1974, box 176).[64]

Catholic clergy and Protestant evangelicals played active roles in a very successful interreligious task force for Soviet Jewry in Louisville.[65] When the Interreligious Council for Soviet Jewry in Louisville requested that Jewish organizations "help a Catholic sister gain her freedom from behind the Iron Curtain" Jerry Goodman of NCSJ objected (Letter, Jerry Goodman to Ted Comet and Abraham J. Bayer, cc: Rudin, box 176).[66]

By March 1974, the Louisville Interreligious Council for Soviet Jewry, headed by Father Stanley A. Schmidt, had been active for almost eighteen months. It was affiliated with the NCSJ, NITFSJ, and the SSSJ (Letter Alan Stark to Abraham Bayer, Jerry Goodman, Sister Margaret Traxler, and Rabbi Mark Tanenbaum, March 8, 1974, box 176; and document of Father Schmidt, "Louisville Interreligious Council for Soviet Jewry").[67] On November 4, 1974, the Council published a letter expressing its understanding that all religions were suffering in the USSR, but that "Jewish community suffers special deprivation" (Louisville Interreligious Council . . . , Form letter to a friend, November 4, 1974, box 210, folder 3). For the next two years, Schmidt headed the local task force and spoke in churches, before Jewish groups, and at seminaries and colleges (Letter, Father Stanley Schmidt to Sister Ann Gillen, April 14, 1976, box 175).[68]

Philadelphia also had an active local task force. Following Vatican II's passage of *Nostra Aetate No. 4*, Cardinal Krol of Philadelphia set up the Cardinal's Commission on Human Relations. The Commission reached out to the Jewish community of Philadelphia and in 1973, Sister Gloria Coleman, a sister from Ann Gillen's order, SHCJ, began to work on the Jewish agenda of the Cardinal's Commission (Sister Gloria Coleman, interviews by author, Rosemont, PA, March 12, 2012 and June 10, 2015).[69] She headed the interreligious affairs unit. Her programs involved Jewish and non-Jewish (Ukrainian) groups with co-religionists in the Soviet Union. She had extensive contact with the local CRC and worked with the AJC, the ADL, local temples, rabbis, and individuals in the Jewish community.

Sister Gillen, however, initially failed in her efforts to initiate a local level interreligious task force in the Philadelphia area. On December 5, 1973, she wrote the Reverend Donald Clifford of Raven Hill Academy in Germantown (box 176) urging him to have St. Joseph's College sponsor a conference on Soviet Jewry.[70] By the summer of 1974, the College agreed to host a program on Soviet Jewry the following academic year (Letter, Rabbi A. James Rudin to Dr. Thomas Melady, Executive VP, St. Joseph's College, Philadelphia, July 24, 1974; and Letter, Sister Ann Gillen to Mrs. Israel Bender, Dropsie College, August 19, 1974, box 176).[71] Eventually, Sister Coleman established a local interreligious task force with the JCRC and the local AJC (Memo, Rita Blume to Murray Friedman re: "Local Interreligious Task Force," July 29, 1975). Over the years the interreligious activity on behalf of Soviet Jewry would expand dramatically in the city of brotherly love. While independent of the NITSF, Sister Coleman often cooperated with the national Task Force and participated with Sister Gillen in many activities, including two visits to the Soviet Union.

Sister Gillen spoke in Miami in December 1973 (Letter, Sister Ann Gillen to Felice Tradmann, December 16, 1973, box 176). By early 1974, an interreligious committee for Soviet Jewry operated there (Letter, Faith Mesnekoff to David Geller, March 13, 1974, box 176). The committee attracted evangelical and mainline Protestants, Catholics, and others. The Greater Miami chapter of the AJC, working with the CRC of the Jewish Federation, and the South Florida Conference on Soviet Jewry, assisted the new group. The AJC of Greater Miami served as its Secretariat and the NITFSJ provided materials. At a preliminary meeting on January 24, 1974, participants elected Reverend Luther Pierce as chair. The committee's declared goal was to "to get as much understanding by Christians of the condition of Jews in the Soviet Union and to secure support of the Christian community for them" (Memo, Walter Zand to Will Katz, November 18, 1974, box 210, folder 3).[72]

In honor of Solidarity Day with Soviet Jewry in June 1974, the group held a silent vigil on the steps of the local courthouse (Letter, Edward Rosenthal, CRC of the Miami Jewish Federation to Sister Ann Gillen, June 5, 1974, box 176).[73] The vigil drew 250 to 300 people, including Catholic and Protestant clergy and African American and white laypersons. The event received widespread television and newspaper coverage.[74] The local task force held a seminar on Human Rights on December 4th at the University of Miami (Zand to Katz, November 18, 1974, box 210, folder 3).[75]

Reverend Luther Pierce resigned when he moved to Connecticut at the end of 1974 (Memo, Reverend Luther Pierce to members of South Florida Interreligious Task Force, January 15, 1975. box 176). The Task Force members decided that that his replacement should come from the Christian community. The Reverend August Kling and Reverend Richard Bailar became co-chairs. They discussed the need to include members of the Greek Orthodox Church and Spanish-speaking clergy, as well as additional membership from the archdiocese. The group sponsored a talk on Soviet Jewry by David Geller on April 7, 1975 (Memo, Brenda Shapiro, Coordination of SFITFSJ, March 24, 1975, box 176).

Finally, Boston is a good example of IAD efforts to help Sister Gillen set up a local interreligious task force (Minutes, Meeting of FAC Steering Committee, March 21, 1974, box 83). The IAD initiated a meeting in Boston on January 25, 1974, with Sister Gillen, Phil Perlmutter, head of AJC's Boston office, and twenty-five to thirty local Jewish Federation and Christian leaders to discuss the idea of a Boston-New England Task Force on Soviet Jewry (Memo, Gerald Strober to Rabbi Tanenbaum, January 10, 1974, box 176). That evening Sister Gillen spoke at Temple Beth Elohim in Wellesley Hills. Two days later she held a lunch meeting on Soviet Jewry at the Paulist Center in Boston (Letter, Sister Ann Gillen to Sister Mary Stanton, Carmelite Monastery, Roxbury, MA, January 10, 1974, box 176).[76] Around this time, Rabbi Roland Gittelsohn of Temple Israel in Boston delivered a sermon, "Strange Bedfellow," about a nun and the

Soviet Jewry movement, which received wide publicity (Letter, Gerald Strober to Rabbi Roland Gittelsohn, April 10, 1974, box 176).[77]

A CLASH IN NEW YORK CITY

A confrontation over "turf" developed between the national Task Force and the Greater New York Conference for Soviet Jewry (GNYCSJ). Established in 1971 by the New York UJA-Jewish Federation, GNYCSJ served as an umbrella for local Soviet Jewish groups in New York City and its suburbs. Its annual Solidarity Sunday Parade along Fifth Avenue became the largest Soviet Jewry advocacy event in the United States.[78]

Rabbi Aaron Decter of the Rockland-Orange Board of Rabbis suggested setting up a local coordinating agency within the GNYCSJ to mobilize the Christian religious community on behalf of Soviet Jewry. In a letter to Malcolm Hoenlein (re: "Religious Coalition and Soviet Jewry," August 20, 1974, box 168) he argued: "There is need for more sustained action, and for a more intensive program of information and of impressing upon the Christian religious leaders and the lay religious leaders that they are witness to spiritual genocide." He also praised the NITFSJ.[79]

Rabbi Decter's proposed "Religious Coalition for Soviet Jewry" would be headed by the GNYCSJ and have local representatives of national Jewish agencies. The Coalition would organize programs and activities on the local level and "interpret the needs of Soviet Jewry and American Jewish feelings." It would "serve the NJCRAC on a consultative basis to help local communities throughout the United States to mobilize local Christian leadership in cooperation with the Inter-Religious Task Force" (Memo to Hoenlein, August 20, 1974). He offered to set up the group under Jerry Goodman's (NCSJ) direction on the national level.

Jerry Goodman forwarded Rabbi Decter's memo to Rabbi Marc Tanenbaum. In an angry response to Goodman (Letter, September 6, 1974, box 210, folder 3), Rabbi Tanenbaum emphasized that an effective organization to involve Christians in the American Soviet Jewry advocacy movement already existed. He attacked Decter's assumption that the Jewish community was "lagging in our efforts to mobilize" Christians. On the contrary he argued, "Christian leadership has responded to the cause of Soviet Jewry far more extensively and consistently than they have to almost any other issue of Jewish concern." He believed that there was no justification to create another body that would seek funds from the same sources and duplicate the efforts of the NITFSJ. Moreover, he continued, "we have succeeded in helping this to become a Christian initiative led by a Christian nun who is concerned, together with her Christian colleagues, about the human rights of Soviet Jewry." He cited the tremendous press coverage that Sister Gillen, Sister Traxler, Father Robert Drinan, and others received every time they spoke out about Soviet Jewry. Despite Decter's good intentions, Tanenbaum concluded, his efforts would "perform a major disservice to the cause of Soviet Jewry." Finally, he noted Sister Gillen's genuine concern and disappointment that she had not been consulted on the matter.

The IAD and NITFSJ tried to establish a local interreligious task force in New York City. They sponsored a lecture by Professor Thomas Bird on the status of religious communities in the Soviet Union on May 30, 1975. The New York Council of Churches hosted the event at NCC headquarters (Form Letter from Sister Margaret Traxler, Professor André LaCocque and Rabbi Marc Tanenbaum, May 19, 1975, n.d. 209 folder 3; Letter, Rabbi A. James Rudin to Tom Bird, June 17, 1975, box 176; and Memo, Arthur Greenberg and Leonard Yaseen [chairs] to members of National Interreligious Affairs Commission, AJC, April 1, 1975, box 469). At the lecture, Sister Gillen led a discussion on the possibility of organizing a greater New York interreligious task force on Soviet Jewry.[80]

As noted in the beginning of this chapter, a Greater New York Interreligious Task Force affiliated with the NITFSJ actively participated in the hunger strike at the Isaiah Wall conducted by Sylva Zalmanson in September 1975 ("NY Women's Coalition on Soviet Jewry...," n.d., Fall 1975, box 176; and NICSJ press release, September 29, 1975, box 176). The NITFSJ hoped to hold a New York City consultation in the fall of 1975 to strengthen its presence in the city and region (NITFSJ, "New developments for 1975–76," n.d.; and RNS, "Her Ailing Father Is in a Soviet Prison," box 175).[81]

A POSSIBLE MOVE TO NEW YORK CITY

In the spring of 1974, the AJC discussed moving Sister Gillen's office in the fall to New York City (Memo, Gerald Strober to Rabbi Marc Tanenbaum, May 23, 1974, box 176; and Minutes of Interreligious Affairs Commission AJC, February 20, 1975 box 469). The attempt by the GNYCSJ to set up a local interreligious task force may have influenced the discussion on whether to move the the Task Force from Chicago to NYC.[82] More importantly, NYC was the home of the AJC (and its IAD), the NCSJ, and other major Jewish and Christian organizations, including the mainline Protestant NCC ("Minutes of interreligious Affairs Commission Meeting, February 20, 1975, box 469).[83]

In August 1974, Sister Traxler wrote Rabbi Tanenbaum (August 20, 1974, box 213, folder 11) that she expected that the office would relocate to NYC. Many favored relocating to the office of the NCC at 475 Riverside Drive (Letter, Sister Ann Gillen to William Weiler and Ms. Claire Randall, NCC, September 30, 1974). Although DuBow believed that housing the local task force within a Christian facility was preferable, he suggested that the AJC house Sister Gillen temporarily in their NYC (Memo, DuBow to Tananbaum, January 13, 1975).

In February 1975, the move to NCC headquarters was still being negotiated (Memo, NITFSJ "Report to co-chairmen," February 1975, box 176). Sister Gillen remained hopeful about a move to either NCC or to the Episcopal Church Center in NYC.[84] The move would never take place.[85] According to Sister Gillen, the available office space was too small and other options were too expensive. It is possible that she opposed the move to preserve her independence from the AJC.[86] A NYC office would bring her, and the Task Force, physically closer to the IAD, the AJC, and the NCC.

TRAVEL TO THE SOVIET UNION

Travel to the USSR became a major activity for the Task Force, with visits by Sister Gillen and others. The Task Force encouraged visits to the Soviet Union by American clergy. Suggested itineraries included visits with persecuted Jews and Christians and offered pre-departure briefings. Sister Gillen and the IAD also became involved with Soviet religious delegations visiting the United States on programs sponsored by the NCC and others.

In the fall of 1972, Representative Robert Drinan (D-MA), himself a Catholic priest, agreed to lead a fact-finding mission to Moscow in early winter to study the problem of Soviet Jews (Office of Representative Robert Drinan, "Press Release," October 29, 1972, box 210, folder 4).[87] He hoped to investigate the proposed educational tax and exit fees. In December, the IAD announced that Rabbi Marc Tanenbaum, Representative Andrew Young, and Margaret Brennan, chair of the Conference of Mothers Superiors, would join Representative Drinan on the trip to Moscow (Telegram, Rabbi Tanenbaum to Dr. Eugene Carson Blake, December 5, 1972, box 176).[88]

In December 1972, the Task Force announced that the planned interreligious delegation would seek amnesty for political prisoners (including Sylva Zalmanson) and report to key Soviet authorities that the American people, and not just the Jewish community, wanted an end the education tax, rights for Soviet Jews to emigrate to Israel or elsewhere, and the right to perpetuate Jewish culture and religion in USSR (Letter, Rabbi Tanenbaum to David Goldstick, December 29, 1972, box 177). The group hoped to leave on February 15th, 1973, if it succeeded in obtaining visas (Letter, Sister Margaret Traxler to Rep. Robert Drinan, January 2, 1973, box 176; and Memo, Strober to Geller, January 17, 1973, box 176).[89]

Due to visa problems, the AJC moved the trip to February 11–19, 1973 (NICSJ, n.d. and; Memo, Strober to Rabbi Tanenbaum, January 23, 1973, box 212, folder 3).[90] The AJC had plans to hold press conferences in

Moscow, London, and New York on the group's return. When Soviet authorities notified the group that there was no hotel space available in Moscow, the Task Force cancelled the trip (RNS, "Interreligious Group Supporting Jews Lash Soviet Cancellation of Visit," February 9, 1973).[91] At a press conference in the Capitol building, Rep. Drinan harshly criticized the Soviet actions, which resulted in the cancellation of the mission (NICSJ press release, February 9, 1973, SMET, series 5 box 7, folders 2–9; and form letter, Rabbi A. James Rudin to Bishop Melvin Wheatly, Denver Co and others, March 22, 1974).[92]

Sister Gillen made her first trip to the Soviet Union in June/July 1974. She travelled with two nuns representing NCAN (Memo, Strober to Rabbi Tanenbaum, May 23, 1974).[93] She visited with Soviet Jews in Moscow and Leningrad and spread the message about the work of the Task Force. In Moscow, she met with well-known refuseniks Tamara and Anatoli Galperin. Anatoli took her to visit another well-known refusenik, Vladimir Slepak (see above n.26), where she also met with Natasha Federov, a Christian, whose husband, Yuri, faced an additional eleven years in prison for the alleged hijacking of the airplane near Leningrad. According to Natasha, Sister Gillen was the first Christian from the United States to meet with them (Letter, Ann Gillen to Margaret Traxler, July 24, 1974, MET, series 1.1, box 1, folder 2; and "Executive Director brings task force message to Soviet Jews," n.d., box 210, folder 3).[94]

Sister Gillen spoke with Slepak about cooperation between Christians and Jews in prison and outside. She then visited Viktor Brailovksy, a scientist whose seminar had been cancelled during Nixon's earlier visit to the USSR. She also met Sasha Lunts, a well-known mathematician and active refusenik.[95] In Leningrad, she met with active refuseniks Varnovitsky, Pauline Eppelman, and Lena and Arkady Rabinov. She met others at a meeting outside the main synagogue in Leningrad. She wrote that Soviet Jews looked to the Jackson-Vanik Amendment and Western help for their freedom. They were free people because they were unafraid (Letter, Sister Ann Gillen to Sister Margaret Traxler, MET, series 1.1, box 1, folder 2).

In Israel, she met with Abraham Harman, President of the Hebrew University, who had a close and active association with the Liaison Bureau (Lazin 2005, 65, 71). She also greeted new immigrants from the Soviet Union at the airport.[96] She later met with Dr. Emil Luboshitz, a recently arrived activist from the USSR. On her way back to the United States, she visited human rights activists in Madrid and Dublin.[97]

In July 1975, Sister Gillen announced that Representative Drinan would be leading an interreligious study tour to the USSR from August 13–24, 1975 "to express the friendship and solidarity of the American people for the Christians and Jews of the Soviet Union." Sponsored by the NITFSJ, the tour would visit Moscow, Leningrad, and Kiev (Form Letter, Ann Gillen to friends, July 1, 1975 box 209, folder 3).[98] She planned to travel with the group (Letter, Sister Ann Gillen to Rabbi Tanenbaum, August 8, 1975).[99] However, the Task Force cancelled the trip in early August when the Soviets agreed to grant a visa only to Representative Drinan (Memo, Rabbi Rudin to Sister Ann Gillen, August 14, 1975; and Letter, Rabbi Rudin to Jerry Goodman, n.d., Spertus, box 48).[100]

Representative Drinan visited the Soviet Union, Romania, and Israel from August 13 to August 31, 1975 (R. Drinan, S.J. "Conversations with Soviet Jews," *The Jewish Advocate*, August 31, 1975, box 209 folder 3). One refusenik in Leningrad told him "If it were not for the Congress of the United States all of us could be in Siberia today" (R. Drinan, SJ, "Conversations with Soviet Jews," August 31, 1975, box 194). While Drinan had known about the affliction of Soviet Jews for years he wrote, "I was still appalled in Leningrad to learn personally of the humiliations and indignities which are inflicted on every individual who makes public his desire to go to Israel." He noted that there were forty-one Prisoners of Zion from Leningrad in twenty-seven different prisons. He reported that he could not disprove the rumor spread by some Jewish groups that the Kremlin was planning an operation to bring about the complete suppression of the Jewish emigration movement. He questioned the Soviet claim that 98.5 percent of Jews that applied obtained visas, suggesting that this figure counted only a small number and neglected 100,000 applicants.

In Moscow, Drinan met with Alexander Lerner, who was denied a visa to become a visiting professor at Case Western University (Beckerman 2010, 263–268).[101] He met with Anatoly Shcharansky, to whom he gave a picture of his wife, Avital, with Jewish activist and Holocaust survivor Elie Wiesel.[102] Drinan noted that the forty-ruble ($55) fee for the application to emigrate violated the Basket III provisions of the Helsinki Accords.

He met with Andrei Sakharov who warned of a revival of Stalinism and the advent of a new wave of oppression (see above n. 35). Sakharov explained to Drinan "that only the Christians of the world, and particularly Christians in America, could so influence world opinion that Russia would simply be required both to allow Jews to emigrate if they so desire and to permit religious freedom in the Soviet Union" (*Congressional Record*, vol.121, #151, October 8, 1975, Human Rights "Congressman Drinan Reports on his recent trip to Russia, Romania and Israel," Spertus, Drinan box 92). The Congressman agreed and argued that the safety and future of Soviet Jews depended on those in the West who cared about them. Sakharov also complained that while Jews in the USSR received help and that there were protests from fellow Jews on their behalf, few, if any, protested the treatment of Christians in the Soviet Union. He talked about the lack of support for his friend, the imprisoned biologist, Dr. Sergei Kovalyov, who would soon be tried in Lithuania (Tracey Early, "Father Congressman Robert Drinan asks commitment for Jews in USSR," RNS, September 23, 1975).

In Israel, Representative Drinan met with recent Soviet immigrants. He hoped that the example of those who had left and those who wanted to leave would "inspire Christians to work diligently to obtain the fulfillment of religious and human freedom in Russia for Jews as well as for Christians" (Letter, Rabbi A. James Rudin to friend, October 9, 1975. box 209, folder 3, with document Robert Drinan, "Conversations in Rumania and Israel trip, August 13–31).

In a talk at the AJC upon his return, Drinan suggested that the Soviets might punish its Jews for the failed trade agreement and predicted that "they could even have another Holocaust." He proposed leveraging the Helsinki Accords on their behalf (Early, "Father . . . USSR," September 23, 1975).[103] He talked of American Jews turning to American Christians "to do something specific, generous and unprecedented." He urged the placement of full-page ads in Catholic newspapers during the four-week Advent period, calling for the rescue of Soviet Jews, because the Soviets might deport all refuseniks to Siberia.

THE TASK NEWSLETTER

The Task Force regularly published a newsletter, *The Task*, which was distributed to Christian organizations, churches, advocates for Soviet Jewry, and individuals. Management of the first issue reflected the AJC's desire to exercise the power of approval over final copy, but not censorship. The Chicago Midwest office of the AJC, in consultation with Sister Gillen, prepared a first draft, which it then sent to Rabbi Tanenbaum, who edited the newsletter and then published it in the name of the Task Force (Memo, Eugene DuBow to Rabbi Tanenbaum, November 21, 1972, box 177).[104] *The Task* was issued quarterly, along with supplemental special alerts.[105]

Eugene DuBow sent a draft of the first edition of *The Task* to the AJC in New York in November 1972 (Ibid.).[106] A final four-sided version of the first issue appeared around February 1973.[107] The masthead read: "*The Task*: The voice of Christian-Jewish Concern; An analytical report on the social, economic, political and cultural plight of Jews in the Soviet Union" (*The Task* (MET, series 5, box 7, folders 2–9). The first article dealt with the setting up of the Secretariat, the first Consultation, the November 1972 meetings, and Sister Gillen's appointment as Chair.[108] The newsletter hoped to inform its readers, arouse the conscience of Christian and Jewish communities, and establish effective communication and collaboration so that Soviet Jews would either be free to live as Jews in the USSR or to leave for a country of their choice.[109] The first issue also described mid-February mission to Moscow that had been cancelled due to a supposed lack of hotel space. The newsletter urged the USSR to show a genuine desire for détente by granting "justice and freedom to the Jews and other deprived religious groups and nationalities." The first issue also reported on plans for the first area NITFSJ conference at Saint Mary's Seminary in Houston, Texas, in February and a planned Second National Consultation in Washington, D.C. in May 1973. Another article dealt with Jewish emigration and exit and educational fees. Another short piece covered the Jackson-Vanik Amendment. A section titled "Aren't all Religious Groups Oppressed in the USSR?" read: ". . . let it be said that the Task Force is deeply concerned about the other oppressed groups in the USSR and indeed, in other parts of the world too. But . . . at this time, it is essential that the cry for help which comes from the Soviet Jews must be heard by the church as well as the synagogue. One group must assume this responsibility as its *only* agenda." While no group in the USSR enjoyed full freedom of worship "the Jewish community suffers special deprivation," and was "not allowed the same advantages as other groups" and in the Nazi Holocaust "the Jewish community lost one-third of its people" and ". . . Christian anti-Semitism was certainly one of the reasons why such inconceivable barbarity could and actually did happen in our time." Finally, the newsletter recommended books by Thomas Bird, Arie Eliav, Yehoshua Gilboa, Lional Kochan, and Ronald Rubin (Memo, Marty Thomas, AJC Chicago, to Rabbi Tanenbaum, February 5, 1973).[110]

The second issue of *The Task* (Vol. 1, No.2) appeared in May 1973 and reported on the May 1973 Consultation in Washington D.C. with the participation of Senator Henry Jackson (D-WA), Representative Charles Vanik, (D-OH), and Representative Robert Drinan (D-MA). The high point was the appearance of Sargent Shriver, who came personally to state his support for Soviet Jewry. Jerry Goodman and Richard Maas of the NCSJ spoke, along with other representatives of Christian and Jewish communities in the United States, and several former Soviet refuseniks. This issue reported on the forthcoming publication of William Korey's *Soviet Cage*. Finally, the newsletter urged Christians to join American Jews who planned to hold a vigil—a national assembly of concern—in the "meadow" opposite the White House if Leonid Brezhnev visited Washington on June 18.

The third issue of *The Task* (Vol. 1, No.3, October 1973), contained a letter from Andre Sakharov supporting the Jackson-Vanik Amendment. It also reprinted articles about Catholic sisters religious supporting Soviet Jews. There was a small note about a local interfaith group in Houston and announcements that Sister Gillen would speak in Miami and Baltimore and about forthcoming visits of the Leningrad orchestra and the Soviet hockey team. The editors of *The Task* urged interreligious participation in protests organized by Jewish women's organizations that would take place in many cities on Human Rights Day in December.

The fourth issue (Vol. 2, No.1, March 1974, box 210, folder 3) focused on Easter and Passover and featured the "Downtown Cluster," an interfaith group in Washington, D.C. in which each congregation renewed a commitment to Lent as a modern liberation experience by "adopting" a Soviet Jewish family or a prisoner of conscience. The group planned a freedom walk on Easter Sunday led by Reverend John Steinbruck, Brant Coopersmith of the AJC, and by others. Another article reported on a sermon by Monsignor John O'Donnell at Holy Name Cathedral who tied the celebration of Lent to the liberation of Soviet Jews.[111] The newsletter reported on the Nixon Administration's pressure against passage of the Jackson-Vanik amendment and listed the names and addresses of Soviet prisoners of conscience.

The fifth issue (Vol. 2, No. 2, November 1974, box 210, folder 3) featured a letter on the first page from Representative Gerald Ford accepting an invitation to be an honorary sponsor of the Task Force.[112] The newsletter also quoted George Meany of the AFL CIO who expressed his hope that the Soviet Union would "stop sabotaging the efforts to build peace in the Middle East." This issue reported on Sister Gillen's recent trip to Europe, the Soviet Union, and the Middle East on behalf of Soviet Jewry, and included a picture of Natasha Federov. Sister Gillen related stories by Vladimir Slepak about harassment and provided news of support for his cause among American Christians and Jews. A second article reported on Irma Chernyak's continued hunger strike, urging people to write and encourage her. The "With Youth" section reported on the success of the Pen Pal Program. Another article reported on the recent release of Sylva Zalmanson and on her arrival in Israel. Her husband and brother remained in jail.[113] Finally, this issue included a list of the names and stories of several prisoners of conscience.

In the following issue, which appeared in November 1975, the lead article focused on Sylva Zalmanson's hunger strike at the UN and her twenty-four-hour vigil and fast at the Chicago Civic Center. The second article contained excerpts from Rep. Drinan's account of his trip to USSR. He emphasized that he learned a great deal from Jews in the USSR about the need for protest in the West. He reported on the one hundred thousand Christian dissidents operating underground and the estimated three hundred activists who had been jailed. In his view, the only hope was that "Perhaps the Kremlin knows that American Christians, haunted by profound guilt at their silence during the Holocaust, may now be prepared to heed the early warning signals which Soviet Jews are sending out to the world." He hoped that "Christians of the world would for once join their voices to the pleas of Jews in Russia to 'Let my people go.'" Finally, the newsletter reported on statements issued by various churches around the United States on behalf of oppressed Christians and Jews in USSR.[114] The editors of the newsletter called for a reduction of sentences for all prisoners of conscience in the Soviet Union and an ending to economic reprisals and to harassment of those wanting to leave.

SOLIDARITY SUNDAYS

From 1973 forward, Sister Gillen and the Task Force participated actively in the National Soviet Jewry Solidarity Sunday program in NYC sponsored by the GNYCSJ in collaboration with the NCSJ.[115] The Task Force encouraged and recruited Christian participation for this program in NYC and for local programs around the country (*The Jewish Press*, May 3–9, 1974, box 210, folder 1).[116] As in previous years, the GNYCSJ very much wanted a large number of Christians to participate (Letter, Malcolm Hoenlein to Rabbi Tanenbaum, February 25, 1974, box 201, folder 1).[117] Malcolm Hoenlein and Rabbi Tanenbaum devised a plan to have forty religious leaders (twenty of them Christian) head the annual march on Fifth Avenue. The NCC vigorously recruited Christians in response to an AJC request (Memo, Claire Randall, NCC, to NCC selected staff, April 16, 1974, box 210, folder 1). Sister Traxler, as chair of the NITFSJ, also circulated a letter (Form letter to Pastor, April 11, 1974, box 201, folder 1) to encourage Christian participation.

Christian leaders in NYC held a press conference at the AJC on April 19, 1974 (RNS, "NY Christians take part in solidarity plea for USSR Jews," April 19, 1974, box 210, folder 1; and GNYCSJ, "Press Release," n.d., box 210, folder 1).[118] At the event, Dr. M.L. Wilson, chair of the National Committee of Black Churchman, called on "Black brothers" to demonstrate on Solidarity Sunday on behalf of Soviet Jews. Rabbi Tanenbaum read a list of Christian theologians and clergy who supported the event. Among the estimated two hundred thousand participants in the Solidarity Sunday program in New York City were many Christian clergy ("Christian Clergy who participated in the Solidarity Day Sunday Jewry April 28," n.d., box 210 folder 1).[119] Senator Henry Jackson (D-WA) and Representative Drinan delivered keynote addresses. In his keynote Congressman Drinan said that he was attending the event:

> "as a Christian . . . plight of Soviet Jews …is the problem of Christians . . . . their neglect and . . . silence . . . has allowed this agony to go on… I implore . . . Christians of America . . . not to be silent as they were during the Holocaust… may the teaching of the Church impel all Christians to realize that if they neglect the Jews of Russia, they neglect Christ Himself."

He quoted Reinhold Niebuhr "no one can be a good Christian until first he is a good Jew" (Press Release, "Address of Robert F. Drinan, MC at Solidarity Sunday, April 28, 1974 NYC," April 29, 1974, box 210, folder 1).

A year later, the NITFSJ joined eighty-five organizations in co-sponsoring the April 13, 1975 GNYCSJ Solidarity Sunday event. A NITFSJ delegation participated (Letter, Ann Gillen to Pastor, March 14, 1975, box 209, folder 4).[120] Sister Gillen came to NYC prior to the event to work on recruitment of Christian clergy and laypersons. NCC provided her with an office (Form letter, NITFSJ to Sisters, April 1, 1975, box 209, folder 4).

Sister Gillen and Rabbi Rudin met with Monsignor James Rigney of the New York Archdiocese about the involvement of Cardinal Terence Cooke and others.[121] Rabbi Rudin also asked for help from the NCC (Letter, Rabbi Rudin to Dr. William Weiler, March 21, 1975, box 209, folder 4).[122] Prior to Solidarity Sunday, the NITFSJ and the GNYCSJ sponsored an interfaith Seder, led by Rabbi Tanenbaum, for Christian and Jewish clergy at the Fifth Avenue Presbyterian Church (RNS, "Symbolic Passover is marked by Christian Jewish clergy in NYC," March 26, 1975, box 176). Rabbi Tanenbaum encouraged those present to participate in Solidarity Sunday on April 13. At the Seder, ministers announced that 3,500 churches in Metropolitan New York City would call on members to support Solidarity Sunday.[123]

In her keynote address (April 1975, box 209, folder 4) at the 1975 event, Sister Gillen recalled her visit to "the home of our sister, Anna Frank . . . ," then to Dachau and then, finally, to meet Soviet Jews "bringing them the pledge of Christian help in their human rights struggle." She pledged that the Task Force would help prisoners of conscience, including Yuri Federov and Alesky Murzhenko, two Christians involved with Jews in the Leningrad trials. She remarked that in front of St. Patrick's Cathedral stood Monsignor James Rigney, rector of the Cathedral, and two Roman Catholic nuns whose Mother General had waited for more than a year to get a passport to leave Czechoslovakia until Jews and Christians worked together for her release.

An estimated 175,000 people marched in the event, including many prominent Catholic and Protestant church leaders and laypersons from the greater metropolitan New York area (Press release of NITFSJ "Christians participate in national solidarity day for soviet Jewry," April 13, 1975, box 209, folder 4).[124] His Eminence Terence Cardinal Cooke issued a statement in support of Soviet Jews "and other persons who are denied their human rights in the Soviet Union." He called on the USSR to free all prisoners of conscience. In the *Amsterdam News*, the Honorable Percy Sutton, president of the Borough of Manhattan, and the Honorable Charles Rangel, chair of the Congressional Black Caucus, issued the following statement. "Their fight is our fight. Their plight is our plight: A statement of Black solidarity with the Civil rights struggle of Russian Jews." "As Black Americans we care about what happens to others." They urged Black Americans to join Americans of all backgrounds on Solidarity Sunday, April 13, 1975. "We identify with them and say that their fight is our fight" ("Black support for solidarity day . . . "—a statement issued in the *Amsterdam News*, n.d., box 209, folder 4).[125]

POLITICAL ACTIVITY: THE JACKSON-VANIK AMENDMENT

The NITFSJ, co-chair Sister Margaret Traxler, and executive director, Sister Ann Gillen, actively supported the Jackson-Vanik Amendment to the United States Trade Bill.[126] Senator Jackson initiated the amendment in response to the Soviet education tax, announced in August 1972, which required Jewish émigrés to repay the state for their education and training. Most potential emigres lacked the resources to pay. The amendment proposed withholding Most Favored Nation (MFN) status from the Soviet Union until it allowed for the free emigration of its Jewish citizens.[127] The Nixon administration opposed the amendment and favored granting MFN to the Soviet Union in the hopes that it would foster détente and trade with the Soviet Union. The Nixon administration also argued that via negotiations it could secure the emigration of greater numbers of Soviet Jews (Lazin 2005).

The leaders of the Task Force worked hard to build public support for the amendment among Christian Americans. For example, in a letter to Sister Rosalie Murphy of Ilchester, Maryland (January 25, 1975, box 176), Sister Ann Gillen urged her to encourage Christians to join Jews in approaching their Congressional representatives to support the Jackson-Vanik Amendment.[128] In another case, Sister Ann Gillen urged Sister Margaret Hohman of the Network in Washington, D.C. (Letter, January 25, 1973, box 176) to lobby members of Congress who were still undecided, suggesting that "some Christian support might mean a great deal with some of them."[129]

An early draft of *The Task* commented on Jackson-Vanik, noting that "... many Jewish groups—and hopefully Christian groups, too—are sponsoring 'write-ins' and 'phone-ins' to add to the list of convinced legislators." The newsletter editors saw this as an excellent opportunity for "practical civic action of Christians and Jews together" (MET, n.d., series 5, box 7, folders 2–9). In June 1973, Sister Gillen sent petitions from concerned Americans to several United States Senators urging support for the amendment (Letter, Anne Gillen to Senator Lloyd Bentsen, June 8, 1973).[130] The Task Force sent a similar note to several members of the House (Task Force Mailgram, September 10, 1973).[131] Local interreligious committees also contacted their Congressional representatives. On September 14, 1974, John Wildenthal, Chair of the Houston Committee of the NITFSJ, wrote to Congressman Bill Archer (R-TX) telling him that Houston was begging him to support the Jackson-Vanik legislation in its original form.[132]

The House Ways and Means Committee invited Sisters Gillen and Traxler, Rabbi Marc Tanenbaum, and Professor LaCocque to testify about the amendment on May 15, 1973 (Letter, Mr. John M. Martin, Jr Chief Counsel, Committee, Ways and Means [HR] to Gerald Strober, AJC, May

4, 1973).[133] Sister Traxler began her testimony: "We come as Easter and Passover people to speak about the real meaning of love. . . . Love is founded on one principle; a cardinal moral virtue and that virtue is justice. There is no charity without justice, and there can be no abiding freedom without both charity and justice." At Passover and Easter, she continued, "we remember . . . the fidelity of a saving God who saw the affliction of his people and found it in his heart to set them free." The amendment represented "a choice between right and wrong . . . between life and death for Russian Jews" ("Oral Testimony of Traxler," n.d., box 212, folder 11). She referred to the three million Soviet Jews killed in the Holocaust and then referenced Abraham and Isaac, noting that "an angel came to stay his hand. I ask you to stay the hand of Russia by supporting the Jackson Amendment." She urged Congress to teach the American people "that church-going and believing people can also learn moral actions from Congressional decision makers who refuse to stand idly by while their brothers' blood cries out from the ground. . . . I appeal to you not to sell your brothers and sisters for a few pieces of silver."

Sister Traxler testified again in Spring 1974 before a Senate Finance Committee hearing (Memo, Gerald Strober to Rabbi Marc Tanenbaum re: "Senate . . . Committee Hearings," March 20, 1974; and Letter Gerald Strober to June Silver, April 11, 1974, box 210, folder 3).[134] She told the Committee that the Task Force was a broad-based coalition of leaders representing all major religious communities in the United States "determined to ameliorate the plight of Soviet Jewry. . . . We are totally committed to the proposition that Soviet Jews should be given the basic human right to live with dignity within the Soviet Union or to be able to leave that nation in an atmosphere of freedom for the nation of their choice." The Task Force "firmly supports the Jackson Amendment . . . and . . . can be a vital factor in aiding the basic aspirations of Soviet Jewry." She then read from the "Statement of Conscience" adopted by delegates to the first Task Force Consultation in March 1972 in Chicago, which was signed by more than two hundred religious leaders of every major faith and denomination. She also cited strong Christian support for Soviet Jewry ". . . in the age after Auschwitz, we as Christians are not going to stand by and allow Jews to be persecuted, intimidate or deprived of their rights in any country."[135]

On June 12, 1974, in response to a request by Gerald Strober, Sister Gillen wrote Senator Russell Long (D-LA) and others in support of the original amendment:

> "I wish to remind you again of the concern that so many Americans feel for Soviet Jews. . . . Our group includes Catholics, Protestants, Orthodox and Jews. . . . We are convinced that the Jackson Amendment continues the tradition of American concern for human rights and support of the oppressed. This is no mere "internal affair" of the USSR. As religious people, we value human life more than financial profits. We

urge your strong support for the Jackson Amendment" (Letter, Gillen to Senator Long, June 12, 1974).[136]

The Jackson-Vanik Amendment passed in December 1973. The Soviet Union rejected a trade agreement passed by Congress and signed into law in early 1975 (Lazin 2005, 50, 51ff0).[137] When President Nixon visited Moscow in June 1975, the Task Force joined the AJC in trying to influence him to raise the issue of Soviet Jews and prisoners of conscience. Sister Gillen urged many nuns and others to send cables to the president (Telegram, Margaret Traxler to President Nixon [in Moscow], June 25, 1974, box 210, folder 3; Cable Bert Gold to US Ambassador Walter J. Stoessel, June 26, 1974, box 173; and Cable, Elmer Winter to President Nixon, box 173).[138]

THE TASK FORCE'S CONCERN FOR SOVIET CHRISTIANS AND DISSIDENTS

While its focus was primarily on Soviet Jewry, the Task Force also took up the cause of other persecuted religious persons, groups, and dissidents, including Andre Sakharov. Rabbi Marc Tanenbaum, head of the IAD, supported this position (Letter, Rabbi Rudin to Rabbi Tanenbaum, July 19, 1977, box 212 folder 1). Within AJC, some departments and individuals disagreed with the IAD position. David Geller of the Foreign Affairs Department (FAD) and coordinator of AJC policy on Soviet Jewry favored limiting concern to Soviet Jews.[139]

However, the head of the AJC, Bertram Gold, expressed early ambivalence about the subject. During a visit to Israel he had discussed the issue with Nehemiah Levanon of the Liaison Bureau. "I told him that I thought it was important that Jews somehow be related to the support for the non-Jewish dissidents and he agreed with the admonition that we keep the issue separate from Soviet Jewry and not take too visible an organizational leadership role" (Memo, Abraham Karlikow to Morris Fine, October 14, 1974, box Bertram Gold 194).[140] Gold allowed the IAD and the Task Force to pursue an independent line on the subject.

In a 1975, the AJC report on "its activities on Behalf of Soviet Jewry," included the activities of the NITFSJ and its function of "carrying out public education, vigils and social action programs on behalf of Soviet Jewry." While the focus was almost exclusively on Soviet Jews, some attention was devoted to the efforts on behalf of prisoners of conscience. The report indicated that the Task Force was seeking to personalize the liberation process by securing commitments from interfaith, ecumenical, or church groups on behalf of a Jewish and Christian family of a prisoner (January 6, 1975, box 209, folder 3).

NOTES

1. In November 1972, Sister Traxler informed the AJC that she was leaving NCCIJ in April, 1973 (Memo, DuBow to Rabbi Tanenbaum, November 20, 1972, box 177). The NCCIJ planned to close its offices in Chicago in 1973 and relocate in Washington, D.C. (Memo, DuBow to Rita Blume "RE NITFSJ," March 7, 1973). After leaving her position at the NCCIJ, Sister Traxler remained actively involved in Task Force activities.

2. Sister Gillen understood that the four national co-chairs of the Task Force approved policy and programs (Summary of conversation of Ann Gillen with Mr. Phillip Klutznick on NITFSJ, July 29, 1975, box 209, folder— Confidential). By mid-1975 Stephanopolous was no longer a co-chairperson. Shriver's role remained symbolic at best.

3. The NCCIJ had provided the Task Force with rent free offices in Chicago (Letter, Rabbi Tanenbaum to Mr. David T. Goldstick, Martin Tananbaum Fund, December 29, 1972, box 177). A very early n.d. proposed budget for October 1972–1973 (box 177) was for $47, 000. The figures were probably inflated.

4. Speaking fees earned by Sister Gillen supplemented the Task Force's funding from the Tananbaum Foundation and from the AJC. Sister Gillen and the Task Force rarely had access to other sources of funding.

5. Sister Gillen requested that the AJC cover Social Security (Letter Rabbi Tanenbaum to Eleanor Katz, December 29, 1972, box 195).

6. Memo, Rita Blume to Eugene DuBow, March 28, 1973 included budget projections for NITFSJ for 1973/1974: Exec. Dir., $10,000; Secretary, $5,720; Social Security, $1,572; Rent, $1,242; Printing (four issues *Task*) $1,200; Total $34,642 plus a contingency of $3,264 for a total of $37,906. A second draft proposed a total budget of $53,075. (Also see Memo, "NITFSJ 1973 operating budget" n.d., box 213, folder 11).

7. The letter contained several documents including "NITFSJ Financial Statement, November 1, 1972–December 21, 1973" which reported on $20,000 in grants from the Tananbaum Foundation and disbursements of $18,701. This included Sister Gillen's salary $7,000 (as of January 1, 1974 it was $1000 per month); a part-time secretary $1,357; fringe benefits $835; rent $700; telephone $1014; travel, conferences and meetings $4,416; printing $1,699; and postage $753. Other documents listed the 1974 NITFSJ budget as $38,500 and the proposed NITFSJ 1975 budget (n.d. Box 210, folder 3) as $49,100. A "Projected Annual Budget NITFSJ 1976–1977 (n.d., box 175) was for $31,710.

8. In a Spring Report (April 2, 1974, box 176) Sister Gillen observed: "The October war took its toll among interfaith groups, too . . . " Strober also wrote to Jerome Cott (January 14, 1974) that the NITFSJ was in a holding pattern due to the Israeli situation. In the fall of 1973, he approached Mr. John Martin of the Hercules Corporation (Letter, November 28, 1973) to support Task Force activities. In February 1975, Bertram Gold asked the Corbett Foundation in Cincinnati for $50,000 for the Task Force (Letter, Bertram Gold to Ralph Corbett, February 11, 1975). Strober and others also approached the AFL-CIO for possible funding (Memo, Strober to Rabbi Marc Tanenbaum, January 7, 1974; and Letter, Strober to Mr. Tom Kahn, AFL-CIO, May 28, 1974, box 213, folder 11); and Letter, Rabbi Jim Rudin to Tom Kahn, AFL-CIO D.C., January 15, 1975). In March of 1974, Sister Traxler asked Stan Adelstein of Rapid City, South Dakota, for financial support for the Task Force. She wrote that the Task Force might close by summer because of a lack of funding (Letter, Sisters Ann Gillen and Margaret Traxler to Stan Adelstein, March 31, 1974). Sister Gillen met with Phil Klutznick about supporting the Task Force. He eventually sent a check for $500 (Letter, Rabbi Marc Tanenbaum to Phil Klutznick, October 10, 1975, box 176).

9. The AJC requested $25,000 for 1976.

10. DuBow reported that Sister Gillen worried about how she would get paid, "was she an employee of AJC"? and wondered about benefits. In New York, she met with AJC's bookkeeper to work out the arrangements. DuBow noted that purchases made by Sister Gillen would be charged to the AJC and thus "we will have control over it."

11. Located in New York City, Strober flew early in the morning to Chicago, spent the day, and returned the same night to New York (Gerald Strober, interview by author, NYC, December 22, 2009). Rabbi A. James Rudin replaced him in 1974.

12. This might also be due to the fiscal crisis following the Yom Kippur War. Rabbi Tanenbaum considered removing her by December 31, 1973 and reorganizing the Task Force.

13. Her community, SHCJ, provided her with secretarial assistance. Sister Gillen had always been interested in using part of her salary to help other sisters pursue employment. In a handwritten note to Sister Traxler (n.d., MET, series 1.2, box 1, folder 2), she mentioned using part of her salary to fund other sisters. She wanted to fund them "As you have helped me get 'launched.'"

14. He raised it from $500 to $1,000 per month retroactively to October 1, 1973.

15. She asked for his permission to send two letters one asking for $100 signed by Rabbi Tanenbaum and Sargent Shriver and a second to Protestant Bishops and NCC leaders signed by Professor André LaCocque and Sargent Shriver.

16. NCSJ informed Strober that in his absence Sister Ann Gillen took on the project of "Operation Redemption."

17. Strober wrote Rabbi Marc Tanenbaum (Memo, May 23, 1974) that "Many items need clarification . . . the possibility of moving to New York in the fall, the location of her office and personal questions related to vacation." He suggested that all three meet in Chicago.

18. The AJC Chicago arranged for her to appear on the November 29 Today Show on WMAQ in Chicago. Her appearance generated mail from all over the country with offers to help in her struggle for Soviet Jewry (Memo, Sheryl Leonard, AJC Chicago, to Sister Ann Gillen, November 14, 1972). Sister Gillen wore a pin which contained a Jewish star with a Christian cross atop it. While many saw it as a "Cross superimposed on the Star of David" in her view it was a "Cross combined with the Star of David" (Letter, Ann Gillen to Jeweler in Riverdale, December 20, 1973, box 176).

19. Graubart noted that few West Coast clergy came to the Consultation. She responded that she had been a dean at Pasadena College. Graubart commented that Neil Sandberg, West Coast head of the AJC, might be an invaluable resource. Sister Gillen suggested that the ADL be enlisted as a co-sponsor in these ventures.

20. In her early visits to Washington, D.C. she often met with officials of Christian religious groups. After her visit to the NCCB they issued a message in support of Solidarity Day. Later, her D.C. visits focused more on politicians and government officials (Memo, Rabbi James Rudin to Marc Talisman, May 15, 1975, box 209).

21. She continued her active involvement with other sisters and the issues that mattered to them; She remained active in NCAN, worked on community projects in child welfare and education and participated in conferences and meetings. In working with fellow Christians, Sister Gillen often urged them to publicize news about Christian clergy in the Soviet Jewry movement. See handwritten note to Sister Margaret Traxler, June 17 n.d. (MET papers, series 1.2, box 1, folder 2).

22. In a form letter to fellow sisters (April 2, 1976, box 209, folder 4) of LCWR, Sister Gillen wrote that 1975 Vatican Council Guidelines on Catholic Jewish relations encouraged cooperation of Christians with Jews in areas of common social concern. An opportunity to translate these teachings into effective action would be Solidarity Sunday May 2, 1976. She invited them to join the Task Force delegation in the Freedom March down Fifth Avenue. At her request, the LCWR circulated a petition urging support for the Jackson-Vanik Amendment. They collected 6,000 signatures (Letter, Sister Ann Gillen to Sister Rose Margaret, Franciscan Sisters of the Poor, Brooklyn, May 18, 1973; NID, "News about the National ITFSJ, box 176; and Letter, Sister Ann Gillen to Sister Maureen Hopkins, SDS, Milwaukee, May 19, 1973. At the Freedom Assembly in D.C. in June 3, 1973 Sister Gillen held a Task Force Banner (note to Sister Helen Waugh, School of Holy Child, Potomac MD, June 3–20, 1973).

23. The sisterhood established an informal coalition of Roman Catholic congregations of sisters, temple and synagogue sisterhoods, Church Women United, and Na-

tional Council of Catholic Women in an interfaith effort to help achieve freedom for oppressed persons as a prelude to nation's bicentennial. Sylva had been arrested along with her husband and others in June 1970 for the alleged Leningrad plane hijacking (Minutes of NJCRAC Executive Meeting on June 13, 1974, box 177 report on "women's Pleas for Soviet Jewry").

24. Many Jewish and Christian leaders representing the Greater New York Interreligious Task force on Soviet Jewry participated, including Professor Thomas Bird; Sister Ann Gillen; Reverend William Harter, Pastor of Margaretville NY; David Hunter of the Council of Religion and International Affairs; Rabbi Jim Rudin; Sister Ann Patrick Ware of the Faith and Order Commission of NCC; and Reverend Dr. William Weiler, Director of Christian Jewish Relations at NCC. Also present were Sister Rose Thering of Seton Hall University and Sister Mary Luke Tobin, Director of Citizen Action for Church Women United. On October 7, 1975 Rabbi Rudin, on behalf of the Greater New York Interreligious Task Force on Soviet Jewry, wrote letters thanking people for participating in the interreligious service at Isaiah Wall for Sylva (box 309, folder 3; and Letter, Rabbi A. James Rudin to Sister Rose Thering, October 9, 1975, box 213, folder 8).

25. Ad Hoc groups of sponsors included the NITFSJ and the Public Affairs Committee of the Jewish Federation (Ann Gillen "NITFSJ: A Report 1972–74," May 1974, MET, series 1.1, box 1, folder 2). This campaign helped to free Sister Elizabeth Pretschener of Czechoslovakia. A "Confidential" memo, July 29, 1975, box 209, folder 3) indicates that Jewish women asked to help free Maria Teresa Allessadro, a Christian social worker in Uruguay.

26. Yuri Federov, a Christian, participated in the alleged Leningrad plane hijacking. The pen pal program was part of the Children of the Otkazniki (refuseniks) program ("Confidential" memo, July 29, 1975). The Mother's Day project focused on Lubov Dinenzon of Chicago whose son was not allowed to leave the Soviet Union. The Fast for Freedom dramatized the plight of the Slepak family of Vladimir and Maria and their two sons Alexander and Leonid. Vladimir was a dissident and Jewish refusenik. The Committee of Correspondence concerned Nijoli Sadunaite an imprisoned Lithuanian Catholic nun (AJC, "Its activities on Behalf of Soviet Jewry," January 6, 1975, box 209/folder 3). Also "confidential" memo of July 29, 1975 refers to adopt a scientist program.

27. She hoped that the NCEA might have a Soviet workshop group in its meetings and school system. She urged him to personally adopt Edward Kuznetsov as "an oppressed brother and work for his release."

28. Operation Write On involved American children writing letters to Soviet children. The Task Force reprinted 150,000 flyers for the New York program.

29. Sister Gillen emphasized that his hunger strike had aroused the interest of Jews and non-Jews. In February 1974, she cooperated with a NCSJ campaign to protest the raising of a Jewish cemetery in Odessa (Telegram/telex, Sister Ann Gillen to Vladimir Kuroyedov, n.d.; and Memo, David Geller to Morris Fine re: "Meeting of Advisory Group of NCSJ . . . ," February 21, 1974, box 194).

30. Vins was a Russian Baptist Pastor persecuted by Soviet authorities for his involvement in a network of independent Baptist Churches. Federov participated in the plane hijacking in Leningrad.

31. Sister Gillen held a special Houston interfaith conference on February 28, 1973, which led to a May Day petition in support of Jackson-Vanik Resolution in Houston. She planned a similar conference in Dallas in the fall.

32. In September 1975, the Zionist Organization of American (ZOA) invited her to speak on a panel at its national convention in Chicago (Letter, Paul Flacks to Sister Ann Gillen, September 23, 1975, box 175).

33. This article noted that she is "touring the country to increase public awareness of the plight of Soviet Jews, ... in encouraging groups and church organizations to protest anti-Semitism and restrictions on the emigration of Soviet Jews." According to Rabbi Rudin, she most enjoyed speaking about Soviet Jewry at parochial schools. Few

others in the Soviet Jewry movement could do this (Rabbi A. James Rudin, interview by author, NYC, July 20, 2015). In 1976, she spent a week in Minneapolis explaining to parochial school students the cause of human rights for Soviet Jews (Letter, Brother Martin Klietz of the Catholic Education Center, Archdiocese of St. Paul and Minneapolis to Sister Ann Gillen, March 16, 1976).

34. For example, in April 1973 Sister Gillen spoke for the Buffalo Niagara Frontier Council on Soviet Jewry (affiliated with the Union of Councils). She spoke on the radio, TV, at synagogues, Hebrew schools, Newman Center, church masses and at an interfaith meeting.

35. Andre Sakharov, a Soviet nuclear physicist, became an outspoken dissident activist for human rights and peace. He won the Nobel Prize for Peace in 1975.

36. She praised him for protesting outrages against Soviet Jews and calling for Christians to join Jews in protest. She hoped to meet him on her forthcoming trip. Also see *RNS*, "Bishop Maher Calls on Christians to Protest Soviet Stand on Jews," January 8, 1973, box 176).

37. State Senator David A. Roberti (Letter to Gillen, April 1, 1974, box 176) wrote that he too supported Soviet Jewry and asked if he could be of help. In a letter of April 29, 1974 (box 176) he offered to help" organize a local Task Force . . . ." In a June 12, 1974 letter he expressed support for the 1972 "Statement of Conscience." He sent a letter to Secretary of State Henry Kissinger (June 12, 1974) signed by 26 members of the Senate and House in California protesting the repression of Soviet Jews.

38. She believed that after the exodus of Jews was assured there would be other oppressed groups asking for help. What follows is from the report.

39. At the Valley Interfaith Council, she urged groups to join the "Sisterhood of Conscience." She wore a chain around her neck with a metal star of David and name of a Soviet Jewish prisoner on back. She urged their children to write Jewish children in Russia. What better Lenten penance for a Christian than to surprise a Jewish friend with "how can I help?"

40. She gave those present copies of a sermon on Soviet Jewry and Lent. She failed to get a resolution introduced on Soviet Jewry at the Priest's Council where she met the Bishop elect of Fresno, Monsignor John Cummins. She raised with him the idea of a state interreligious task force which would also take up the plight of farm workers.

41. Spokane was to host an international exposition with participation of the USSR and expected four million visitors in the following six months. The local Jewish community wanted her to return when it opened.

42. Abraham Karlikow of AJC's office in Paris recommended writing letters on behalf of prisoners of conscience. Zvi Netzer of the Liaison Bureau gave him the names of prisoners.

43. He noted several events coinciding with Human Rights Day (December 10) and the anniversary of the Leningrad Trials. Ads had been placed in newspapers. Geller wrote that it would be a coup if they obtained statements from similar persons in England, France, Italy, and in Latin America.

44. In commenting on a draft for *The Task*, Geller wrote that since they hoped "to enlist the support of the Christian community in appeal for amnesty for Soviet Jewish prisoners of conscience," it would be "wise to highlight the project by having it in a box on the first page." In the draft of the first edition (Memo, Eugene DuBow to Rabbi Marc Tanenbaum, November 21, 1972, box 177) the second article "Free them now" noted that on the fiftieth anniversary of the Soviet Union, Soviet leaders would free prisoners. At this time, the NITFSJ focused on giving Jewish prisoners amnesty.

45. Leonard Schroeter and Sister Gillen spoke at the event. It was one of fifty demonstrations organized by the NCSJ for "freedom month "for Soviet Jewish prisoners of conscience. Many were sponsored by Women's Pleas for Human Rights (of the Soviet Jewish Prisoners of Conscience) (Claire R. Aronson, "Prisoners of Conscience" *Jewish Post & Opinion*, December 8, 1972, box 176). Finally, in writing about Drinan's mission to the USSR, Rabbi Tanenbaum emphasized that the focus would be on seeking amnesty for Jewish prisoners (Telegram, Rabbi Marc Tanenbaum to Dr. Eugene Carson

Blake, December 5, 1972). Chicago's AJC office assisted in organizing the local protest (Memo, Judah Graubart to David Geller, re: Women's Plea for Soviet Jewry, December 21, 1973, box 177).

46. Jerry Goodman (interview by author, NYC, August 16, 2011), former head of the NCSJ, expressed surprise that Rabbi Rudin would have copied Izo Rager of the Liaison Bureau.

47. The author was not able to determine whether the mission ever took place.

48. Strober had proposed a two-day event and asked Sister Gillen for her thoughts. She consulted with Reverend Steinbruck. (Also, Letter, Rabbi Tanenbaum to Martin Gang, April 6, 1973; Letter, June Silver, NCSJ, to Mr. Jacob Levy (Israeli Consulate), April 13, 1973, box 174; and Memo, Sister Ann Gillen, December 20, 1972. box 176). The AJC's Washington lobbyist, Hyman Bookbinder, recruited D.C. speakers (Memo, Gerald Strober to Hyman Bookbinder, April 18, 1973, box 174). The AJC sent an additional five invitations to each regional director for distribution to local contacts (Letter, Gerald Strober to AJC area directors re: NIFSJ 2nd Annual Meeting D.C., May 14, 15," April 20, 1973 , box 174).

49. Rev. Dr. Jack E. McClendon, NY Avenue Presbyterian Church, Most Rev. William Baum, Archbishop of D.C., and Rev. Edward H. Flannery (Executive Secretary, Secretariat for Catholic Jewish relations (NCCB) also offered greetings.

50. At the church, Reverend Steinbruck read from the book of Exodus and Misha Shepshalovich, a former prisoner of conscience, and Representative Drinan spoke.

51. At lunch, Sister Traxler praised Jackson and others in Congress for supporting human rights. At the meeting with Armitage, the group expressed support for East-West trade and for the Jackson-Vanik Amendment.

52. ". . . Leave for a nation of his choice" is a departure from the Liaison Bureau position which favored "Leave for his homeland-Israel."

53. Sisters Gillen and Traxler represented the Task Force at a Freedom Assembly in D.C. on June 18 protesting the visit of Leonid Brezhnev (Letter, Sister Ann Gillen to Allan L. Start, June 8, 1973; Letter, Sister Ann Gillen to Sister Helen Waugh, June 20, 1973; Letter, Richard Maass to Sister Margaret Traxler, June 22, 1973; and Letter, Sister Ann Gillen to Dan Asher, June 20, 1973).

54. AJC, NEC Meeting, December 1–3, 1972, Hollywood FL, box 174). Summing up two years of activities in 1974, Sister Ann emphasized the hope of establishing local interreligious task forces in Houston, Seattle, Spokane, Miami, Louisville, Washington D.C., San Diego, Scranton, Tulsa, Denver, Minneapolis-St. Paul, St Louis, Philadelphia, Chicago, and NYC (Ann Gillen "NITFSJ: A Report 1972–74").

55. On early efforts that fell short of success see Letter, John Pawlikowski to Sister Margaret Burke, November 14, 1972 (box 177); Memo, Sister Ann Gillen to colleagues, February 11, 1974 (box 176); "Participants," Chicago Conference on Soviet Jewry, NITFSJ, March 5, 1974 (box 176); Memo, Eugene Du Bow, "Midwest Regional . . . ." ND and Letter, Judah Graubart to Mrs. Morton Blitstein, June 14, 1974. Rabbi Marc Tanenbaum addressed a newly formed Chicago Interreligious Task Force, on July 22, 1975. The sponsors decided to organize the Illinois Interreligious Task Force on Soviet Jewry.

56. She asked David Geller to speak at the event.

57. More people attended a follow-up meeting on May 1, 1973. Members of the Houston Committee Task Force included John Wildenthal (chair), Rev. Warren Dicharry and David Askanse (co-chairs), Dan Asher, Rev. John Craig, Sister Ann Gillen, Sherman Harris, Rev. Clifford Kirkpatrick, Phillip Libby, June Mabry, Rev. Edwin D. Peterman, Barbara Youngssettle, Ms. Edward Stern, Rev. Nicholas Triantafilou, and Ms. Mason Woods. Co-sponsors included the ADL, the Catholic Commission for Ecumenism and Interreligious Affairs, the Greek Orthodox Cathedral, the Houston Chapter of the AJC, Houston Metropolitan Ministries, the Jewish Community Council, and the NCCJ (Letter, Sister Ann Gillen to John Wildenthal, May 24, 1973). In June, Sister Gillen coordinated the placement of newspaper ads with the Jewish Community

Council of Houston with the expected visit of Leonid Brezhnev to the city (Letters, Sister Ann Gillen to Dan Asher, June 6 and June 29, 1973).

58. In a letter to Dan Asher of the JCC (January 22, 1974, box 176), she discussed the Otkazniki project, a Sisterhood of Conscience meeting to be held on February 6 in Houston, and a possible world day of prayer at Rothko Chapel with a focus on persecuted Soviet Jews and Christians. She also thanked Reverend Warren Dicharry of St Mary's Seminary in Houston (January 21, 1974, box 176) for speaking at Memorial Senior High School about Soviet Jewry. Dan Asher thanked Reverend John L. Morkovsky, Diocese of Galveston (February 8, 1974, box 176) for helping with local NITFSJ activities and for having the speaker Sima Kaminsky interviewed by the *Catholic Texas Herald*. Sister Gillen returned in March 1976, doing two newspaper interviews and speaking at a breakfast at Central Presbyterian Church and at Friday night services at a Jewish temple (Letter, Michael Rapp to Sister Ann Gillen, March 17, 1976, box 175).

59. Reverend Steinbruck sponsored an open house at the parsonage in Alexandria, VA in December 1972 requesting that visitors leave "a modest Christmas contribution to ransom Soviet Jews" (Blessed Advent," December 8, 1972, box 210, folder 4). His congregation adopted Valerie Kukuy, a prisoner of conscience.

60. Reverend Steinbruck wrote Dr. Robert J. Marshall, President of the Lutheran Church in America (LCA) (April 18, 1974) that he saw no point in serving on the Task Force "unless it is as a representative or liaison capacity for the LCA." Marshall disagreed. He praised Reverend Steinbruck's involvement in the struggle for Soviet Jewry, which was important for the Lutheran Church. He himself however chose to focus on isolated and unregistered communities of Lutherans in the Soviet Union. He was not in a position "to compare the suffering of these groups to the suffering of Jewish people in the Soviet Union. I do believe that it is important that some of us pursue the possibilities of greater freedom for Lutheran people just as I consider it important that others lay their emphasis upon greater justice and freedom for Soviet Jewry" (Letter, Dr. Robert J. Marshall to Rev. John Steinbruck, March 12, 1976, box 211, folder 8).

61. The event focused on Soviet Jewish prisoners of conscience. Reverend Steinbruck (letter to Sister Ann Gillen, February 19, 1974) suggested that she relate Passover and Holy Week to individual congregational support for a particular Soviet Jewish prisoner which would provide "a powerful and authentic meaning to our celebration of the Resurrection—"liberation" in Christ—and hopefully result in benefits to some Jews who have in the past borne the brunt of Holy Week horrors and pogroms in that part of the world."

62. In terms of local Soviet Jewry advocacy efforts, Indianapolis resembled Milwaukee. Shortly after becoming director, Sister Gillen spoke in Indianapolis where she hoped to set up an interreligious Task Force. She worked with the local JCRC on a program for the Women's Pleas for Soviet Jewry. In April 1976, the NITFSJ held a state wide LCWR workshop in Indianapolis.

63. Sister Gillen asked the local Jewish sponsors to invite Christian groups, including Church Women United and the Diocesan Council of Catholic Women (Letter, Sister Ann Gillen to Mrs. Herman Tuchman, November 20, 1972, box 177; and "Task Force Head to Hear Testimony on Soviet Jewry" *Wisconsin Jewish Chronicle*, December 1, 1972, box 176). Prior to her arrival, AJC's Chicago director Eugene Du Bow notified the Milwaukee AJC that Sister Gillen would be available for additional meetings.

64. Dr. Thomas Bird gave the keynote. Sister Kathleen Feeley, President of Notre Dame, presided. Gerald Strober, Sister Ann Gillen and Reverend Chester Wickwire, chaplain at John Hopkins, responded to Bird. After lunch, Rabbi Marc Tanenbaum summed up the sessions (Letter, Sol Goldstein to Sister Ann Gillen (May 2, 1974).

65. The participation of Evangelicals initially caused some waves in the local Jewish community. The Mideast Israel Affairs subcommittee of the local CRC approached evangelical Protestant ministers to mobilize their concerns for Israel and Soviet Jewry. The local Rabbinical Council, however, argued that contact with Christians should only be with establishment groups as "contact with Evangelicals who may be pro-Israel is inappropriate, since their ultimate aim is the conversion of the Jews." The

director of the local federation sought advice from the NJCRAC (Letter, Marshall Jacobson, to Dr. Walter Lurie, NJCRAC, January 23, 1973, box 177). Lurie replied that issue was complex saying it depended with which evangelical group and for what purpose. He asked for more details (Letter, Walter Lurie to Marshall Jacobson, January 25, 1973, box 177).

66. Sister Gillen and the NITFSJ took up the case of Sister Elizabeth Pretschner who was not allowed to leave Czechoslovakia (Sister Ann Gillen, Letter to Friends, January 21, 1975). Goodman argued that, based on human compassion, individuals and Jewish organizations should do whatever they could to help the Sister but said "I question the wisdom of a group like the Louisville Interreligious Council on Soviet Jewry to undertake this activity. It seems to me that all sorts of unrelated problems are raised and crisscrossing of lines will be confusing" (Letter, Jerry Goodman to Ted Comet and Abraham J. Bayer, CC, Rudin, box 176). Sister Gillen invited the Jewish Federation and Father Stanley A. Schmidt, director of the Louisville Interreligious Council for Soviet Jewry, to attend the June 1973 Freedom Assembly events in Washington D.C. (Letter, Ann Gillen to Allan Stark, Jewish Community Federation of Louisville, June 8, 1973).

67. Schmidt emphasized that in addition to five council meetings, the interreligious council prepared a letter to local newspapers defending Jackson-Vanik; on June 18, held a television press conference during Brezhnev's visit to Washington urging an end to the education tax; on October 5, called Jewish activist David Abele in Moscow; on October 10, distributed flyers at a local performance of the Krasnayarsk Dance Company of Siberia; on October 15, jointly sponsored with the Jewish community a Simchat Torah unity observance with Soviet Jewry; on December 7 called the Soviet prosecutor in the Leonid Zablishensky trial; on December 10 participated in the Women's Pleas for Human Rights of Soviet Jews and with two local councilwomen on television concerning women's plea month; on December 13, Gita Comer presented a public service announcement on the radio (which aired seven times daily); on December 24, Sister Mary Frances Lottes appeared on local television with a "viewpoint on behalf of interreligious Council for Soviet Jewry."

68. Schmidt attended Brussels II (see below).

69. She would be involved for over twenty years with the Commission, which later became the Office of Ecumenical and Interreligious Affairs.

70. She asked him to meet with Gerald Strober and Murray Friedman of the Philadelphia AJC. She also wrote that Dr. Richard Firster (Baptist) and May and Murray Biddle (of John XXIII Center) would be of assistance. Clifford, Freidman, Strober, and Gillen (Memo, Strober to Tanenbaum,, January 10, 1974, box 176) met on January 23, 1974 to discuss a possible regional meeting for the NITFSJ in the spring.

71. Sister Gillen spoke at Dropsie College on October 21, 1974 on the subject of "A sisterhood of Conscience for Soviet Jewry."

72. Task Force members included representatives of the Baptist Association, Episcopalians, the Catholic Archdiocese, the Metropolitan Fellowship of Churches, and the NCCJ.

73. Attending were representatives of the NCCJ, the St. Louis Church, the Center for Dialogue, the Miami Springs Baptist Church, the Union Congregational Church, the Kendal Methodist Church, the AMC, the Women's American ORT, the Chancery-Archdiocese of Miami, and the South Florida Conference on Soviet Jewry.

74. Task Force Chair Reverend Luther Pierce made Soviet Jewry and Solidarity Sunday the subject of his regular one-half hour television program on June 2. It was also the subject of a television program of the local rabbinical association and a three-hour radio talk show. In addition, many local rabbis and Christian clergy spoke about Soviet Jewry in their weekly sermons.

75. Speakers included three University of Miami faculty members and Father John Vereb of the Archdiocese of Miami. The Reverend Luther Pierce moderated.

76. The LCWR had endorsed cause of Soviet Jewry as a human rights issue. The Contemplative Sisters expressed a similar concern.

77. Rabbi Gittelsohn probably attended the earlier meeting with Sister Gillen.

78. The GNYCSJ organized the annual demonstration (parade) for the NCSJ. The first parade was held in 1972. Some suggested that the GNYCSJ had national aspirations when it later changed its name in the 1980s to the Coalition for Soviet Jewry (Lazin 2005:38, 39). Malcolm Hoenlein headed the GNYCSJ.

79. He assumed that it had relocated to NYC. See discussion below. Earlier, in a memo to Rabbi Tanenbaum (May 23, 1974), Gerald Strober asked him to speak to Sister Gillen about the "possibility of moving to New York in the fall." (Also see letter, Sister Margaret Traxler to Rabbi Tanenbaum, August 20, 1974, box 213, folder 11).

80. A note from Eugene Gold to the NY Conference and Community Leadership, June 16, 1975 (Gold box 194) referred to a "NY interreligious Task Force on Soviet Jewry" as a sponsor of the May 30 event.

81. By December 1975, the AJC, the GNYCSJ, and the NITFSJ were involved together in a protest involving Msgr. James Rigney, Rector of St. Patrick's Cathedral, and Lilu Butman and her mother, whose father/husband were in a Soviet labor camp. Butman was a member of the Leningrad hijackers group. Congressman Norman Lent (R-NY) had adopted the Butman family.

82. In a memo to Rabbi Tanenbaum (January 13, 1975, box 209, folder 3), Eugene DuBow referred to "more radical Soviet Jewry groups" in NYC who were also considering an interreligious task force. He believed it was imperative to "move to New York as soon as possible." Other agencies, he warned, saw a truly fertile field "for themselves in the area of interreligious activity, and as long as Sister Ann is not on the scene in New York, they feel as if they can go ahead and set up their own organization." Sister Gillen had told DuBow that Malcolm Hoenlein of the GNYCSJ had invited her to help set up the New York City interreligious task force on the condition that she resettle in New York. If she did not, he would set up the local task force without her.

83. At the meeting, Rabbi Tanenbaum stated that he favored the move to NYC because of the presence of many church organizations.

84. Sister Ann Gillen wrote Rabbi Rudin (Letter, February 3, 1975, box 176) that the NCCIJ would be moving their offices to Washington after Easter. She hoped that by then the Task Force would have an office either at the NCC or the Episcopal Church Center in NYC. She noted her depleted budget and asked if the AJC would pay for the office move even though she did not work for the AJC.

85. In a note to Margaret Traxler (n.d., MET, series 1.2, box 1, folder 2) Sister Gillen wrote "DuBow encouraging me to stay in Chicago" and to move the office near the AJC in Chicago.

86. Rabbi Rudin, interview by author, NYC, July 30, 2015. Rudin stated that Sister Gillen opposed moving the office to NYC. She very much wanted her independence from the AJC and other church groups.

87. The next day Sister Traxler sent a telegram to Drinan (October 30, 1972 (Box 177) ". . . I formally request you to undertake the fact-finding trip to Russia in order to inform our committee regarding the status of Soviet Jewry."

88. Earlier Rabbi Tanenbaum suggested that the mission include Sister Traxler, Rep. Drinan, Sister Gillen, himself, and possibly Professor LaCocque (Memo, Judah Graubart to Rabbi Marc Tanenbaum re "National ITFSJ," November 1, 1972, box 177). Sister Traxler and Professor LaCocque wrote Rabbi Tanenbaum (November 21, 1973, box 177) that they wanted the proposed mission to "be a broadly based task force including leaders from the religious, academic and socially oriented community. . ."

89. In a letter to Dr. R. Dean Goodwin of the American Baptist Convention (January 26, 1974, box 176), Gerald Strober asked for letters of introduction to Baptist contacts in USSR. Goodwin wrote Reverend Alexie Bichkov, General Secretary of the All Union Council of Christian Evangelical Baptists, (February 2, 1973) about the American delegation. A revised memo listing members of the group on January 26, 1973 (box 18, folder 8) included Rep. Drinan, Dr. Arnold Olson, Mother Margaret Brennan, Dr. Milton Curry, Sister Traxler, Rev. Edward Flannery, Professor Bird, Strober, Professor Ursula Niebuhr, and Rabbi Marc Tanenbaum. The AJC provided funding for Profes-

sor Bird, Professor Niebuhr, and Strober (Letter, Rabbi Marc Tanenbaum to Goldstick, February 2, 1973 and "Three Christians not pay way," February 1973, *The Task*.)

90. In late January, Jerry Goodman of the NCSJ agreed to brief the group at a New York airport.

91. On January 24, Intourist officials had reported that hotel accommodations had been reserved ("Statement of Congressman Robert F. Drinan Responding to Messages from the Kremlin, Challenges the USSR to Issue Visas for Ten American Religious leaders," April 21, 1973).

92. Rabbi Marc Tanenbaum and Father Edward Flannery were in attendance. Rabbi Tanenbaum wrote Rep. Drinan (February 12, 1973) that the State Department officials doubted that visas would be forthcoming for a possible rescheduled trip in April 1973. He closed " . . . I pray constantly for your continued good health and strength. You are the best Catholic the Jews ever had in Congress (like Pope John was the best Pope the Jews ever had)."

93. She arrived in Leningrad on June 27. She left Moscow on July 4 and then visited Israel for seven days.

94. She asked Sister Gillen to obtain a Bible in Russian for her husband who was in a prison camp. For more information about the refuseniks see Beckerman 2010 (on Brailovsky: Beckerman 2010: 420–21; on Federov: Beckerman 2010: 194–5, 203, 205; and on Slepak: Beckerman 243–4, 246–250). In a note to Sister Traxler (n.d., MET, series 1.2, box 1, folder 2), Sister Gillen tells of going to a dinner with Rabbi Rudin at an NCC event for Russian clergy. There, at the suggestion of David Hunter, she gave the Bible to Metropolitan Yuvenali who asked her to tell Federov to contact him in Moscow. He promised to give her the Bible for her husband.

95. On Lunts, see Beckerman 2010, 314.

96. She visited with the Catholic scholars at the Tantur Institute and participated in meetings with Israeli television (Kol Israel), David Prital, Father Josepi Stiassney, and the Sisters of Sion (Zion). She also visited Neve Shalom.

97. In a note to Rabbi Tanenbaum (around Simchat Torah 1974, box 176), she wrote that her effort to meet Soviet Jews in the USSR and in Israel with those working with Soviet Jews had been very successful. She had been far less successful in raising consciousness among Christian groups in key West European cities. However, she had made some important initial contacts.

98. Representative Drinan had planned to visit the Soviet Union in 1975. Rabbi Rudin wrote him (June 17, 1975, box 176) inquiring about his intentions: "Do you see it (your forthcoming visit to the USSR) as an interreligious delegation that will be led by you?" He and Sister Gillen were willing to assist in any preparation or briefing.

99. Her provincial superior agreed to finance her ticket ("as an implementation of the Vatican guidelines").

100. Around this time, Sargent Shriver was going to the USSR. Rabbi Rudin spoke to his associate, Christopher Whitney, about the trip (Letter, Rabbi A. James Rudin to Sargent Shriver, August 28, 1975, Spertus, box 48).

101. Soviet authorities refused to give his son an exit visa on grounds that he had knowledge of "secrets." His daughter had left the country and was at the Weitzman Institute of Science in Israel.

102. Shcharansky, born in 1948, earned a degree in applied mathematics. After being denied an exit visa to Israel he became a refusenik and human rights activist. He worked as a translator for Andrei Sakharov and spokesman for the Moscow Helsinki Monitoring group. In March 1977, Soviet authorities arrested him for treason and spying for the United States. In 1978, he received a thirteen-year prison sentence. Following Gorbachev's rise to power, he was released in Berlin in a prisoner exchange involving former Communist spies held in the West and several prisoners in Soviet jails. On arriving in Israel, he changed his name to Natan Sharansky (Snyder 2018, p. 185, n.13). He became active in Israeli politics.

103. He personally opposed the Stevenson Packwood bill to limit credit to $300 million (See Lazin 2005, 50).

104. DuBow suggested that Graubart write the first draft, with copies sent for comments to Rabbi Tanenbaum, Sister Gillen, David Geller, Gerry Strober, William Katz, Samuel Katz, Isaiah Terman, Sister Traxler and Professor LaCocque. DuBow expected that in time and with experience Sister Gillen could write it by herself.

105. Later the Task Force issued, without prior AJC/IAD review, mimeographed copies of articles and reports under the title *"The Task."*

106. David Geller (Memo to Rabbi Marc Tanenbaum, Gerry Strober, Judah Graubart and Eugene DuBow, November 28, 1972, box 177) favored a two-page format having regular features; one section on information on Soviet Jews, another on undertakings of some Christian groups, and one on activities of Jewish groups (NCSJ), and a paragraph of in-depth analysis.

107. The AJC files contain a different earlier four-page draft version of the first issue of *The Task"* probably prepared by Graubart. (Graubart draft of "The Task," June 1972, box 174.) The first article covered the Consultation in Chicago. The second dealt with Kremlin conservatives versus dissidents and crackdowns on Jews and dissidents. The third dealt with Solzhenitsyn's protest letter to Patriarch Pimen the head of Russian Orthopox Church in which he bemoans the lack of true Christian Spirit within contemporary Russian Orthodox Church. The fourth covered a petition signed by seventeen thousand Lithuanian Catholics to UN Secretary General Kurt Waldheim about the absence of freedom of conscience, the inadequate number of functioning priests, and the fact that article eighteen of the Universal Declaration of Human Rights allows for religious freedom. The final article contained the "Statement of Conscience" from the Consultation.

108. It noted that it sent out a special report in December on the amnesty issue. It also listed as Task Force Co-Chairs Traxler, LaCocque, Stephanopoulos, and Tanenbaum.

109. The quote is significant. The standard Liaison Bureau line was "let them live as Jews in the Soviet Union or leave to be Jews in their homeland Israel."

110. She wrote: "I understand you are to give your permission to print as is or make corrections."

111. The issue publicized the "Matzo of Hope" prayer issued by the GNYCSJ. It offered copies at eight dollars per thousand. It also offered Prisoner of Conscience kits for twenty-five cents each.

112. Sister Gillen (Letter, to Senator Jackson, November 22, 1973) recruited Senator Henry Jackson (D-WA) to become an honorary sponsor, but his name never appeared on stationery or in publications. He replied (November 29, 1973) "I am delighted and I accept."

113. The issue reported on the pledge by Jewish women to work for the release of Maria Tersa Alessandro, a Christian social worker in Uruguay who was arrested and tortured in the name of "national security," along with 3,500 others. Sister Suzanne Noffke led an effort to collect ten thousand names on a petition.

114. It cited the NCC protest of the persecution of two Christians in the USSR and the call of the ecumenical and interreligious concerns division of the United Methodist Board of Global Ministries for a reconciliation and renewal of freedom and human dignity for Jews and others who were denied human rights in the Soviet Union.

115. In 1974, the Task Force became a co-sponsor of the Solidarity Sunday event in NYC. (GNYCSJ "In Brief," n.d., box 210, folder 1) report Christian community mobilizing thanks to efforts of Jerry Strober (AJC).

116. The rest of the country celebrated Solidarity Sunday on June 2, 1974 (Letter Abraham Bayer to NJCRAC and CJFWF Member Agencies, May 14, 1974). Father Edward H. Flannery (May 9, 1974 (box 210, folder 3) called for Christians to support the event. His letter included a "Statement of Support" by Reverend Reid C. Mayo, President, National Federation of Priest's Councils, representing one hundred and thirty councils of priests in forty-five states. On this occasion Sister Gillen wrote Sister Francis Borgia Rothleubbuer of Milwaukee (box 176) asking her to reaffirm her support in some special way, either issuing a statement or joining other groups in signing

the statement of conscience (Zeesy Schnur, phone interview by the author, June 26, 2014).

117. Hoenlein met with Rabbi Tanenbaum to "stimulate a large Christian participation" (Letter, Malcolm Hoenlein to Rabbi Marc Tanenbaum, March 11, 1974, box 210, folder 1). He suggested that if the New York Cardinal did not want to speak at the rally, he could hold a press conference before the rally to urge the participation of Christians.

118. Among those present were Father Edward Flannery, Executive Secretary of Secretariat for Catholic Jewish Relations of NCCB; Dr. Bryant Kirkland, senior minister of the Fifth Avenue Presbyterian Church; Rabbi Harold Gordon of the NY Board of Rabbis: and Rt. Rev. Stuart Wetmore, Suffragan Bishop of the Episcopal Diocese of NY.

119. Rev. Maurice M. Bell, United Church of Christ; Dr. Thomas Bird, special counselor to Vatican; Eleanor Bowker, NCC; Dr. Richard Butler, NCC; Joseph Conrad Pastor, St Matthias Roman Catholic (RC) Church, Ridgewood Queens; Rev. Edward H. Flannery, NCCB; Dr. Mary Jane Fried, United Farm Workers; Sister Ann Gillen, NITFSJ; Rev. Blahoslav Hruby, Editor; Rev. Horace Hunt, the Metropolitan Ecumenical Ministry; Dr. David Hunter, NCC; Rev. Dr. J. Oscar Lee , NCCJ; The Most Rev. R. Dunham Merrick, the Archdiocese of NY and Eastern provinces of the US; Rev. John Morely; Rev. Leo Niato, United Farm Workers; Dr. Christopher Niebuhr; Rev. Joe Perry, Williamsburg Christian Church; Rev. Louis Rios, Our Lady of Esperanza, RC Church; Rev. John Rodano; Rev. Herbert Rogers, Fordham University; Sister Rose Albert Thering, Seton Hall; Rev. Paul Stagg, New Jersey Council of Churches (NJCC); Rev. Charles Straut, Council of Churches of NYC; Rev. Nathan H. VanderWerf, NCC; Sister Ann Patrick Ware, NCC; and Rev. George Webber, the NY Theological Seminary.

120. Again, the AJC and the NITFSJ recruited Christian participants. The AJC staff sent a letter prepared and signed by Sister Gillen to Christian clergy and leaders (Letter, Ann Gillen to Rabbi Marc Tanenbaum re: "Solidarity Day," March 11, 1975, box 209, folder 4; Letter, Rabbi Rudin to Rev. Paul L. Stagg, NJCC, box 209, folder 4; and Letter, Rabbi Rudin to Rev. Dan Potter NCC, March 14, 1975, box 209, folder 40). In one version of her letter (to Bishops, March 24, 1975, box 176), Sister Gillen invited the recipients to join other Christian leaders to issue statements on behalf of Soviet Jewry. She emphasized the urgency due to the decline in emigration, increased harassment, trials, and the problems of prisoners of conscience, including two non-Jews and "The Holy Year stress on reconciliation and the Vatican Guidelines urging us to cooperate with Jews in common causes."

121. Rabbi Rudin wrote Msgr. Rigney (March 21, 1975, box 209, folder 4) " . . . enclosing a draft text that the Cardinal may find helpful in preparing his public statement."

122. He asked if Claire Randall could issue a letter as she did the previous year. The NCC agreed to send a letter signed by Sister Gillen to 4,000 churches in the New York and northern New Jersey area. The AJC paid the NCC $74.13 for the postage. On April 4, the NCC issued an office memo from Reverend William L. Weiler to NCC elected and appointed staff (Box 209 folder 4) urging all to be Christian witnesses on Solidarity Sunday to declare "your solidarity with the repressed minorities living in the Soviet Union. . . . Their fight is our fight." Weiler himself could not attend the event.

123. The *New York Daily News*, the *New York Post*, JTA, and RNS covered the Seder. According to Rabbi Rudin (Letter, to Ms. Randy Shuman, April 17, 1975, box 209, folder 4) Msgr. James Rigney Rector of St. Patrick's Cathedral would review the march from the steps of the Cathedral along with Rabbi Ronald Sobel of Temple Emanu-El, Dr. Dan Potter of the Council of Churches, and Sister Joan McMullen, LCWR. Thirty Christian leaders would march on April 13. Dr. Paul Stagg, NJCC, sent letter from Sister Gillen and a flier to 1,000 clergy members in New Jersey, Dr. Dan Potter sent a similar letter. Rep. Drinan would place a Solidarity Day statement in the *Congressional Record*. WINS Radio Commentaries were scheduled for that day on forty-five stations around the country. Sister Gillen was to be one of the speakers, along with Jesse

Jackson, Hubert Humphrey, Sen. Bill Brock (R-TN) and Governor Hugh Carey (Memo, Rabbi Rudin to Rabbi Tanenbaum, April 10, 1975, box 209, folder 4).

124. The *NYT* of April 14, 1975 (box 209, folder 4) estimated that 100,000 people participated and RNS estimated the crowd to be 150,000 (April 14, box 176). Members of the Interreligious Task Force delegation Solidarity Day, April 13, 1975 (box 175; version also in box 209, folder 4) included: Sister Natalie Barton, St. Johns University; Reverend Maurice M. Bell, United Church of Christ; Professor Thomas Bird; Sister Ann Gillen; Bishop R. Dunham, the Council of Churches; Reverend Herbert Rogers, Fordham University; Reverend Isaac Rottenberg, the Reform Church of the USA; Rabbi James Rudin; Eleanor Schnurr, UN Office, American Baptist Churches; Sister Rose Thering, Seton Hall University; Sister Luke Tobin, Church Women United; Reverent Nathan H. VanderWerf; Sister Ann Patrick Ware, NCC; Reverend George Webber, NY Theological Seminary; Reverend William Weiler, NCC; Ida Altman; Marshall Miller, the Catholic Jewish Relations Council of Flushing NY; Johan Garra, the Catholic Interracial Council of NY; Terry Lampropoulos; Sister Ann Joyce Peters, Sisterhood of Conscience; Sister Elizabeth Butler; Sister Elizabeth Loomis; and Sister Diana Trebbi.

125. The list included African American political and religious leaders. It stated that Blacks suffered as slaves while today Russian Jews that wanted to emigrate were treated as traitors. There were required to carry ID cards that singled them out for discrimination. They felt the need to speak out and in doing so recalled that in their struggle "for human rights, we found many friends outside of our communities who saw the wrong and spoke out against it."

126. The Liaison Bureau, the AJC, and most mainstream American Jewish organizations supported the amendment.

127. See Snyder (2018, 35–39) for a discussion of Jackson's motivations for proposing the amendment. The wording banned the granting of MFN to any nation that restricted the freedom of emigration and other human rights.

128. She asked her to copy and distribute legislative kits for Congressional Representatives which had been developed by a Chicago Committee on Soviet Jewry.

129. She cited names from the Illinois Congressional delegation (Morgan Murphy, Hanrahan, Samuel Young, and O'Brien).

130. She sent the same letter to Senator John Tower. The letter noted: "These are only a few of thousands of Christians (Catholic, Protestant and Orthodox as well as Jews who are united in support of Jackson-Vanik"). Earlier in the year, The Task Force had collected six thousand signatures from sisters in support of the Jackson-Vanik amendment (See above, n. 22).

131. "We appreciate your continuing support for the Mills-Vanik legislation . . ." Sent to US Representatives Joseph Karth (D-MN), Joel Broyhill (R-VA), Donald Brotzman (R-CO), Donald Clancy (R-OH), and William Archer (R-TX).

132. Also see "News about the NITFSJ," n.d., Fall 1974, box 176). They sent out additional telegrams in October 1973.

133. The AJC coordinated the response to the invitation. Strober replied (May 9, 1973) that Sister Gillen would not appear but that she would submit written material.

134. David Geller and Gerald Strober briefed her before her testimony. At the time, AJC staff were very concerned about "Jewish issues" in Washington, D.C. Geller (Memo, David Geller to Morris Fine re: "Advisory Group of the NCSJ," February 19, 1974, box 1974) noted several hostile Senators, including Russell Long, and wrote " . . . for fear that these senators would see the presence of Jewish spokesmen to air accusations and opinions that may be hurtful to us, it has been suggested that . . . Jewish organizations not testify orally." Geller and Strober advised Traxler to read into the record a cross section of names of honorary sponsors of the Task Force indicating "the American consensus which has formed around the issue of Soviet Jews;" signal Task Force support for Jackson-Vanik; and close with a personal statement reflecting her own views, as a committed Christian leader, on the plight of Soviet Jewry (Memo Gerald Strober to Sister Margaret Ellen Traxler, March 28, 1974, box 210, folder 3). She followed their instructions (NICSJ, Press Release," April 10, 1974, box 176).

135. In a memo to Rabbi Tanenbaum, Bertram Gold, and others (April 11, 1974, box 210, folder 3) Strober cited praises for Sister Traxler by Senator Packwood and noted that her appearance gave "important and highly positive visibility to the Task Force." She was interviewed by Israeli telvision, JTA and RNS. Her written testimony was circulated to the press and to every member of the Senate. Representative Drinan entered it into the *Congressional Record*. "As a result of Sister Traxler's appearance, [wrote Strober], the Task Force has taken a major step toward establishing itself as a significant force in the struggle for Soviet Jewry."

136. See Memo, Gerald Strober to Ann Gillen, June 6, 1974 (box 176).

137. When the Soviets broke off trade negotiations, Sister Gillen argued that they probably did so "because they resent the three hundred million ceiling on loans" ("Ann Gillen, form letter, January 21, 1975). See above n. 103.

138. Sister May Daniel Turner, SND, told Strober (Letter, July 2, 1974, box 210, folder 3) that Sister Francis Borgia Rothluebber sent a cablegram to Nixon: "Request intervention in the question of rights and freedom of Soviet Jews. . . ." Similarly, Sister Angela Rees of Servants of the Immaculate Heart of Mary, Northeast Province, MI, wrote Strober on July 10, 1974, that Sister Luanne Yocke had sent a telegram to Nixon (box 210, folder 3): "Am deeply concerned over the present plight of the Soviet Jews. Please use your power to intervene on their behalf."

139. He noted in 1973 that the AJC had been asked to associate with various nationalist movements including the Ukrainians and Lithuanians. The AJC's response, he stated, had been: "It would be strategically inadvisable for the Jewish 'Movement' to be associated with either of the other two, because the nationalist movements are seeking to dismember the Soviet Union and the dissidents are seeking to change and restructure the Soviet system of government." Geller admitted that in the Jewish community there was a "profound concern and sympathy for the dissidents" (Letter, David Geller to Elmer Winter, September 11, 1973, Bertram Gold box 193). He reiterated this position in a December 1976 memo opposing the linking of Soviet Jews with Ukrainians, Lithuanians and dissidents seeking freedom under the banner of human rights. He did, however, suggest cooperation with others. He emphasized that, at that time, the AJC policy was to maintain the separation between the Jewish issue and others (Memo, David Geller to AJC Area Directors, December 16, 1976, box 175).

140. Karlikow reported on a meeting of French Jewish communal leaders about the extent to which the fight on behalf of Soviet Jews should extend to other minorities. They pushed the issue aside and warned of the danger of this activity.

FIVE
The Brussels II Conference

In the early 1970s, the Israeli Liaison Bureau and Jewish advocacy groups for Soviet Jewry from around the world organized a conference for activists in Brussels, Belgium. Later known as Brussels I, the Conference, held on February 23 and 24, 1971, attracted more than one thousand people and received wide media coverage. The Conference established the Presidium for Soviet Jewry, which brought together leaders of Soviet Jewry advocacy groups from different countries twice yearly (Lazin, 2005, 35ff.).[1] In early 1975, the Presidium began to plan a follow up conference—Brussels II. In addition to Jewish advocacy activists from around the world, conference organizers wanted to invite Christian advocates for Soviet Jewry from the United States, Europe, and Latin America. During the planning stage, the AJC representative lobbied for a meaningful role for Christians, Sister Ann Gillen, and the Task Force.

Despite the effort to involve Christian advocates, Soviet Jewry remained the exclusive focus of Brussels II. Concern and comments about persecuted Christians and others were peripheral, at best. When mentioning other persecuted religious groups in the Soviet Union, Sister Gillen and other Christians at Brussels II made it clear that Soviet Jewry remained their primary concern.

The catalyst for Brussels II may have been the worsening situation of Jewish activists in the USSR and the decline of emigration following the late 1974 Soviet rejection of the trade pact with the United States.[2] The Soviets allowed fewer Jews to leave for Israel (Bernard Weintraub, "Pressed on Soviet Jews," *NYT*, February 18, 1976).[3] This, in turn, contributed to a slackening of the Soviet Jewry advocacy movement in the United States and Europe. The new situation frustrated and depressed activists in the Soviet Union and their advocates in the West. Finally, there had been an increase of anti-Semitism in the USSR following the November 10, 1979 UN General Assembly resolution equating Zionism with racism (Bernard Weintraub, "Moscow Is Berated on Eve of Brussels Meetings on Soviet Jews." *NYT*, February 17, 1976).

In July 1975, the Presidium for Soviet Jewry invited advocates for Soviet Jewry to meet in Paris in September to plan the Brussels II Conference scheduled for February 15 and 16, 1976 (Note, David Geller to Morris Fine, re: "Report of the Soviet Jewry Program Advisory Groups," July 23, 1975, box 194). Abe Karlikow, head of the AJC office in Europe, found many matters at the meetings " . . . fairly cut and dry given that our Israeli friends had come with a definitive idea of what they wanted and put this through without any difficulty" (Memo, Abraham Karlikow to David Geller, re: "Preparatory meeting in Paris for Brussels II," September 3, 1975, box 195).[4] The Paris meeting set up a Brussels II Presidium and Secretariat (Memo, Abraham Karlikow to Morris Fine, September 4, 1975, box 195).[5]

The organizers hoped for more than one thousand delegates, including a contingent of Soviet Jews now living in Israel. They also wanted ". . . non-Jewish participation in the conference." It was not a question of whether they would participate, but rather, of the extent and nature of their participation. At the September meeting, some favored inviting one or two prominent Christians, while others favored a full non-Jewish section. In the end, they agreed to host thirty or forty "prominent non-Jewish figures." The steering committee would approve the Christian participants and national delegations could invite other non-Jews with whom they collaborated. Nevertheless, they agreed that the Christian presence should not detract from the idea that Brussels II would be an unprecedented "mobilization of the Jewish world" (Memo, Karlikow to Geller, re "Prep. . .").

At the suggestion of Arye Dulzin of the Jewish Agency, former Israeli Prime Minister Golda Meir became the Honorary Patron of Brussels II. Participants at the planning sessions also discussed inviting other political leaders, including Senators Henry Jackson (D-WA), Jacob Javits (R-NY) and Abraham Ribicoff (D-CT). While not wanting an anti-Soviet tone—a problem with Senator Jackson—some mentioned that the strong and negative Soviet response to Brussels I contributed to widespread press coverage of the event (Lazin 2005, 65).[6]

Finally, the planners agreed that the plight of Jews in the USSR must be presented as a critical test of The Helsinki Accords (Lazin 2005, 52).[7] In her keynote address at the Conference, former Israeli Prime Minister Meir would argue that the Helsinki agreements had not facilitated Soviet Jewish emigration ("Mrs. Meir Pleads for Soviet Jews," February 19, 1976, *NYT*.)

Following the September meeting, Abe Karlikow urged the AJC to lobby for program issues at the proposed Brussels II Conference that were relevant for the Task Force and the AJC, such as which non-Jews and which politicians to invite and the Task Force's policy regarding Soviet Jews wanting to emigrate to countries other than Israel (Memo, Abraham Karlikow to Morris Fine, September 4, 1975, box 195).[8] He argued that most advocates had pushed for emigration, but that some thought the focus should now turn more to the cultural and religious rights of Jews who would remain in the Soviet Union. These concerns would fall under the Helsinki Accords, which covered cultural and religious freedoms, as well as the right of emigration. Finally, he raised the issue of ties with dissidents and persecuted non-Jews in the Soviet Union, who were waging a campaign for greater freedom (Memo, Abe Karlikow to David Geller, October 17, 1975, box 195).[9]

Karlikow attended a second planning meeting in Paris on November 3. The recent signing of The Helsinki Accords probably influenced the meeting. Participants wanted a program to "demonstrate general political and moral support for the cause of Soviet Jewry—as contrasted with Brussels I which was strictly a Jewish meeting—and to re-demonstrate Jewish support."[10] They discussed inviting prominent politicians to speak.[11] There would be four special commission meetings for jurists, parliamentarians, scientists, and one on interfaith matters.[12] The workshops reflected an emphasis on the plight of Soviet Jewry to the neglect of dissidents and other persecuted religious groups in the Soviet Union. One workshop, for example, focused on Prisoners of Zion with no reference to non-Jewish prisoners of conscience (Memo, Abe Karlikow to David Geller, November 5, 1975, box 194).[13]

A call for delegates for Brussels II, circulated by NJCRAC in November, emphasized the importance of creating "a dramatic message to the world and to Soviet authorities of the unity of the Jewish world in its struggle for Soviet Jews, at a time when critics claim that there is a lack of cohesion." While emphasizing the Jewish character of the struggle outside the USSR, the call for delegates did mention that the movement in the West "includes new people, young leadership and non-Jews" and cited the role of the Task Force in the United States (Letter, Lewis Cole, NJCRAC to Member Agencies and CJFWF, re: "A Call for the Designation of Delegates...", November 26, 1975, box 195).[14]

In December 1975, Sister Gillen announced that the Task Force had the responsibility "for inviting Christian participants" to Brussels II (Letter, Ann Gillen to "Christians concerned about the cause of Soviet Jewry and Human rights in the USSR," re "Christian participation in Brussels II...., December 2, 1975.[15] Rabbi Rudin wrote (Form Letters, December 1975 and February 18, 1976, box 177) to Christian clergy and lay persons asking them to join the NITFSJ delegation for Brussels II led by Sister Gillen.[16] In early January 1976, the Task Force delegation included Sisters Ann Gillen and Margaret Traxler, Reverend John Steinbruck, Father Stanley Schmidt, Dr. Robert Pruitt, Professor Thomas Bird, Sister Marie Erst (SHCJ) from Dublin, and Professor André LaCocque (Memo, Rabbi Rudin to Rabbi Tanenbaum, January 7, 1976, box 208, folder 4).[17] At the time, Rabbi Rudin and Ann Gillen were preparing a "Christian Call for Conscience" for Brussels II (*The Task* (Special Issue), March 1976 (box 208, folder 3).[18] Rabbi Rudin asked Karlikow (Memo, January 13, 1976, box 208, folder 4) to make sure that the role of the Task Force in Brussels received "the attention that it deserves."[19]

Following a meeting of the Brussels II steering committee in late January, Karlikow complained to David Geller (Memo, re: "Brussels II," January 27, 1976, box 195) about the quality of the expected participants. He described them as being "woefully short of quality, particularly non-Jewish quality" and even more so with respect to American statesmen or Nobel prize winners. He suggested that the AJC recruit former Vice President Senator Hubert Humphrey (D-MN) to speak at Brussels II.[20]

He also criticized a draft of a Brussels II Declaration written by Holocaust survivor, author, and Jewish activist Elie Wiesel, which dealt as much with "Zionism as racism as it did with Jews in the Soviet Union" (Memo, Karlikow to Geller, January 27, 1976).[21] He remarked that Wiesel's draft referred to reunification with families in Israel. He urged the AJC to support the position of several American Jewish groups including the NCSJ, which favored the idea of freedom to resettle in a country of choice. Finally, he called on the AJC to take up his as-yet unsuccessful fight for a more prominent role for non-Jews at plenary sessions (Ibid.).[22]

He suggested that there might be greater Christian visibility at a plenary on "Soviet Jewry and World Conscience," where both Jews and non-Jews were to issue statements. He hoped that Sister Gillen and Professor Tom Bird might participate. He also suggested that Rabbi Rudin work with Jerry Goodman and Dick Cohen (who oversaw publicity at Brussels II) to create a special mini event around the "Christian Call to Conscience." Finally, he hoped that the Christian delegation would have the opportunity to "express its views and shine in the Interfaith Commission that will be meeting on Thursday morning, February 19th" (Ibid.).

A January 28, 1976, Task Force press release (box 195) on Brussels II focused on the "Christian Call to Conscience" being prepared by Rabbi Rudin and Sister Gillen. The Call demanded that Soviet authorities provide full human rights to Soviet Jews, including the right to emigrate as provided in the Helsinki Accords. The press release also announced that Sister Gillen would lead the Task Force delegation to Brussels II.[23] Sister Gillen wrote: "Our Christian delegation, by its presence in Brussels, will bear witness to the universality of the struggle to secure the legitimate human rights of Soviet Jews" (NITFSJ Press Release, January 28, 1976, box 195).

The conference was held on February 17–19, 1976. Twelve hundred delegates from thirty-two countries participated. Among them were fifty non-Jews from eight countries representing various religious denominations and including parliamentarians, scientists, and jurists (*The Task*

[Special Issue], March 1976 (box 208, folder 3).[24] According to the NITFSJ, the Christians participating in Brussels II reflected the broad spectrum of Church support for Soviet Jewry ("A Report on the Second . . . *The Task* . . . March 1976 (www.ajcarchives.org/AJC_Data/files/773.pdf, Accessed April 27, 2016.[25] Thirty-five new Israeli immigrants from the Soviet Union also participated.

The subject of the Helsinki Accords took center stage. Participants believed that the major task now for many Jewish communities was to monitor Soviet implementation of both the Helsinki Final Act and the UN Covenant on Civil and Political Rights.

On the first night of the conference at a gala that included members of the Brussels Jewish community, the "Brussels II Declaration" was read in five languages. The message declared a "great family feeling" of Jews of the world with Soviet Jewry. It expressed empathy and admiration for the struggle and the faith and courage of Soviet Jewry. The message saluted the non-Jews of every sector of society, race, and religion who joined the cause for Soviet Jewry at Brussels II. It noted that one generation after the Holocaust "that they dare not remain silent in the face of the renewed threats confronting the Jewish people." The Declaration condemned anti-Semitism in the Soviet Union, which included prejudice against Jews and Judaism and "false accusations against Israel and Zionism." It saw the equation of "Zionism and racism" by the Soviet government and other regimes as a "calumny against Israel" and Jews everywhere. The final section focused on emigration and resettlement in Israel, hoping that many more Soviet Jews would follow the "one hundred thousand. . . who have succeeded in reaching the Jewish State." It vowed that ". . . for the sake of our brethren in the Soviet Union, we shall not remain silent nor shall we hold our peace" (*The Task* (Special Issue), March 1976, box 208, folder 3).

The NITFSJ delegation participated in the Interfaith Commission meeting, which discussed how international interreligious cooperation addressed Soviet Jewry ("Participants in Interreligious Commission of Brussels II Meeting on Soviet Jewry–Feb 19, 1976," February 19, 1976, box 195).[26] Rabbi Arthur Herzberg served as chair. The Commission discussed a draft of the Call to Christian Conscience prepared by Rabbi Jim Rudin and Sister Gillen (Report of SR Ann Gillen Regarding Brussels II Conference, n.d., box 208, folder; and Memo, Rabbi A. James Rudin to Bert Gold. February 13, 1976, b ox 195). Representative Drinan wanted the statement to be more critical of church leadership. Sister Gillen defended what she had written telling him to fulfill "this need from his position as a prophet in Congress." Others expressed the "need to stress more our concern for Christians in the USSR, too." Rabbi Arthur Hertzberg said: "our group will lack credibility with the Christian community unless this were done" (Report . . . Gillen . . . Conference, n.d., box 208, folder 3).[27] He also stressed the need to focus on the right of free association for Jews in the USSR and their right to choose their own leaders, urging advocacy for these same rights for the Christian communities in the Soviet Union ("A Report on the Second. . . . *The Task* (www.ajcarchives.org/AJC_Data/files/773.pdf (Accessed, April 27, 2016). Minor revisions were made to the draft; the focus of the document remained on Soviet Jewry (Rabbi Rudin "Christians make strong impact at Brussels Conference on Soviet Jewry," March 20, 1976, Spertus, box 48, Rudin file).[28]

At the commission meeting, Sister Margaret Traxler spoke about the foresight of the AJC and the NCCIJ in organizing the Task Force in 1972 (*The Task* (Special Issue), March 1976, box 208, folder 3). Père Michel Riquet of France spoke about the "shining example" of the Jewish people in their concern for Soviet Jewry. He suggested that Christians had "much to learn from this movement to help Soviet Jews, asking why similar movements have not been organized by Christians for other Christians when their human rights are denied" ("A Report . . . March 1976"). This theme would be articulated in the future by Sister Ann Gillen, Rep. Robert Drinan, and the NITFSJ.

Following the commission meeting, the Christian delegation approved the "Call to Christian Conscience" prepared by the NITFSJ with minor revisions. It began "We Christians, Catholics, Protestant, and Evangelicals meeting thirty years after the Nazi Holocaust recognize that our fellow Christians of that time did not heed the 'ominous signs' of escalating Nazi attacks on European Jewry which resulted in the death of six million Jews." The Call emphasized that this generation of Christians would not "be silent as we raise our voices in support of the struggle to prevent the cultural and spiritual annihilation of the Jews of the Soviet Union." It noted that Christians join with Jews to express anguish and concern about the continued denial of human rights for "Soviet Jews, and . . . other deprived groups and nationalities."[29]

The document called on Soviet leaders to respect the "human rights provisions of the UN Charter" and to "implement those provisions of the Helsinki Agreement which relate to freedom of thought, conscience, religion and belief as well as to the right of people to emigrate."[30] The appeal asked the Soviets to allow religious, cultural and educational institutions to perpetuate Judaism and Jewish culture in their country.[31]

Realizing their own failures on human rights, the signers pledged not to be silent "or indifferent in the face of the grave and dehumanizing injustices that have been inflicted upon the Jews and other groups in the Soviet Union." However, they made it clear despite the "harassment and persecution of our Christian brothers and sisters," that they were "convinced that the oppressed condition of our Jewish brothers and sisters is unique and in all specifics more vigorous than that faced by the Christian communities." They urged churches to make 1976 Easter an occasion to demonstrate solidarity "with all believers in the Soviet Union and the inauguration of a new exodus."[32]

The document pledged solidarity with all those who were "denied religious liberty in the Soviet Union. . . We will not rest until human rights and justice prevail in the Soviet Union. . . ." In the spirit of the prophet Isaiah, the Call appealed to Christians to help free an entire people. It slightly modified a standard position of the Liaison Bureau: "Let the Jews of the Soviet Union leave or let them live as Jews" ("Call to Christian Conscience, "Brussels February 19, 1976 submitted by NITFSJ and Memo, Rabbi A. James Rudin to Bert Gold, February 13, 1976, box 195).[33]

A high point and special experience for Sister Gillen and the Task Force delegation involved a ceremony in which the former Israeli Prime Minister Golda Meir presented a special medal to each member of the Christian delegation. Sister Gillen and Prime Minister Meir embraced, and Sister Gillen apologized for Meir's alleged ill treatment during her private audience with Pope Paul (Memo, Gene DuBow to Bert Gold, February 27, 1976, box 208, folder 4; and Sister Margaret Traxler "A personal report of the Brussels conference," MET, series 5, box 7, folders 2–4). Sister Gillen told Prime Minister Meir:

> . . . you have won respect, admiration, and affection . . . all over the world by your heroic leadership. Your . . . concern for Soviet Jews has deep roots . . . implanted when you were . . . Ambassador to the Soviet Union, and . . . because of that concern . . . we are all here in Brussels. We . . . pledge . . . our commitment to this human rights cause, and as a sign of this commitment, may I present . . . a copy of this 'Call to Christian Conscience' . . . We look forward to continued cooperation in the whole area of civil, religious and human rights ("A Report . . . *The Task* . . . March 1976).

Mrs. Meir responded:

> I am anxious for the sake of our Jewish children to see that our often very cruel and dangerous dialogue with the non-Jewish world shall not be the *only* dialogue. . . There has never been a period of history when some non-Jews . . . stand by our side. . . . I would ordinarily say "thank you," but I cannot say "thank you" about a cause of this kind. I know you are preoccupied with this problem because you have made it yours. I praise God in these hours that we are not left alone. Just as we are found together today, so also somewhere, someplace may we meet again when we have won (Rabbi Rudin "Brussels II Conference on Soviet Jewry," March 9, 1976, box 195).

At the end of the conference, a "Declaration of Principles" was issued. It emphasized world Jewry advocating for Soviet Jewry and the struggle for Jews to emigrate and resettle in Israel. There was no mention of dissidents or other persecuted religious minorities in the USSR.[34] The Declaration called for the freedom of all Jewish prisoners of conscience. The document urged the Soviet Union to follow its own constitution and international laws and agreements on human rights and freedom, including the Final Act of the Helsinki Conference. It called for free emigration for Soviet Jews and their reunification with their brethren in the historic Jewish homeland, Israel (David Geller, "AJC report on the 2nd Brussels Conference," February 17–19, 1976, n.d., box 195).[35] It asked for religious and cultural freedom for those Jews that remained in the Soviet Union and demanded an end to anti-Semitism and allowing Soviet Jews to maintain ties with Jews abroad ("Declaration of the Second World Conference of Jewish Communities on Soviet Jewry," February 19, 1976, box 195).

A *New York Times* report on Brussels II did not refer to the "Christian Call to Conscience." Rather, the article cited a more general declaration from the Conference: "We call on all men and women of conscience . . . to speak out on behalf of Jews in the USSR" (Bernard Weintraub, "Meeting Appeals to Soviet Jews," *NYT*, February 20, 1976). In contrast, the Jewish Telegraph Agency mentioned the "Call to Conscience" issued by Christian delegates at a seminar held in Brussels (in connection with Brussels II), which demanded that the Soviet regime cease persecution of Jews ("Christians Issue 'call to Conscience'" February 20, 1976 JTA (http://www.jta.org/1976/02/20/archive/christians-issue-call-to-sonscience (accessed, April 27, 2016).[36]

Writing from Brussels, *Scripps-Howard* staff writer William Steif focused on the Christians at Brussels II. He cited Sister Ann Gillen's suggestion that "Jewish unity on behalf of Soviet Jewry shows the Christian community the way to organize similar campaigns for similarly oppressed Christians" (William Steif, "Telex from Brussels," February 22, 1976, box 208, folder 3).[37]

A *Jewish Week* report from Brussels quoted Protestant ministers Robert Pruitt and John Steinbruck:

> "Our presence was an act of seeking forgiveness from our older brother, whom we and our community persecuted and hurt . . . and whose current special suffering behind the Iron Curtain in the USSR (while not justifying the evil and inhumane atrocities of the Soviets upon the innocent Jewish citizens (is in tragic measure the legacy of Christian anti-Semitism of the 19th and early 20th centuries in Czarist Russia prior to the October revolution" ("Christians from D.C/ area sing Brussels appeal," *Jewish Week*, February 26–March 3, 1976 (box 175).

AJC personnel considered Brussels II to have been a very successful event for Sister Gillen and the Task Force (David Geller, "AJC report on the Second . . .," n.d., box 195). According to Rabbi Rudin: "By all accounts, the Christian impact at Brussels II was extraordinary and powerful. . . . More and more Christian leaders perceive the Soviet Jewry struggle as being much more than a 'Jewish issue,' rather they see it as a part of the global human rights question. Seen in these terms, we can help mobilize an increased Christian commitment to the cause of Soviet Jewry" (Rabbi Rudin, "Brussels II . . ." March 9, 1976, box 195).

Eugene DuBow (Letter to Bert Gold, February 27, 1976, box 208, folder 4) wrote that Sister Gillen had "established herself and the NITFSJ as *the* Christian voice on the subject of Soviet Jewry." In her own way, he suggested, she had become "sort of an international Jewish superstar—one of our hottest projects."[38] AJC Executive VP Bert Gold wrote Sister Gillen (March 4, 1976, box 208, folder 4) that "Everyone who was at Brussels II with whom I spoke was unstinting in their praise of the tremendous contribution made by the Christian contingent and the leadership which you helped provide. I look forward to our continued association."

Ironically, some in the AJC criticized the organization's own role at Brussels II. David Geller said that many people told him that the AJC should have had a greater presence at this most important "world Jewish event."[39] Eugene Du Bow wrote similarly to Bert Gold (February 27, 1976, box 208, folder 4) that some thought that the AJC was insufficiently represented.[40] On the other hand, some in the AJC preferred a silent, behind-the- scenes role (Jim Rudin, "Brussels II . . ." March 9, 1976, box 195).[41]

In their thank you notes to the Christian participants, Sister Gillen and Rabbi Rudin urged them to work on obtaining a large number of "Christian signatures" for the ""Call to Christian Conscience" to have maximum impact" (Letter, Ann Gillen and Rabbi Rudin to Rep. Drinan, n.d. (Spertus, box 92, Drinan file).[42]

NOTES

1. The Israeli Liaison Bureau coordinated and likely controlled this organization.

2. On January 10, 1975, the Soviet Union informed Secretary of State Kissinger that "it had decided to scrap the October 1972 trade agreement with the United States" (Lazin 2005: 51). While the Jackson-Vanik amendment and American pressure on the issue of Jewish emigration mattered, the Soviets may have been most upset by "the passage of routine U.S. Export Import Bank funding bill with an amendment by Senator Stevenson . . . {limiting}. . . Soviet import credits. . . ." (Ibid.).

3. Senator Frank Church (D ID) at Brussels II noted that thirty-five thousand had been allowed to leave in 1973, twenty thousand in 1974, and only thirteen thousand in 1975.

4. "Our friends' steamroller operated a little too efficiently, perhaps creating certain irritation in the American group." "Our friends" is a reference to the Liaison Bureau.

5. The Paris Secretariat included Stanley Lowell (NCSJ), Eugene Gold, (GNYCSJ), Mr. Krone (Jewish Agency), Abe Karlikow (AJC) Sergio Nudelstejer (Latin American Jewish Congress), Marc Turkow (WJC), Al Chernin (NJCRAC), Jerry Goodman (NCSJ), and Yehuda Hellman (Presidents' Conference). Members of the Brussels II Presidium were the heads of the West European Council for Jews in the USSR, Public Council for Soviet Jewry in Israel, Latin American Congress, NCSJ, Presidents Confer-

ence, B'nai B'rith International (BB), David Susskind of Brussels and one representative of the Secretariat. Tentative Sponsors of Brussels II were Australian Board of Deputies, the Canadian Jewish Congress, and the World Union of Jewish Students. Karlikow failed in his effort to have the AJC become a sponsor. The suggestion that the South African Board of Jewish Deputies be a sponsor was rejected, because it would make it difficult for some Blacks to participate. The Israelis opposed a World Zionist Organization proposal that Soviet *Olim* (immigrants) be given a representative on the Presidium.

6. "Soviet criticism and threats . . . gave the conference (Brussels I) publicity." According to Professor André LaCocque "Brussels II was a success even before it began, judging from the international press accounts of reactions from the USSR and several Arab countries" ("A Report on the Second World Conference of Jewish Communities on Soviet Jewry, Brussels, February 17–19, 1976." *The Task: A Voice of Christian-Jewish Concern*, Special Issue, March 1976 (www.ajcarchives.org/AJC_Data/files/773.pdf), last visited April 27, 2016).

7. On August 1, 1975, representatives of the United States, Canada, the USSR and thirty-two European governments signed the Helsinki Agreements which finalized the European borders established after the Second World War. Basket III of the Agreements contained several humanitarian aims including facilitating and expediting approval of exit visas for achieving family reunification and religious and cultural rights.

8. He also talked about the controversy around the issue of Soviet "*Yordim*" (new immigrants from the Soviet Union who were leaving Israel). "I scarcely dare bring it up?"

9. Karlikow wrote Rabbi Rudin (October 24, 1975, box 176) that it was very important that "an appropriate place be found on the Brussels program for Sister Ann Gillen." Jerry Goodman of the NCSJ, he believed, would support such a proposal. At the October 13, 1976 NCSJ Plenum Meeting in Philadelphia, participants discussed a proposed interfaith component at Brussels II and a request to have President Gerald Ford speak about the relevance of the Helsinki Final Agreements for Soviet Jews (Letter, David Geller to Morris Fine, October 14, 1975, box 209, folder 3).

10. They also want to give a more prominent role to new *olim* (immigrants to Israel) from the Soviet Union.

11. They rejected George Meany to avoid the "Cold War" image. They hoped to invite Willy Brandt to speak on human rights and the spirit of Helsinki. Senator Jackson was not available, but Senator Ted Kennedy (D-MA) was. President Ford agreed to have his message read by Senator Javits. They also discussed inviting former British Prime Minister Edward Heath, British MP Ian Mikado, British jurist Lord Oliver, former French Premier Pierre Mendes-France, former Canadian Prime Minister John Diefenbaker, and several Nobel prize winners.

12. Some Europeans objected to the interfaith component, but they were outvoted. Karlikow hoped to find a place for Sister Gillen in a special interfaith commission meeting at Brussels II.

13. The five scheduled workshops were public action and public relations, prisoners of Zion and refuseniks, anti- Semitism, rights of Jews in the USSR, and implementation of Helsinki Accords, and contacts with Jews in the USSR.

14. It contained an NCSJ memo, "World Assembly of Jewish communities on Jews in the Soviet Union," February 17–19, 1976, Brussels report #1.

15. Shortly thereafter, Sister Traxler wrote to the AJC (December 9, 1975, box 210, folder 3)) that the School of Sisters of Notre Dame would provide $200 for Gene DuBow to attend. He wrote Bert Gold (December 11, 1975, box 210, folder 3) that it was great public relations having nuns fund his trip.

16. The earlier letter went to Dr. William L. Weiler, executive director, Office on Christian Jewish relations (NCC), and to others. A second letter went to Dr. Cynthia Wedel, The Right Reverend Jonathan Sherman, Ursula Niebuhr, David Hyatt (president, NCCJ), Dr. Thomas Bird, David Hunter, Episcopal bishop of Long Island Jonathan Sherman, Bishop Bernard Law of Springfield, NJ, and to others.

17. The Louisville AJC covered Schmidt's expenses.

18. Professor Tom Bird translated it into Russian, and Professor André LaCocque translated it into French.

19. The NCSJ agreed to allow Rabbi Meir Kahane of the Jewish Defense League to address Brussels II but in the end, he was not allowed to participate (Telegram, Elmer Winter to AJC, January 22, 1976, box 195; and Richard Cohen, "Report on Brussels II: World Jewry: United in Solidarity with the Jews of the USSR," *Congress Monthly*, March 1976, box 195). A ten-minute melee erupted when Kahane was removed from the lobby of the conference hall. When asked why he could not speak, Golda Meir responded, "he is a demagogue" ("Mrs. Meir pleads . . ." *NYT* February 19, 1976). The decision caused far less a stir than his not being allowed to speak at Brussels I (Lazin 2005:65 n.94 and Naftalin 1999:231).

20. On January 7, 1976, Rabbi Rudin wrote Rabbi Tanenbaum (box 208, folder 4) that given the quantity and quality of Christian delegation it is "imperative that we immediately discuss some public relations aspects of the Brussels meetings."

21. The Liaison Bureau (and government of Israel) viewed advocacy for Soviet Jewry in "Zionist" terms—it was an Aliya (immigration to Israel) movement; Soviet Jews wanted to return to their homeland. The consensus of the steering committee was that it should be modified to avoid the broader issue of "Zionism as racism." Karlikow added, "I nonetheless have the impression that some hard-liners like Charlotte Jacobson and (Nehemiah) Levanon (of Liaison Bureau) will be pushing Lowell (NCSJ) behind the scenes, through Rager (Israeli Consulate in NYC and Liaison Bureau operative), to come down heavily on Zionism-Racism."

22. Karlikow urged Geller to lobby for the appointment of non-Jews as chair or rapporteur for the interfaith commission at Brussels II. He hoped that Rabbi Rudin would be the consultant for the Interfaith Commission, chaired by Rabbi Arthur Hertzberg and with Rabbi Elio Toaff of Rome as rapporteur. He explained his failure to get more visibility for Sister Gillen and other non-Jews. First, some on the Steering Committee felt strongly that emphasis should be on a Jewish conference. Second, the lack of *yichus* (status) posts for Jews led to the decision that Jews should serve as chairs and rapporteurs of all plenary sessions.

23. Participants included Sister Margaret Traxler, Prof Andre LaCocque, Prof. Thomas Bird, Rev Dr. Thomas G. Fahy, President of Seton Hall; Mr. Walter Hubbard, President of National Organization of Black Catholics (NOBC); Dr. David Hunter, Council on Religion and International Affairs (CRIA); Rev Robert Pruitt; Rev Paul Stagg; Rev John Steinbruck; Rev Stanley A. Schmidt; and Msgr. Ralph Kuehner and Msgr. Bernard Gerhardt of the Washington, D.C. Archdiocese. Sister Marie Erst, SHCJ of the Irish Commission for Justice and Peace of Dublin also joined the delegation. Sisters Traxler and Gillen requested that the AJC allow Rabbi Rudin to participate (Telegram, Margaret Traxler and Ann Gillen to Bert Gold, February 10, 1976, box 195). Bert Gold replied that Rudin could not go (Letter, Bert Gold to Ann Gillen, February 11, 1976, box 195).

24. American political leaders included Congressmen Robert Drinan (D-MA), Joshua Eilberg (D-PA), Hamilton Fish (R-NY), Felix Hebert (D-LA) and Peter Peyser (R-NY), Senator Frank Church (D-ID) and civil rights activist Bayard Rustin of the AFL-CIO's A. Philip Randolph Institute. The *NYT* published four articles about the conference. One noted the Protestant and Roman Catholic religious leaders from the United States without mentioning Sister Gillen or the Task Force by name (Bernard Weintraub, "Moscow is Berated on Eve of Brussels Meetings on Soviet Jewry," February 17. 1976).

25. Representing "the institutional church" were Rev. Rufus Cornelson (Philadelphia Metropolitan Council of Christian Ministries); Rev. Charles Devlin (Philadelphia Cardinal's Commission of Human Relations); Monsignors Bernard Gerhardt and Ralph Kuehner (Roman Catholic Archdiocese of Washington DC); Dr. Thomas Fahy (President of Seton Hall University); Mr. Walter Hubbard (President, NOBC); Virgil J. Parker (President, Church of Jesus Christ of latter-Day Saints); Rev. William Weiler

(Director of Jewish /Christian Relations of NCC); and David Hunter (CRIA). The Rev. Luc Dequeker represented Belgian bishops; M. Helene Fournier, the Sisters of Sion; Sister Ann Marie Erst the Irish Commission on Justice and Peace; Lord Donald Soper the English Methodists; Dr. Charles Favre the International Council of Christians and Jews; and Rev. Père Michel Riquet the French clergy ("Special to Church News," *Desert News,* Salt Lake City, Utah, February 24, 1976, box 175).

26. Participants included Saul Amias, UK; Rev. and Mrs. Bakker, Rotterdam; Levy Becker, Canada; Joan Bennett, 35's England; Prof. Thomas Bird; Père Roger Braun, *Revue Recontre* (Chr. Et Juifs); Brant Coopersmith, AJC DC; Jean Paul David, International Christians and Jews (ICJ) Boulogne; Moshe Davis, Office of Chief Rabbi, London; Rev. Luc Dequeker, Belgium,; Jacques Dreyfuss, France; Rep. Robert Drinan; Eugene DuBow; Rabbi Colin Elmer, England; Rabbi Joseph Ehrenkranz, Stamford, CT; Sr. Ann Marie Erst; Msgr. T.G. Fahy; Dr. Charles Favre, ICJ, Lyons; Mother Helene Fournier, Belgium; Dan Gerber, Canada; Msgr. Bernard Gerhardt, DC; David Geller; Sr. Ann Gillen; Rabbi Oscar Groner DC; Rabbi L.H. Hardman London; Walter Hubbard; Dr. David Hunter; Norman Krasne, Mt Vernon NY; Msgr. Ralph Kuehner D.C.; Prof. Andre LaCocque; Rabbi Dan Marmur, England; Claude Mura "Dernieres Nouvelles" Colmar, France; Jean Nardmann, Fribourg; Rabbi Morton Narrowe, Stockholm; Rabbi Herbert Pannitch, Milwaukee, WI; Dr. and Mrs. Virgil Parker Church of Jesus Christ of Latter Day Saints, Belgium; Serge Perc, *Revue Recontre* Paris; Elaine Pittell, Hollywood, FL; Rabbi Joachim Prinz, NJ; Rev. Robert Pruitt; A. C. Ramselaar, Utrecht; Dr. G. N. Riegner, WJC; Seymour Reich, NY; Père Michel Riquet, France; Father Jewan Roger, Jerusalem; Bayard Rustin (Honorary co-sponsor of the Task Force); J. Schonberg, London; Lord Donald Soper; Maria Swings, Brussels; Rev. Stanley Schmidt; Rona Schwaat, Brookline, MA; Rev. John F. Steinbruck; Rev. Paul L. Stagg; Percy Sutton, NY; Sr. Margaret Traxler; Ms. Charlotte Turner, Morristown, NJ; R. Urban, B'nai B'rith, Great Britain; Rev. William Weiler; and Myrtle Zackian, Havertown, PA.

27. Herzberg became emotional. He spoke as a survivor of a Galician family: "Would that such meetings had taken place not too far from here in the 1940s. Thank God you are here, standing together against the cultural and religious genocide in atonement for how badly we failed to stand together in times past."

28. A NITFSJ Press Release on Brussels II issued on February 20, 1976 (box 195) noted that the Call to Conscience listed many varieties of persecution against Jews and others in the USSR.

29. It quoted Pope Paul VI on human rights, dignity, the right of religious liberty, and the repudiation of the denial of human rights in the Soviet Union from the WCC 1975 General Assembly in Nairobi, Kenya.

30. The document then appealed to Soviet authorities to end harassment of persons applying for exit visas, kidnapping of Jewish children and sending them to compulsory boarding schools, drafting of young Jewish men into military as a punitive measure, sending of men and women to prison on false charges, transfer of prisoners to psychiatric wards for alleged mental illness, denial of educational opportunities for Soviet Jews, denial of exit visas to soldiers and scientists based on security clearances, and exorbitant taxation of gift monies from abroad. It also urged an end to imprisonment of Jewish and Christian prisoners of conscience and freedom for jailed prisoners of conscience.

31. They asked for an end to the ban on publishing Hebrew Bibles and prayer books and to allow the production of religious articles, to permit the training of Rabbis and Jewish teachers, and to allow Soviet Jews to communicate with co-religionists abroad.

32. This was one of the amended clauses. "A Report on the Second . . . *The Task* . . . March 1976).

33. It closed: "I the Lord have call you for the victory of Justice. I have grasped you by the hand; I formed you and set you as a covenant of the people, a light for the nations to open the eyes of the blind, to bring prisoners out from confinement, and

from the dungeon, those who live in darkness (Isaiah: 42:6–7). A later version is contained in a NITFSJ press release, (February 20, 1976, box 195).

34. These "Principles" had originated at the Paris planning meetings. Karlikow had prepared a draft and Abe Harmon (affiliated with the Liaison Bureau) prepared the final version. Nehemiah Levanon, head of the Liaison Bureau, had brought to Paris his own version of a declaration which did not cite the Helsinki Agreements.

35. While some favored the right to resettle anywhere, the final version mentioned only Israel by name ("the Jewish historic homeland").

36. It listed the specific demands cited above, all referring to Soviet Jews except for the call to end the "ruthless and brutal imprisonment of all Prisoners of Conscience, both Jewish and Christian."

37. He noted that the American delegation had twenty-five Christians including four African- Americans. He noted that Sister Gillen referred to the desire by Germans, Latvians, and Lithuanians in the USSR to leave for resettlement in the West.

38. He added that if they decided not to continue funding her, then another twenty Jewish groups would do so.

39. He argued that to say that AJC's Board of Governors was meeting in Israel was not a satisfactory response (Memo, David Geller to Morris Fine. February 25, 1976, box 195).

40. He wrote that some thought that AJC President Elmer Winter and representatives of IAD should have been present. Even though Richard Maass, Abraham Karlikow, David Geller, Sergio Nudelstejer and he himself were present, they were "not seen as the *top* leadership."

41. In speaking of the key role of Sister Ann Gillen and the NITFSJ's Christian delegation, Rudin argued "for obvious reasons, we did not publicize our AJC role."

42. The Task Force also issued a special edition of *The Task* reporting on Brussels II (see above).

SIX

The Helsinki Accords and Persecuted Christians in the Soviet Union

A major issue for the AJC and the Task Force following Brussels II was the question of the linkage between the persecution of Jews and Christians and, to a lesser extent, dissidents in the Soviet Union. From the start, while advocating for Soviet Jews, Sister Gillen consistently expressed concern for persecuted Christians and some dissidents, such as Andrei Sakharov. In time, she also supported the cause of captive nations. However, two other activists, Professor André LaCocque and Father John Pawlikowski, favored an exclusive focus on Jews. Rabbis Tanenbaum and Rudin of the IAD accepted the linkages among all persecuted groups and spoke often about the persecution of both Soviet Jews and Christians. On the other side of the issue, David Geller of the FAD and AJC coordinator of Soviet Jewry policy, often favored maintaining an exclusive focus on Soviet Jews.

Importantly, as will be shown in this chapter, the Helsinki Accords reinforced the position of Sister Gillen and others in the Task Force that emphasized human rights in their advocacy for Soviet Jews and others in the Soviet Union.

THE HELSINKI ACCORDS

The United States, Canada, the USSR, and thirty-two European nations signed the Helsinki Final Act on April 1, 1975, which recognized the post-WWII boundaries in Europe. Basket III of the Accords included a list of human rights to be observed by the signatory nations. The most important concerned facilitating and expediting approval of exit visas for achieving family reunification and religious and cultural rights (Lazin

2005, 52). In effect, Basket III codified a set of principles by which to measure Soviet behavior toward its citizens ("Helsinki Accord and the Soviet Union: Effects on Human Rights Seem Mixed," *NYT*, July 31, 1976, box 175). Importantly, the Soviet Union had previously defined these human rights issues as internal matters. The Accords also established a regular review process involving follow-up conferences to evaluate the implementation of Basket III provisions by signatory nations. The first follow-up conference was scheduled to take place in Belgrade in the autumn of 1977 (Ann Gillen, "Interreligious Cooperation in Human Rights: a working model," paper presented at University of Michigan seminar of Human Rights, February 8, 1978, box 175).

Sister Gillen believed that Basket III reaffirmed a commitment to human rights by the signatory nations. Almost immediately, the Task Force charged the Soviet regime with "gross violations of the Helsinki Accords through a series of denials of human rights to Jews" (NITFSJ press release, November 3, 1976, box 208, folder 1).[1] Sister Gillen and the Task Force lobbied for passage of a Congressional bill that established the Commission on Security and Cooperation in Europe (CSCE or the United States Helsinki Commission) to monitor compliance with the Helsinki Accords. Congressman Dante Fascell, a Democrat from Florida, served as chair (Letter, Sister Ann Gillen to Colleagues, n.d., 1976).[2]

The AJC served on a committee sponsored by the Presidium and Steering Committee of the World Conference on Soviet Jewry to monitor the Helsinki Accords. In a September 1976 meeting, participants discussed the implication of the Helsinki Accords to broaden the issue of Soviet Jewry to one of human rights covering Jewish and non-Jewish groups (Memo, Sidney Liskofsky to Abe Karlikow re: "Meeting of Committee on Helsinki Monitoring . . .," September 30, 1976).[3] They decided to prepare a report on the repression of Jewish culture in the Soviet Union for the Helsinki follow-up conference in Belgrade (Memos, Abe Karlikow to Sidney Liskofsky re: "Meeting of Committee . . .," October 13, 1976, box 194; and re: "Meeting on Soviet Jews," March 22, 1977, box 194).[4]

The AJC and the Task Force collaborated with the CSCE and Congressman Fascell (Memo, David Geller to Rabbi Jim Rudin et. al. ". . . Program Priority Report . . .," August 31, 1976, box 209, folder 3).[5] Sister Gillen and the Task Force proposed holding public hearings on alleged Soviet violations of The Helsinki Accords involving Jewish and Christian prisoners of conscience. They hoped to present the findings either to the CSCE or at Belgrade (Memo, Rabbi Rudin to Bert Gold, re "Chicago II Follow Up . . .," December 22, 1976, box 208, folder 1).[6]

The AJC organized the hearings (Memo, Rabbi Rudin to Rabbi Tanenbaum, February 3, 1977, box 212, folder 1).[7] Rabbi Rudin met with Professor Tom Bird to discuss who should be invited and the proposed program, which would deal with Baptists, Uniates (Ukrainian Catholics),

Roman Catholics (Lithuanian), members of the Russian Orthodox Church, and Soviet Jews.[8]

The hearings on "Religious Liberty and Human Rights" in the Soviet Union were held on March 16, 1977, in NYC as a public tribunal modeled on the Nuremberg Nazi War Crimes Tribunal (NITFSJ, "Alter to editors, broadcasters," March 10, 1977 and "Religious Liberty in the Soviet Union" report on testimony given in NYC on March 16 submitted to CSCE, "Basket Three" GPO).[9] The first witness, Professor Bird, an expert on religion in the Soviet Union, described the situation of Jews in the USSR as being "equal to every other religious and national group in the USSR under the law, but grossly ... unequal in the arbitrariness with which the law is applied."[10] He urged his fellow Christians to "understand their own self-interest in supporting the cause of Soviet Jews." The implication was "first the Jews and then us. . . . We Christians, in an age that has witnessed the Holocaust, have a profound historical, moral obligation to stand guard over the destiny of the children of Israel wherever its existence is threatened. . ." He urged American pressure on the USSR on "emigration, liberalization of religious education and expansion of places of worship" (Judy Cummings, "Religious Group Asks . . . put Pressure on Soviets . . . Helsinki Accords" *NYT*, March 17, 1977). He also presented an overview of the situation of Catholics in the Soviet Union and expressed his belief that the Helsinki Final Act might be helpful in easing their plight. He explained that religious groups must register but had no right to exist as such, religious societies were denied property rights, the government forbade missionary and cultural activities, and that it was a crime to educate religiously one's children and grandchildren ("Basket Three . . ." GPO, May 9, 1977, 80).

The second witness Ilya Kevkov, a Soviet Jewish émigré and researcher for the NCSJ, focused on the problems of family reunification and recent anti-Semitism. Professor William Fletcher, director of Soviet Studies at the University of Kansas and a Baptist, followed. He reiterated Professor Bird's three points about the lack of freedom of movement, freedom of worship, and freedom of religious education. NYU law professor Howard Greenberger next argued that The Helsinki Accords (along with other protocols) meant that the lack of religious freedom was no longer an internal Soviet matter. He wanted more done to ensure a meaningful Jewish life for those who remained. Next, the Reverend A. Veinbergs of Washington, D.C., talked about the destruction of churches and persecution of Lutherans and others in Latvia. He thanked the Task Force "for its bold and effective efforts to defend human rights regardless of nationality or religious conviction."

Walter Dushnyck, editor of the *Ukrainian Quarterly*, described Soviet destruction of Ukrainian churches. He argued that the government denied religious freedom to members of the Ukrainian Orthodox Church, the Ukrainian Catholic Church (Uniate Church), "underground" Ukrainian Catholic communities, Roman Catholics, Evangelical Christians, and Baptists.[11] He was followed by Reverend Blahoslav Hruby of the Research Center for Religion and Human Rights in Closed Societies who talked about the struggle for religious freedom and human rights in the USSR and Czechoslovakia. He criticized the WCC for failing to act against charges of religious persecution in the Soviet Union.[12]

The AJC submitted a transcript of its New York hearings to a CSCE hearing on the Helsinki Accords in Washington, D.C. on April 28, 1977 ("Religious Liberty . . ." March 16 submitted to CSCE, Basket Three, GPO).[13] Several Task Force and AJC members testified at the CSCE hearings about the persecution of Jews and Christians in the Soviet Union. Sister Traxler focused on religious persecution and the closing of churches (Vol. II "Religious liberty and minority rights in the Soviet Union" April 27–28, 1977; Helsinki Compliance in Eastern Europe, May 9, 1977. GPO, 1977). She explained that setting up the NITFSJ did not mean that they were "not equally concerned about Christians who were also denied religious liberties." She called for action regarding the freedom of movement, including the right to leave, relaxation of the registry of houses of worship, and fewer restrictions on religious education.

In her testimony, Sister Gillen claimed indifference by most people to the struggle for religious freedom in the Soviet Union. She hoped that the agreements made in Belgrade would make a difference (Ibid.).[14] Professor LaCocque said it was a miracle that after a half century of repression "not to say persecution, one still finds such a liveliness of faith and belief everywhere, and especially among the Jews, which have so often shown the way to others" (Ibid.). Rabbi Marc Tanenbaum referred to the "spiritual genocide" of Soviet Jewry when he described the lack of religious liberty and freedom of conscience in the USSR (Ibid.). He also told the Senators about the existence of local task forces in cities throughout the United States, which had brought together Roman Catholics, mainline Protestants, Greek Orthodox, evangelical Christians, African American churches, Hispanic churches, and Jews. He argued that in considering the issue of the Helsinki Accords these groups wanted to "make real impact . . . on public opinion, and . . . to make sure that the American government and leadership understand the [commitment] . . . of our people to this cause" (Testimony on Human Rights, DC, CSCE, Congress of US April 28, 1977, box 212, folder 1).

SISTER ANN GILLEN'S US SPEAKING ENGAGEMENTS

From March 1976 through March 1983, Sister Gillen attended meetings, demonstrations, and protests and lectured at parochial schools, college campuses, churches, synagogues, parlor meetings, and JCRC events in towns and cities throughout the country.[15] She also lobbied in Washington, D.C. and ran the Task Force office in Chicago.

Sister Gillen's extensive personal and professional ties with sisters religious and Catholic clergy continued to facilitate her invitations to speak. During a March 1976 weeklong visit to St. Paul and Minneapolis, she presented the cause of human rights for Soviet Jews before the Catholic Archdiocese (Letter, Bro. Martin Klietz..., Archdiocese of St. Paul and Minneapolis to Ann Gillen, March 16, 1976, box 175).[16] In July 1976, she spoke about Soviet Jews at the Bicentennial Convocation on Global Justice sponsored by the NCCB in Maryknoll, New York. Here she met Reverend Casimir Pugevicius (Letter, Casimir Pugevicius to Ann Gillen, August 9, 1976, Spertus Archives, box 109, misc. cor.).[17] In May 1976, she and Rabbi Rudin spoke at the Newman Club in St. Louis, Missouri. A month later, she addressed the Bellwood Il Clergy Association, describing the Co-adoption Program. She visited Philadelphia in May, June, and July 1976 for various Soviet Jewry activities ("Update...," Summer 1976).

In September 1978, the IAD arranged for Sister Gillen to speak about human rights and Soviet Jewry at a series of joint Jewish-Southern Baptist Conferences in Virginia and North and South Carolina (Memo, Rabbi Jim Rudin to Rabbi Marc Tanenbaum. June 15, 1978, box 211, folder 19; and Letter, Rabbi Rudin to Ann Gillen, March 14, 1978, Spertus, box 48, Rudin). In 1979, Sister Gillen spoke at a one-day Task Force-sponsored leadership conference at the Church Center at the UN in New York City.[18]

The AJC also encouraged Sister Gillen's involvement with national Jewish organizations. In May 1976, she participated on a panel at NCSJ meetings in Washington, D.C. (Memo, March 31, 1976, box 175 and Spertus, Box 48, Rudin).[19] She coordinated many Task Force activities with the NCSJ (Memo, Rabbi Rudin to Rabbi Tanenbaum, March 23, 197, box 211, folder 19).[20] Sister Gillen also had very close ties with the grassroots Union of Councils and later served on its board. They collaborated with her on speaking engagement at the Ohio Human Rights Council in Cincinnati, a San Francisco area meeting with a panel, including Andrei Sakharov's daughter, and at several meetings in East Rockaway, New York, and on Long Island in 1981 ("Batch of Borscht," Catholic *Telegraph* Cincinnati. December 5, 1980, box 303, folder 3).[21] In cooperation with the BB, she addressed a Manhattan Garment Workers group. In June 1976, the AJC arranged for Sister Gillen to address the National Conference of Jewish Communal Service in Washington, D.C. (Letter, Herbert Schneider to Ann Gillen, June 10, 1976, box 175; and Memo, Eugene DuBow to Sam Katz, "re National Conference of Jewish Communal Service," April 19, 1976). She spoke in Buffalo for the NCCJ-sponsored "Women's Pleas for Soviet Jewry" in December 1981 (Flyer, NCCJ, Western NY Region, Buffalo chapter, November 23, 1981, box 303, folder 1).[22]

The IAD arranged for Sister Gillen to speak at many AJC national gatherings. She addressed the AJC Interreligious Affairs Meeting in

Washington, D.C. on May 13, 1976. Typically, the AJC initiated and organized her trips and often coordinated them with regional staff, most of whom were very happy to have her speak (Memo, Eugene DuBow to Sam Katz, April 19,1976, box 175). On many trips she did outreach to the Jewish and Christian communities. On a two-day trip to Houston in March 1976, the local AJC arranged for two newspaper interviews, a breakfast at Central Presbyterian Church, and a talk at a Jewish synagogue on Friday night (Letter, Michael Rapp, AJC Houston, to Sister Ann Gillen, March 17, 1976, box 175).[23] The print media and television stations covered her AJC-organized speaking visit to Denver and its suburbs in October 1976 (Letter, Bette Lande, AJC Los Angeles, to Ann Gillen, September 14, 1976, box 175; and Letter, Bette Lande to Bob Kerbel, October 19, 1976, box 175).[24]

In November 1981, she joined AJC Midwest regional director Adam Simms in an off-the-record consultation with Ukrainian and Lithuanian religious and nationalist leaders. They hoped that their consultation would lead to future meetings focusing on religious liberty and the cultural rights of Jews and Christians in the USSR and Eastern Europe (Ann Gillen, "Report to co-Leaders, November 23, 1981, box 302, folder 3). The off-the-record character of the event may have been an indicator of the sensitivity of the outreach on the part of the AJC and the Task Force to captive nation groups.

In 1982, Sister Gillen spent three days in Cleveland and its suburbs. She spoke at the Jewish Federation, a multi-ethnic forum at Our Lady of Perpetual Help Church, the Newman Center, the JCRC, several high schools, civic groups, and a radio show, and participated in four newspaper interviews.[25] The Mayor of Cleveland, George V. Voinovich, designated January 27, 1982 "Sister Ann Gillen Day." Her visit resulted in an AJC effort to launch "a petition drive to collect signatures on behalf of a closed church in Klaipeda, Lithuania and . . .to begin to work on a campaign on behalf of Soviet Jews and relatives of local ethnics here" (Memo, Marty Plax. AJC to Rabbi James Rudin, "re Sister Ann Gillen," February 1, 1982, box 302, folder 2).[26]

Sister Gillen spoke at local JCRCs from coast-to-coast including, Des Moines, Iowa; San Diego; Tulsa; Scranton, Pennsylvania; and Albany, New York.[27] She was the featured speaker in Canton, Ohio at the opening of an art exhibit from the underground in the Soviet Union in early 1978 (Talk by Ann Gillen, April 8, 1978, box 175). In Portland, Oregon she spoke about persecuted Soviet Jews and Christians at Westminster Presbyterian Church and at Congregation Neveh Shalom ("Soviet Jews Face Tough Plight" *Portland Oregon Catholic Sentinel*, February 26, 1982, box 302, folder 2; and *The Task*, December 25, 1982, box 302, folder 2; article by Charlotte Graydon of the *Oregonian*, "Nun Fights for Jewish Emigration"). She spoke in Phoenix in December 1982 for a local Soviet Jewry advocacy group and in Boston in February 1983 for the Jewish Community Council of Metropolitan Boston (JCCMB) (Letter, Dr. Judith Wolf, JCCMB, and Rabbi Murray I. Rothman to Sister Ann, February 2, 1983, box 301).[28]

She visited Washington, D.C. several times each year for a variety of activities. In May 1976, she lobbied for passage of the bill to establish the CSCE (Letter, Rep. Barbara Jordan to Ann Gillen, May 20, 1976, box 176). In 1978, she presented a paper on the Helsinki Accords and Human Rights at the United States State Department (Gillen paper at State Department, February 28, 1978, box 175).[29] In 1981, she joined a Union of Councils delegation in meetings with Senator Charles Percy (R-IL) ("Report to Co-Leaders," November 23, 1981, box 302, folder 3).[30] She also wrote frequently to State Department officials and to the President about American policy and individual cases (Letter, Hodding Carter III, Assistant Secretary of State to Ann Gillen, September 22, 1977, Spertus, box 3).

In Chicago, Sister Gillen ran the Task Force office, spoke at churches, synagogues, JCCs, and at JCRC meetings and kept in contact with those concerned with the plight of persecuted Jews and Christians in the Soviet Union ("Update. . ." Summer 1976).[31] In May 1976, she appeared on a television program with former Prisoner of Conscience Alexander (Sasha) Lunts, and participated in Solidarity Day in Chicago and a planning session for the Task Force's Chicago II Consultation.

LOCAL TASK FORCES

During this period Sister Gillen and the AJC continued to cultivate local interreligious task forces. In her appearances around the country she urged her listeners and sponsors to establish local interreligious task forces.[32] The AJC directed its regional directors and offices to cooperate with Sister Gillen's efforts to establish local task forces (Memo, Rabbi Marc Tanenbaum to Phyllis Sherman, "NITFSJ," May 11, 1976, box 209, folder 2). The new task forces joined a very loose network of mostly independent bodies responsible to local level sponsors. Almost all focused on persecuted Jews and Christians in the Soviet Union (and sometimes also in Eastern Europe). While Sister Gillen urged the inclusion of national (ethnic) groups who suffered persecution in the Soviet Union, the concern for non-Jews focused mostly on denial of their religious freedom (Memo, Sister Ann Gillen to Rabbi Marc Tanenbaum, Rabbi Jim Rudin and Eugene DuBow re "Memo regarding Task Force . . . by Eugene DuBow," n.d., c1976, box 175).[33]

The local Jewish CRCs, supervised by the NJCRAC in NYC, cooperated with Sister Gillen's efforts to establish local task forces ("Interreligious Task Force. . . .", Minutes of Meeting, JCC Scranton PA, December 15, 1976, box 175).[34] In several larger communities, the CRCs worked with the local AJC. Very few had reservations about Sister Gillen's speaking about the persecution of Christians in the Soviet Union. The events in 1976 in Cincinnati were typical.[35] The local CRC wanted to form a local task force. They invited Sister Gillen to address a gathering of about sixty people including Christian clergy, rabbis, and lay leaders. Afterward, the local JCRC recruited an influential Christian clergyperson to head the local task force (Letter, Jane B. Holzman. JCRC of Cincinnati, to Al Chernin, Abe Bayer, and Jerry Goodman, re "Visit of Sister . . . Gillen . . . on May 25, 1976," June 7, 1976, box 175).[36]

The JCRC led the effort to set up a local task force in Philadelphia. Initially they organized a women's interfaith task force on Soviet Jewry with a full-time staff person (Letter, Murray Friedman, Philadelphia AJC, to Isaiah Terman "re Task Force . . . ." June 28, 1976, box 175).[37] By December 1976, Sister Gloria Coleman, SHCJ, headed the Philadelphia Task Force on Soviet Jewry (Memo, Sister Gloria Coleman, chairperson to colleagues, December 21, 1976, box 175). She announced a forthcoming meeting with Professor Bird speaking on the issue of Human Rights in the Soviet Union. Rabbi Rudin spoke at their awards ceremony in May 1981. Sister Coleman recruited local Ukrainians, Lithuanians, and Jews, Philadelphia ITFSJ, May 27, 198, box, Interreligious Affairs 1980s, 303, folder 2; and Ann Gillen, "Challenge of this to the Western Religious Community and to the US," n.d.).

In Los Angeles, AJC director Neil Sandberg established a local interreligious task force on Soviet Jewry, which included the JCRC. He noted that "for the moment" it kept the Christian and human rights dimensions outside its purview (Memo, Neil C. Sandberg to Will Katz, March 28, 1977, box 194). In contrast, the Knoxville Inter Religious Task Force on Religious Freedom and Human Rights in the Soviet Union dealt with all persecuted religious groups in the USSR (Minutes of Executive Committee of Knoxville Interreligious Task Force . . ., March 5, 1980, box 303, folder 1).[38] They kept in close contact with Sister Gillen and Rabbi Rudin.

In Dallas, the local AJC formed "a coalition on behalf of Christians and Jews in the Soviet Union" (Memo, Miles Zitmore to Will Katz, "Dallas Interfaith Consultation for Religious Freedom and Human Rights in the Soviet Union," March 16, 1977, box 194).[39] The coalition held a Consultation on May 7, 1977, chaired by Judge Oswin Chrisman, a Baptist; Bishop Thomas Tschoepe of the Catholic Diocese; and Carl Lee of the AJC (Memo, Miles Zitmore to Rabbi Tanenbaum, December 9, 1976, box 175).[40] Judge Chrisman presided.[41] Bishop Tschoepe delivered the invocation and Sister Gillen spoke about the human rights problems facing Soviet Jews. Rabbi Rudin then addressed the problems of Christian prisoners of conscience in the USSR. Tony Martins of the Baptist Christian Life Commission gave the benediction, which included the Hebrew *Shema*. The local press, newspapers, and radio and television stations covered the event.[42] The consultation hoped to draft a "Declaration of Support" for the Helsinki Accords, to participate in a project of co-adoption, and to conduct an interfaith consultation annually.[43]

AJC's Southeast Director William A. Gralnick worked actively on behalf of the Task Force and its outreach activities to the Christian community.[44] He held the view that the Soviet Union persecuted Christians as well as Jews.[45] He helped local Jewish welfare federations organize local interreligious task forces in Atlanta, Charleston, Greensboro, Memphis, Nashville, and Birmingham. He encouraged them to attend Chicago II (Letter, William Gralnick to Marvin B. Schpeiser, Atlanta Jewish Welfare Federation. August 24, 1976, box 208, folder 1).

Gralnick coordinated the activities of the Atlanta Interreligious Task Force on Soviet Jewry and Human Rights, which had been founded in 1970. In June 1980, it joined the Georgia Office of the NCCJ in calling for the immediate release of two Christian prisoners of conscience, Aleksi Murzhenko and Yuri Federov, and the Jewish prisoner of conscience, Yosef Mendelovitch (Memo, Rabbi Rudin to Rabbi Tanenbaum, June 24, 1980, box 303, folder 3).[46] He believed the three prisoners "symbolically speak to the issue of religious persecution as a whole" and that there was "an alarming lack of knowledge about the persecution of Christians in Eastern Europe and the Soviet Union." Many Christians, he argued, viewed the religious issue as a Jewish one, which he believed it was not ("Two Religious Groups Seek Freedom for three," *Atlanta Journal*, July 19, 1980, box 303, folder 1).[47]

During 1975 and 1976, the local task force in Miami functioned on an *ad hoc* basis. In the fall of 1976, the AJC and CRC reorganized the local task force and broadened the agenda by focusing on the Helsinki Accords (Memo, Brenda Shapiro, director, Miami AJC, to Will Katz, March 31, 1977, box 194).[48] They selected Reverend Richard Bailar, a local United Church of Christ minister, to serve as chair.[49] Task Force members wanted the organization to address a wide spectrum "of human rights problems," including Soviet Jewry, Anglican oppression in Uganda, and repression of Catholic Clergy in Latin America. In March 1977, they restricted membership to clergy and renamed the task force the "Interfaith Committee on Human Rights." They elected Reverend Richard Bailar as chair.[50] The group sent letters to President Carter in favor of the Jackson-Vanik Amendment, discussed participation in the May 22 Solidarity Day in Dade County, and coordinated activities with the South Florida Conference on Soviet Jewry. They hoped to have Sister Gillen speak. They also had the support of the NCCJ, which saw the new groups as "a vehicle for taking action" (Memo, Brenda Shapiro to Will Katz "Interfaith Commission ... of Greater Miami," March 31, 1977, box 194).

The Interfaith Committee on Human Rights and the greater Miami AJC co-sponsored a conference "Religion: Right or Risk" on March 3, 1982 in Coral Gables to celebrate the tenth anniversary of the NITFSJ. Co-sponsors included JCRC, the South Florida Conference on Soviet Jewry,

NCCJ, Southern Baptist Home Mission Board, Metropolitan Fellowship of Churches, Episcopal Diocese, three Jewish temples, Catholic churches, several Protestant churches and a Greek Orthodox church. Both Sister Gillen and Rabbi Rudin spoke. Sister Gillen suggested that Christians duplicate the new Jewish custom of Bar/Bat Mitzvah children adopting a Soviet Jewish teen (Robert Wilcox, "Russia Killing Christianity: Nun Says Catholics Singled out..." March 8, 1982, *The Voice*, box 302, folder 2).

At a meeting in April 1982, local task force participants discussed the lack of large audiences at many of the sessions of its March interfaith conference in Coral Gables (Minutes of Interreligious Task Force, April 12, 1982, box 302, folder 3). Arguing that that clergy are too overburdened, they wanted to focus on laypersons. They proposed issuing a newsletter with a description of "the issue of Christian persecution... and methods by which help can be obtained for them." They would focus, possibly, on Roman Catholics (particularly ethnic Catholics), Eastern Rite religions, Baptists, and Pentecostals. Bill Gralnick of the AJC would organize the next meeting.

Efforts by Sister Gillen and the AJC to establish a local task force in NYC continued to be problematic. Negotiations between the AJC and the GNCSJ resumed in January 1977. The new GNYCSJ executive director, Margy Ruth Davis, invited Sister Gillen and Rabbi Rudin to a January 11, 1977 program of a New York interreligious task force affiliated with the GNYCSJ (Memo, Margy-Ruth Davis to Ann Gillen and Rabbi Rudin, December 1, 1976).[51] Two years later, Rabbi Rudin explained that efforts to set up a local task force during the past two and one-half years had failed. He believed that the GNYCSJ had been interested but "the GNYCSJ itself wants to control any interreligious activities on behalf of Soviet Jewry." Nevertheless, he and Sister Gillen had managed to establish a modest local NYC task force comprised primarily of academics (Letter, Rabbi Rudin to Sister Ann Gillen, March 14, 1978, Spertus, box 48, Rudin folder; and Memo, Rabbi Rudin to Rabbi Tanenbaum. November 13, 1978 box 211, folder 19).[52]

THE CHICAGO II CONSULTATION

The Second Consultation of the NITFSJ (Chicago, II) took place in November 1976 after the signing of the Helsinki Accords. While Sister Gillen played a key role, the AJC organized the event.[53] After consulting with Rabbi Marc Tanenbaum about dates, she invited a group of local Catholic, Protestant, and Jewish clergy to a planning meeting for the Consultation on May 20, 1976 (Memo, Sister Ann Gillen to Rabbi Tanenbaum, March 10, 1976, box 175). Chairpersons of the Chicago Task Force on Soviet Jewry and local AJC staff also attended (Form letter, Ann Gillen to participants, April 28, 1976, box 175). Participants at the planning meeting named the event "The Chicago II Consultation on Soviet Jewry: Human Rights/Helsinki/Religious liberty" (Memo, Rabbi Rudin to Rabbi Tanenbaum, May 28, 1976, box 174; and Memo, Sister Ann Gillen to Rabbi A. Jim Rudin, August 26, 1976, box 208, folder 1).[54] In August, the name of the event became "Second National Interreligious Consultation on Soviet Jewry" on the theme of "The Helsinki Accords, Human Rights, and Religious Liberty in the USSR" (Memo, Sister Ann Gillen and Rabbi Rudin to Margaret Traxler, August 5, 1976, box 208, folder 1).[55] The Helsinki Accords had taken center stage in the Task Force's advocacy for Soviet Jewry.[56]

The AJC urged its regional directors to recruit non-Jewish participants. It suggested organizing a local task force involving Christian clergy and ethnic organizations representing captive nations from the USSR and Eastern Europe who would then send a delegation to Chicago II (Memo, DuBow to Rabbi Tanenbaum, June 21, 1976, box 175 and Spertus, box 48, Tanenbaum file; and Memo, Rabbi Rudin to Bert Gold, October 22, 1976, box 208).[57]

The Consultation opened on Monday evening November 29 at the University of Chicago ("Chicago II Participants," box 208, folder 2).[58] Sister Traxler presided. Reverend Robert Pruitt gave the invocation. Representative Robert F. Drinan and Dr. Cynthia C. Wedel, president of the WCC, gave the keynote speeches. Representative Drinan called for "immediate and forceful action by the American Government to bring about increased compliance with . . . the Helsinki Accords." There was an urgent need, he insisted "to enforce . . . provisions, lest Soviet Jews and other minorities suffer ever greater repression." By its actions since enactment of The Accords, he argued, the "Soviet government demonstrated its clear intention to ignore the Agreement's human rights provision and to pursue its inhuman emigration policy unchanged, if international pressure does not require a change" ("Précis of Remarks by Cong Robert F. Drinan. . . , Second National . . . Soviet Jewry," November 29, 1976, box 208, folder 1).[59]

Dr. Cynthia Wedel articulated the WCC's stand on religious liberty and Soviet Jewry (Cynthia Wedel, "The WCC and Religious Liberty," November 29, 1976, box 208, folder 2).[60] She feared that antagonizing the Soviet Union would result in the closing of churches, greater religious persecution, and the cutting of ties with the WCC. She emphasized that Christians throughout the free world were "deeply concerned about the severe problems faced by Soviet Jewry . . . the WCC . . . stands ready to be helpful . . . if it could find any concrete way of doing so." She said that "those church leaders in the Soviet Union who are still able to function are in no position to make effective overtures to the government. *Nor is there any possible reason to suppose that any attempt at intervention by WCC itself would be effective*" (emphasis is the author's). She concluded by saying the WCC was "deeply committed to the principle of religious freedom . . . that applies to *all* religious groups. Soviet Jews will be in our minds in all our conferences, discussions and actions. . . . We feel sure that your concern, in the same way, is for freedom of religion for all groups in the Eastern European lands."

In her keynote address the next day, Sister Gillen reasserted the focus on Soviet Jewry (The NITFSJ, 1972–1976: "A report. . ."). She noted the strong representation of the Greek Orthodox Church at the first Consultation and its absence at the second. She described Task Force programs, including the Children's Pen Pal Program, the Call to Christian Conscience, and Project Co-Adoption. She expressed pride in the establishment of a national interreligious network of groups and individuals and *The Task* newsletter. She noted the many regional and local meetings throughout the country, activity in Washington, D.C., including Sister Traxler's testifying on the Jackson-Vanik Amendment. She recalled Brussels II. She cited the Sisterhood of Conscience for Sylva Zalmanson, which had helped free Zalmanson and Sister Elizabeth Pretschener; the support for the Christian prisoner of conscience Yuri Federov; a Mother's Day project which had focused on Luboc Dinenzon who waited in Chicago for the freedom of her son; the fast for freedom for the Slepak family, and the letter-writing campaign for Nijoli Sadunaite, a Lithuanian Catholic woman imprisoned for her service to the Church.

She closed with a question: *was she also concerned about Christian suffering in the USSR?* She answered *yes* and then explained that "the . . . Jews seek to return to an ancient homeland; Christians seek to liberate their homelands; our focus is specific—on one human right, the freedom to emigrate. If we work for one group and human right, we lift the horizon of hope for all groups and all rights. . . . The Soviet Jewry group has sired many groups to adopt similar measures to obtain the right of religious liberty."[61]

Senator Charles Percy (R-IL) addressed participants at lunch. He focused on The Helsinki Accords and the role of Voice of America (VOA) in dealing with discrimination in the Soviet Union.[62] Later in the day, Task Force co-chair Professor André LaCocque presented a brief theological discourse on Soviet Jewry ("Perspectives," a speech delivered at Chicago II by André LaCocque, November 29, 1976, box 208, folder 1). During the last twenty centuries, he argued, the Jews had lost every battle, but not the war. All of their enemies had fallen, including Spain and Portugal. "Tomorrow another Jewish prophet . . . will shout out his joy because the Soviet persecution of Jews and other peaceful and innocent minorities is no more."

He praised the involvement of Christians and Jews collaborating in the important work of the Task Force. He emphasized "our movement must remain a Task Force for Soviet Jewry. My preceding remarks made bare the foundation of such a dedication to the Jews *qua* representative's *par excellence* of humanity." It was important, he said, to be concerned about all humanity and about suffering in all countries ". . . where a Jew is denied his Jewishness, man is denied his humanness. Where a man is debased, the Jew in him . . . is put on the stake. . . . Like in love affairs, universalism is found only in particularism."

He closed by saying that the history of the past two thousand years teaches that:

> . . . a political regime stands or falls on its dealing with the Jewish question. Anti-Semitism always amounts to committing suicide. We dare warn the Soviet Union that it will not escape the doom of Nazi Germany if it persists in such a disposition rendered so ultimately infamous by their former enemy. . . . We proclaim our faith and trust that no totalitarianism will last. . .Nothing ultimately can prevail against man, because he is the image of God (Ibid.).

At the closing plenary session, Alfred Friendly of the CSCE and Rabbi Marc Tanenbaum spoke. Rabbi Tanenbaum related the plight of Soviet Jews to the millions of Lithuanian Catholics, Latvian "Catholics," Poles, Estonians, Russian Orthodox, and Anglican Baptists in the Soviet Union. He predicted that what had happened to the Jews if the world remained silent, could also happen to them (Rabbi Tanenbaum's Consultation Address, November 29, 30, 1976, box 208, folder 2). Father John T. Pawlikowski gave the final benediction.

After the Consultation, Eugene DuBow, praised Sister Gillen for the event's success (Memo, DuBow to Rabbi Tanenbaum, December 9, 1976, box 208, folder 2).[63] AJC's executive director, wrote to her: "However, if the truth be told, it has been the effective and dedicated leadership that you have given to the Task Force which has made it as important as it is" (Note, Bert Gold to Ann Gillen, December 17, 1976, box 208, folder 1).[64]

DuBow also commented on the lack of media coverage. He believed that the real target was not "so much the general American population but rather the 'Christian professionals' who have the power to put the issue of Soviet Jewry on the American Christian agenda where presently it rates down near the bottom." He focused on the problem of broadening the context in which the subject of Soviet Jewry was discussed in many of the sessions. He wrote:

> I guess . . . we must expect that issues of Christian importance will be increasingly introduced to the partial exclusion of Soviet Jewry. . . . The implications . . . are that we must do more careful planning of agendas . . ., I hope the AJC is finally convinced that the NITFSJ is one of its most important priorities. The Consultation . . . proved it (Letter, DuBow to Rabbi Tanenbaum, December 9. 1976, box 208, folder 2).[65]

An unexpected controversy arose around comments made by Father Casimir Pugevicius, executive director of the Lithuanian American Catholic Services, who had participated on a panel at the Consultation (Letter, Casimir Pugevicius to Ann Gillen, August 9, 1976, Spertus, box 109, misc.

cor. 1975–76; and Memo, Sister Ann Gillen to Rabbis Tanenbaum and Rudin, July 23, 1976).[66] Judy Edinger a reporter with the National Catholic News Service (NCNS) and RNS quoted him as saying that some participants at the Consultation seemed "insensitive to the Lithuanians' problems and he disagreed with the statement that the Jews have suffered more than anyone else in the Soviet Union" ("Consultation on Soviet Jews sought Lithuanian Input, Sister says," NCNS, January 3, 1977, Spertus, box 42).[67] Sister Gillen denied the charges. She argued that she and other Task Force leaders shared his concern about the oppression and persecution of Lithuanian Catholic people (Letter, Sister Ann Gillen to Richard Daw, NCNS, and Miss Lillian Block RNS, December 21, 1976, box 174). She explained that the Task Force had invited him to raise the issue of the plight of Lithuanian Catholics at the Consultation, which brought together two hundred and fifty Jewish and Christian leaders from all over the United States. Moreover, the theme of the conference was deliberately chosen to include consideration of oppressed Catholics, Russian Orthodox, and Baptists, in addition to Jews in the USSR and Eastern Europe. "To suggest that the victims must fight one another, or that Americans should choose to support one victimized group at the expense of another is to nothing less than to confound the victimization and to play into the hands of the enemies of both Christians and Jews." She went on to emphasize that the Task Force worked with "church groups in seeking the liberation of all prisoners of conscience, whatever their faith, in the Soviet Union," and concluded:

> Our regret over the . . . stories is not only because it distorted reality, but because it may lead . . . to the pollution of the atmosphere between Christians and Jews who need each other desperately in the common struggle to preserve the sacred image of men and women created in the image of God which is being defiled daily in these oppressive, totalitarian societies (Ibid.).

LOCAL CONFERENCES

A year later, the AJC and the Task Force organized a one-day Task Force Leadership Conference at the Holiday Inn near Chicago's O'Hare airport on November 14, 1977. The Conference brought together Task Force leaders with AJC area directors from Chicago, Cleveland, Milwaukee, St. Louis, Dallas, Miami, Washington D.C., Louisville, and Scranton (Memo, Rabbi Rudin to Rabbi Tanenbaum re: "Proposed Leadership Conference of Task Force," September 28, 1977, box 212, folder 1). The Task Force conducted the workshop. In a letter of invitation to its supporters, the Task Force referred to Edward Kuznetsov, Anatoly Shcharansky, Nijole Sadunaite, Georgi Vins, and other prisoners of conscience (Form Letter, NITFSJ to Friend, October 14, 1977, box 207, folder 4; and Memo, Rabbi

Rudin to Area Directors, October 24, 1977, box 207, folder 4). Task Force Co-Chair Sister Traxler welcomed the attendees. In the morning, Rabbi James Rudin presented an update on the "Current Status of the Jews in the Soviet Union." Professor André LaCocque led a panel on community reports from around the country. In the afternoon, Sister Gillen talked about the priorities for 1977. Reverend John F. Steinbruck, Reverend Stanley A. Schmidt, and Lorel Pollack, chairperson of Chicago Action for Soviet Jewry, responded to Sister Gillen's presentation.

Rabbi Rudin planned a one-day mini conference for Task Force leadership in New York City for October 30, 1979 at the Church Center at the United Nations (Memo, Rabbi Rudin to Rabbi Tanenbaum, June 6, 1979, box 211, folder 18). Speakers included Matthew Nimetz from the State Department, Representative Drinan, Sister Gillen, Rabbi Rudin, Jerry Goodman, Bayard Rustin, Rabbi Tanenbaum, and Professor Bird (Letter, Margaret Traxler, Rabbi Marc Tanenbaum and Andre LaCocque to friends, August 1979, box 208, folder 4).[68] The conference ended with a vigil at the Isaiah Wall. More than hundred religious leaders from around the country attended (NITFSJ, "News and Photo Alert" October 24, 1979 and NITFSJ, Press Release. ". . . Matthew Nimetz at Luncheon address . . ." October 30, 1979, box 194).[69]

THE AJC AND THE TASK FORCE

Upon return from Brussels II, Sister Gillen began to recruit people for Task Force committees. She envisioned committees on education, liturgy, and international affairs (Letter, Sister Ann Gillen to Rabbi Rudin, March 9, 1976, Spertus, box 1, folder, some cor.).[70] These never materialized. The Task Force remained, in many ways, a one-person operation.

In a telling May 1976 memo about the AJC and the Task Force, Rabbi Marc Tanenbaum admitted "Thus far, we have dealt very casually with its existence and have practically taken its activity and value for granted. Are we prepared to help staff it, fund it, and promote it as an integral part of our pro-Soviet Jewry program?" He wondered if the AJC was prepared to accept a "program through the Task Force for work with Christians on an international level in Europe" and South America?" (Memo, Rabbi Tanenbaum to Phyllis Sherman "NITFSJ," May 11, 1976, box 209, folder 2).[71]

Importantly, in addition to the Task Force, the IAD was engaged in many other activities and programs with mainline and evangelical Protestant, Catholic, and Eastern Orthodox religious groups in the United States and overseas. Some of these activities involved advocacy for Soviet Jewry. The Task Force was either a minor concern or one of several components of its programmatic activities (Memo, Rabbi Rudin to Rabbi Tanenbaum, "Major events since 1973 that we involved in," June 6, 1977, box 212, folder 1).[72]

Indicative of the Task Force's standing within IAD is Rabbi Rudin's 1979 schedule which is representative of the period from the mid-1970s though the late 1980s during which time he supervised the Task Force for the AJC (Memo, Rabbi Rudin to Rabbi Tanenbaum, re: "IAD calendar," July 17, 1976, box 211, folder 18). In late July, he and Sister Gillen lobbied for Soviet Jewry in Washington, D.C. for two days. He then traveled to Israel for the President's Holocaust Commission. In September, he attended a conference on Christians and Jews sponsored by the Episcopal Church in Denver, a Polish American Jewish Community leadership meeting in Detroit, an IAC dinner meeting in New York City, and the Minneapolis Foundation meeting. In October, he attended a US Army Chaplains conference in Louisville, a Christian Jewish conference in Detroit, and a meeting about the Vatican and Jews in Regensburg, Germany, followed by meetings of AJC's IAD and the NEC in San Francisco. At the end of October, he attended the NITFSJ leadership conference in New York City. In November, he participated in a two-day meeting of the board of the NCC in New York City, followed by the "Faith Without Prejudice" conference in Miami and he gave a major address in Indianapolis on November 14th.

Frequently, other subjects took precedence over the Task Force within the IAD. In his address at the NEC of the AJC in December 1976, the IAD's chairman, Maynard I. Wishner, focused on Catholic and Protestant text books and improved relations with Evangelicals, referring to a recent conference with Baptists, and the obtaining of a statement from Reverend Billy Graham "declaring there should be no proselytizing of Jews." He mentioned that the Task Force was monitoring the Helsinki agreements (Comments by Maynard Wishner at AJC's NEC. December 20, 1976, box 175). Three years later at the AJC National Interreligious Affairs Commission meeting in Chicago, Sister Gillen participated but the main topics were Muslims in America and Middle East issues and not Soviet Jewry and the Task Force (AJC Chicago Press Release, March 29, 1979, box 211, folder 18).

During the 1970s, outreach to evangelical Protestants became a major activity of the IAD (IAD Program Plans 1976–1977, Background for Staff Cabinet Meeting, February 15, 1977, box 211, folder 6).[73] The IAD and the AJC encouraged involvement of Evangelicals in the advocacy for Soviet Jewry and in Task Force activities. They cooperated with the Task Force in reaching out to the Christian community in the United States (See discussion above about joint Jewish-Southern Baptist Conferences). In January 1980, the AJC asked the Task Force to organize a program in NYC on "Human Rights and Religious Liberty" in honor of Cuban exile Hubert Matos (Letter, Ann Gillen and Rabbi Rudin to general mailing, January 8, 1980, box 303, folder 4). (See above n. 52.) The desire to reach out to Evangelicals may have influenced the IAD to focus on persecuted Christians, as well as Jews, in the Soviet Union. Bill Gralnick remarked that Soviet religious persecution once synonymous with Soviet Jewry, was now "bringing brutal pressure to bear on Soviet Christians" (Letter, William Gralnick to *Miami Herald*, March 16, 1983, box 301).

Significantly, however, the AJC and IAD often acted on the issue of Soviet Jewry directly with Christian clergy and communities without the involvement of the NITFSJ (AJC press release, April 19, 1978, box 194).[74] In October 1976, the AJC and NCC announced the cancellation of a planned interreligious trip to Poland, the USSR, and Israel.[75] The Task Force had not been involved in the trip (NCC Press Release, October 28, 1976, box 208 folder 1; and AJC press release, October 28, 1976, box 194). Rabbi Rudin, nevertheless, often pushed for a larger role for the Task Force and for Sister Gillen in AJC activities.[76]

David Geller served on a committee to review recommendations from Brussels II (Memo, David Geller to Rabbi Jim Rudin, "Proposals re: Interreligious Activities," April 13, 1976, box 208, folder 3). He discussed his report with Sister Gillen, Rabbi Rudin, Professor Bird, and others at Brussels II. Sister Gillen's perspective was clearly evident in his suggestions, which included developing local interreligious task forces linked with the NITFSJ, encouraging interreligious task forces in other countries, and an international interreligious task force. He also suggested developing one or two internationally coordinated programs around projects such as the Call to Conscience and the Co-adoption of Prisoners of Conscience. He advised concentrating on the religious aspects of the Helsinki Final Act: "We must ensure the inclusion of an interreligious dimension along with the legal dimension." He recommended several activities already operated by the Task Force (Letter, Sister Ann Gillen to Brussels II colleague, n.d., box 175; and Letter, Mary Danile Turner, executive director, LCWR, to Ann Gillen, March 30, 1976, box 175; and Letter Rabbi Jim Rudin to Dr. Paul L. Stagg, May 3, 1976, box 175).[77]

In late summer 1976, David Geller recommended greater AJC cooperation with the NCSJ, mobilization of non-Jewish public opinion, and utilization of the Task Force (supported by AJC chapters) in a maximum number of local communities (Memo, David Geller to Rabbi Rudin, Eugene DuBow, and Michael Rapp re: "Program priority report Soviet Jewry," August 31, 1976, box 209, folder 3). He emphasized, however, a focus on programs relating to Jews who remained in the USSR, as these projects had "a great deal of institutional benefit, as well as fund raising potential."

In his response, Eugene DuBow said that in mobilizing non-Jewish public opinion, Geller should have provided more information about the Task Force (Memo, to David Geller, re: "Soviet Jewry as a program priority," September 9, 1976, box 175). He criticized Geller for not mentioning the upcoming Second Consultation planned for Chicago. If the organization was going to look upon matters of Soviet Jewry as "an international human-rights problem" then it had to move Ann Gillen closer to leaders of the NCSJ (Minutes, Meeting of Steering Committee for Program Strategy Staff Meeting, December 24, 1976, box 301).[78]

Finally, the IAD and AJC saw the value of having Sister Gillen and the Task Force joining them when lobbying for Soviet Jewry in Washington, DC. Sister Gillen often accompanied Rabbi Rudin when he lobbied members of Congress, State Department officials, and others (AJC, Minutes AJC Interreligious Affairs Commission. September 18, 1978, box 469; and Memo, Rabbi Jim Rudin to Ann Gillen, June 12, 1980, box 303, folder 4). In testimony before Congress on Soviet Jewry, the IAD would often send Sisters Gillen and Traxler, Professor Bird, and Professor LaCocque.[79]

CONCERN FOR OTHER PERSECUTED GROUPS IN THE USSR

The AJC coordinated its advocacy efforts on behalf of Soviet Jewry with the Israeli Liaison Bureau, which focused exclusively on Jews in the Soviet Union. The Bureau did not concern itself with dissidents, persecuted Christians, and captive nations, arguing that "the others" wanted regime change and/or an end to Russian (Soviet) domination of their homelands. Soviet Jewish activists, they argued, wanted their constitutional rights of cultural and religious freedom. If the Soviets could not provide them, then the Liaison Bureau demanded their right to emigrate and to return to their ancient homeland, Israel. The slogan "Let them live as Jews or leave to be Jews in Israel" captures the Bureau's perspective. To support "the others," argued the Liaison Bureau, jeopardized the legitimate demands of Soviet Jews.

With the passage of the Helsinki Accords, Sister Gillen increased her advocacy for persecuted Christians in the Soviet Union, including Catholics in Lithuania and in the Ukraine, and Pentecostals, and Baptists in non-registered churches.[80] She acted cautiously in her initial contacts with advocates for captive nations in the Soviet Union and Eastern Europe. She took up their case by focusing on religious persecution of Catholics and Evangelicals in the Soviet Union.[81] For example, the Task Force campaigned to have the Soviet Union reopen five closed Catholic Churches in Lithuania (Letter, Ginte Damusis to Sister Ann Gillen May 21, 1981, Spertus, box 81, Lithuania).[82] During these years, the Task Force issued hundreds of reprints of articles, letters and reports about the plight of persecuted Christians in the Soviet Union.[83] In a Task Force reprint of an article about "Soviet Catholic Oppression," the author quoted William Gralnick on the problem of religion in the USSR: "It's not just a Jewish problem but one that faces all people of faith" (Tersa Gernazian. "Soviet Catholic Oppression," *Georgian Bulletin,* January 1, 1980, box 302, folder 1).

The Task Force also circulated reprints of articles about Andre Sakharov "(Flyer on Sakharov protest," n.d., box 303, folder 4).[84] The Liaison Bureau and the American Jewish establishment had avoided contact with him in order not to antagonize the Soviet regime.[85] On a Task Force mission to the USSR, Representative Drinan had visited Sakharov. Later as a member of the Interreligious Task Force on Human Rights in Chicago, Sister Gillen would become more involved with the Sakharov case (*The Task*, June 11, 1982, box 301).[86]

In the late 1970s, not everyone affiliated with the Task Force agreed with Sister Gillen's increasing concern about persecuted Christians in the Soviet Union. Abe Bayer of the NJCRAC, wanted the Task Force to limit its concerns to Soviet Jews; he opposed Task Force involvement with Soviet Christians (Memo, Rabbi Rudin to Rabbi Tanenbaum. July 12, box 194, copy July 19, 1977, box 212, folder 1). Rabbi Rudin and Jerry Goodman of the NCSJ met with Bayer on this issue in July 1977. Jerry Goodman disagreed with Bayer but urged the Task Force to change its name to "National Interreligious Task Force Against Religious Oppression in the Soviet Union." He asked Rabbi Rudin to discuss the idea with AJC leadership. Rabbi Rudin opposed the idea and argued that "we have enlisted more Christians in the cause of Soviet Jewry when we broaden the Task Force's appeal to include Soviet Christians as well." He argued that Carter's broad human rights policy encouraged Christians to speak out about Uganda, Chile, and the Soviet Union. The "genie is out of the bottle... We cannot go back to 1972, 1973."[87] Abe said that as a staff member of NJCRAC he would "no longer be recommending Sr. Ann" to speak in the various communities because she spoke not just about Soviet Jewry but also about Soviet Baptists.[88]

In May 1978, at a Task Force meeting in Chicago, Sisters Gillen and Traxler, Eugene DuBow, Professor LaCocque, Father John Pawlikowski, Rabbi Jim Rudin, and Adam Sims (AJC) discussed the issues of linkage and a possible name change (Minutes of NITFSJ Leadership Meeting, Chicago IL of April 20, 1978, May 4, 1978, MET, series 1.1, box 1, folder 2). Sister Traxler favored the Task Force being concerned with Christians as well as Jews in the Soviet Union. Father Pawlikowski disagreed saying that the primary focus should remain on Soviet Jewry. He later suggested taking up a few symbolic cases of Christians. He opposed a name change. He also warned: "we should not get too close to the far out evangelical Christians on the Cold War or ethnic groups." He opposed the Task Force's sponsoring or convening a Helsinki monitoring commission. He favored more ties with mainline churches. Professor LaCocque concurred and urged sticking with "our original name and purpose. Our definite focus is on Soviet Jewry." In response Sister Gillen emphasized that she felt a "commitment to Soviet Christians."[89] Rabbi Rudin summed up, suggesting that "the Task Force should continue as it has been but with perhaps greater focus on Soviet Jewry and greater selectivity regarding

Soviet Christian cases." He also felt that the group opposed the Task Force moving into other areas outside the USSR and Eastern Europe.[90] Importantly, Rabbi Rudin seemed to be the source of authority among Task Force leaders including Sister Gillen. In the future, however, a more independent Ann Gillen would lead the Task Force in the direction she favored.

Rabbi Marc Tanenbaum, who headed the IAD until the early 1980s, frequently mentioned other persecuted religious minorities when discussing the plight of Soviet Jewry ("Sister Ann" WINS Religious Commentary. May 7, 1979, SHCJ Archives, folder Misc. Soviet Jewry).[91] Rabbi Tanenbaum was concerned about how AJC policy against linkage might adversely affect the Task Force. He noted "the limited success of the Task Force has stimulated Christians to ask if we can cooperate with them in support for the human rights of Catholics, Orthodox, Baptists. . . who are also suffering deprivation in Eastern Europe . . .?" He wanted AJC to develop clear guidelines "on how we work and with who we work—legitimate ethnics but not captive nation groups, for example, in this country and abroad?" At what point should they think "of creating and giving leadership to a national interreligious task force on human rights?" (Letter, Marc Tanenbaum to Phyllis Sherman, AJC, "NITFSJ," May 11, 1976, box 209, folder 2).[92]

Importantly, by the mid-1970s, if not before, individuals, organizations, members of Congress, the mainstream American press, and religious publications raised the issue of and advocated for, persecuted Christians in the Soviet Union (see Chapter 3 above).[93] Some advocates for Soviet Jewry also took up their cause.[94]

In July 1978, seven Pentecostal Christians from two families in Siberia took refuge in the American Embassy in Moscow. They had been denied permission to emigrate. The United States granted them asylum and they remained in the Embassy until 1983 when Soviet authorities allowed them to leave for Israel. Their refuge in the embassy created widespread publicity in the United States about the plight of persecuted Christians in the Soviet Union, which led many Evangelicals and others, including members of Congress, to take up their cause.[95] Sister Gillen took up the cause of the Siberian Seven.[96] She integrated their story with the general picture she presented of religious persecution in the Soviet Union and of the common struggle of Jews and Christians for religious freedom (Ann Gillen, "Light out of Darkness "in *The Church Woman*, June July 1979, box 175).[97]

Sister Gillen and others associated with the Task Force frequently argued that American Christians could learn from American Jews about advocacy on behalf of their persecuted religious brethren in the Soviet Union. She argued that "the religious community in the West had done little or nothing to relieve, let alone, liberate, their Christian brothers and sisters under Marxism."[98]

Representative John Buchanan (R-AL), who had introduced a resolution about persecuted Christians, appeared to agree with the criticism. He noted "a great deal has been said about the persecution of Soviet Jews and intellectual dissidents. Unfortunately, the plight of Christians has received little notification" (Letter, William A. Gralnick to James Rudin, August 25, 1976, box 208 folder 1).[99] The American evangelical activist advocates for their brethren in the Soviet Union wanted to change this. As we shall see below some looked to Sister Gillen and the Task Force as a model to emulate (Kent Hill, phone interviews by the author, October 30, 2014 and October 15, 2018).

The early 1980s saw significant growth in the United States of advocacy groups concerned about the persecution of Christians in the USSR and Eastern Europe. Three groups had dominated the field for the past two decades: The Center for the Study of Religion and Communism at Keston College in England, supported by the Church of England; and the more militant Research Center for Religion and Human Rights in Closed Societies, founded in New York by Reverend Blahoslav Hruby, a Czech-born Presbyterian minister who had fought in the anti-Nazi underground; and the less vocal Interfaith Appeal of Conscience Foundation, headed by Rabbi Arthur Schneier of New York City, which worked quietly behind the scenes for religious liberty in Eastern Europe (William Bole, "A growing lobby of evangelical human rights organizations is focusing on religious repression in the Soviet bloc" RNS, March 4, 1983, box 301).

Now several evangelical Protestant groups with broad goals joined these three. They organized letter-writing campaigns on behalf of specific dissidents, sent food and clothing to relatives of prisoners of conscience, and monitored the human rights situation. They included an Indiana-based group that represented a dissident evangelical Baptist denomination in the Soviet Union led by its recently exiled leader Georgi Vins; the Evangelical East-West News Services; and CREED, a private Washington group headed by Dr. Ernest Gordon (Ibid.).[100] At times, the mainline Protestant NCC and other churches criticized these evangelical groups as being politically motivated. They doubted the ability of these groups to influence the situation in the Soviet Union (Ibid.).[101]

Christians inside the Soviet Union also protested religious persecution. In 1976, Christian clergy and laity signed an appeal to the Supreme Soviet Government for freedom of religious worship.[102] They protested their inability to voice opinions on matters of church policy, the circulation of anti-religious publication, the need for the government to approve religious activity, the forbidding of religious teaching, the inability to provide welfare services, forbidding of religious literature, and too few places of religious worship. They cited rights of religious freedom in the Soviet Constitution, which "guaranteed" the noninterference of the State in religious affairs and equality between believers and militant atheists

(*RNS*, "Christian Leaders in the Soviet Union Cite Repressions to Western Reporters," July 19, 1976, box 211, folder 1).[103]

From its establishment, the primary mission of the Task Force was the plight of Soviet Jewry.[104] When comparing the common plight of Jews and Christians in the Soviet Union, Sister Gillen acknowledged that Soviet Jews had a unique and more difficult status as a persecuted minority. In the May 1978 meeting of Task Force leaders in Chicago Sister Traxler emphasized that "the Task Force's primary goal is Soviet Jewry" (Minutes of NITFSJ Leadership Meeting, . . .", May 4, 1978, . . box 1 Folder 2). By the early 1980s, Sister Gillen believed that concern for persecuted Christians complemented the Task Force's primary concern with Soviet Jewry (Form letter, Ann Gillen to Catholic Bishops, October 1981, box 302, folder 3).[105] She put it best in May 1983 when she explained that the Task Force had "striven to educate, sensitize and organize Christians and Jews to respond to the plight of Soviet Jews." Christians in the Western World had "subsequently become aware that in addition to Jews, Christians in the Soviet Union are suffering also and are denied their human right of religious freedom. It is in this framework that people of all faiths need to work together to help those in USSR to obtain religious freedom and to be allowed to emigrate" (Sister Ann Gillen, "Interreligious Concern for Soviet Jewry" in *Interfaith Perspectives: Occasional papers*, vol. IV#1, Published by Interfaith Committee JCCMB, May 1983.

NOTES

1. They cited denial of visas to Vladimir Slepak and his family and the harassment, beating, and arrest of Jewish protestors who protested in Moscow.

2. It consisted of nine members each from the House and Senate and one each from the Departments of State, Defense, and Commerce. Also see Gillen talk at Temple KAM (Chicago) "From Helsinki to Belgrade," March 29, 1978, box 175). Snyder (2018, 40) argues that the setting up of the CSCE reflected increased Congressional involvement in US foreign policy.

3. Two or three of the eight participants were affiliated with the Liaison Bureau.

4. Professor Dinstein of Tel Aviv University and a Liaison Bureau operative suggested that Moshe Decter prepare it. Dr. Roth of WJC prepared the draft (Memo, Abe Karlikow to Morris Fine and David Geller, September 9, 1977, box 194). Liaison Bureau recommended printing several thousand copies in English, French, and Russian with release in New York, London, Paris, Brussels, Rome, and Ottawa (Memo, Albert Chernin, NJCRAC to NJCRAC and CJFWF Agencies, "re recommendations. . . .," September 9, 1977. According to Morris Fine (Memo, to Ira Silverman, December 2, 1977, box 194), the Institute of Jewish Affairs in London coordinated the preparation of a "Blue Book" on Soviet Jewry for Belgrade by a team of five persons including AJC's Sid Liskofsky and Abe Karlikow.

5. The AJC and NCSJ provided information to the CSCE. AJC's Sidney Liskofsky of AJC served as a consultant to CSCE (Memo, Morris Fine to Ira Silverman, December 2, 1977, box 194).

6. The CSCE may have asked the Task Force to hold the hearings. David Geller supported idea of emphasizing both Jewish and Christian prisoners of conscience. At Chicago II (November 1976) (see below) Alfred Friendly Jr., CSCE, suggested holding

hearings ("Basket Three: Implementation of the Helsinki Accords," Hearings before the CSCE," 95th Congress, First session on implementation of the Helsinki accords, Vol II "Religious liberty and minority rights in the Soviet Union" April 27 and 28, 1977; Helsinki Compliance in Eastern Europe, May 9, 1977. GPO, 1977). "Rabbi Tanenbaum endorsed the holding of hearings" (Memo, Eugene DuBow to Rabbi Tanenbaum, December 9, 1976, box 208, folder 2). Also see NITFSJ Press Release, March 16, 1977 (box 194) and NITFSJ invitation, March 10, 1977.

7. The AJC (and Task Force) scheduled hearings in NYC (March16), Chicago (March 31) and Los Angeles. AJC files only contain documents from the hearings held in NYC.

8. Professor Bird wanted to show that the Soviets violated their own laws and the Helsinki Accords. He continued to look for appropriate experts on Muslims, Jehovah Witnesses and Lutherans in the Soviet Union. Professor Bird and Rabbi Rudin left open the question of whether to include Eastern European nations.

9. Sister Gillen, Rita Hauser, David Hunter (CRIA), The Honorable Thomas P. Meladay (President, Sacred Heart College), Bayard Rustin, and Rabbi Marc Tanenbaum served as panelists who listened to testimony.

10. Active in Task Force activities, at the time he taught Slavic languages and literature at Queens College. He specialized in religion (Roman Catholic, Eastern Orthodox, and Oriental Orthodox Churches. He served on several Catholic Church interfaith committees (Professor Thomas Bird, email message to author with "Biography," December 21, 2017).

11. Since WWII the government had banned the Ukrainian Evangelical Reformed and Ukrainian Lutheran Churches. He noted the activity of Pentecostals and Jews in Ukraine. The latter had no central or regional organization, no cultural centers, could not produce religious articles, and had no seminaries.

12. He cited a conference in Nairobi, where WCC officials stonewalled a request by Revs. Gleb Yakunin and Lev Regelson to demand international inspection of psychiatric hospitals and to aid Christians wanting to emigrate.

13. The report emphasized that since 1972 the Task Force worked for emigration of Jews and Christians. After Helsinki, its concerns expanded "to focus on religious liberty in USSR. . . ."

14. In a Q&A with Senator Pell (D-RI), she said that there was groundswell among religious people in the USSR against compromises made by the Russian Orthodox Church.

15. She gave seminars on campus and appeared at Newman clubs and Hillels ("Update activities of Task Force Director May 1976," Summer 1976, box 175). In January 1982, she spoke at UCLA (Memo, Rabbi Rudin to Neil Sandberg. January 22, 1982, box 301). In the early 1980s, she spoke at the Universities of Manitoba and Winnipeg (Sister Gillen, "Report to co-Leaders." November 23, 1981, box 302, folder 3).

16. She spoke at several parochial schools. She also spoke at Cornelia Connelly School in Anaheim, CA and St Leonard's School in Rosemont CA (AJC Biographical Sketch Sister Ann Gillen. September 25, 1982, box 300).

17. At the convocation, he spoke about the persecution of Catholics in Lithuania. When Sister Gillen asked why he did not mention Soviet Jews, he asked if anyone raised questions about Christians at Jewish meetings. She replied that she did. He was "glad to hear it." She arranged for him to meet with Professor Bird about possible cooperation (Memo, Ann Gillen to Rabbis Tanenbaum and Rudin, July 23, 1976). See Chapter Two for Pugevicius's earlier contact with Rabbi Tanenbaum. An American born priest, Pugevicius directed the Lithuanian Catholic Aid group from 1975–1992 (www.articles.baltimoresun.com/2000-0003030119__1-lithuanian-catholic-roman-catholic-catholic-church , Accessed, December 5, 2016).

18. Sister Gillen contacted the NCCB about the Task Force, June 6, 1979; Memo, Rabbi Jim Rudin to Rabbi Marc Tanenbaum (box 211, folder 18) and "Update . . . ," Summer 1976. She frequently attended meetings at the NCC in New York City (Memo, Rabbi Rudin to Rabbi Tanenbaum, June 6, 1979, box 211, folder 18).

19. Rabbi Rudin urged Jerry Goodman to involve Sister Gillen in national NCSJ meetings. Also see "Update. . .,." In spring 1985, she spoke at the national convention of the Rabbinical Assembly in Miami (Letter Rabbi Akiba Lubow to Sister Ann Gillen, May 13, 1985, Spertus, box 54).

20. In 1976, Sister Gillen and Rabbi Rudin coordinated the Washington, D.C. and Houston visit of a sister of the Soviet Jewish prisoner of conscience Yosef Mendelovitch.

21. She returned to Cincinnati in late 1980 for the Women's Pleas for Human Rights at Isaac M. Wise Temple sponsored by Church Women United and the Adath Israel Synagogue. She criticized the American press for not publishing stories about persecuted Christians and Jews (Shannon Flynn, "Activist nun protests. . . . The USSR" Catholic *Telegraph*, December 19, 1980). This trip also involved an evening program in Louisville (Ann Gillen, "Report to co-Leaders. November 23, 1981, box 302, folder 3). Here she had contact with the state's Attorney General David L Armstrong who later wrote her (January 20, 1981) about forming interreligious legal Committee for Helsinki monitors of prisoners of conscience (Ann Gillen, "Report to co-Leaders. November 23, 1981, box 302, folder 3). Sister Gillen spoke for the Rockaway Catholic Jewish Council on October 1, 1986 (Letter, Ralph Leinoff, RCJC, to Ann Gillen, November 17, 1986, Spertus, box 54, correspondence folder).

22. Jewish, Christian, and interfaith groups sponsored the event at Daemen College in Amherst, NY in honor of National Human Rights Day. Sister Gillen spoke along with Ina Levin, sister of refusenik Vladimir Prestin.

23. She returned in July 1976 to work on a regional conference on religious liberty in USSR ("Update . . ." Summer 1976). In December 1983, Sister Gillen spoke at an CRC interfaith program in Houston. She wrote: "With other speakers, I sat in the sanctuary of St. Thomas More Catholic Church. seeing a large Hanukah Candelabra. A procession of Jews and Christians brought in the candles, calling out the names of Ann Frank, Ida Nudel, Anatoly Shcharansky, Martin Luther King, JFK and RFK. . ." (Memo, Ann Gillen to Rabbi A. James Rudin, December 20, 1983, Spertus, box 48).

24. She appeared with Senator Birch Bayh (D-IN) at a community assembly. The *Denver Post* interviewed her. Later (Letter, October 19, 1976, box 175) Bayh offered to lend a hand.

25. One event was co-sponsored by the interreligious affairs committee of the Cleveland Chapter and the Ohio Helsinki Accords Council and the Community Relations Board of City of Cleveland.

26. Marty Plax described her visit and speaking as phenomenal. She also did work with AJC in Seattle and a number of other cities (Letter, Ann Gillen to Arthur Abramson, March 11, 1982, box 302, folder 2). In a memo dated February 5, 1985, Rabbi Alan Mittleman asked about the time and place to present the petitions about the Lithuanian church in Klaipeda to the Soviet Ambassador. He asked whether to include Cardinal Bernadin and an interreligious delegation including Lithuanian religious leaders (Spertus 122/48).

27. The latter was co-sponsoring The Women's pleas for Soviet Jewry in December 1976.

28. Letter, Lorna Michelson to Ann Gillen, July 19, 1976 (box 175); Letter, Morton Schrag, Director, CRC San Diego, to Ann Gillen, September 20, 1976 (box 175); Letter, Yolanda Charney CRC (Tulsa, OK) to Ann Gillen, October 25, 1976 (box 175); Letter, Gloria Herzberg, Scranton Lackawanna Jewish Council to Ann Gillen, November 5, 1976 (box 208, folder 1); Program Albany NY Women's Pleas for Soviet Jewry, December 12, 1976 (box 175); Letter, Dr. Steven Windmueller to Ann Gillen, September 12, 1976 (box 175). Letter, Lorene N. Schecter to Ann Gillen, May 24, 1982 (box 302, folder 2); and Richard Lessner, "Nun leads drive to aid Soviet Jews," *The Arizona Republic*, December 15, 1982 reissued by the NITFSJ, box 302, folder 2).

29. She focused on Jews and Christians in the Soviet Union. She called for freedom of movement, the right to leave and return, the freedom of parents to educate children, and freedom of worship. She joined Rabbi Rudin in Washington in July 1979 and June

1980 to meet with State Department officials, members of Congress, the US NCCB, and Sargent Shriver (Memos, Rabbi Jim Rudin to Rabbi Marc Tanenbaum. July 17, 1979, box 211, folder 18; and June 24, 1980 box 303, folder 3). She cultivated a relationship with Assistant Secretary of State for Human Affairs, Elliott Abrams. In 1982 for example, she arranged for him to speak for the Task Force in the Chicago area (Letter, Ann Gillen to Elliott Abrams, February 11, 1982, Spertus 122/86, folder 0342).

30. She also met with Senator Paul Tsongas (D-MA). The Task Force lobbied Congress in October 1981. She also noted the formation of CREED, a newly active advocacy groups for Evangelicals in the Soviet Union supported by Senator Roger Jepsen (R-IO) and Congressman Jack Kemp (R- NY) and directed by Dr. Ernest Gordon.

31. In June 1976, she attended a meeting at the Chicago Institute of Interreligious Research and demonstrated against the exhibit on Science in Siberia at the Chicago Museum of Science and Industry. She spoke at Congregation KAM on March 29, 1978. In June 1980, she spoke about dissidents at annual meeting of Council of Hyde Park and Kenwood Churches and Synagogues (Letter, Pastor Thomas J. Havard to Ann Gillen, June 7, 1980, box 303, folder 3).

32. Sister Gillen wrote Rabbis Tanenbaum and Rudin ("Task Force Update," July 23, 1976) that Sister Katherine Hargrove in Westchester and Sister Joyce Rowland in Minnesota each wanted to organize local task forces.

33. On organizing a local task force Sister Gillen wrote: "Utilize your religious 'ethnic' contacts as well. . . . Ethnic leaders understand" . . . "religious peoplehood" or "religious liberty." She urged focusing on Human Rights Day events.

34. In Scranton, PA in response to a request from Sister Gillen, George Joel of the Scranton Lackawanna Jewish Council, Rabbi Simon Shoop, Msgr. Constantin V. Siconolfi, and Father Victor Donovan of the Catholic Diocese set up a local Interreligious Task Force. Rabbi Shoop chaired a committee with Msgr. Siconoli, and Rev. Jonathan King of Congregations in Christian Mission. King attended the second Consultation in Chicago.

35. The documents in the AJC archives determined the choice of communities discussed here. Dozens, or more, other cities organized interreligious task forces during this period.

36. She wrote: "a dynamic speaker, a warm and sensitive human being and totally sympathetic to the plight of the Jews in the Soviet Union."

37. Eileen Sussman directed the Soviet Jewry Council of the JCRC of Philadelphia. She attended the Task Forces Chicago II in November 1976. Having limited resources, the local AJC deferred to the JCRC. A member of the AJC served as co-chair of an advisory committee. Sussman (Letter, August 24, 1976, box 175) kept Sister Gillen informed. She reported that the task force distributed thirty thousand pieces of literature (including a "project co-adoption" flyer) at a Eucharistic Congress in the city).

38. Members were Reverend Bill Bruster, Rabbi Matt Derby, and Phil Ericson. They met at Temple Beth El in Knoxville.

39. They hoped to send a delegation to the Second National Interreligious Consultation in Chicago. The local CRC provided funding, but no one went. As noted above in Chapter Three, Sister Gillen helped set up a Task Force in Houston. In 1976 the local head of Houston's AJC organized a conference on religious liberty in the USSR. It involved Houston Baptist Minister Ken Chafin who set up Baptist Ministers for Baptist prisoners of conscience in the USSR.

40. Temple Baptist Church hosted the Consultation. Dallas Cowboy coach Tom Landry, state and local officials, leaders of the African American and Hispanic communities and prominent clergy served on the sponsoring committee. The Consultation focused on the persecution of religious activists including Russian Baptist Pastor Georgi Vins along with refusenik and participant in the alleged plot to hijack a plane in Leningrad, Mikhail Korenblit, the Dallas Jewish community's adopted prisoner of conscience (Memo, Zitmore to Katz, March 16, 1977).

41. He read Mayor Folsom's proclamation declaring March 7, Human Rights and Religious Freedom Day.

42. Stories appeared in *Baptist Standard Weekly*, *Texas Jewish Post*, and *Dallas Times Herald*.

43. Sister Gillen went on to visit San Antonio, Fort Worth, and El Paso where she spoke at churches, synagogues, and at women's and youth groups. In Fort Worth the General Ministers Association agreed to organize an interfaith task force on behalf of prisoners of conscience. At an event in El Paso co-sponsored by the JCRC, the Catholic Diocese, and the NCCJ, participants agreed to establish a local interreligious task force (Memo, Miles Zitmore to Will Katz "Dallas Interfaith . . ." March 16, 1977, box 194). In 1982 Sister Ann Gillen (Flyer, December 12, 1982, box 302, folder 2) spoke at the 12th annual Women's Plea "Light their way to freedom" at St. Mark's Episcopal Church in San Antonio.

44. He began working in 1974 as AJC regional director in Atlanta and then moved with the office to Miami and later to Palm Beach, Florida.

45. In the name of the Atlanta Interreligious Task Force on Soviet Jewry and Human Rights, he wrote President Carter (July 10, 1978, box 195), "Remember that Christianity will next be repressed to the point of extinction once Judaism is dealt with." In a letter to Mr. Charles Whited of *Miami Herald*, March 16, 1983, box 301) he noted that "Soviet persecution of Jews masks their determined persecution of Christians."

46. A petition had been initiated by an Atlanta interfaith advocacy group for religious freedom, RESCUE.

47. The AJC Atlanta urged joint activities between the local task force and the Interfaith Women's Pleas for Soviet Jewry (Letter, Sherry Frank to Mr. Willis Johnson, chair, of Interreligious Task Force Atlanta, September 25, 1980, box 303, folder 1. The Atlanta Task Force, Atlanta Jewish Federation, and the NCCJ (February 24, 1982, box 302, folder 2) sponsored program with former refusenik Yacov Ariev. The Atlanta Task Force published *"Watchline"* to "alert religious groups to the plight of their coreligionist in the Soviet Union" (November 1981, box 303, folder 1). The 1981 issue (mimeo) reported on prisoners of conscience Ivan Tetrovich Fedotov, a Christian, and Vytautas Skoudis, a Lithuanian American.

48. Rosenthal of the CRC felt that "Jewish members of the Task Force (should) . . . address themselves to matters on the Christian agenda as well as the plight of Soviet Jews."

49. The CRC provided $250 and the AJC $50 to fund his participation in Chicago, II in December. He had previously served as co-chair (see Chapter 4).

50. They also elected AJC to serve as its secretariat and began forming a steering committee with Protestant, Catholic, and Jewish clergy.

51. Davis had returned from the Task Force's Consultation in Chicago where the idea of a greater New York City task force may have been discussed. Rabbi Rudin wrote Sister Rose Thering (January 10, 1977, box 213, folder 8) thanking her for agreeing to come to "our" meeting at Fordham to explore possible organization of a greater NY interreligious task force with Margy Ruth Davis and Reverend Paul Stagg, of the NJCC. Reverend David Hunter, (CRIA) wrote Sister Gillen that we were ready to organize a "prisoner of conscience task force" (Letter, January 4, 1977, box 208, folder 1).

52. Madeleine Rice, a retired Hunter College Professor and a Roman Catholic, led the local NITFSJ/AJC sponsored group, which met at her home on May 25, 1978. The group sponsored a January 1980 reception for the Cuban exile Hubert Matos (General Mailing from Sister Ann Gillen and Rabbi Jim Rudin. January 8, 1980, box 303, folder 4). Among the eight attendees were Pol Castel, Ginte Damusis, Rev. B. Hruby, Dr. David Hunter, Rev. Gareth Miller, Rev. Casimir Pugevicius, Dr. Madeleine Rice, and Dr. George Sheridan.

53. Sister Traxler, affiliated with NCAN, remained active in the Task Force. But the NCCIJ was present in name only.

54. Rabbi Rudin may have attended the planning meeting. After meeting with Sister Gillen and DuBow, Philip Klutznick hosted a luncheon which raised $2,735 for the Consultation (Draft memo, Philip M. Klutznick and Joel J. Sprayregen, n.d. and Letter,

Sister Ann Gillen to Philip Klutznick, November 18, 1976, box 208, folder 1). SHCJ donated one thousand dollars for the Consultation. (Letter, Sister Elizabeth Fitzmaurice SHCJ to Rabbi Tanenbaum, October 7, 1976, box 208, folder 1).

55. Several people recruited speakers. DuBow approached Senator Percy (R-IL) suggesting that the issue of Soviet Jewry might help him reconnect with the Jewish community (Memo, DuBow to Sue Rubin, "re: Senator Percy," June 14, 1976, box 208, folder 2; and Letter, DuBow to Mr. Scott Cohen, Office of Sen. Percy, July 2, 1976, box 208, folder 2). Sargent Shriver decided not to attend (Letter, Sister Gillen and Rabbi Rudin to Sargent Shriver, August 5, 1976, box 208, folder 1). Rabbi Rudin contacted Rep. Drinan, Rev. Hunter, Jerry Goodman, and others. Rabbi Tanenbaum invited the Reverend Billy Graham and Father Hesburgh (Memo, Rabbi Rudin to Rabbi Tanenbaum, June 22, 1976, box 212, folder 2). A June AJC draft program's "hoped for" participants (Memo, Rabbi Rudin to Rabbi Tanenbaum, June 22, 1976, box 212, folder 2) included Cardinal Cody, Mayor Daley, Rep. Robert Drinan, Rep. Millicent Fenwick (R-NJ), Rev. Billy Graham, Rev. Theodore M. Hesburgh, Philip Klutznick, Rev. Robert Pruitt, Senator Percy, Rabbi Tanenbaum, and Dr. Cynthia Wedel.

56. A Task Force press release (November 3, 1976, box 208, folder1) indicated that the consultation would determine if the Soviet Union is living up to human rights commitment under the Helsinki Accords. Sister Gillen, Sister Traxler, Professor LaCocque, and Rabbi Tanenbaum charged the Soviet regime with "gross violations of the . . . accords through a series of denials of human rights to Jews." Also, see NITFSJ press release, November 12, 1976, box 175; and in MET, series 5, box 7, folders 2–4). They hoped to plan a national and international strategy and program for the further implementation of human rights for Jews, Christians and Muslims in Communist dominated countries. Sister Gillen declared that "these Soviet actions, coupled with their continuing harassment of Jews and other activists, makes it clear that further action is called for by world bodies if the Helsinki accord is to mean anything."

57. The Task Force issued a new letterhead. Sargent Shriver remained Honorary Chair, National co-Leaders were Professor André LaCocque, Sister Margaret Traxler, and Rabbi Marc Tanenbaum. Sister Ann Gillen was Executive Director with Rabbi James Rudin as Executive Chair, Eugene DuBow as Consultation Coordinator, and David Geller as Chair of the Coordinating Committee. The names of the Founding Sponsors, many of whom were now deceased, remained. It listed a Task Force in Formation including Prof. Tom Bird, Prof. Jerald, Brauer, Sr. Gloria Coleman, Msgr. Charles Devlin, Rev. Ed Flannery, Howard A. Golbert, Msgr. John Gorman, Rev. David R. Hunter, Bro. Martin Klietz, Richard H. Levin, Dr. Clyde Manschreck, Sr. Suzanne Noffke, Rev. John Pawlikowski, Rev. Robert Pruitt, Prof J. Coert Rylaarsdam, Rev. Stanley A. Schmidt, Prof. Joseph Sittler, Rev. Paul Stagg, Rev John Steinbruck, Sr. Rose Thering, Sr. Ann Patrick Ware, Rev. William Weiler, and Elmer Winter. This Task Force never became operational (Memo, Rabbi Rudin to Ann Gillen, August 24, 1976, box 208, folder 2). Jon Reich (AJC Chicago office) and Sister Gillen wanted to involve representatives of ethnic groups from Eastern Europe and the Soviet Union including Lithuanians and Ukrainians (Memo, John Reich to Gene DuBow and Sheryl Leonard, "re Meeting . . . to clarify ethnic role in Chicago II" October 28, 1976, box 208, folder 3). They met with Stanley Balzekas Jr, an activist in the Lithuanian community in Chicago, in August 1976 (Note, Jon Reich to Eugene DuBow, re: "Meeting with Lithuanian Community Leader," August 9, 1976, box 211, folder 1). But Reich noted that Peter Foote of the Archdiocese and David Roth (AJC program on ethnicity) argued "that the ethnics haven't been sympathetic in the past because they perceived the base of our movement as too narrow, as unsympathetic to their concerns, that there are standing animosities that have yet to be fully healed, that if we are to succeed in working with them, they must see their cooperation as being in their interest; therefore we should seek to occupy a middle ground, stressing themes of religious liberty and human rights" (Ibid.). This effort failed to achieve meaningful results (Memo, Jon Reich to Rabbi Tanenbaum and Irving Levine re: "Greely, Lithuanians et al." September 9, 1976, Spertus, box 109, miscellaneous correspondence 1975–76).

58. Almost two hundred and eighty persons participated. Approximately seventy came from Jewish communal and religious organizations, including seven rabbis. Seventeen nuns and six Catholic clergy attended along with twenty-two Protestant clergy and seminary students and twenty lay members of various Protestant religious and social organizations. There were five members of interfaith organizations, four representatives of local task forces, and two members of organized labor. Four members of the press attended. Stanley Balzekas Sr., President of the Balzekas Museum of Lithuanian Culture in Chicago, participated.

59. When Drinan left Congress in 1980, AJC and the Task Force honored him at AJC headquarters (Letter, Rabbi Rudin to Robert Drinan, October 7, 1980, box 303, folder 4).

60. Six Soviet based churches including the Russian Orthodox Church were affiliated with the WCC.

61. Jerry Goodman then spoke about the future for Soviet Jewry and Professor Bird spoke on "Christians, Jews and Muslims in the USSR." Seven concurrent panels followed: "Soviet Jewry, Political Legislative, and Migration Issues" with Joseph Edelman of HIAS, David Geller of the AJC and Joel Sprayregen, NCSJ; "Educating for Human Rights" with Professor Stephen Feinstein, University of Wisconsin; Rev. David Hunter, CRIA; Reverend John T. Pawlikowski, CTU; Professor Ronald Sider, Messiah College, Philadelphia; and Sister Rose Thering, Seton Hall University; "Religion and Ethnic communities in the USSR" with Professor Thomas Bird; Rabbi Arnold G. Kaiman, CCAR, Reverend Casimir Pugevicius, Lithuanian American Catholic Services; and Dr. Walter Sawatsky, Keston College; "Communication and Travel to the USSR," with Reverend Donal Dohrn, Church of Annunciation, Chicago; Lorel Pollack, the Chicago Soviet Jewry Action Committee; Glen Richter, SSSJ; and Reverend Nathan VanderWerf, (NCC); "Special Projects: Cultural and Liturgical Models" with Sister Gloria Coleman, Cardinal's Commission on Human Relations; Reverend Robert Pruitt; Reverend John F. Steinbruck and Stuart Wurtman, UCSJ; "Organizing in Communities" with Abraham J. Bayer, NJCRAC; Margy Ruth Davis, GNYCSJ; Brother Martin Klietz; and "Christian Initiatives" with Dr. Glen Iglehart, Home Mission Board of Southern Baptist Convention, Reverend Stanley A. Schmidt, Sister Ann Patrick Ware, NCC; and Dr. William Weiler, NCC.

62. After the Consultation, Rabbi Tanenbaum (Letter to Sen. Percy, December 7, 1976, box 208, folder 2) sent him materials about prisoner of conscience Benjamin Levich for a meeting Percy would have with the Soviet ambassador.

63. He noted that Chicago II drew double the number of participants as Chicago I (two hundred and fifty versus one hundred and twenty). Also, whereas the Jewish Christian ratio of participants was sixty-five to twenty-five at I, at Chicago II, it was reversed. He credited Sister Gillen with doing her job. He also noted a very moving moment when a conversation between Sister Gillen and Professor Levich in Russia was piped over the PA system. Rabbi Rudin praised the hard work of AJC's Eugene DuBow for the success of Chicago II. The AJC offices in Chicago and NY had done most of the organizational work (Memo, December 17, 1976, box 208, folder 1).

64. Sister Gillen also earned the appreciation of the NCSJ. In 1981, it awarded the Task Force a National Agency Activities Awards in recognition of its interreligious efforts on the local and national levels on behalf of Soviet Jews. It cited the "dynamic and untiring leadership, in the person of Sister Anne Gillen, the plight of Soviet Jews has reached Christians of all denominations" (Letter, Burton S. Levinsonm, NCSJ, to Mr. Maynard Wishner, AJC, April 29, 1981, box 303, folder 1).

65. He noted that keynote speaker Senator Charles Percy focused on Voice of America (VOA) which was of greater importance to advocates for Eastern European "captive nations" and Catholics in the United States. In turn, the media coverage focused on Percy's comments on VOA and not on what he said about Soviet Jewry. "I frankly do not know how to safeguard against this kind of thing. But it is something we should be thinking about."

66. See above n.17.

67. He also stated that Jews" have broken some barriers" that would make it easier to free Lithuanians and others and that." . . . he did not mean Christian should not champion the rights of Jews."

68. In a memo to Rabbi Tanenbaum (September 25, 1979, box 211, folder 18), Rabbi Rudin suggested bringing in Sister Traxler and Professor LaCocque—"We have not done much with these two co-leaders and this will be a good opportunity to bring them into New York for our conference."

69. Both Nimetz and Drinan focused on the Helsinki Agreements. Vice President Mondale sent a message of support (Letter, Sister Ann Gillen and Rabbi Rudin to VP Mondale, November 18, 1979, box 208, folder 4).

70. She asked Brother Martin Kleitz to be on the education committee. She asked John Steinbruck (Letter, March 13, 1976, box 211, folder 8) to join a liturgical committee. She also consulted with Professor Tom Bird about committees.

71. From 1976 to 1983, the AJC obtained most of the Task Force funding from the Martin Tananbaum Foundation. It provided $17,500 for 1975 (Draft, Rabbi Tanenbaum to David Goldstick, n.d., C June 1976 box 175). The foundation approved grants of $20,000 for 1976 and 1977 (Letter, Arnold Alperstein to Rabbi Tanenbaum, April 28, 1976, box 194 and Memo, Rita Blume to Rabbi Tanenbaum, box 194). In 1979, it provided a $20,000 grant (Memo, Rabbi Rudin to Rabbi Tanenbaum. May 1, 1981, box 303, folder 2). In 1979, the Task Force had a budget of $45,935 with a deficit of $8,093 which the AJC absorbed (Memo, re: "NITFSJ," Rabbi Rudin to Rabbi Tanenbaum. May 1, 1979, box 303, folder 2). The Foundation gave AJC $22,000 in 1981 for the Task Force. In 1982, it increased the grant to $29,500 after AJC honored Foundation Trustees (Letter, Rabbi Tanenbaum to Arnold Alperstein. November 3, 1981, box 303; and Memo, Rabbi Rudin to Gene DuBow. September 24, 1983, box 302, file 3; and Letter, Rabbi Tanenbaum to Mr. Arnold Alperstein, August 9, 1982, box 301 folder 4). Sister Gillen and the Task Force received some smaller donations including honorariums for her speaking; $1,145 in 1979, $400 in 1980, and $495 in 1981 (NITFSJ Project Budget 1982, n.d., box 302, folder 3). The AJC encouraged Sister Gillen to apply for financial support and grants (Letter, Rita Blume, AJC, to Ann Gillen, April 20, 1976). She applied to Pew for a grant of $100,000 in October 1981 (Letter, Ann Gillen to Robert I Smith, October 30, 1981, box 303 folder 2). She received small grants from the Raskob Foundation for Catholic Activities and from SHCJ, $1,000 from Philip Klutznick of Chicago, and $5,000 from the AHS Foundation in Cleveland (Sr. Virginia Gaine SHCJ to Mr. Gerard S. Carey, December 13, 1977; Ann Gillen Papers 1972–1994, Folder Corr. business and personal letters), Letter, Rabbi Jim Rudin to Sister Elizabeth Fitzmaurice (SHCJ), October 6, 1982, box 302, folder; and Memo, Rita Blume to Rabbi Marc Tanenbaum January 25, 1977, box 208, folder 1; and Letter, Bert Gold to Mr. and Mrs. Leland Schubert, July 10, 1978, box 195). Sister Gillen appealed for funds in a form letter on *The Task* stationery during Passover Easter 1985, Spertus, box 32).

72. For example, in 1976, the IAD dealt with Vatican guidelines on Jews/Judaism, an interreligious coalition of World Hunger Conference in DC, countless meetings of NCC committees, Jewish -Episcopal national consultation in Cincinnati, Armenian Church meeting on genocide, National Faith without Prejudice Conference (in St. Louis), annual meeting of American Baptist Church National Mission Society (WI), National Ecumenical Meeting in North Carolina, REA convention in Philadelphia, a meeting on Zionism with Bishop Paul Moore and a national Evangelical-Jewish conference.

73. A 1976 IAD report gave priority to Evangelical Jewish relations and the emergence of the South. Other priorities involved Arabs, Muslims, and the Greek Orthodox Church. It also noted a major program push for the Task Force to organize several local/regional conferences and hearings on the Helsinki agreements. Bill Gralnick, director of AJC's Southeast region, actively worked with Evangelicals.

74. In April 1978, Rabbi Rudin conducted a "Seder for Soviet Jewry" under the auspices of AJC's NYC chapter with the participation of many Christian leaders. Absent was the Task Force. In 1980, the AJC established an annual fellowship in the name

of Andrei Sakharov. It was sponsored by the AJC's Jacob Blaustein Institute for the Advancement of Human Rights. Sister Gillen was not involved (AJC Memo, May 18, 1980, box 301, folder 1).

75. In a joint news conference, Rabbi Rudin and Reverend Nathan H. VanderWerf, Director of the NCC Commission on Regional and Local Ecumenism, charged that the Soviet denial of visas to three American Rabbis was a flagrant "violation of the Helsinki Final Act." VanderWerf called Soviet action "anti-Semitic" ("Protest urged over canceled visit to USSR" *Washington Post*, November 5, 1976, box 194); and Letter, Eugene DuBow, coordinator of NITFSJ, sent to the of editor *Chicago Tribune, Chicago Sun Times, Daily News and Chicago Sentinel*, November 15, 1976, box 208, folder 1).

76. The IAD participated in the annual National Christian Jewish Dialogues sponsored by the Secretariat for Catholic Jewish Relations, the Office of Christian Jewish Relations of the NCC in cooperation with the AJC, the ADL and local organization of the sponsoring city (Brochure 3rd National Workshop . . .: " Living Together in an age of pluralism." April 19–21, 1977, box 177). The AJC put Sister Gillen on a panel at the third conference (Letter, Sherwood San Weiss to Rabbi Tanenbaum, November 10, 1976, box 177). It failed to include her on the program for the fourth (Letter, Dr. Carl Segerhammar, Fr. Royale M. Vadakin and Rabbi Alfred Wolf to Rabbi Marc Tanenbaum. May 12, 1978, box 177). The IAD often kept Sister Gillen informed. When Rabbi Jim Rudin asked Dr. Thomas Bird to prepare a fact sheet on "religions in the Soviet Union" for a Eucharistic Congress in Philadelphia, he asked Bird to send a copy to Sister Gillen (Letter, Jim Rudin to Dr. Thomas Bird, June 25, 1976, box 175).

77. He urged greater contact with the Christian media, providing speakers for Christian groups, and distributing the Christian Call to Conscience. He later suggested that they might come closer to other groups seeking greater liberty for their groups in the USSR. This is surprising as he often favored advocating exclusively for Soviet Jews (Memo, David Geller to Morris Fine, "Programs and Projects re Soviet Jewry for AJC. April 20, 1976, box 194).

78. This group planned AJC strategy for Soviet Jewry. In a follow up memo to Bertram Gold (January 12, 1977, box 194) Phyllis Sherman reported that Geller would present a paper on Soviet Jewry advocacy at the planned February 11 program strategy meeting. She hoped that Gold would end the session "with one of your brilliant summaries." Rabbi James Rudin (interview by the author, NYC, July 31, 2015) described Bert Gold's policy style. He would hold senior staff meetings on Monday mornings. Each participant could speak his/her mind; there were often sharp debates. At the end he would sum up and set the direction of AJC policy.

79. In a memo to Rabbi Tanenbaum (re: "Twelve-month projection for NITFSJ," February 27, 1979. box 211, folder 18b) Rabbi Rudin suggested that the AJC hold a national leadership conference for the NITFSJ to bring Task Force leaders from around the country to meet and lobby Congress, the State Department, and the White House. This would occur in 1982 (see below).

80. In writing members of Congress, Sister Gillen typically provided information about the "plight of Soviet Jews and others who face religious persecution in the Soviet Union" (Letter, Rep. Raymond J. McGrath (R-NY) to Ann Gillen, October 26, 1981 and Letter, Rep. Michael Barnes (D-MD) to Ann Gillen. November 25, 1981).

81. This approach was evident, as we have seen, in the March 1977 hearings on "Religious Liberty and Human Rights" in Chicago. In November 1981, when Sister Gillen joined the AJC regional director in talks with Ukrainian and Lithuanian American "nationalist" leaders, the talks were "off the record" (Ann Gillen, "Report to Co-Leaders," November 23, 1981, box 32, folder 3).

82. Sister Gillen had asked Father Pugevicius for assistance in this matter. According to Damusis, Father Pugevicius searched for common ground with advocates of others being persecuted in the Soviet Union (Ginte Damusis, phone interview by the author, December 16, 2016). Damusis directed the Lithuanian Information Center sponsored by Pugevicius's Lithuanian Catholic Religious Aid. The Information Center focused on the human rights of Lithuanian Catholics but its publication *The Chronicle*

of the Catholic Church in Lithuania also printed information about civil rights violations of other religious groups in the USSR including Jews.

83. In September 1978, it reprinted Vasyl Makus's "Another forgotten dissident," (September 5, 1978, *Chicago Tribune,* box 301) about several Ukrainian Christians who wanted to emigrate. A "Task Force Alert" (c 1980, box 303—mimeo) publicized the persecution of Seventh Day Adventists, the trial of three members of All Union Church of Faithful, the passing of the eighty-four-year-old Seventh Day Adventist Vladimir Shelkov who died in a strict regime camp and the arrest of Olga Petrovna Bynyak, charged with distributing religious literature. Finally, it reported on a new Soviet Christian emigration committee set up in May 1979. In the spring of 1981, the Task Force circulated reprints from *Ukrainian Weekly,* No. 18 about a meeting in New York of the Israel-based society of Ukrainian Jewish relations with activists of Ukrainian Democratic Movement and the Organization for the Rebirth of Ukraine (ODVU). A second article was about group formed in Jerusalem in 1980 for collaboration for human rights and mutual support for national liberation of our peoples. They held a ceremony at Babi Yar. A third reported that Anatoly Shcharansky joined eight Ukrainians and Yuri Orlev in a letter to the Helsinki Review Conference in Madrid. A typical Task Force newsletter (mimeo with information and reprints, September 12, 1980 , box 303, folder 7) discussed a Lithuanian Catholic nun to be released in Siberia, a report on Jewish emigration figures, Soviet census data on Lithuania and Latvia, a report of a meeting of Hebrew teachers in the USSR, information about Roman Catholics in the USSR, and a report on United States Helsinki Watch Committee meetings in D.C. (Reprint, March 27, 1981, MET, box 92, folder, correspondence 1982; and *The Task* (mimeo reprint), July 16, 1982 and March 5, 1983, MET, box 80) concerned a Lithuanian priest and Lithuanian Helsinki groups.

84. They also reprinted an appeal from Lithuanian Helsinki groups protesting his treatment.

85. This may explain the early reluctance of the NCSJ and the Liaison Bureau to support Anatoly Shcharansky (see Dershowitz 1991, 252–55 and Lazin 2005). They mistrusted his close ties with Sakharov. See above n. 74 about an AJC group honoring Sakharov in 1980.

86. Sister Gillen had contact with Sakharov's step daughter Tatyana Yankelevich (Form letter, Sister Ann Gillen to Jim Rudin. January 27, 1981, box 303, folder 2).

87. Loeffler (2018, 292) discusses President Carter's commitment to human rights.

88. In a later phone call to Rabbi Rudin, Abe retreated. He said that he had not represented NJCRAC policy. He would discuss the issue at NJCRAC Interreligious Affairs Commission and that he did not include his comments in summary of his meeting with Rudin and Goodman. Rabbi Rudin felt that the comments at the meeting indicated "how uneasy the establishment Soviet Jewry groups and specialists are with the entire interreligious Task Force. This is due, in my opinion to our continued policy of maintaining the Task Force's independence from both the NCSJ and NJCRAC. By remaining independent, we are not controlled or dominated by them and thus we are freed to develop a flexible policy in a rapidly changing situation" (Memo, Rabbi Jim Rudin to Rabbi Marc Tanenbaum, July 12, 1977). Interestingly Bertram Gold wrote Rudin about the meeting with Goodman and Bayer that it might be "worthwhile for some of us to get together to look ahead to the implications of both Abe and Jerry's comments for the continuance of our work with the task force" (Memo, Bert Gold to Jim Rudin, July 20, 1977). Apparently, Bayer later changed his attitude toward Sister Gillen. She wrote him a warm note on October 26, 1983 (Spertus, box 54) thanking him for recommending her as a speaker for the Tucson Freedom weekend.

89. Pawlikowski suggested setting up a Board of Directors for the Task Force consisting of influential persons in various religious communities. Sister Gillen retorted that she hoped "this would not mean a heavy bureaucracy which would impede the Task Force programs." In 1981, in discussing the tenth anniversary of the Task Force, the three national co-leaders, Professor André LaCocque, Rabbi Marc Tanenbaum, and Sister Margaret Traxler noted: "As a major expression of human rights concerns that

are shared by Christians and Jews, the Task Force's ten year record has focused on an intensive program of education, interpretation and action to achieve freedom for Soviet Jews and other oppressed people" ("National-Co-Leaders' Press Conference Addresses Soviet Emigration, Human Rights Problems, Tenth Anniversary Plans," November 3, 1981, box 303, IAD 1980s, folder 2).

90. In June 1980, in a meeting with Sister Gillen and Rabbi Rudin, Sargent Shriver suggested either changing or expanding the name so "that it does not appear to be limited solely to Soviet Jewry." He felt that they should work to free all "religious hostages" wherever they be." Sister Gillen and Rabbi Rudin explained that they had set up the Task Force solely "on behalf of Soviet Jewry" but that they had broadened their "concern to include Soviet Christians and Muslims as well." He responded that this was commendable but that the title should reflect this fact.They promised to discuss his suggestion with Task Force leadership (Memo, Rabbi Jim Rudin to Rabbi Marc Tanenbaum, June 24, 1980, box 303, folder 3). An early memo discussing a tenth anniversary conference for the Task Force again raised a possible name change. (Memo (AJC) "Items for discussion" April 30, 1981, box 303 interreligious affairs 1980s, folder 2).

91. On WINS Radio on May 7, 1979, Rabbi Tanenbaum referred to the five recently released Soviet prisoners whose "shared convictions about human freedom lit up the heavens in a blaze of unified hope." He noted that those released are "ecumenical and pluralist in their identities" and so are those that fought for their release. He praised Sister Gillen and her ecumenical organization NITFSJ. The five were Alexander Ginzburg, a dissident; Valentyn Moroz, a Ukrainian activist; Georgi Vins, a Baptist activist in the Ukraine; and Mark Dymshits and Edward Kuznetsov, Jewish activists in prison for the alleged Leningrad plane hijacking (Edward Walsh, "Soviets Exchange 5 Dissidents for 2 Spies," *Washington Post,* May 28, 1979). Kuznetsov was the husband of Sylva Zalmanson. In contrast to Tanenbaum's view of the five, the GNYCSJ only invited the two Jewish members of the group to appear at the 1979 Solidarity Day parade. The five arrived in NYC prior to the parade.

92. The May 1978 AJC policy statement adopted at the Seventy-Second Annual Meeting only referred to Soviet Jews ("AJC Statement on Soviet Jewry," May 21, 1978, box 194). It asked the Soviet Union to free "Prisoners of Conscience" and to release Anatoly Shcharansky. It referenced the plight of Jews in the Soviet Union: ". . . will remain a top priority for AJC. Together with Christians, whose support and solidarity have been so crucial, we shall continue our efforts in this historic struggle for human rights." It made no mention of other persecuted religious or dissident groups.

93. Several Congressional Representatives expressed concern for Christians as well as Jews in the Soviet Union. Representative Michael Barnes (D-MD), chair of the Congressional Vigil for Soviet Jewry, wrote Sister Gillen (November 25, 1981) that he wanted to help "these brave persons," including Anatoly Shcharansky, Ida Nudel, The Vashchenko family, and Vytautas Skuodis. On February 4, 1983, *Christianity Today* published ("Time to Cry Enough" by Bud Bultman and Bonnie Ward Elson, box 301) a guide on how to protest persecution of Christians in the Soviet Union. It cited "Persecution in Lithuania," *Commonweal,* July 1976, Harvey Fireside "The Trial of Sergei Kovalev"(about Catholics) and Fred S. Belk, "Soviet Mennonites want to Emigrate," *Liberty,* March, April 1976. See, Sister Ann Gillen to Rabbi Jim Rudin, November 10, 1976, box 208, folder 2).

94. George Novotney, "Back specific (Vins) and general (believers) stands; Witnesses advise Congress on Resolutions condemning Religious Repression in the USSR," RNS, July 1, 1976, box 311, folder 1). Testifying were Rep. John Buchanan (R-AL) chief sponsor of HR Concurrent Resolution 626 on Pastor Vins; Prof. John Dunlop of Oberlin who appeared for the Rt. Rev. Alexander Kiselev, chair of Committee for the Defense of Orthodox Christians persecuted in the USSR; Prof. Lev Dorbiansky of Georgetown, and George Dobczansky of Human Rights Research Inc. Rev. Stanley A. Schmidt of the NITFSJ affiliated local interreligious Task Force in Louisville, wrote Senator Walter D. Huddleston (D-KY) (February 26, 1977, box 211, folder 1) urging the

Senate to pass a resolution about Pastor Maksimilians Grivans, who wanted to join his wife and daughter in Sweden. The Jewish Community Council of Greater Washington lobbied Congress for a private immigration bill for the relief of the Pentecostal Seven (Letter, Rep. Elizabeth Holtzman [D-NY] to Bert Silver, President JCC of Greater Washington, September 11, 1980, box 303 folder 1).

95. Preston writes (2012, 595) that the Siberian Seven "attracted widespread sympathy in the U.S." He noted that Rep. Barney Frank (D-MA) and Sen. Tom Harkin (D-IA) got their colleagues to sign a petition urging action by President Reagan. Reverend Dr. Cecil Williamson set up a support and advocacy organization on their behalf in Alabama. Rabbi David Baylinson, Rep. William L. Dickinson (D-AL) and Rep. Richard Shelby (R-AL), Senator Carl Levin (D-MI), Governor Fob James (D-AL), Sister Gillen, and the Rev. Blahoslav S. Hruby joined the steering committee. The journal *Religion in Communist Dominated Areas* took up their case as did Kevin Lynch in "Russian Christians in the Catacomb: Down and Out in the American Embassy," *National Review* and "The Siberian Seven: The guests in the basement" (*CR*, vol. 126 no. 108 part II, Legislative day June 12, 1980, June 27, 1980). American and Western European media covered extensively the dissident movement (Jacques Amalric "Following a Campaign of Intimidation . . . reduced dissident activities" *Le Monde*. May 15–17, 1977, box 194). Also see "Million Russian Baptists see new hope in Carter," *Chicago Tribune*, December 12, 1976, box 211, folder 1. See testimony of Senator Carl Levin and Representative Barney Frank on the Siberian Seven in the *CR* of June 29, 1982. Also see *CR*, Vol 126 no., 108 Part II, June 12, 1980. A bill to grant both families permanent residency (S 312) passed in the Senate but was held up for two years in the House (Form Letter, President of Society of Americans for Vashchenko Emigration, Alabama, c June 1980, box 303, folder 3).

96. Letter, Ann Gillen to William T. Shinn, State Department, June 7, 1979 (MET, box 86, folder 0342) and Notes on the Meeting of Interreligious Attorneys Task Force on Human Rights in the Soviet Union, June 30, 1982 (Ibid., box 85, folder 0349, correspondence 1979–82).

97. The Task Force reprinted flyers on the "Siberian 7" (Reprint of June 1980, box 303 folder 3). *The Task*, June 25, 1982 (box 302, folder 2) saluted "the bravery of Jews and Christians who started the emigration movement in the USSR." It cited the two Pentecostal families in the embassy and the spirit "of Soviet Jews like Ida Nudel and Vladimir Slepak."

98. In contrast, she praised world Jewry for launching a modern Exodus to "Save Soviet Jewry" (Ann Gillen, "Patience or Prophetic Protest," 1977).

99. Representative Buchanan wanted to be invited to Chicago, II.

100. Dr. Gordon emphasized the growing awareness among Christians "of their responsibility toward Christians in atheistic countries." See above n. 30.

101. While the Baptist World Alliance and official Soviet Baptist body regarded public protest as counterproductive, Georgi Vins, disagreed. (See C May 1977, draft on " The Task Force and Christians in the USSR," box 211, folder 1).

102. They came from officially recognized Russian Orthodox and Lithuanian Roman Catholic churches and the unrecognized "Unregistered" Baptists, Pentecostals, Adventists, and Fundamentalist Church of Christ.

103. The *NYT* ("Soviet Religious Groups Report Beating of 150," September 8, 1977, box 211, folder 1) reported on a six-hour clash between the KGB and Baptists in Bryansk, southwest of Moscow. A Moscow based Christian Committee for the Defense of Believers Rights reported the incident to the *NYT*.

104. As noted in Chapter Three, the first issue of *The Task* in 1973 stated that Soviet Jewry was the sole agenda item of the Task Force because the "Jewish community suffers special deprivation."

105. In October 1981, she described the Task force as being the voice of Jews and Christians "working together for their brothers and sisters in the USSR and Eastern Europe."

SEVEN

International Conferences and the Interreligious Legal Task Force on Human Rights

This chapter covers the period from the aftermath of Brussels II through the early 1980s, beginning with the participation of Sister Gillen and the Task Force in two follow-up conferences, one in Belgrade and the other in Madrid, on the implementation of the human rights provisions of the Helsinki Accords. The Accords shifted the focus of the advocacy efforts for Soviet Jews to issues of human rights. This shift strengthened Sister Gillen's position of concern for persecuted Christians and dissidents in the Soviet Union, along with her advocacy for the rights of Soviet Jews.

An incident in 1978 involving seven evangelical Christians who took refuge in the American embassy in Moscow highlighted the plight of persecuted Christians in the Soviet Union and fostered greater advocacy by American Evangelicals for their religious brethren in the Soviet Union. Evangelical Protestants became very critical of the mainline Protestants in the NCC and WCC who favored accommodation with the Soviet Union and the Russian Orthodox Church.

In Chicago Sister Ann Gillen and the Chicago AJC set up a National Interreligious Task Force on Human Rights together with Jewish, Catholic, and Evangelical legal fraternities. This further shifted the focus of advocacy to one of universal human rights and enhanced Sister Gillen's concerns and contacts with captive nations groups.

The chapter concludes with a discussion of Brussels III, held in Jerusalem in March 1983. At this meeting the standing and status of Ann Gillen and the Task Force in the Soviet Jewry advocacy movement were considerably diminished from their prominence at Brussels II. At the same time

AJC's IAD continues an active Soviet Jewry advocacy agenda for Soviet Jewry.

THE BELGRADE CONFERENCE ON SECURITY AND COOPERATION IN EUROPE

On May 17, 1977, Rabbi Rudin and Sister Gillen attended a briefing at the State Department for the first follow-up conference on the implementation of the Helsinki Accords scheduled for Belgrade. State Department counselor Matthew Nimetz suggested that at the initial meetings in Belgrade in June participants would set the agenda, select the dates, and choose the committees. Later, during the second stage in September or October, he expected a substantive review of all three baskets of the Accords but that he believed that "human rights would be given special emphasis."[1]

In the summer of 1977, President Jimmy Carter appointed former Supreme Court Justice, and past AJC president, Arthur Goldberg, to head the American delegation to the Belgrade meetings (Letter, Bert Gold to Arthur J. Goldberg. September 12, 1977, box 194). Rabbi Rudin recommended organizing a large interreligious delegation involving all branches of Christianity, African Americans, and whites, and including both men and women to visit Belgrade, which "would symbolize the deep commitment of American Christians and Jews to the cause of human rights. . . . It would give visibility to the Task Force and it would serve notice to the Russians that the American religious community is committed to the full implementation of the Helsinki Final Act" (Memo, Rudin to Tanenbaum, June 3, 1977).[2] Rabbi Rudin hoped that the delegation would also visit Soviet Jewry processing center in Vienna, confer with Soviet Jewry groups in Europe, and meet with Soviet émigrés in Israel.

At the initial meetings in Belgrade in June, the Soviets failed to limit the scope of the follow up meetings scheduled for the fall (Memo, A. Karlikow to Morris Fine, "Belgrade Conference," October 13, 1977, box 194).[3] They had argued that what happened in the USSR was a domestic matter and should not concern outsiders. According to Abraham Karlikow, the West won a tactical victory in June, which opened the meetings for a full and thorough review of Basket III. It became a major human rights victory. He noted that while Soviet Jewry had been the main issue of dissidents in the past, the perspective had widened and "human rights protests there have become more general." Karlikow noted that "human rights precedents and processes are on the way to being established, on a regular basis, that provide powerful weapons for the future."[4]

Led by Sister Gillen and Rabbi Rudin, the Task Force delegation visited Belgrade and Rome from November 19–27, 1977. Members of the delegation included Professors Thomas Bird and André LaCocque; William R. Phillippe, executive director of the United Presbyterian Synod of Piedmont; Rev. Msgr. John A. Radano of Seton Hall University; and Judge Charles Z. Smith, president of American Baptist Churches and associate dean of the University of Washington Law School (NITFSJ "Press Release" November 23, 1977, box 194).[5] They received observer status and, as Sister Gillen noted, spoke "for the thousands, even millions of our coreligionists in the USSR and Eastern Europe who seek to obtain religious liberty or to leave for lands where they can live freely as Christians and Jews" (Charles Z. Smith, "Report of the President to the General Board, American Baptist Churches in the USA," December 5, 1977, box 303 folder 7). They met with several national delegations to urge their unflagging support for human rights (emigration and religious liberty).[6] They also distributed documents about Protestant, Catholic, and Jewish prisoners of conscience.[7]

They first met with Goldberg, who emphasized that only the United States had spoken out about individual cases of human rights violations (Memo, Rabbi Rudin to Rabbi Tanenbaum, January 30, 1978, box 303, folder 7).[8] He spoke about Anatoly Shcharansky, Eduard Kuznetsov, Josef Begun, and other Jewish prisoners, as well as about Baptist Pastor Georgi Vins and other Christians imprisoned in the Soviet Union (Rabbi Rudin, "Did the Belgrade Conference Make a Difference?" August 18, 1978, box 301, folder 11).[9] He discussed the rights of emigration, maintaining houses of worship, and parents giving their children religious education. They also met with Ambassador August H. Croin of the Netherlands, who affirmed his government's commitment to "human rights, religious liberty and Basket III." British Ambassador Peter Summerscales told the delegation that he favored "quiet diplomacy" and "discreet interventions." They pushed him to speak up for Shcharansky, Vins and the right of emigration, but he and his human rights deputy remained "always positive but guarded." The Spanish delegation, at a meeting with the Task Force delegation, expressed support for Basket III.

The delegation had a "cordial and candid" meeting with the Vatican delegation, comprising the Papal Nuncio to Yugoslavia, Archbishop Michel Cechinni, and Msgr. Fausino Sainz-Munox from the Vatican Secretariat of State. The Vatican declared itself to be the "voice of believers," representing all religions at Belgrade (Memo, Rabbi Rudin to Rabbi Tanenbaum, January 30, 1978).[10] Professor Bird urged the Holy See to speak out "publicly and clearly on the wretched condition of Soviet prisoners of conscience, both Jewish and Christian." He mentioned Anatoly Shcharansky and the Lithuanian Catholic nun Nijole Sadunaite. The Vatican representatives expressed concern for them (Ibid.).[11]

Although the Task Force delegation failed to secure a meeting with the delegations from Poland and Romania, they did meet with five senior Hungarian diplomats. Hungarian Ambassador Janos Petran Kadar expressed a commitment to religious freedom and to Basket III and noted that Jews in Hungary had a rabbinical seminary. One of the delegates asked why Hungarian Jews could not visit relatives overseas and Msgr. Radano asked about family reunification in Canada. Sister Gillen brought up the banning in 1950 of Roman Catholic orders and pressed for full development of all religious orders. The Ambassador promised to investigate these issues. He also extended an invitation for the delegates to visit Hungary (Ibid.).

The Task Force delegation also met in Belgrade with Senators Robert Dole (R-KS), Claiborne Pell (D-RI), and Representative Millicent Fenwick (R-NJ). All three expressed support for Soviet Jewry and the struggle for human rights in the USSR and Eastern Europe (Ibid.).

The issue of human rights was discussed in Belgrade and remained on the agenda for the follow-up meetings in Madrid in 1980.[12] This gave East European Communist Governments and dissidents' movements leverage against Moscow and showed Moscow that trade and economic collaboration was inevitably tied to questions of "political freedom and intercourse between East and West" ("What the West Accomplished," *Business Week*, January 30, 1978, box 195).

The Task Force delegation arrived in Rome on November 23 to confer with Vatican officials about Soviet Jews and other oppressed people (Memo, Rabbi Rudin to Rabbi Tanenbaum, "re Rome report," March 9, 1978, box 195) and (box 211, folder 19, marked "Confidential not for distribution).[13] They first met with Msgr. Charles Moeller, vice-president of the Commission for Religious Relations, with the Jewish people, and with Father Jorge Mejía of the Secretariat for Promoting Christian Unity. They urged both men to press for "a more public and specific stance on Soviet Jewry, human rights and religious liberties." The group held a well-attended news conference on the afternoon on November 24 with representatives from *United Press International (UPI)*, the *NYT*, the *Chicago Sun Times* and RNS. They met subsequently with Msgr. Achille Silvestrini, Undersecretary at the Secretariat of State, and his associate Msgr. Audrys Bakis. Msgr. Charles Moeller and Father Mejía also joined the meeting. Silvestrini told them that the Holy See was committed to religious freedom for all believers, which included the right to emigrate and internal liberty within Eastern bloc nations (Memo, Rudin to Tanenbaum, March 9, 1978).[14] He noted that the Vatican was floating two proposals at Belgrade and would present them at the right time.[15]

Sister Gillen asked about the possibility of the Vatican's speaking out at Belgrade on behalf of Christian and Jewish prisoners in the USSR. Silvestrini responded that the Vatican would not intervene publicly for any prisoner, Jewish or Christian, but would employ "quiet diplomacy" The Vatican would be discreet and conduct private interventions (Ibid.).[16]

In Rome, the delegation participated in the Second Session of the International Sakharov Hearings at the Palazzo di Congressi, "staged to focus international public attention on human rights and religious liberty . . . focusing . . . to those human rights sanctioned by the Universal Declaration of Human Rights and by the International Covenants on Civil and Political rights" (Charles Z. Smith, "Report of the President . . . USA," December 5, 1977, box 303, folder 7). Simon Wiesenthal chaired the hearings, which heard the testimony of witnesses from the Soviet Union and Eastern Europe (Memo, Rabbi Rudin to Rabbi Tanenbaum, March 9, 1978, box 195).[17]

THE MADRID CONFERENCE

The second follow-up conference on the implementation of The Helsinki Accords took place in Madrid in the fall of 1980 (Letter, Mathew Nimetz to Sister Ann Gillen, June 30, 1978, Spertus, box 3).[18] President Carter appointed attorney Max Kampelman to head the American delegation (Memos, Rabbi Rudin to Rabbi Tanenbaum {confidential}, July 24, 1978, box 211, folder 19; and June 11, 1980, box 303, folder 4).[19] Efforts by Rabbi Rudin and the AJC to have Sister Gillen appointed to the American delegation failed (Letter, Rabbi Rudin to Sargent Shriver, June 26, 1980, box 303, folder 6).[20]

Rabbi Rudin and Sister Gillen led a Task Force delegation of observers supported by the AJC, and coordinated with the NCSJ (Memo, Rabbi Rudin to Rabbi Tanenbaum, August 11, 1980, box 303, folder 6).[21] It included Professor Charles Z. Smith; Rev. Msgr. John Radano; Reverend John Steinbruck; Sister Ann Marie Erst (SHCJ), a member of the Bishop's Commission on Justice and Peace in Dublin; Reverend William Phillippe, pastor of Bower Hill United Presbyterian Church (Pittsburgh); and Dr. Thomas P. Melady, President of Sacred Heart University (Memo, Rabbi Rudin to Rabbi Tanenbaum, June 11, 1980, box 303, folder 4).[22] Sister Gillen remarked that the delegation represented "the sentiments of millions of our fellow Americans who are appalled by the Soviet Union's dismal human rights record . . . concerned about the virulent new campaign of anti-Semitism . . . in the USSR. . . . Our interreligious group is a visible sign of our solidarity with all peoples who are oppressed in the Soviet Union and other Eastern European nations." She mentioned Anatoly Shcharansky, Andrei Sakharov, Ida Nudel, and the Orthodox nun Sister Valeriya Makeeva, who were "symbolic of all who are imprisoned, banished and silenced by the Soviet Union" (Natalie Flatow, NITFSJ, Press Release, November 19, 1980, box 283).[23]

Jerry Goodman of the NCSJ and Dr. William Korey of B'nai B'rith (BB) briefed the Task Force delegation on their arrival in Madrid. Later at the United States Commission on Security and Cooperation in Europe

(CSCE) headquarters, they received briefings from Ambassadors Warren Zimmerman and Jerome Shestack (Letter, Rabbi Rudin to Meg Donovan, March 3, 1980, box 303, folder 7).[24] The delegation met with the heads of delegations from West Germany, Sweden, and Denmark (John Steinbruck, "Jottings on a Journey—Madrid Rome and Home." December 4, 1980, box 303, folder 5).[25] In these meetings, the delegation stressed the importance of unified East-West support for human rights, of personalizing human rights, and of naming persons who symbolize the struggle of whole groups.[26] They gave the Swedish group copies of Task Force materials about Raoul Wallenberg (Ibid.).[27]

The delegation flew to Rome on Thanksgiving where they met with representatives of the Vatican Secretariat of State, the liaison for Jewish Christian Relations, and with William Murphy, an American with the Vatican's Justice and Peace Commission. They asked the Vatican officials to ". . . take a vigorous stance at Madrid in favor of human rights and religious liberty for oppressed Soviet Jews and Christians" (Telegram or Press Release, November 29, 1980, box 303, folder 6).[28]

VISITS TO IRELAND AND ENGLAND

Sister Gillen visited Ireland in 1977 to speak out on Soviet Jewry and human rights. In August, she held a meeting of the Task Force in Dublin with representatives of the Thirty-fives Women's Campaign for Soviet Jewry, Amnesty International, Pax Christi, Working for Peace, the Irish Commission for Justice and Peace, and the Dublin Jewish community ("Persons Attending Task Force meeting at Shelburne Hotel Dublin on Aug 16, 1977," August 16, 1977, Spertus, folder correspondence 1968–1991, Jewish Christian). In December 1978, she visited Dublin, Leeds, and London to urge Christians and Jews to work together for their co-religionists in USSR and Eastern Europe ("Form from Ann about history of NITFSJ," n.d., box 302, folder 4).

Later in 1979 in London, Sister Gillen visited the Soviet embassy to present a letter to the Soviet Ambassador offering to exchange herself for Ida Nudel, who had been exiled to a prison camp in Siberia (Thomas Johnson, "Prisoner of Conscience: Sr. Ann Gillen keeps alive the hopes of Eastern European Jews and Christians," *AJC Journal*, Spring 1985, SHCJ archives). The plan was for Sister Gillen to request the release of Ida Nudel and for Rita Eker, an English Jewish activist affiliated with the "Thirty-fives," to request the release of Sister Makeeva (Letters, Kevin P. Greenan to Sister Ann Gillen, September 12, 1979, Spertus, box 79; and Rosalind Gamal to Ann Gillen, November 8, 1980, Spertus, box 107, corr. Israel).[29] This event, as well as the August 1977 meetings, may have been organized by—or coordinated with—the Liaison Bureau, which had helped to organize the "Thirty-fives," a British Jewish advocacy group for Soviet Jewry.

Ida Nudel wrote Sister Gillen (transcribed . . ., 1979–1980. SHCJ archives, Special Ann Gillen Personal Folder) shortly thereafter that when she heard the news "My back began to shiver. You cannot imagine, dear Sister Ann, feeling of someone who knows that other person is ready to bring freedom to you by sacrifice of his own." She added, "only pressure of people of good will keep me alive. . . . These words are full of tears and meaning. If not for you, and many other people of good will, it wasn't possible for so many people to fulfill their dream. It wasn't possible even to speak in a loud voice about human rights for Soviet people."

During this time, Sister Gillen received an honorary doctorate from Lenoir Rhyne College of Hickory, North Carolina (Letter, Raymond M. Bost, President of the College, to Sister Ann Gillen, April 13, 1976, box 175). In 1981, *Pioneer Women* in the United States gave her the Golda Meir Human Relations Award for contributing to ". . . bridging the gap between the United States and Israel in any of the following areas: Literature, science . . .; promotion of *aliya* . . . promoting closer relations between the Christians in the US and Israel, and Soviet Jewry" (Letter, Edythe Rosenfield, *Pioneer Women*, to Ann Gillen, April 27, 1981, SHCJ Archives).[30]

SISTER ANN GILLEN IN THE SOVIET UNION

Sister Gillen and Sister Gloria Coleman travelled together to the Soviet Union from June 9–25, 1978. They met with thirty Jewish and non-Jewish activists in Moscow, Leningrad, Riga, and Vilna (Letter, Bert Gold to Mr. and Mrs. Leland Schubert, July 10, 1978, box 195; and NITFSJ information sheet about 1980, n.d., box 283).[31] A police matron at customs conducted a body search on Sister Ann before she left the Soviet Union.[32]

Upon her return, Sister Gillen joined a Task Force delegation for a meeting on July 5 at the White House with Counsel Robert Lipshutz, Joyce Starr, former Congressman Ed Mezvinsky (D-IO) and a representative from Hamilton Jordan's office (Memo, Rabbi Tanenbaum to Bert Gold, "Interreligious Task Force activity on Vladimir Slepak, etc.," confidential).[33] Sister Gillen described her recent experience of meeting with dissidents in the Soviet Union. She urged intervention on behalf of Slepak and Nudel. Later, Sister Gillen and Rabbi Rudin met with Matthew Nimetz at the State Department. He promised to send a report to Secretary of State Cyrus Vance. He advised them to hold a press conference to share Sister Gillen's experiences in the Soviet Union.

At a later press conference, Sister Gillen reported that they had found a much-worsened situation in contrast to her 1974 visit. She charged Soviet leaders "with the deliberate destruction of refusenik families, with a policy of cruelty which is causing the loss of human lives, not only the denial of human rights" (Text of Statement by Sister Ann Gillen at AJC press conference, July 6, 1978, box 175). She called on the president to recall the ambassador, urged the US Helsinki Commission to present Congress with a review of all programs of cooperation with the USSR, and called for curtailment of all concessions made too rapidly. She urged minor "harassment" of Soviet tourists visiting in the United States: they should be searched as she and Sister Coleman had been. She urged the government and labor unions to close thirty-seven ports open to Soviet shipping, leaving only three open.

In discussions about a possible boycott of the 1980 Moscow Olympics, Sister Gillen was more cautious.[34] In July of 1978, she expressed the view that the Task Force should urge athletes and visitors to the 1980 Olympics to ask questions of Soviet authorities and visit refuseniks. She said: "We urge athletes to give serious consideration to their cooperation in these games of honor in a country which plays games of dishonor with its people's human rights and human lives" (Text of statement by Sister Ann Gillen at AJC press conference in NYC, July 6, 1978, box 175). David Geller argued that the consensus was that it would be impossible to bring about the withdrawal of American participation in the Moscow Olympics. He argued that most people agreed that the Olympics should be used as a vehicle for public discussion and dissemination of information and statements that could be used to mobilize public opinion against the Soviet Union. He proposed that NBC be urged to broadcast programs regarding the treatment of Jews in the USSR and other human rights violations during the days when they would be broadcasting the Olympics.[35] He urged the NEC of the AJC to adopt a resolution on the Olympics, as a form of protest, deliver it to the Olympic Committee, and release it to the press (Memo, David Geller to Morris Fine, "re Steering Committee Meeting on Soviet Jewry on July 20," July 20, 1978, box 194).[36]

Senator Wendell Anderson (D-MN) and Representative Jack Kemp (R-NY) introduced a Congressional resolution to have the Olympic games moved from Moscow. Geller urged low-key support for the resolution (Memo, David Geller to Bert Gold, "recap of . . . meeting of July 31, 1978" [revised by Morris Fine], August 1, 1978, box 194). President Carter went on record saying that he hoped that the US athletes would participate in the Moscow Olympics. The decision, he said, would be made by the US Olympic Committee and not by the US government (www.jta.org/1978/07/24/arachive/congressional-action-tomove-Olympic-games-out-of-Moscow, accessed December 23, 2014).

In September 1978, Rabbi Rudin argued that the Anderson-Kemp bill was not practical, since no country would agree to hold the Olympics at that point. He felt that the boycott was not standard AJC policy. He noted that athletes could bring religious materials into the USSR. He suggested Rabbi Tanenbaum speak to NBC and urged that a large number of Jews

International Conferences and the Interreligious Legal Task Force on Human Rights   153

and Christians on the Task Force attend the Olympics and visit refuseniks (Minutes of the AJC Interreligious Affairs Commission, September 18, 1978, box 469).[37] Later in November, Sister Gillen and Rabbi Jim Rudin rebuffed requests by Leo Henzel and Rabbi Leonard Goldstein of the 1980 Committee of Human Rights to cooperate in boycotting the Olympics (Memo, Rabbi Rudin to Rabbi Tanenbaum. November 14, 1978, box 211, folder 19).

COPENHAGEN, JULY 1980

In early July 1980, Sisters Traxler and Gillen represented NCAN at the United Nations-sponsored International Women's Conference in Copenhagen (Elizabeth Mary Stub SHJC, "Elizabeth Mary Stub Attends Copenhagen Meetings, Reports on UN Conference and on Open Forum" in the *SHJC NEWS*, SHCJ, American Province, vol. 5, #2, reprinted by NITFSJ c1980).[38] In Copenhagen, the Sisters appealed to women of all faiths to make the conference "an opportunity to dialogue about the women's agenda" (NCAN Press Release issued by Margaret Traxler and Ann Gillen. July 8, 1980, box 208, folder 4).[39]

Outside the Bella Conference Center, Sister Gillen, together with other delegates and representatives of the local Danish Jewish community and local women's groups, conducted a demonstration on behalf of Soviet Jewry. Sister Gillen spoke about Ida Nudel and offered to serve out the two remaining years of her sentence. Her participation in the demonstration, and possibly at the conference, may have been coordinated by the Israeli Liaison Bureau.[40] This demonstration led by a nun in blue wearing a Jewish Star made the front page of many local and European newspapers. The news coverage reported that the protest was on behalf of both Jewish and Christian women being persecuted in the USSR. One reporter quoted Sister Gillen as saying, "It's too late to help the Jews who died in the Holocaust but it's not too late to try to turn the direction of history in the Soviet Union" (Anders Jerichow, "A Nun wants to give two years of her life in Siberia" translated from *Berlingske Tidende* p. 2. July 17, 1980, box 281; and "A Little Group demands freedom for a Soviet Jew," *Berlingske Tidende*, July 17, 1980, NITFSJ reprint).

THE LAWYERS LEGAL PROJECT

For many years, the NCSJ recruited lawyers to become involved in the legal cases of Soviet Jews charged with violating laws related to emigration and religious and cultural practices. The organization funded the expenses of some lawyers to observe trials and to meet with clients and with Soviet officials.[41]

In June 1978, Jerry Goodman of the NCSJ asked the AJC to run the project (Letter, Jerry Goodman to Bert Gold, June 22, 1978, box 195).[42] Around this time Sister Gillen and the Task Force became involved in a project to engage the legal community of Chicago in the struggle for civil rights in the Soviet Union (Letter, Sister Ann Gillen to Prof. Ralph Ruebner, n.d., box 301). Sister Gillen appealed to religious oriented legal fraternities to help liberate Soviet laws and lawyers by bringing to the attention of their colleagues the denial of civil rights in the Soviet Union. She asked them to challenge Soviet lawyers regarding systematic abuses of the ideals of the legal profession. She urged them to attend trials in the Soviet Union and to help prepare defense briefs to be submitted to Soviet officials.[43]

In early 1982, Sister Gillen and the Task Force began to organize an Interreligious Legal Task Force on Human Rights in the Soviet Union. The Chicago AJC and the Task Force invited representatives of Jewish, evangelical Protestant and Catholic legal fraternities and interested individuals to a meeting in Chicago on March 22, 1982.[44] At the meeting, AJC Area Director Jonathan Levine welcomed everyone and Sister Gillen spoke. Attorney Bert Meyers of the Decalogue Society then reported on his efforts to help refuseniks during his recent trip to USSR. Lynn Buzzard, director of the Christian Legal Society, described his visit to the Siberian Seven in the basement of the American Embassy in Moscow. Those present discussed issuing a proclamation on religious freedom for all peoples in the Soviet Union on Law Day on May 1, sending representatives to visit refuseniks and dissidents in the USSR (in cooperation with a similar AJC program), and forming a committee to investigate ways to "use" the Soviet legal system to enhance human rights. They also discussed the preparation of a writ of *habeas corpus* on behalf of Andrei Sakharov (Meeting of ITFSJ, Catholic, Jewish, and Protestant Lawyers in Chicago, March 22, 1982, box 302, folder 2).[45]

By the end of June 1982, the lawyers had discussed setting up an executive committee for a legal task force with representatives of the Catholic League for Religious and Civil Rights, the Christian Legal Society, the Decalogue Society of Lawyers, the AJC, and the Task Force.[46] The formal organization became the National Interreligious Legal Task Force on Human Rights (NILTFHR/Legal Task Force); (AJC, Notes on meeting of Interreligious Attorney's Task Force on Human Rights in the Soviet Union, June 30, 1982, Spertus, box 86, folder 3).[47] The organization's declared purpose was to support international human rights agreements, foster public awareness of these rights, and within the legal community "to gather and disseminate information about human rights violations," to establish ties with human rights organizations and to redress these violations.

In April 1982, a delegation of the Legal Task Force, including Sister Gillen, presented the Soviet Embassy in Washington, D.C. with a writ of *habeas corpus* on behalf of Andrei Sakharov (AJC news release "Midwest Attorneys petition Soviet court for Sakharov's immediate Release," April 23, 1982).[48] The Soviets refused to accept it and the State Department sent it to the American Embassy in Moscow. On July 11, 1982 Warren Zimmerman, the Chargé d'Affairs at the Embassy, wrote Sister Gillen (box 302, folder 2) that "Our embassies are prohibited by regulation from serving legal processes, except when an individual is being summoned to appear before US Federal Court proceedings." He added, however, that her actions helped Sakharov as the Soviet authorities were aware of her efforts, protest, and criticism and said that her efforts were "another element of pressure on the Soviet authorities to eventually resolve the case."[49]

The Legal Task Force organized a two-day legal seminar "Human rights Violations in Eastern Bloc Countries: Practical Legal Responses" at the University of Chicago on September 11 and 12, 1983 (Ibid.).[50] They sponsored a lecture by Professor Cherif Bassiouni in January 1984 at DePaul University Law School (Memo, Ralph Ruebner, January 20, 1984, Spertus, box 86). In September 1984, the Legal Task Force sent a telegram to the Procurator General of the USSR to end the detention and harassment of Andrei Sakharov (Ibid.). In October 1985, the organization filed a petition with the UN Centre for Human Rights on behalf of seventeen persecuted Soviet citizens (Letter, Arthur Matthews, Jr. to Hon. Jakob Th. Moller, October 14, 1985, Spertus, box 86). In a memo dated September 20, 1985, Professor Ralph Ruebner of John Marshall Law School, and Sister Gillen, in the absence of a chair, invited Legal Task Force Members of the first meeting of the year and to the election of officers on October 2, 1985 (Spertus, box 86).

For years, Sister Gillen had argued that the Soviets fabricated charges of collaboration with the Nazis to defame émigré critics of the Soviet Union residing in the United States and Canada. In her role in the Legal Task Force, she took an interest in this issue. It surfaced in denaturalization cases in the US and Canada in the early 1980s.[51] Defendants were charged with lying on applications for asylum and citizenship by not admitting to having served in the military, police, and/or axillary forces of the Third Reich. A guilty verdict could result in loss of citizenship and deportation, often to the Soviet Union (Letter, Sister Ann Gillen to Rabbi Rudin, July 1, 1982, box 302, folder 3).[52] The Office of Special Investigations (OSI) of the Justice Department investigated and tried persons suspected of having lied on their US citizenship applications. A 1980 agreement between the US Justice Department and the Procurator General of the Soviet Union allowed for "Soviet supplied evidence and eyewitnesses to be used in government's denaturalization cases." Within a few years, the activities of the Legal Task Force would dominate the public advocacy efforts of Sister Gillen and would embroil her in a controversy with some important individuals and institutions of the American Jewish community.

In a related incident, Sister Gillen criticized Morris Abram, head of the NCSJ, for his recent reference to "Ukrainian" anti-Semitism (Letter, Sister Ann Gillen to Morris Abram, n.d., Spertus, box 54).[53] She argued that Abram stressed "Ukrainian" more than "anti-Semitism." She criticized him and others for failing to make the point that Moscow "controls and directs all the media in the USSR" and that "a large segment of Ukrainians abroad maintain that they do not control their own country." She affirmed that she understood the past Jewish experiences of suffering in the Ukraine and that anti-Semitism still existed among Ukrainians, but she urged dropping the phrase "Ukrainian anti-Semitism . . . as a crowd pleaser, thus fanning the flame of traumatic memories at the expense of better intergroup relations in the present."[54] In effect, she favored dropping a phrase that would remind people of traumatic memories and hurt the chances for improved relations among Jews and Ukrainians in the United States and Canada advocating for their brethren in the Soviet Union. Importantly, Sister Gillen viewed the Soviet defamation of émigré critics as a plot to drive a wedge between Eastern European Catholic communities and American Jews.[55]

Finally, she attacked the stance of the NCSJ and other establishment advocacy groups for Soviet Jewry for lacking empathy for the plight of captive nations and others (Ibid.). She noted that the *Ukrainian Weekly* published information about Jewish prisoners of conscience, which was not reciprocated in the Jewish press, except by the Task Force because the Jewish press had "opted to focus solely on the emigration issue."

THE TASK FORCE CELEBRATES ITS TENTH ANNIVERSARY

The Task Force and the AJC held a Tenth Anniversary Leadership Consultation Conference on November 23, 1982 in Washington, D.C. to mark the founding of the Task Force (Memos, "Items for Discussion," April 30, 1981, box 303, folder 2; Rabbi Rudin to Rabbi Tanenbaum, "Agenda for November 23 meeting," November 16, 1982; box 302, folder 3, and "AJC tentative schedule for 10th . . . NITFSJ," March 8, 1982, box 302, folder 3).[56] They planned a two-day event with panel discussions, a briefing at the State Department, meetings with members of Congress, an evening awards dinner, and a vigil at the Soviet Embassy (Memo, Rabbi Rudin to Rabbi Tanenbaum, November 16, 1981). Sister Gillen assisted the national AJC and its Washington lobbyist, Hyman Bookbinder, to secure most of the speakers (Memo, Rabbi Rudin to Hyman Bookbinder, August 17, 1983, box 302, folder 4).[57]

AJC and Task Force publicity for the event emphasized the plight of Soviet Jewry in the context of violations of the Helsinki Accords. In invitations to potential speakers, Rabbi Rudin described the Task Force as bringing together Protestants, Evangelicals, Roman Catholics, members of the Greek Orthodox Church, and Jews "in the common struggle to achieve human rights and religious liberty in the Soviet Union" (Letter, Rabbi Rudin to Hon. Elliott Abrams, Assistant Secretary of State . . . , July 14, 1982, box 302, folder 4). In publicity for the event, Sister Gillen argued that the Soviets were "continuing their sabotage of the Helsinki human rights process. The latest immigration figures, . . . are an outrage. Both Jews and Christians are suffering severe repression in their struggles to maintain their religious and cultural traditions." She called on religious leaders to speak out on behalf of prisoners of conscience and refuseniks who had been waiting "more than ten years for their visas" (Memo, Natalie Flatow to Rabbi Rudin. August 16, 1982, box 302, folder 3).[58]

As in the past, AJC staff downplayed the Jewish and AJC's visible presence at the Task Force event. In rejecting a regional director's request to bring two staff members to the conference, Eugene DuBow wrote "it is not only the cost . . . We really do not want the thing to turn into an AJC staff retreat. There will be a few of us there and that is enough. The idea behind the meeting is to turn out others—especially Christians. It is supposed to be their thing" (Note, Eugene DuBow to Jon Levine, July 19, 1982, box 302, folder 3).

The Conference took place on September 13–14, 1982 at the Dupont Plaza Hotel ("Rededication and Recommitment: 10th Anniversary National Leadership Conference NITFSJ," box 300). AJC area director Rabbi Andrew Baker presided at the opening lunch. Dr. Eugene Fisher, executive secretary of the Secretariat for Catholic Jewish Relations of the United States Conference of Catholic Bishops (USCCB), gave the invocation.[59] Sister Gillen spoke on the "The State of the Task Force" and Professor Thomas Bird discussed the "Current Religious Situation in the Soviet Union." A briefing at the State Department followed with Reverend John Pawlikowski presiding over presentations by Meg Donovan, CSCE; Richard Pipes, director of Eastern Europe and Soviet Affairs of the National Security Council, and Elliott Abrams, assistant secretary of state.

Rabbi Rudin presided at a gala banquet in the evening. Dr. William H. Harter, Pastor of Falling Spring Presbyterian Church of Chambersburg, Pennsylvania, gave the invocation. Jerry Goodman of the NCSJ reported on the forthcoming Third International Conference on Soviet Jewry planned for Paris in October. Other speakers included Kissye Ratner, mother of refusenik Judith Ratner-Byaly, and Lynn Singer, president of the Union of Councils of Soviet Jewry. The evening ended with The Honorable Walter T. Hubbard Jr., chair of the National Organization of Black Catholics, presenting a Task Force award to Sargent Shriver, the honorary chair of the Task Force (Letter, Margaret Ellen Traxler to Rabbi

Tanenbaum, August 24, 1982, box 302, folder 3).[60] Rabbi Tanenbaum also presented an award to civil rights activist Bayard Rustin.

The next day Patrick Monoghan, general counsel of the Catholic League for Religious and Civil Rights, presided at breakfast. Sister Veronica Grover of SHCJ, gave the invocation. Sister Gloria Coleman, William Gralnick, and the Reverend John Steinbruck spoke on a panel about organizing in local communities. A series of working groups followed (Letter, Sister Anne Mary Dooley SSJ, Niagara University, to Rabbi Rudin, December 14, 1982, box 302, folder 2).[61]

After breakfast, a Task Force delegation led by Professor LaCocque attempted to present a list of names of prisoners of conscience to the Soviet Embassy. They were not received (Letter, Rabbi Rudin to Gerald Fitzgerald, RNS, September 20, 1982, box 302, folder 3). A plenary session followed. Lunch with several members of the House and Senate took place in the Gold Room at the Sam Rayburn building.[62] Hyman Bookbinder of the AJC chaired the lunch and Reverend David E. Simpson, executive director of the Office of Christian Jewish Relations of the NCC, gave the invocation. Rep. Sidney Yates (D-IL) and others spoke (Letter, Rabbi A. James Rudin to Hon. Sidney Yates, September 23, 1982, box 302, folder 3).[63]

In the afternoon, former Representative Robert F. Drinan, Reverend Robert Pruitt; Reverend John Steinbruck; and Rabbi Marc Tanenbaum led a prayer vigil on the steps of the Capitol.[64] At the vigil, Eugene DuBow read the "Tenth Anniversary Manifesto." It presented a balanced concern for Jews and Christians in the Soviet Union. Each demand was inclusive of both ("Tenth Anniversary Manifesto," September 14, 1982, box 302, folder 3). The Task Force was working, the Manifesto stated "to bring freedom to the Soviet Jews and Christians. [We protest the] . . . cultural and spiritual repression of Jews and Christians in the Soviet Union . . . [the continuing] denial of human rights and religious liberty of Soviet Christians and Jews [it called on Soviet authorities to] give Christians and Jews their rights to leave for countries of their choice." It called on Jews and Christians in every country to join with the Task Force in this vital effort.[65] After this session, participants visited offices of their respective senators and congressional representatives.

Rabbi Rudin sent out most of the thank-you notes under his name. Sister Gillen did not co-sign.[66] This may indicate AJC's increasingly independent role in the interreligious advocacy for Soviet Jewry. By 1982, it may have begun to downgrade the role and status of Sister Ann Gillen and the Task Force.

International Conferences and the Interreligious Legal Task Force on Human Rights

BRUSSELS III WORLD CONFERENCE ON SOVIET JEWRY

The follow-up conference to Brussels II was scheduled for October 1982 in Paris (Letter Rabbi Rudin to Rabbi Tanenbaum, August 16, 1982, box 302, folder 1).[67] The Presidium and Steering Committee of the World Conference on Soviet Jewry worried about how the press would cover the conference after Israel's July 1982 invasion and occupation of Lebanon. They also feared that rising anti-Semitism in Europe might keep delegates away. They rescheduled the conference for March 1983 in Jerusalem (Letter, David Geller to Donald Feldstein "Paris Conference-Soviet Jewry," August 12, 1982, box 302, folder 1).

Abe Karlikow, head of AJC's European operations, participated on the planning committee for Brussels III (Letter, Abraham Karlikow to Dr. Donald Feldstein, David Geller, Rabbi Marc Tanenbaum, and others, January 16, 1983, box 301, folder 2). There were to be four major sessions: Jewish identity, public awareness, anti-Semitism, and human rights.[68] An interfaith meeting would be organized by Rabbi Israel Miller.[69] There was no mention of the Task Force or of Sister Ann Gillen. More significantly, according to Rabbi Rudin, Rabbi Miller "especially expresses anxiety about the Christians speaking out on the status of Soviet Christians." Rabbi Rudin told him that "this was now part of the interreligious scene and that one could not expect Christians to remain silent about their co-religionists inside the USSR."[70]

The organizers had asked Rabbi Rudin to draft a text "of the Christian appeal" (Rabbi Rudin to Rabbi Tanenbaum, January 14 . . .).[71] Sister Gillen helped him prepare the document which he viewed as an appeal to the Christian community on Soviet Jewry (Letter, Rabbi A. James Rudin to Myrna Sheinbaum, February 10, 1983 box 301, folder 2).[72] The final document was titled "A call from Jerusalem to all People of Conscience."[73]

It read:

> We Christians and Jews from many lands in Jerusalem . . . . symbol and sign of the heart's homeland, the exile's longing, God's call and the human family's quest for holiness and we boldly affirm this call to conscience. . . .
>
> We rejoice in the freedom to emigrate from the USSR won by more than three hundred thousand persons, including Soviet Jews, German Christians and others. who . . . return to their own homelands and/or to be reunited with their families. . . . We deplore the recent actions of Soviet officials in closing the doors of emigration . . . disregard . . . principles enshrined in the 'Universal Declaration of Human Rights.' . . . We are appalled by the denial of human rights to hundreds of thousands of Jews, Christians and others unjustly imprisoned in the U.S.S.R. whether by prison bars, like Anatoly Shcharansky, Yuri Federov and Alexei Murzhenko or by prolonged exile, like Andrei Sakharov

and Ida Nudel or bound by the borders of that land which denies so many persons their right to emigrate . . . We protest the third trial of Josef Begun for teaching "the Hebrew language and the cultural heritage of the Jewish people. . . . We remind Soviet leaders that in all these matters they have failed to honor the promises of the Helsinki Accord . . . We pledge our renewed commitment to the cause of our brothers and sisters who are denied their basic religious and cultural human rights by the USSR as well as their right to leave. . . . We will not be silent, whether in prayer for God's help or in protest against the inhuman oppression inflicted upon them by Soviet officials. We will not rest until human rights and religious liberty prevail.[74]

Approximately fifteen hundred delegates from thirty-one countries attended the opening ceremony at Jerusalem's National Convention Center (Dr. Robert O. Freedman. "Observations on Third World Conference on Soviet Jewry," March 14–16, 1983, box 301).[75] Israeli President Navon spoke, along with the American Ambassador to the United Nations, Jeanne Kirkpatrick, and Simone Veil, former president of the European Parliament.[76] Former refusenik Yosef Mendelovitch urged Israel to grant Soviet Jews *de jure* status as Israeli citizens. Greetings from British Prime Minister Margaret Thatcher were read. The next morning historian Martin Gilbert described the proliferation of anti-Semitic literature in the Soviet Union. Following a plenary session four parallel workshops were held on Jewish identity in the USSR, public action on behalf of Soviet Jewry, official Soviet anti-Semitism, and Soviet human rights violations. In the afternoon two additional workshops were held—one an interfaith colloquium and a second dealing with activities of scientists on behalf of Soviet Jewry.[77]

In his keynote address, Representative Drinan summarized the role of the Task Force and Christians in the struggle for Soviet Jews in the United States (Address of Robert F. Drinan, Third Conference, Jerusalem. March 17, 1983, box 301). He explained how, reading Wiesel's *The Jews of Silence*, moved him to work for the liberation of Soviet Jewry. He rejoiced at the press coverage of the First Brussels Conference on Soviet Jewry but was disappointed at the absence of Christian participants. During his August 1975 visit to the Soviet Union, Anatoly Shcharansky served as his guide and translator. "He taught me about the cruelty of the Kremlin to the Jews in Moscow, Leningrad, Riga, Kiev and elsewhere. He took me to visit Doctor Sakharov. . . . That week changed my life."[78] He attended Brussels II in 1976 with thirty-five Christians who presented to Prime Minister Golda Meir the Task Force's statement of solidarity and commitment to work for the deliverance of Soviet Jews. He praised NITFSJ and Sister Ann Gillen for the presence of Christians at Brussels II.[79]

He saw a moral awakening in Christian churches, along with a sharp rise in the "level of grief and guilt about what Christians have done to Jews through the centuries." In 1965, the Second Vatican Council for the first time in twenty centuries condemned anti-Semitism in every form. This resulted in more dialogue and fewer misunderstandings. All too slowly, he claimed, "Christians are beginning to understand the centrality of the Jewish people . . . to the world." Christians today he said recognize "the beauty of Judaism and the majesty of Israel."[80]

He suggested that Christians had to be asked and urged to action. He had a vision of hundreds of meetings with thousands of Christians producing millions of petitions to free the prisoners of Zion. Christians were beginning to understand, he stated, the profound statement of Reinhold Niebuhr that "no one can be a good Christian until first he is a good Jew." He closed by citing what Andre Sakharov told him during a 1975 visit "only the Christians of America can save the Jews of Russia." He urged the Christians of America to speak out against the crime of humanity that could be seen in the attempted destruction of the Jewish people in the Soviet Union.[81]

In 1976, Sister Gillen and the Task Force had played a central role in Brussels II. The high point of the gathering may have been the embrace and exchange of words between former Israeli Prime Minister Golda Meir and Sister Gillen. Now, at Brussels III in Jerusalem in early 1983, Sister Gillen and the Task Force were peripheral participants. Ironically, a Jesuit Priest who served in Congress and taught law at Georgetown, reminded those present of the role that Sister Gillen and the Task Force had played in the movement to liberate Soviet Jewry. He predicted that that the destiny of Soviet Jewry lay in the hands of Christians in America.[82]

NOTES

1. Among the eighty guests were Jerry Goodman (NCSJ), Phil Baum (American Jewish Congress) William Korey (BB), Irene Marensky of the Soviet Jewry Council, and representatives of "captive nations" in the Soviet Union and Eastern Europe. Ambassador Albert W. Sherer Jr, head of the American delegation to Belgrade, stated: "We have no high expectations for Belgrade but we intend to hold the Soviet Union's feet close the fire on the question of human rights" (Memo, Rabbi Rudin to Rabbi Tanenbaum, "Interfaith Role in Belgrade," June 3, 1977, box 212, folder 1).

2. At its annual meeting in May 1977, the AJC called on signatory "governments of the Helsinki Agreements meeting in Belgrade to insist that the Soviet Union . . . take concrete steps to carry out their human rights commitments under the accord, particularly those relating to family reunification and the rights of religious and national minorities to practice and perpetuate their own religion and culture" (Statement on Soviet Jewry of AJC, May 13, 1977, box 194). A second version adopted on May 15, 1977 called on signatories "to ensure that the issue of human rights of Jews in the Soviet Union is placed on the agenda of the . . . conference." In appealing to US Presidential candidates in 1976 several Jewish refuseniks referred to the Helsinki Accords and human rights (Press Release, "Georgetown Appeal to President Ford and Carter," September 16, 1976, box 175).

3. The Belgrade Conference began officially on October 4, 1977 and concluded on March 9, 1978.

4. His view was confirmed by Leopold Unger writing in the *International Herald Tribune* (*IHT*) of March 24, 1978 (with Letter, Abe Karlikow to Goldberg, March 24, 1978, box 195). "All the efforts deployed to eliminate any illusion to human rights had a diametrically opposite result: The rights of man became the leading issue of the conference." Matthew Nimetz (Letter, Matthew Nimetz to Elmer Winter, April 3, 1978, box 195) of the State Department argued that Belgrade was successful: "while the concluding document did not fully reflect our hopes and expectations, . . . (succeeded in most important part of program) a thorough, honest and open review of the record of implementation of the Final Act." The human rights and human contacts provision "discussed . . . an historic breakthrough . . . a precedent . . . procedures established which should encourage future efforts to implement the Final Act more concretely . . . . The Final Act and Belgrade meeting 'have demonstrated, . . . that it is legitimate to discuss human rights." Representative Dante Fascell was less optimistic. He wrote that post Belgrade Soviet violation of human rights did not bode well for the Helsinki process (Form letter, July 19, 1978, box 195).

5. They spent three days in Belgrade.

6. They referred to Anatoly Shcharansky, Eduard Kuznetsov, Pastor Georgi Vins, Nijole Sadunaite, Vasyl Roamyuk, and others. Sister Gillen ("interview of June 3, 1991," SHCJ Archives, folder Ann Gillen,) recalled that at Belgrade their delegation joined in effort "to name names, cite facts."

7. The AJC helped prepare a "Blue Book" showing that Soviet performance toward its Jews fell short of its Helsinki commitments. In May, the forty-six-page volume (and eleven appendices) was delivered to most foreign offices and the delegation at Belgrade. (See chapter 6 n.4.) Karlikow believed that Goldberg's opening address brought up all five concerns of the "Blue Book." Goldberg noted "restrictions on the right of individuals to travel or emigrate;" cited interference with international broadcasts; urged that people should be free to worship without fear or state interference; supported "required respect for unique cultural and linguistic heritage;" and said that it was important to register "vigorous disapproval" of repressive measures against those seeking to promote final act's goals (Memo, A. Karlikow to M. Fine, "Belgrade conference," October 13, 1977, box 194).

8. Abe Karlikow set up meetings for them in Belgrade and Zach Shuster arranged meetings at the Vatican.

9. Rabbi Rudin wrote that Shcharansky and Pastor Georgi Vins hovered over the Sava Center (site of the Conference) like Banquo's ghost. He credited Goldberg with making Shcharansky a central concern.

10. In his opening remarks at Belgrade, Msgr. Achilles Silvestrini, Vatican Under Secretary of State, declared "'Millions of believers be they Catholic, Orthodox, Evangelical Christians, Jews, Muslims all felt that they were included, understood and interpreted in the Helsinki Declaration on motives of common aspirations to liberty."

11. Professor Bird asked the Vatican to speak out about Roman Catholics in Lithuania and Ukraine, noting that their ethnic co-religionists in America were concerned about the "spiritual welfare of their brothers and sisters . . . " He added that the current Vatican détente with the Soviet Union did not include "re-birth of a Ukrainian Roman Catholic Church or the sustaining of a viable Lithuanian Church." In his view, the Vatican after WWII had been aggressive against the USSR in Italy, Hungary, and Poland. He felt that it now preferred quiet diplomacy.

12. In his January 30 memo to Rabbi Marc Tanenbaum, Rabbi Rudin wrote: "while we were in Belgrade but three days we felt that something was happening." The Soviet Jewry issue came up all the time and the names of prisoners of conscience were mentioned. In contrast, William R. Phillippe of the Task Force delegation, wrote in a note, "Trifling with Human Rights," was more skeptical. He felt that most delegates were more concerned "with boundaries and trade . . . , very few have investment in pressing the issues of human rights." He expressed shock that the religious community in the United States was not aware of the Final Agreements and that they had no

International Conferences and the Interreligious Legal Task Force on Human 163
Rights

plan to press for the advance of these discussions in Belgrade. He felt that the voice of the Vatican had been muted in Belgrade.

13. They joined Sister Gillen and Rabbi Rudin in an ecumenical prayer on the floor of St. Peters and in an ecumenical Eucharist celebrated by Msgr. Radano, Sister Gillen, and Professor Bird.

14. Rabbi Rudin described Bakis as a Lithuanian Catholic, completely Vaticanized; he showed no emotion or interest in the plight of Lithuanian Catholics.

15. Professor Bird asked him about Roman Catholic prayer books and he replied that they were available in Russian and Lithuanian but not in Byelorussian or Ukrainian.

16. He said that the Vatican was working on behalf of Shcharansky. In response to negative comments about Vatican Israel relations, Silvestrini said that issue of Jerusalem was not simple because the city belonged to three religions. He said that the Vatican did not recognize Israel's final borders but it had " . . . more than de facto recognition of Israel." Rabbi Rudin commented that "Msgr. Silvestini's seeming inability to understand the Jewish commitment to Israel in other than "emotional terms" was depressing and a disappointment." Rabbi Rudin believed that the Vatican was pursuing a careful but risky policy vis a vis USSR and Eastern Europe. They apparently had written off Ukrainian and Lithuanian Roman Catholics.They wanted substantive victories in Eastern Europe including ties with Hungary, and coexistence with the Soviet government so that they could distribute Russian language liturgy. The price it paid was to remain publicly silent on human rights cases in Eastern Europe and the USSR. The Vatican would not intervene publicly. Its overall strategy was rapprochement with the Soviet Union and, by implication, with the Russian Orthodox Church. The Task Force delegation then met with Father William Murphey and Dr. George Filibeck of the Pontifical Commission for Justice and Peace. At the US Embassy, they met with Alan Holmes, as the Ambassador was out of the country.

17. Mario Corti, an Italian Catholic, organized the hearings. Journalists, lawyers, parliamentarians, labor officials, religious leaders, and human rights activists from the US and Europe participated. Professor Bird considered Corti's group,"Ecumenica Russiya" to be "conservative Christian." Among the non-Italian *Membri della commissione* were Task Force delegation participants Sister Ann Gillen, Professor André LaCocque, Rabbi James Rudin, and Charles Z Smith.

18. Nimetz had been updating Sister Gillen on CSCE supervision of Helsinki since Belgrade.

19. Max Kampelman of Washington, D.C., was a law partner of Task Force Honorary Chair Sargent Shriver. Former Congressman Edward Mezvinsky (D-IA) had asked the AJC to lobby for a strong replacement for Arthur Goldberg. Rabbi Andrew Baker of the AJC in D.C. and Task Force Coordinator (Letter, January 15, 1980, box 303, folder 4) asked President Carter to appoint the Honorable Dante Fascell. A similar letter was sent by Julian Kulas, vice president of the Ukrainian National Congress Committee, Chicago Division.

20. Rabbi Rudin asked Shriver to mention the appointment of Sister Gillen to Kampelman. At least two AJC area directors wrote to Kampelman about appointing her (Letter, Adam Simms to Max Kampelman, June 30, 1980, box 303, folder 4; and Letter, William Gralnick to Max Kampelman, July 8, 1980, box 303, folder 5).

21. The NCSJ advised the AJC as to what it "expected" from the Task Force at the Madrid meetings (Memo, David Geller to Morris Fine, "Steering Committee meeting . . . Soviet Jewry . . . ," July 10, 1978, box 194; and Memo, Rabbi Rudin to Rabbi Tanenbaum, June 11, 1980 box 303, folder 4). The NCSJ submitted a report documenting violations of human rights involving Soviet Jews with a focus on the denial of the right to emigrate (NCSJ, Aide Memoire submitted to President Jimmy Carter, September 4, 1980, box 283). Many American NGOs representing Jewish, East European captive nations, and human rights organizations sent delegations (Madrid CSCE Review meeting: An Interim Report . . . January 6, 1980, box 303, folder 5). US Helsinki Watch, the World Federation of Free Latvians, the Joint Baltic American National Committee,

the Estonian American National Council, the Lithuanian American Council, the Supreme Committee for the Liberation of Lithuania, the Coordinating Committee of Hungarian organizations in North America, Philadelphia Human Rights for Ukraine, the Ukrainian Congress Committee of America, the Slovak World Congress, Free Czechoslovakia, the American Bar Association, the Committee of Concerned Scientists, Helsinki Monitoring of Chicago, the Committee for Persecuted Orthodox Christians, and the AFL-CIO sent delegations. The Union of Councils had a small staff in place. Professor Alan Dershowitz, Joan Baez, and Avital Shcharansky attended. Professor Bird participated as a representative of the St. Sophia Religious Association of Ukrainian Catholics, and Sidney Liskofsky of the AJC represented the International League for Human Rights.

22. The AJC covered expenses for Rabbi Rudin and Sister Gillen. They arrived in Madrid on November 23 and left for Rome on November 27.

23. The Task Force prepared a report (Aide Memoire) for Madrid which detailed Soviet violations of human rights provisions in the Helsinki Final Act. It reaffirmed support for compliance with Helsinki Act Basket III provisions that guaranteed respect for "fundamental freedom including the freedom of thought, conscience, religious or belief" ("Aide Memoir to the Madrid CESC," November 24, 1980; box 283; also in box 303, folder 1, "International Affairs" box). It charged that the USSR implemented the right of emigration "in an excessively narrow manner. {placing} . . . obstacles in the path of those that wish to depart." New Soviet regulations make family reunification more difficult. In violation of the Final Act it cited cases of American clergy prevented from meeting co-religionists while visiting the Soviet Union. They demanded the release of the Christian Pentecostals residing in the American Embassy. They condemned the current anti-Semitic campaign in the USSR. They protested the Soviet ban on the religious education of youth (including the teaching of Hebrew) which violated Principle VII of the Final Act. They criticized the Soviet policy of restricting the registry of houses of worship. Finally, they charged that some Jews and Christians were denied the right to work, tried for economic parasitism, and exiled in violation of Principle VII of the final Act.

24. Jerome Shestack, a Philadelphia lawyer, served as Chairman of the International League for the Rights of Man (ILRM) (Snyder 2018, 25). Rabbi Rudin coordinated the visit with Meg Donovan of CSCE. She set up meetings for the Task Force delegation with delegations from France, Holland, Hungary, Ireland, Malta, Spain, the Vatican, United Kingdom, United States, and West Germany. Rabbi Rudin divided the delegation into two groups for these meetings. Sister Gillen and Rabbi Rudin had also sent formal letters to the heads of various delegations requesting meetings (Letter, Ann Gillen and Rabbi A. James Rudin to Ambassadors in Rome,1980, box 283).

25. Steinbruck commented that even after two scotches the head of the German delegation "couldn't be moved." On Kampelman he wrote "simply outstanding. A magnificently compassionate, brilliant and courageous human being."

26. At Madrid, participating countries could raise specific cases and mention the names of victims. Recalling Madrid in 1991 (Sister Ann Gillen Interview, June 3, 1991) Sister Gillen felt that the Europeans, who suffered from "burnout," were impressed that the Americans cared about rights. Flora Lewis commented in the *NYT* of November 21, 1979, that this time the Soviets had made tactical and diplomatic mistakes. They stonewalled but "managed to solidify the bickering allies, disgruntled the Warsaw Pact and drew even more attention to the central issues than they would otherwise have attracted from a speech sated world." Sister Gillen urged the Vatican to speak out for Soviet Jewry and to intervene on behalf of Ida Nudel. They registered her concern but felt "the possibilities of such an intervention by the Holy See, and moreover one which produces a positive outcome, are severely limited, almost to the point of being non-existent" (Letter, Apostolic Delegate to D.C. to Ann Gillen, March 12, 1980, SHCJ Archives, Ann Gillen Papers).

27. The Swedish diplomat Raoul Wallenberg, working in cooperation with the United States War Refugee Board, saved the lives of tens of thousands of Jews in

Budapest, Hungary in 1944. He disappeared when Soviet forces liberated the city (https://www.ushmm.org/wlc/en/article.php?ModuleId=10005211). They met with his sister Nina Lagergren who thought he might still be alive. The delegation focused on the Jewish Tsitverblit family of Kiev and the Christian Pentecostal Vaschenko-Chymkhalov family currently living in the cellar of the United States Embassy. Reverend John Steinbruck had visited both families earlier in the year. At a NCSJ reception, the Task Force renewed its pledge to help Feiga Shkolnik obtain a visa for her husband and the mother of Marc Nashpitz to get a visa for her son. At the American Embassy, the Task Force delegation promised Avital Shcharansky to continue efforts on behalf of her husband.

28. The Vatican issued no details of the meeting. Steinbruck ("Jottings . . . " December 4, 1980) found Vatican officials "punctual, proper, courteous and reserved. And in a word, safe."

29. Greenan insisted that Sister Gillen wear her veil at the Embassy for public relations reasons.

30. The term *aliya* refers to immigration of Jews to Israel. Previous recipients were Hubert Humphrey and Isaac Stern ("Sister Ann Gillen Speaks out for Soviet Jewry," *Pioneer Women*, November December 1981, pages 21, 34, box 302, folder 2).

31. They visited the Slepaks, Lerners, Ida Nudel, and others. In a return visit in 1980 Sister Coleman met with refuseniks in Moscow, Kiev, Odessa and Leningrad (Sister Gloria Coleman SHCJ Soviet Union Trip, May 14–28, 1980, n.d., box 208, folder 4).

32. Sister Gloria Coleman, interview by author, Rosemont, PA., March 12, 2012. She said, "Ann was very aggressive, I told her to calm down or we might not leave."

33. Rabbi Rudin arranged the meeting with Joyce Star of the White House. Ed Mezvinsky succeeded Al Lowenstein at the UN Human Rights Commission. Tanenbaum wrote (Memo, to Bert Gold, July 7, 1978 {confidential) that "Ann Jim and I came away with the feeling that that group had little notion as to how to proceed, apparently caught between the "hard line" and the "soft line" irresolution toward the Soviet Union."

34. Karlikow in a memo to Arthur Goldberg (March 24, 1978, box 195) mentioned a possible boycott of the 1980 Moscow Olympics along with a boycott of scientific cooperation with the Soviet Academy of Sciences.

35. Geller hoped to coordinate a meeting with NBC and the NCSJ. He also discussed a possible meeting with ABC and CBS concerning a documentary on Soviet Jews and human rights violations.

36. Geller was even more cautious about taking action against scientific and technical cooperation. Dr. Sol Davidson of Iowa proposed a similar idea about using NBC (Telegram, Dr. Sol Davidson, Chair, Greater Des Moines Committee of Concern for Human Rights in the Soviet Union, to Eugene Gold. July 25, 1978, box 195).

37. Finally, he urged the AJC to make it clear to the Olympic Committee how they feel about Israeli and Jewish athletes and journalists having full and equal participation.

38. At the time, both were NCAN board members. An earlier World Conference of the International Women's Year in Mexico City in 1975 called for the "elimination of colonialism, and neo-colonialism, foreign occupation, Zionism, Apartheid and racial discrimination in all its forms" (Loeffler 2018, 293). Also see Preston 2012, 558.

39. They deplored (PLO) efforts to politicize the current meetings and denounced its support of terror. Laila Khaled, former airline hijacker, represented the PLO. Sister Gillen told the delegation of Palestinian women, "I speak to you like one woman to another. Don't you realize . . . , that you, the Palestinian women are . . . in the hands of the man. It is their game you are playing, when you show such an uncompromising attitude. I have myself worked in the countries surrounding Israel and I know that many Palestinian women have a completely different attitude to Israel and their Jewish fellow sisters than what you express at this conference" (NCSJ reprint "Hypocrisy to invite PLO," Svenska *Dagbladet*, July 17, 1980, box 303, folder 4).

40. Rosalind Gemal of The 35s in London wrote Sister Gillen on October 8, 1980 (Spertus, box 107, Israel correspondence), "Sister Ann Gillen's presence in Copenhagen was the most tremendous help to us . . . her participation at the demonstration made all the difference." On their own and sometimes encouraged by the AJC, Sisters Gillen and Traxler defended Israel. For example, Rabbi Rudin asked Traxler to reply to an article critical of Israeli policy on Jerusalem in the Catholic press (Note to Margaret Traxler, July 25, 1974, box 213, folder 11). Following the Yom Kippur War, Sister Gillen urged Secretary of State Kissinger to intervene on behalf of the Israeli prisoners in Syria (Letter, Sister Ann Gillen to Eric Martin and Henry Kissinger, February 20, 1974). The NJCRAC commended the Task Force for bringing attention to prisoners of war in Syria which evoked "substantial Christian denunciation and protest" (NJCRAC Report by Commission Chair Milton Goldstein, April 22, 1974, box 177). In March 1975, Traxler wrote Sister Mary Daniel Turner (LCWR) in Washington D.C. (March 17, 1975) asking her to appraise the executive committee of her concern regarding a whole and fair approach to any study she undertook regarding the Israeli Arab questions. She urged the LCWR to involve Israeli consuls and Rabbi Tanenbaum in programs on Israel. In early 1976 Sister Gillen criticized the Vatican UN delegate for silence on the UN resolution equating Zionism with racism. She also attacked the Vatican's criticism of Israeli retaliation against Palestinians while saying nothing about Palestinian raids on Israel (*RNS*, "Nun scores Vatican UN Delegate for Silence on Zionism Vote," January 12, 1976, box 176; and "Vatican criticized on Zionism Silence," *Washington* Post, January 23, 1976, box 175).

41. The Liaison Bureau helped recruit Professor Telford Taylor for this project. He served as the chief US Prosecutor at the Nuremberg Trials. See Lazin 2005: 59, n.39. He later wrote *Courts of Terror*. In the early 1980s the GNYCSJ also became involved in legal advocacy for Soviet Jewry ((Newsline, newsletter of GNYCS, February 27, 1980, box 301).

42. The large city budget conference of the Council of Jewish Federations and Welfare Funds (CJF) would provide funding.

43. Sister Gillen urged the adoption of Lev Lukianenko, a Lithuanian lawyer, serving a long sentence for his Helsinki human rights activities. David L. Armstrong, Attorney General of Kentucky (Letter, January 20, 1981, box 303, folder 2) wrote her that he was willing to help liberate Soviet lawyers.

44. In a 1982 report (AJC NITFSJ Project budget, n.d., box 302, folder 3), the Task Force discussed a special legal program focusing on injustice of the Soviet legal system.

45. The 1982 report also contained a draft: "In the Supreme Court of the Union of Soviet Socialist Republics Andrei Sakharov Petitioner vs. the Procurator General Respondent Petition for habeas corpus." In May of 1983, the Decalogue Society of Lawyers, gave Sister Gillen its annual award for "tireless efforts on behalf of human rights and the cause of Soviet Jewry." (Minutes of meeting of the NILTFHR of February 17, 1983, box 301). The award had been given previously to Eleanor Roosevelt, President Harry S. Truman, and Albert Einstein. Also, see "St Conrad's Community, Melvindale," May 1983 (box 301).

46. The Decalogue Society of Lawyers of Chicago is a legal fraternity for lawyers of the Jewish faith established in 1934 in Chicago. See, http://legal-dictionary.thefreedictionary.com/Decalogue+Society+of+Lawyers . Accessed, June 1, 2016). The Christian Legal Society (CLS) is an American non-profit, non-denominational organization of Christian lawyers, judges, law professors, and law students "committed to acting justly, loving mercy, and walking humbly with God (Micah 6:8). Founded in 1961, CLS defends the religious liberties of all Americans in the legislatures and the courts and serves those most in need in our society through Christian Legal Aid." (https://www.christianlegalsociety.org, accessed March 21, 2018). The Catholic League for Religious and Civil Rights is an American Catholic anti-defamation and civil rights organization. Founded in 1973 the Catholic League for Religious and Civil Rights is an anti-defamation and civil rights organization (https://www.catholicleague.org).

International Conferences and the Interreligious Legal Task Force on Human 167
Rights

47. Ralph Ruebner reported on the Sakharov *writ* and Robert Jacobs on the Blaustein Sakharov award. Lynn Buzzard proposed that either Arthur Goldberg or Leon Jaworsky present the Sakharov writ of *habeas corpus* in Moscow. The first executive meeting was held on July 19, 1982 at the AJC offices in Chicago (AJC Memo, Ralph Ruebner and Harriet Bogard to Exec Comm. of NILTFHR, July 23, 1982, Spertus, box 86, folder 8, corr. 1979–82). According to the By-Laws of August 9, 1982 (Ibid.) and NITFSJ information sheet C 1982 (box 301), "by-laws of the National Interreligious Legal Task Force for Human Rights" eligible for membership were the American Jewish Congress, the AJC, the ADL, the Catholic League for Religious and Civil Rights, the CLS, the Chicago Conference on Soviet Jewry, the Decalogue Society of Lawyers, and any other organization concerned with human rights. Individuals at large could join if they were approved by a three-fourths vote of the executive.

48. Other members were Bertram Meyers of the Decalogue Society, Ralph Ruebner of John Marshall Law School, and Lynn Buzzard of CLS. Representative John Edward Porter (R-IL) placed a copy in the *Congressional Record* (Letter, Rep. John Edward Porter to Sister Ann Gillen, May 24, 1982, box 302, folder 2). He also requested from the State Department that her letter to Warren Zimmerman be delivered in a diplomatic pouch.

49. In a letter to Alan Wynn on March 28, 1985, (Spertus, box 107) Sister Gillen regretted not being able to attend the Fifth International Sakharov meeting in London.

50. On the program were Professor Anthony D'Amato of Northwestern Law School, Professor Cherif Bassiouni of DePaul Law School, Michael Posner of the Lawyers Committee for International Human Rights, and Meg Donovan of the United States CSCE. The NITFSJ became an affiliated member of the NILTFHR.

51. The most notable "victim" was John Demjanjuk, accused of being the guard "Ivan the Terrible" at the Treblinka death camp in Poland during WWII.

52. Sister Gillen sent Rabbi Rudin several articles about Soviet falsification of evidence in denaturalization cases in the US and Canada of Eastern Europeans accused of collaboration with Nazis in WWII. In a *Chicago Tribune* article ("Ex KGB Spy Testifies in Kairys "Nazi Trial," June 24, 1982), Robert Estad reported that the KGB engaged in propaganda against Latvian émigré communities in the late 1960s. A second article was a reprint from *Ukrainian Weekly* of June 13, 1982 "Ukrainians, Balts form new group to monitor denaturalization cases" (NITFSJ's project on Holocaust Education and Reconciliation run by Sister Erst in Sister Gillen's office circulated this).

53. The letter was written sometime between 1983 and 1984. She argued that the "USSR is today the ultimate source of terrorism, a real enemy of Israel responsible for orchestrating anti-Semitism as anti-Zionism through the UN." Abram served as NCSJ president from 1983 to 1988. While President of the AJC in the 1960s, Abram headed the US delegation to the UN Commission on Human Rights. There he criticized the anti-Semitic publication of the Ukrainian Communist Party Trophim Kichko's *Judaism without Embellishment*. The Soviets withdrew the book (See Lazin 2005:27 and n.41, p. 59).

54. She cited Ukrainian Jewish efforts in US to bring about mutual understanding and respect. She mentioned an AJC project on "white-ethnics."

55. In a note to Rita Hauser (November 19, 1985, box 301, folder 8) she complained about legal problems causing so "much tension and divisiveness among Jewish and Eastern European groups at present . . . these current problems may have made intergroup cooperation far more difficult. I hope not, of course, but at present the problem looms larger than any possible solution." Earlier on July 1, 1982 (box 302, folder 3) Sister Gillen sent Rabbi Rudin a joint statement issued by the United Ukrainian Organizations of Cleveland and the Jewish Federation of Cleveland which addressed the issue of Ukrainian collaboration with the Nazi atrocities against Jews in the Ukrainian and Stalin's planned famine in the Ukraine in the 1930's. Both sides demanded "appropriate legal action against all who participate in acts of genocide and crimes against humanity." Both sides hoped to continue the dialogue between them.They emphasized that the Russians would not succeed in turning Jews against Ukrainians.

168 Chapter 7

56. AJC staff met with Sister Gillen, Sister Traxler, and Professor LaCocque to plan the conference. Initially they chose to hold it in Chicago, but by the fall of 1981 decided to move it to Washington, D.C.

57. They failed to get Vice President George Bush to speak at the event (Memo, Rabbi A. Jim Rudin to Hyman Bookbinder. July 1, 1982, box 302, folder 4).

58. In a form note (about 10th anniversary, n.d., box 302, folder 4)) Rabbi Rudin and Sister Gillen argued that Jewish emigration rates declined by ninety percent and added that Christians too were caught in "this unjust emigration limbo." While mentioning four hundred thousand Jews wanting to emigrate they also noted that " . . . fifty thousand Pentecostals have signed their names to statements for emigration."

59. Reverend Dr. Tommy Watson of the First Baptist Church in Perrine, FL turned down Rabbi Rudin's earlier invitation to give the invocation (Letters, Rabbi Jim Rudin to Tommy Watson, July 29, 1982, and Tommy Watson to Rabbi Rudin, August 3, 1982, box 302, folder 4).

60. Sister Traxler was to present the award but was unable to attend. She noted that Hubbard had been president of the board of NCCIJ when it established the Task Force and that he was the first to champion the idea.

61. These included Legal and Professional Groups led by Bertram Myers, the Decalogue Society, and the NILTFHR; Religious and Academic Groups led by Reverend John Radano, Seton Hall University; Women's Groups led by Sister Ann May Dooley of Niagara University. Ralph Ruebner of the NILTFHR participated on a panel (NILTFHR Minutes, September 30, 1982, Spertus, box 86, folder 3, corr. 1979–1982).

62. Representative Barney Frank (D-MA) arranged the luncheon but did not attend.

63. Senator Robert Dole (R-KS) and Representative Millicent Fenwick (R-NJ) may have spoken (Charles A. Wood, "Human Rights Situation "dismal" in Soviet Union, says Dole, " *Catholic News Service*, September 14, 1982, box 302 folder 3). Dole served as co-chair of CSCE (Letter, Rabbi A. James Rudin to Mr. Gerald Fitzgerald, RNS, September 20, 1982, box 302, folder 3).

64. After leaving Congress in 1981, Robert Drinan, SJ, joined the faculty of the Georgetown University Law Center (Schroth 2011, 317).

65. It closed: "I the Lord have called you in righteousness. I have grasped you by the hand, I have formed you and set you as a covenant for the people, a light for the nations. To open the eyes of the blind, to bring prisoners out from confinement. And from the dungeon those who live in darkness" (Isaiah 42: 6–7).

66. She may have sent out notes of her own. They are not in the files of the AJC. He and not Sister Gillen had sent out most of the invitations to people speaking at the Conference. At the time, he served as Executive Chair of the Task Force.

67. The AJC approved Rabbi Rudin's request to fund Sister Gillen's participation. Rabbi Rudin and Sister Gillen urged Task Force supporters to attend (box 302 folder 1).

68. The latter would be led by Irwin Cotler of Canada, D. Jacobi of France, and M. Azbel of Israel (Ibid). Karlikow noted that an effort would be made to contact the NCC, local Anglican leaders, and representatives of mainline churches.

69. Israel Miller was an American Orthodox Rabbi, past president of the Rabbinical Council of America, and Conference of Presidents of Major American Jewish Organizations, and active in advocacy for Soviet Jewry (https://www.nytimes.com/2002/03/23/nyregion/rabbi-israel-miller-83-aided-holocaust-survivors.html , accessed June 5, 2018).

70. They spoke with each other at a January 13 meeting hosted by the NCSJ to plan the interreligious program for the Jerusalem Conference (Memo, Rabbi Rudin to Rabbi Tanenbaum, January 14, 1983). Attending were Jerry Goodman and Myrna Sheinbaum of NCSJ, Abe Bayer of NJCRAC, Sarah Frankel of the Israeli Consulate (and Liaison Bureau), Rabbi Balfour Brickner (CCAR) and Rabbi Israel Miller. The group agreed to a pre-conference interreligious consultation in Jerusalem on March 15. Representative Robert Drinan, SJ, would chair the first panel with Father Marcel DuBois of Hebrew University, and a leader of the Dutch Protestant Community, speaking on

"The Meaning of the Soviet Jewry Movement for Christians." The second part of the Conference would consist of "action" responses from Sister Gillen and a British Methodist Bishop. After the sessions, the Christian delegation would be received by Israeli President Navon at his residence.

71. A March 17 plenary session ("window dressing" event) would have Episcopal Bishop Paul Moore of New York and the Apostolic Delegate in Jerusalem Archbishop Carew reading "an Appeal from the Christian Conscience." Myrna Sheinbaum of the NCSJ, in a letter to Sara Frankel, (with a copy to Sister Gillen, February 16, 1983, box 301, folder 2) listed expected potential "Christian" participants from the US: Three clergy from Allentown, Reverend Charles James Parr, RC Diocese of Patterson NJ, Sister Rose Thering, Father Robert Drinan, Reverend John Steinbruck, Sister Anna Marie Erst, and Sister Ann Gillen. On the copy in AJC files, the names of Sister Gloria Coleman and Franklin Littell are added in ink. In a NILTFHR memo of April 4, 1983, Sister Gillen stated that she attended Brussels III with thirteen Christians, including a French priest and a minister from Costa Rica (Spertus, box 86, folder 3).

72. They referred to it as the "Call to Christian Conscience." Sister Gillen shared a draft with Sister Gloria Coleman who made changes (Letter, Sister Gloria Coleman to Rabbi Rudin, February 25, 1983, box 301 folder 11).

73. "A call from Jerusalem to all people of conscience," March 1983 (box 301).

74. It ended: "Long for day when vision of Psalmist will prevail for entire world."

> "Kindness and truth shall meet, Justice and peace shall kiss, Truth shall spring out to the earth And justice shall look down from heaven" (Psalm 85) ". . . we call upon all people of conscience in every land to join us in this great endeavor, a continuation of the call given long ago to the Prophet Isaiah, to "open the eyes of the blind, to bring prisoners out from confinement, and from the dungeon, those who live in darkness" (Isaiah 42.7).
> A note with the "Call" asked for it to be signed after the line "I support 'A Call from Jerusalem to all people of Conscience' and returned to Sister Gillen.

75. The Task Force (*The Task*, week ending January 14, 1983, box 301) urged its followers to register. In February 1983, the NCSJ reported that three hundred and fifty people had registered with others coming *via* B'nai B'rith International (Memo, Ted Mann, Chair NCSJ, February 22, 1983, box 301, folder SJ82-83). He cited the noteworthy response of the AJC, the GNYCSJ, and the Soviet Jewry Council of Jewish CRC of Greater Philadelphia. The Christian Embassy participated in Brussels III. In the early 1980s, several American Evangelical groups established a Christian Embassy in Jerusalem in response to the refusal of most governments to recognize Jerusalem as the capital of Israel (https://int.icej.org , Accessed, August 9, 2016). "During the Easter of 1981 the Christian Embassy organized demonstrations around the world in support of imprisoned Soviet Jews and Prisoners of Zion . . . marched to the Russian compound and 'nailed' their protest to the closed doors of the Russian Orthodox church . . . {in Jerusalem} "(https://int.icej.org (last visited August 9, 2016). Around the time of Brussels III, they sponsored a press conference in Jerusalem as the first event of Christian Embassy project "Mordecai Outcry" in support of Soviet Jews. Attending were Senators David Boren (D-OK), Charles Grassley (R-IA); Representatives Jack Kemp (R-NY), Chris Smith (R-NJ), and Steve Bartlett (R-TX); and two Soviet Jews, Mikail Marenko and Avigdor Eskin. The US Congressional Representatives disassociated themselves from comments by Mikail Marenko, which were sharply critical of United States government policy. Jerry Goodman of the NCSJ disapproved of their anti-Soviet stance (Letter, Mark Levin to Jerry Goodman re "Soviet Jewry Press Conference . . . ," March 18, 1983, box 301). The Christian Embassy participated in Soviet Jewry events in Seattle and Atlanta and probably in other cities ("Seattle Area Christians in rally . . . . Free Soviet Jewry." *Jewish Transcript*. April 14, 1983, box 301, folder "Soviet Jewry 1982–83). See below note 6, chapter 8, November 1, 1983 program in Seattle with Sister Gillen, Max Kampelman, and George S. Weigel. Co-sponsors in-

cluded the Christian Embassy for Israel-Seattle Consulate and others. Also see Note of Rabbi Ilene Schneider, Director of Jewish Education at Atlanta JCRC, October 24, 1983, box 301, file 2).

76. Veil noted that as Israel was seeking justice for Soviet Jewry, she urged Israel to "do justice to the Palestinian people."

77. Among the notable speakers were Governor Thomas Kean (R–NJ), former Congressman Robert Drinan; Newman Flanagan, president of the National Association of American District Attorneys; Professor Inga Fischer-Hjalmars, vice-president of the Royal Swedish Academy of Science; American Nobel Laureate Paul Flory; Avital Shcharansky; and Israeli political leaders Abba Eban, Shimon Peres, and former Prime Minister Menachem Begin.

78. He said he would never forget Shcharansky, Ida Nudel, Vladimir Slepak, and Dr. Alexander Lerner. He had never seen "such faith, hope and love."

79. He recounted of the efforts of the Task Force to send delegations to the Helsinki follow-up conferences in Belgrade and Madrid, the establishment of local Task forces involving Jews and Christians in over twenty cities, and getting statements from prominent clergy for Shcharansky and others. He cited activities of the NCAN on behalf of Shcharansky and noted that Muhlenberg College, a Lutheran institution, would offer honorary degree in absentia to refusenik Alexander Paritsky.

80. "As guilt becomes clearer in our consciences we shrink from its revelations. We want first to deny it. But when we can no longer deny our guilt we turn to God — to ask for forgiveness — and then do restitution."

81. "Inspirations and divine graces are coming to Christians in America and around the world. The God of Israel is speaking to them, reminding them of their sins and their guilt. He is teaching them about the dreams and visions of Zionism."

82. Professor Freedman (Ibid.) noted that a "general conclusion to emerge from the conference was that a greater effort should be made to include non-Jews in the Soviet Jewry movement." The Conference established an international human rights advocacy center "inter-Amicus" to be based in Canada to provide legal defense for all Soviet Jewish prisoners of conscience. In an addendum to Freedman's memo listing specific suggestions to aid Soviet Jewry," number eighteen instructed readers to involve non-Jews in Soviet Jewry activities "to a degree."

EIGHT

Continuity and Change in the Mid-1980s — An Alliance with Evangelical Protestants

In 1983, Rabbi Alan Mittleman joined the staff of the IAD, now headed by Rabbi Jim Rudin. Rabbi Mittleman supervised Sister Gillen and the Task Force. He and Sister Gillen led a Task Force mission to the Soviet Union in January 1986. Professor Tom Bird joined them (Form letter, Sister Ann Gillen to friends, April 1986, box 300; and Memo, Rabbi Alan Mittleman to Rabbi Jim Rudin re "Proposed . . . Mission to the USSR." November 19, 1985, box 300).[1] They visited Minsk, Kiev, and Moscow from January 5–18, where they met with Jewish and Christian activists. In Moscow, they visited the residences of Alexander Lerner and Viktor and Irina Brailovsky, refusenik scientists who had spent five years in exile and were still denied exit visas. In Kiev, they visited several churches that had become museums, the baptismal site of Prince Vladimir, and Babi Yar at the Dnieper River (Form letter, Ann Gillen, April 1986).[2] They learned that the "Russian Orthodox Church has swallowed up the Ukrainian Orthodox Church and the Ukrainian Catholic Church exists only in secret" (Ibid.). In Moscow, at the All Union Office of Visa and Registration (OVIR), Mittleman made a personal appeal for his cousin and her family to leave the USSR ("NITFSJ program report for 1986," n.d. and Alan Mittleman, email message to the author, March 23, 2015).[3]

Sister Gillen remained active through 1985, speaking at Jewish Community Centers, churches, temples, universities, women's groups, and human rights forums around the country. In December 1982, she spoke in San Antonio at the 12th Annual Women's Plea "Light their Way to Freedom" event at St Mark's Episcopal Church (Flyer, "Light their way to freedom," December 12, 1982, box 302, folder 2).[4] A few days later in a press interview in Arizona, she spoke about anti-Semitism and the plight of persecuted Jews and Christians in Russia (Richard Lessner, "Nun Leads drive to aid Soviet Jews," the *Arizona Republic*, December 15, 1982, reissued by NITFSJ, box 302, folder 2). In February 1983, she spoke before the Soviet Jewry Committee and the Interfaith Committee of the JCC of Metropolitan Boston (Letter, Dr. Judith Wolf and Rabbi Rothman to Sister Ann Gillen, February 2, 1983, box 301). In April, she participated in the NCSJ Annual Leadership Conference in Washington, D.C. (Letter, Theodore Mann and Jerry Goodman to Sister Ann Gillen, May 10, 1983, box 301). In May, she gave a public lecture about "The Plight of Soviet Jews" at a Dallas Interfaith "Pleas for Soviet Jewry" conference (Flyer, "Dallas 'Interfaith Pleas . . . '", May 13, 1983).[5] In August 1983, Sister Gillen urged US Senators to sign a letter to President Yuri Andropov repudiating the allegations of a newly formed anti-Zionist Committee (Letter, Ann Gillen to Senators, August 11, 1983, box 301).

In several appearances in Seattle in November 1983, Sister Gillen spoke on human rights in the Soviet Union. At one talk, she focused on "the tragic assaults on freedom of conscience and the denial of basic human rights in the Soviet Union" (Memo, Barbara, Hurst, Director of AJC Seattle to members, October 21, 1983, box 301). At another event, she joined Ambassador Max Kampelman and Professor George Weigel Jr. of St. Thomas the Apostle Seminary School of Theology on a panel about "Human Rights in the Soviet Union and Eastern Europe: Strategies for Action in the Post Jackson Era."[6] While in Seattle, she worked to reestablish the defunct local Seattle task force ("Report on the Activities of the Task Force: Year 1983," n.d., box 301). Later in the month, she participated in an interfaith forum with Rabbi Rudin, organized by Sister Gloria Coleman in Philadelphia.[7] In December, Sister Gillen joined Representative Richard Gephardt (D-MO) for a program in St. Louis (Memo, Sister Ann Gillen to Rabbi Rudin, December 20, 1983, Spertus, box 48) and Flyer, "Human Rights Week," December 7, 1983 (box 301).[8] In February 1984, she spoke at a program on Soviet Jewry at Temple Bet El Zedek in Indianapolis.

In February 1984, she testified before a Congressional hearing in Chicago about the Soviet Union's disruption of mail service. She explained the special concern of the Task Force "for Jews and Christian seeking the right to leave and/or the right to live as Jews and Christians in the USSR and Eastern Europe" ("Testimony before the US Congress Subcommittee on Postal Operations: Special Field Hearing" in Chicago, February 3, 1984, box 301, folder 7). Also, early in 1984, she worked on the issue of human rights violations and prisoners of conscience in the Soviet Union and in Eastern Europe with Eastern European ethnic groups in Canada (Ibid.).[9] Sister Gillen visited Detroit for a program for the Human Rights Plea on December 2, 1984, sponsored by the NCCJ (Memo, Sister Gillen to Rabbis Rudin and Mittleman, December 3, 1984, box 301, folder 7).[10]

She continued speaking and traveling in 1985. In late January, she participated in activities of the Union of Councils and the NCSJ in New York City and Washington, D.C. (Report on NITFSJ 1985, n.d., box 301, folder 8). On March 31, she spoke before the Women's Pleas for Soviet Jews in Omaha, Nebraska. In a prior phone interview, she focused on the suppression of Hebrew in the USSR, as well as the oppression of Christians and Jews in the Ukraine, the Baltic States, and Poland (Carol Katzman, "Women's Pleas . . . features Sister . . . Gillen," *Jewish Press of Omaha NE*, March 22, 1985, box 301, folder 8; and "Report on NITFSJ 1985).[11]

In early April, Sister Gillen met in Baltimore with the Trinitarians who were reorganizing and studying the Task Force as a modern model to emulate (Letter, Sister Ann Gillen to David Ziomek, Keston College USA, December 30, 1985, Spertus, box 111, folder 1).[12] In May, she gave the keynote at an AJC-sponsored interfaith meeting honoring a leader in the perfume industry (NITFSJ 1985).[13]

In early July 1985, Sister Gillen traveled to Dublin to attend a meeting of the International Council of Christians and Jews. She went on to participate in the International Religious Liberty Working Group on Law in London from July 24–26. While in England she attended a charismatic prayer group in Blackpool.

After attending a meeting at the State Department in early September 1985, she participated in a gathering of Polish and Jewish Americans in Philadelphia.[14] On September 15, she visited Sacred Heart University in Bridgeport, Connecticut, where she established an interfaith group with the NCSJ and University President Thomas Melady (NITFSJ 1985). She was back in Washington, D.C. in October to attend meetings of the NCSJ. In November, she participated in a religious liberation dialogue at Haverford College, and held meetings in Washington, D.C. and Annapolis with representatives of Keston College. In December, she returned to NYC for AJC meetings. On December 10, she participated in a Women's Plea program in Montgomery, Alabama. On December 15, she gave a keynote address at the Women's Plea for Soviet Jewry at Temple Beth El in Springfield, Massachusetts. She told participants that while it was too late to help the Jews who died in the Holocaust, it was not too late to help "Soviet Jews and other Russians who are being denied the right to emigrate and other basic rights." She insisted that denial of rights was "not limited to the Jewish community" and described the experience of two Catholic priests who were sentenced to ten years in prison in Lithuania. She added: "Nor is the drive for the right to emigrate simply a matter of concern for Jews" (Peggy Weber "Chicago Sister urges help for Soviet Jews," *Catholic Observer,* Springfield MA, January 3, 1986, SHCJ archives). Three days later, she spoke in West Palm Beach, Florida, and then in South Bend, Indiana.

PROJECT LIFELINE

Around 1983, the Task Force announced the launch of Project Lifeline. The program was similar to Project Co-Adoption, in which Jewish synagogues and Christian churches adopted prisoners of conscience of the other faith. In the new program, the Task Force asked participating individuals to write to prisoners of conscience. Later, participating newspapers encouraged their readers to write letters of support to prisoners of conscience (Jewish and Christian) whose pictures and bios they published. A goal of the program was to educate non-Jews about religious persecution in the Soviet Union (Report on the Activities of the Task Force-Year 1983," n.d., box 301).[15]

After Sister Gillen talked about the project in Miami, Bill Gralnick, then director of the AJC's Southeast Office, approached the *St. Petersburg Evening Independent* about participating (Bill Gralnick, phone interview by author, November 4, 2014).[16] Sister Gillen supplied him with the information that he needed for the project.[17] Individual readers and organizations responded warmly. The paper ran the Lifeline Letters again in December 1984 (Kay Masters, "Life of Valeri Marchenko ends with a tragic finale," *St. Petersburg Evening Independent,* December 12, 1984). The AJC publicized the project as a joint AJC-Task Force project.[18]

A few years later, Sister Ann Gillen became angry with Gralnick when a local newspaper running Project Lifeline urged readers to respond to the paper and or the NCCJ. It made no mention of the Task Force. (Letter, Sister Ann Gillen to William A. Gralnick, February 20, 1987, box 1, folder, some correspondence). She implied that he had hijacked the program from the Task Force.

TASK FORCE HEARINGS

In May 1983, the AJC announced that the Task Force would hold three seminars on the theme of anti-Semitism in the USSR. The title became "Anti-Semitism, Religious Liberty and Human Rights in the Soviet Union" (Draft, NITFSJ Program Proposal and Budget 1983–1984, May 1983, box 301; and Memo, Rabbi Rudin to Rabbi Tanenbaum, June 22, 1983, box 301). Rabbi Alan Mittleman took charge of the program (Memo, Sister Gillen to Rabbi Mittleman, February 19, 1985, Spertus, box 48). Sister Gillen assisted Rabbi Mittleman, and AJC regional directors cooperated. The Task Force hoped that the conferences would focus on the building of interreligious coalitions to combat Soviet anti-Semitism and put the issue of Soviet Jewry on the agendas of Christian churches (Report on . . . Task Force Year 1983, box 301).[19] Significantly, all three conferences dealt with the persecution of Jews and Christians in the Soviet Union.

The first conference was held in a Philadelphia synagogue for an audience of interfaith women organized by Sister Gloria Coleman of the Cardinal's Commission on Human Relations and the Philadelphia Interreligious Task Force. Sister Gillen and Rabbi Andrew Baker, the head of the AJC in Washington, D.C., spoke. A second conference took place at Reed College in Oregon on February 26, 1984 titled "Two faces of Soviet reality, anti-Semitism and religious repression" (Letter, Laurie Rogoway, AJC, to Sister Ann Gillen, "Soviet Jewry conference," December 9, 1983).[20] The third conference occurred in October 1984 in Dallas on the theme "The Right to Print, Publish and Write in the USSR," with a focus on cultural deprivation for Soviet Jews and Christians, who were denied access to media and subjected to strong negative propaganda by the media ("NITFSJ Report on Activities," September 10, 1984, box 301).

In 1985, the AJC and the Task Force held a series of public hearings about religious and cultural persecution in the Soviet Union. They wanted to gather data about the repression of Soviet Jews and Christians and to submit their findings at upcoming meetings of the Commission on Security and Cooperation in Europe (CSCE) (Letter, Ginte Damusis to Rabbi Mittleman, December 10, 1986, box 283). Following the meetings in Belgrade and Madrid, "mini" meetings were held on disarmament in Stockholm, on human rights in Ottawa, on cultural links in Budapest, and on human contacts in Bern prior to a scheduled Review Conference in Vienna in November 1986.[21] Again, these hearings dealt with religious persecution in the Soviet Union involving Jews, Christians, and Muslims.

They held the first hearing "Culture and Community: The Struggle for Religious Liberty in the USSR" at Loyola Marymount University in Los Angeles on April 18, 1985. Rabbi Mittleman moderated. He remarked that while during the Holocaust Jews stood alone and the world abandoned them, in the case of Soviet Jewry "one of the main signs of hope is the increased level of cooperation between the Jewish and Christian communities; the increased level of sensitivity to one another's concerns." He explained that the Task Force had sponsored this event "to sensitize Christians to the dire problems of Soviet Jewry and to sensitize the Jewish community to the problems that Catholics, Protestant, and Orthodox face in the Soviet Union. The Task Force is pledged to human rights education as well as activism on behalf of the prisoners of conscience of all faiths in the USSR" (Beverly Beyette, "How they keep the faith behind the Iron Curtain," *Los Angeles Times*, April 25, 1985, box 301, folder 4).[22]

Presenters included Dr. Yuri Yarim-Agaev, an exiled Soviet physicist and member of Moscow Helsinki Monitoring group.[23] He spoke about the persecution of dissidents, the problems of emigration, the exploitation of psychiatry for political purposes, and the violation of international covenants. He insisted: "Nothing has improved since Gorbachev came to power."[24] He urged the United States to be "sober minded about the Soviet Union." Too many Americans were tempted to see Gorbachev as opening a new era, he said. He emphasized the worsening condition of prisoners and the increased use of torture in the Ukraine and Armenia (Memo, Sister Ann Gillen to Rabbi Alan Mittleman, "Recommendations to the CSCE Delegates Attending the Ottawa Human Rights Meeting," April 29, 1985, box 300). He spoke of new waves of repression against Muslims and Jews. He urged protests because the Soviets were sensitive to Western opinion and might let more people leave if they perceived that people in the United States disapproved of their policies (Beyette, April 25, 1985). Ginte Damusis of the Lithuanian Catholic Religious Aid Society spoke about Roman Catholics in the USSR. She cited arrests of priests and the dismantling of Lithuanian Helsinki groups and argued that Ukrainian Catholics wanted to see their church restored (Memo, "Gillen to Mittleman . . . ," April 29, 1985). She reported on the existence of twenty-five hundred underground nuns in a country that had banned all Catholic religious orders. She argued that Catholics suffered religious persecution because they resisted and maintained contact with the Vatican.[25]

In her talk titled "Samizdat Publication: Reporting on Suppression of the Russian Orthodox Church and other religious groups," Olga Stacevich, a member of the Russian Orthodox Church, noted the substantial number of closed churches that had become museums.[26] She spoke about the closure of monasteries where fewer than 1,500 religious people remained (Memo, Gillen to Mittleman . . . April 29, 1985).

The historian Kent Hill of Seattle Pacific University spoke on the "Present Plight of Evangelicals in the Soviet Society." He reported on the 336 known Christian prisoners of conscience, mostly Baptists (Ibid.).[27] He argued that the NCC had done a disservice to Christians in the Soviet Union by "buying the Soviet line" as handed to them by official Soviet church leaders and insisting that the situation would only get worse if protests were made. The truth, Hill said, was that speaking out "protected the dissidents" (Beyette, April 25, 1985).[28] Hill emphasized the problem of indifference among American Christians toward persecution of Christians in the Soviet Union. While many feared a nuclear confrontation, when they heard of the persecution of Christians, they asked if these people were Pentecostal. He wanted to know if Jews ask if a persecuted Jew was reform or conservative?[29]

Ed Robin, vice chair of the NCSJ and chair of the Commission on Soviet Jewry of Jewish Federation Council of Los Angeles, talked about the "Struggle for Jewish Religion and Culture within the Soviet Union." He referred to "the most serious harassment of Soviet Jews since . . . the early 1960s," including the cessation of emigration, escalation of attacks on Hebrew teachers, and an alarming upsurge of anti-Semitism in the media and by the anti-Zionist Committee (Gillen to Mittleman . . . April 29, 1985). He argued that the plight of Jews in the USSR was unique (Beyette, April 25, 1985 and "A public hearing . . ." April 18, 1985).[30]

A second hearing on "Culture and Community: The Struggle for Religious Liberty in the USSR" was held at De Paul University in Chicago on October 3, 1985 (Flyer, "Culture and community . . . October 3, 1985, box 301, folder 9).[31] AJC's Chicago office organized the afternoon meeting. Sister Gillen moderated (Letter, Jonathan Levine to Prof. John Woods, August 20, 1985, box 301, folder 9).[32] She focused her remarks on the persecution of Roman Catholics in Lithuania ("Sister Ann Gillen's comments," October 3, 1985, box 301, folder 9) and Letter, Sister Ann Gillen to Rabbi Rudin, September 3, 1987, Spertus, box 48).[33] She cited various petitions by Catholic priests in Lithuania protesting the injustice toward the Roman Catholic Church, a protest by Father Antana Ylius against slander against Catholics in the *Encyclopedia of Lithuania* of 1981, the pressure on Catholics not to allow their children to attend Christmas celebrations, teachers spying on pupils, the lack of priests, and limits on the numbers of students at seminaries. She argued that a small but sizeable number of priests had been "viciously attacked or murdered by unknown persons." She referred to the current Pope as a refusenik, since he was not allowed to visit his congregation in Lithuania.[34]

Natasha Vins, international representative for the Council of Evangelical Baptist Churches in the Soviet Union, spoke about the incarceration of ministers and believers since 1917 when atheists had come to power and tried to eradicate religion ("Persecution of Evangelical Christian Baptists in the Soviet Union," October 3, 1985, box 301, folder 9). The regime battled against Christians with arrests, trials, and beatings, and took children from religious families. Legislation against religious cults in 1929, she argued, led to the arrest and torture of tens of thousands of Christians. She noted that one hundred and seventy Baptists were in jail or confined in psychiatric hospitals.[35]

The third public hearing, titled "Culture and Community: The Struggle for Religious Liberty in the USSR," took place in Seattle on April 8, 1986. The official sponsor, the Seattle Interreligious Task Force on Religious Freedom issued invitations (Rabbi Anson Laytner, press release, Seattle Interreligious Task Force for Religion Freedom, n.d., box 284).[36] The local AJC office coordinated the event (Letter, Zev Kessler, AJC, to Kent Hill, April 4, 1986, box 300, and Press Release, Greater Seattle Chapter of AJC, April 12, 1986, box 284).[37] In his introduction, Alan Mittleman stated that the purpose of the three hearings was to gather testimony on the persecution of religious believers and communities in the USSR and to raise the level of public awareness about the problem. He believed that the public's appreciation of the problem was low ("Culture and Community: The Struggle for Religious Liberty in the USSR: A public hearing," stenographic minutes by William Macauley RPR CM Court reporter April 8, 1986, box 211, folder 2).

Sister Gillen focused her remarks on Roman Catholics in the Ukraine and Lithuania where the Catholic Church had made great sacrifices "to maintain what small degree of religious freedom is still permitted to it" ("Testimony of Sister Ann Gillen, "Culture and Community . . .").[38] She argued that the Catholic Church in the Ukraine had been "dealt . . . sledgehammer blows during 1939 and 41" when "all monasteries, convents, church schools, publications, charitable institutions and lay work organizations were suppressed." Three seminaries were closed, and church property nationalized, and then on April 11, 1945, the Soviet secret police "arrested the entire hierarchy of that Catholic church, plus hundreds of clergy and lay leaders." Of 3,600 priests and monks, only 216 remained to attend the staged, forced synod, which dissolved the Ukrainian Catholic church. Yet the Roman Catholic religion survived and was now growing thanks to "sacrifices and sufferings of laity as well as clergy." She talked about an active church underground in the Ukraine (Ibid.).

She described a comparable situation in Lithuania where almost 75 percent of the population remained Catholic. The number of diocese priests had fallen from 1,271 to 693, many of whom were elderly and infirm and should have retired. 144 parishes had no priest. While, there were once four seminaries with 470 students, there was now only one with 104 students that produced twelve ordained priests each year. She recounted protests by priests (Ibid.).[39] In closing, she reiterated a common Task Force theme that "Roman Catholics throughout the world have failed to really respond to the plight of the Catholics in the Soviet Union." She was happy to learn that American Catholic Bishops had "called for support to be given to the campaign for the restoration of the Church in Klaipeda" (Ibid.).[40]

Irene Barinoff, a member of Seattle's Russian Orthodox community, testified that religious oppression was a problem for the 60 percent of Russians who were Orthodox. Church leaders were forced to toe the party line at home and abroad (John McCoy P-I Reporter "Soviets try to stifle religion, speakers at hearings charge," April 12, 1986, http://www.seattlepi.com/archives/1986/860180597.asp , accessed November 30, 2010).[41]

Kent Hill, in his testimony, emphasized that "unregistered" evangelical churches incurred special persecution." In his opinion, churches "registered" with the state mean the end of Evangelism. He argued that Soviet Christians preferred religious freedom in the USSR and did not want to emigrate like the Jews.[42]

The AJC published a report containing excerpts from the testimony at the three hearings. In his introduction, Rabbi Mittleman addressed the long-running issue of the proper concerns of the Task Force ("Report of Task Force Activities for 1985," box 301, folder 8) and Rabbi Alan Mittleman (ed.), ("The Struggle for Religious Survival in the Soviet Union; Testimony Presented at Hearings of the NITFSJ, 1985–1986," box 283).[43] He argued that the NITFSJ was principally concerned with the dangerous situation of Soviet Jews, which could be solved by allowing the Jews to leave. The solution to the problems of Christians and others required a liberalization of Soviet society, if not regime change. He insisted that the "Jewish struggle for culture, community, and religious liberty is a struggle to leave and to achieve those blessing elsewhere. The struggle of the various Christian and Muslim groups involves the achievement of their goals at home." He believed that the Task Force remained committed to securing Soviet Jews their right to emigrate (Mittleman, "The Struggle ... ").[44]

He went on to say that the Task Force was part of the international human rights movement. For the first-time, the treatment of people was "no longer normatively considered to be a purely internal matter. . . . States . . . have obligated themselves to a human international order grounded on human rights" through adoption of various UN covenants and the Helsinki Final Act. In democratic states human rights activists bring "violators to account before the bar of international public opinion and seek to influence their own government's policies toward the offending states." He concluded that the Task Force places the problem of Soviet Jewry:

> within the broad context of human rights activism . . . it finds the linkage of Jewish with other Soviet minority concerns a natural one. As an interreligious, human rights organization. . . . Task Force works . . . to raise public awareness of Soviet human rights violations . . . with respect to Soviet Jews, and to build coalitions of conscience with other like-minded groups.

THE PHILADELPHIA CONFERENCE

Around this time, Sister Gloria Coleman of the Cardinal's Commission on Human Relations approached Lorraine B. Meyer at AJC's office in Philadelphia about co-sponsoring a conference on religion in the Soviet Union (Memo, Lorraine Meyer to Alan Mittleman re: "Proposal for a conference on religion in the Soviet Union," February 18, 1986, box 283). She wanted to focus on the persecution of Soviet Jews and members of the Russian Orthodox, Ukrainian, Greek Orthodox, Lithuanian, Protestant, and Muslim faiths. Each group would have a member of local clergy present its concerns.[45] The Conference, to be held on September 25, would end with a "call to action" for specific ways the groups could continue to work together in Philadelphia (Minutes, "Planning committee . . . on religion in the Soviet Union," February 26, 1986, box 283) and (Letter, Lorraine Meyer to Richard L. Weiner, Louis N. Marks, and Rabbi Alan Mittleman, "Planning meeting . . . ," February 27, 1986, box 283).[46]

The conference focused on the deteriorating situation of Jews and Christians in the USSR (Program Brochure, "Religious Persecution in the

USSR, 1986"; AJC [NY], Press Release, "News from AJC, September 25, 1986, box 283; and "Planning committee . . . corrected list," n.d., box 283).[47] The Reverend Kajatona Sakalauskas, pastor of St. Andrew Roman Catholic Church, gave the invocation and Sister Coleman introduced the program. Ambassador Michael Novak, who had headed the American delegation to the Experts' Meeting on Human Contacts of the CSCE in Bern, gave the keynote address. Professor Bird responded. A panel chaired by Rabbi Mittleman followed. Participants included Ginte Damusis; Dr. Nina Strokata-Karavansky, a former Ukrainian prisoner of conscience and an external representative of the Ukrainian Helsinki monitoring group; Vadim Sheheglov, a Russian Orthodox member and foreign representative of the Christian Community for the Defense of Believers' Rights in USSR; and Joseph Dorfman, a former refusenik. A question and answer session followed, moderated by Terese Gecys of the Philadelphia chapter of the Lithuanian American Community of USA, Inc. Professor Thomas Bird summarized the day's events. The Call to Action was led by Orsysia Hewka of the Ukrainian Human Rights Committee. Rabbi David Wortman, the executive director of the greater Philadelphia Board of Rabbis, gave the benediction (Memo, Rabbi Mittleman to Rabbi Rudin, "Religious persecution . . . " September 26, 1986, box 283).[48]

SISTER ANN GILLEN AND EVANGELICAL ADVOCATES IN THE UNITED STATES

During the 1980s, Sister Gillen found common cause with anti-Soviet Evangelical advocacy groups in the United States. She began a collaboration with Dr. Kent R. Hill, executive director of the Institute on Religion and Democracy in Washington, D.C.[49] In October 1986, Dr. Hill invited her and the Task Force to join an "Ad Hoc Committee for Religious Liberty in the U.S.S.R." The Committee wanted to organize a protest in Washington, D.C. on "the plight of the persecuted religious believers in the Soviet Union" during the anticipated summit between President Ronald Reagan and General Secretary Mikhail Gorbachev. The Committee hoped to organize a "chain of hope" of thousands of Christians and Jews encircling the Soviet Embassy. Initially the Ad Hoc Committee consisted of Christians and Jews working together "on behalf of each other" (Letter Ad Hoc Committee for Religious Liberty in the U.S.S.R. to Sister Ann Gillen, October 1, 1986, Spertus, box 42). Sister Gillen agreed to have the National Interreligious Task Force on Soviet Jewry join the list of sponsors (Letter, Sister Ann Gillen to Dr. Kent Hill, October 21, 1986 [Ibid.]. By February 1987, the Ad Hoc Committee became a coalition of Christian groups that planned to hold a major "event in support of Christians in the USSR on May 1st." As a sponsor, the Task Force was listed as "National Interreligious Task Force" minus the words "on Soviet Jewry" (Letter,

Sister Ann Gillen to Rabbi Mittleman, February 23, 1987, Spertus, box 48).[50]

Kent Hill became chair of the steering committee of the Coalition for Solidarity with Christians in the USSR, which organized the May 1 rally (Memorandum, Kent Hill to Steering Committee-Coalition for Solidarity with Christians in the USSR, C March 1987, Spertus, box 42, file DC corr. 1985–1988).[51] The Coalition hoped to raise the nation's consciousness about the difficulties facing Christians in the Soviet Union, to update the public on recent releases of Christian prisoners and pending cases, and to suggest ways people could help individual prisoners. The demonstration took place on May 1, 1987, with three hundred people in attendance. In his talk, Dr. Kent Hill pledged not to rest "until 'glasnost' also means liberty to all who are captive, and an end to discrimination against all religious believers." Senator Pete Wilson (R-CA) urged that the USSR "Let 'glasnost' be practiced, not simply preached." Congressman Frank Wolf (R-VA) representing the Congressional Human Rights Caucus, pledged to work with the Coalition "until all the prisoners are released and free." Ginte Damusis encouraged participants in the demonstration to write to Christian prisoners of conscience, which numbered two hundred and thirty at the time. "Not only will letters help sustain the prisoners but they will also put the jailers on notice that Christians around the globe are concerned about them."[52] In closing, Dr. Hill praised the impressive record of Jewish groups who were working on behalf of Soviet Jews: "We have not thus far been adequate advocates for our brothers and sisters in Christ. Our national and international ecumenical organizations have far too often been shamefully silent about the suffering of those persecuted for their religious beliefs. And many of the rest of us have remained apathetic, divided and parochial in our concerns."[53]

By allowing the Task Force to become a sponsor of an organization and an event representing Christian groups in America concerned specifically about the religious persecution of Christians in the Soviet Union, Sister Gillen had aligned herself—and the Task Force—more closely with their cause. She had accepted inclusion of the Task Force as a sponsor without the inclusion of "for Soviet Jewry" in its name.

After the event, Dr. Kent Hill encouraged the Coalition for Solidarity with Christians in the USSR to reorganize and expand its activities. Sister Gillen and the Task Force did not remain on the on the steering committee (See Minutes of the Steering Committee Meeting, Coalition for Solidarity . . ., October 23, 1987 [Ibid.].[54] The Coalition planned to hold a joint press conference with the Congressional Human Rights Caucus during the Gorbachev-Regan summit in Washington in December 1987. Speakers would include several members of Congress, Dr. Kent Hill, Ginte Damusis, and Dr. Ernest Gordon, head of the Evangelical advocacy group CREED (see chapter 6 above) (Memo, Kent Hill to Members of the

Coalition for Solidarity with Christians in the USSR, November 19, 1987 [Ibid.].

THE NATIONAL COUNCIL OF CHURCHES IN CHRIST (NCC) AND THE SOVIET UNION

After its founding, the Task Force had close ties with the NCC. The NCC cooperated with and supported Task Force programs and activities. Rabbi James Rudin of the IAD often represented the Task Force in its dealings with the NCC. At times, the interests of the NCC and Task Force vis a vis the Soviet Union did not overlap. The NCC had excellent ties with the Russian Orthodox Church, which was recognized by the Soviet government. The Russian Orthodox Church and its members enjoyed a degree of religious freedom within the confines of an environment of strict regulation and restrictions on religious organizations and their members. In contrast, un-recognized Christian churches faced greater harassment, persecution, and suppression. The NCC believed that close ties with the Russian Orthodox Church helped it to influence favorably matters related to religion for Christians and others in the Soviet Union. To end this special relationship, the NCC argued, would add to the isolation and greater persecution of Soviet Christians and others.

In late November 1982, the AJC learned of a planned NCC delegation visit to Moscow and Leningrad as guests of the Russian Orthodox Church (Memo, Rabbi Rudin to Rabbi Tanenbaum, December 3, 1982, box 301). The NCC delegation included its President, Bishop James Armstrong of Indianapolis, and his wife; Dr. Bruce Rigdon of Chicago's McCormick Theological Seminary, a specialist in American Soviet relations; and its general secretary, Dr. Claire Randall.

Bishop Armstrong agreed to be briefed by Abe Bayer of the NJCRAC about the condition of Soviet Jewry, prior to his departure.[55] At the urging of the AJC, Sister Gillen had several productive conversations with Claire Randall before she flew to the Soviet Union.[56] Bayer and Sister Gillen found the NCC leaders "most receptive to the briefings they received . . . they promised to press the cause of Soviet Jewry during their trip." Both were aware of the "Billy Graham episode" earlier in the year and vowed that they would not repeat his mistakes ("Letter, Sister Ann Gillen to Fred Smith," July 19, 1983, Spertus, box 109).[57] During their trip to the USSR, the NCC delegation discussed plans for increased cooperation with leaders of the Russian Orthodox Church and the All Union Council of Evangelical Christian Baptists. They met with government officials, attended Orthodox services, and visited two Baptist churches and synagogues in Moscow and Leningrad. They sought an interview with a Jewish refusenik but were "unable to see him." They also visited two Russian Orthodox seminaries and made a pastoral visit to the Pentecostals who had taken refuge in the American Embassy. Bishop Armstrong remarked that everyone he met was interested in peace as the Soviet Union had twenty million casualties in WWII.

Upon the delegation's return from the Soviet Union, the NCC announced plans for an intensified program of joint actions in peacemaking and other issues with churches in the USSR.[58] There would be exchange visits of large delegations from both countries.[59]

The NCC arranged for several hundred clergy to visit the Soviet Union in June 1984 (Memo, Jerry Goodman to Rabbi Rudin, December 20, 1983, box 301, file 2). After being contacted by Rabbi Jim Rudin, Professor Bruce Rigdon agreed to have the NITFSJ be part of the team to brief the group before their trip (Letter, Rabbi Rudin to Prof Bruce Rigdon, January 6, 1984, box 301, folder 10).[60]

The NCC Ecumenical Seminar in the Soviet Union, with 266 American church leaders, toured fourteen cities from June 8–21, 1984.[61] The group included Protestants, Orthodox, and Roman Catholics, with twice as many laypersons as clergy. On the final day, the delegation attended a reception given by Patriarch Pimen, the head of the Russian Orthodox Church (News of the News Service of United Methodist Church, June 26, 1984, box 301, file 10).[62]

The visit caused controversy in the United States. The *NYT* reported that the American church leaders praised ". . . the status of religion in the Soviet Union and condemnation of the American role in the arms race. . . . Leaders of the group, . . . also voiced irritation that the harmony of their visit had been marred when two demonstrators, demanding religious freedom, held up banners during a Baptist church service" (Seth Mydans, "US Visitors Praise the Status of Religion in Soviet," *NYT*, June 21, 1984).[63] According to the news report, the tour pointed to a "growing role assigned to the controlled churches in representing the Soviet Union to the outside world." Russian church figures spoke out on themes such as deploying American missiles in Western Europe "that echo their government's foreign policy positions."

Charles Perry, provost of the Washington National Cathedral told the *NYT*: "I was impressed by the numbers of people, the numbers of children, the numbers of middle class people attending church services . . ." (Ibid.).[64] John Lindner, program director of the American Soviet Church Relations Office of NCC, added: "We discovered vital religious communities wherever we went, from Tallinn to Tashkent." These remarks reflected the perceptions of many on previous officially sponsored tours who were surprised to find officially recognized churches crowded. Seth Mydans of the *New York Times* added: "Several of the group's statements echoed those of Reverend Billy Graham, who aroused controversy on visit here two years ago, when he said 'It would seem to me that in the churches I visited—and there are thousands of them—services can go on freely.'" The newspaper story noted, however, that several members of the delegation, who asked that their names not be used, criticized their leaders "for what they said was an insufficiently forceful presentation of human rights issues. . . . 'The message we got right from the start was not to do anything that might insult our Soviet hosts' said one."

During a visit to a church two demonstrators unfurled banners that read: "This is a persecuted church."[65] They were hustled from the hall. One visitor reported a scuffle with six-to-eight people on the floor. At a news conference Bruce Rigdon, the tour's leader, said that the demonstrators " . . . were asked to leave and they were conducted out by members of the congregation. We believe they are free. I understand that in the United States a situation like this would have been handled by the police." The *Wall Street Journal* (*"Deferential . . ."*) reported that the two women with banners began to speak to the group but that "this brief conversation was cut off by . . . John Lindner, and by Intourist guides."

Tracey Early of *RNS/Catholic News Service* provided a somewhat more nuanced report on the Catholic participants in the mission ("Mixed Impressions follow Ecumenical Tour of Soviet Churches." June 26, 1984, box 301, folder 10). Benedictine Sister Mary Catherine Shambour said that, based on contacts with individuals, the situation of religion was the best it had been in their lifetime.[66] One priest told her, she said, that the religious situation was "excellent." But Mary Frances Flood, a youth minister at St. Edward's Church in Bloomington, Minnesota, said that, based on her contact with a priest in another city, it would be misleading to take "excellent" as a description of the religious situation in general. Among the Catholic members of the delegation was Ginte Damusis. In contrast to her 1979 trip to Leningrad and Lithuania, she did not sense the watchful eye of the secret police on this visit. She reported, however, that the authorities did not want them to contact Catholics in Lithuania, who were strongly resistant to state control.[67]

In a letter to the *NYT* Rabbi Rudin expressed disbelief at Rigdon's dismissal of the protest ("Draft letter to *NYT* on trip to USSR, June 21, 1984, box 301, folder 10).[68] He added that "unregistered groups of believers, such as Jehovah's Witnesses, Seventh Day Adventists, Pentecostals, some Baptists . . . are harassed at schools, dismissed from work and imprisoned for violating Soviet Laws on religion." He added that Soviet law prohibited religious believers from engaging in charitable activities and from "providing religious training to children" and religious believers who did not operate under the strict constraints imposed by the state could be charged "under the vague category 'anti-state activity' or 'anti-Soviet slander.'"[69]

Rabbi Rudin warned that the false picture of the status of religion in the USSR presented by the leaders of the NCC tour would lead to harsher treatment of believers. Soviet officials would gain the confidence to attack believers with impunity and Western acquiescence.[70] Rabbi Rudin argued: "turning a blind eye to repression of religious believers in USSR betrays moral obligation that people of faith in the West have toward activists in the USSR who courageously bear the burden of maintaining religious faith under repressive Soviet rule."

On return to the United States, Reverend Rigdon held a press conference in NYC on June 22nd (The News Service of the United Methodist Church offices in Dayton, Nashville NY and DC. "News," June 26, 1984, box 301, folder 10) and (News Release Wrap up. Release #8481 "US Church Members seek Trust During visit to Soviet Union." June 29, 1984, box 301, folder 10).[71] In response to a question about what he learned on the trip, Father Berzonsky replied that in contrast to an earlier visit in 1975, he found younger people attending church and much younger clergy in Odessa and Kiev. In conversations with both church and government officials, Americans had asked about the policy regarding those being detained by Soviet government. He reported that the delegation had not visited any unregistered churches.[72]

Reverend John Lindner reported that Reverend Alan Geyer, another trip participant, had raised questions during the trip about Andrei Sakharov, "a scientist allegedly being detained by the government."[73] Georgi Arbatov, head of the Institute for United States and Canada Studies in Moscow, told the delegation that the Sakharov affair was an internal matter, but that Sakharov and his wife were both well and were both eating.

Both Rigdon and Lindner reported that there remained "many problems for Soviet Christians and other religious groups . . . there are too few churches . . . also a shortage of Bibles and other religious literature" (Weekly News Rap, June 29, 1984 [#8481], "US Church Members seek trust during visit to Soviet Union," box 301, folder 10).[74] Reverend Robert White said there was a tendency of church officials to refrain from criticizing government policy.

The highlight of the trip for Rigdon was celebrating Pentecost Sunday at Zagorsk where they were joined by thousands of Soviet "brothers and sisters in Christ. . . . Our time was not spent in political discussion but in worship and fellowship with each other, talking about our life and the unity in Christ given to us and the whole world."

Lindner said that "peacemaking and human rights questions were principle issues on the agenda of discussions," giving Soviet officials a clear message of the importance of "justice and rights for all peoples. . . . The ability of Soviet Christians to exercise freedom in the exercise of their religious will have a direct correlation to our ability to succeed in our joint peacemaking efforts as Christians."

Ludmilla Thorne of *Freedom Appeals* asked if the group had made an effort "to also visit unregistered churches." Rigdon answered that they had, and that they attempted to obtain information about them and had raised questions throughout their travels in the USSR. He recalled the incident at a Baptist church service in Moscow where three or four people stood up with signs in English referring to the two hundred pastors and lay Christians who were in prison. The protestors were asked to leave by a member of the congregation. Everyone present, he argued, saw this as a disturbance. "My impression is that a shock went through the entire congregation—Americans and Soviets alike. I can tell you that we were, and we continue to be, deeply troubled by that event."[75]

Rigdon argued that Americans would "probably be better prepared to listen to, and enter into some dialogue with, fellow believers in the Soviet Union than with the Soviet population or its government. . . ." If people valued the attempts by Christians to change the climate and ethos of relations with USSR, he said, then it was important to understand that ". . . the degree to which Christians and others in the Soviet Union are fully free to exercise everything . . . in their faith is in correlation to the degree of trust . . . established in the United States . . . so long as there are cases of violation of human rights, oppression of religious groups . . . this makes much more difficult the task of communication between those groups and hence for the good which they can do overall" ("Weekly news wrap up contents," June 29, 1984, July 1984, box 301, folder 10).

At the press conference, Rabbi Rudin criticized the leaders of the tour (News release wrap up. Release #8481 "Us . . . " June 29, 1984, box 301, folder 10).

> "I think you all missed a rare opportunity to be prophetic witnesses. . . . I was also stunned to hear that you did not visit one unregistered church . . . some of us in the Jewish and Christian world . . . find it unacceptable that two-hundred and sixty people of goodwill did not make a prophetic witness for unregistered churches, for Soviet Jews. . . . Did you speak out for Pentecostals who were arrested? Did you speak out for {Alexander} Smachenko who is a registered Baptist who was sentenced to three or four years in Moscow . . . for 'distributing Christian literature'? Did you 'speak out for Anatoly Shcharansky?' 'Were you a prophetic witness?'"[76]

Lindner responded to the criticism that ". . . an enormous percentage of our time was devoted to dialogue about human rights issues. . . . Every time we met with a major Soviet official, or key political official . . . we took an opportunity to send some very clear message about our concern for individuals, for Soviet policy and the credibility and justice that needs to be established" ("Weekly News Wrap Up").

Rabbi Rudin answered: "You said you went there for "Christian unity . . . but the [*New York*] *Times* story yesterday had an enormous amount of anti-American comment made by members of the delegation. Also, a reference in the story to a group who didn't want their names used . . . who felt that the leaders of the group of the NCC had not been vigorous enough in pressing for human rights . . . ?" (Ibid.).[77]

TRENDS

In the 1980s, while remaining committed to advocating for Soviet Jewry, Sister Gillen and the Task Force focused more and more on human rights. This led to greater cooperation with those advocating for the human rights and religious freedom for persecuted Christians in the Soviet Union. Her initiative to establish the Legal Task Force in Chicago is an important example of this shift. The Legal Task Force placed the issue of Soviet Jewry in a more universal context of violations of human rights.

In Washington, D.C., Sister Gillen found evangelical Protestant allies in her advocacy for Soviet Jewry and human rights for all in the Soviet Union. She initially joined a coalition of evangelical Protestants in their struggle for the rights of Jews and Christians in the Soviet Union. When the ad hoc group led by Kent Hill decided to focus only on persecuted Christians, whom he felt were neglected by rights activists in the US, who advocated almost exclusively for Soviet Jews, Sister Gillen joined with him and his coalition. In doing so, she altered temporarily the name of the Task Force, dropping "For Soviet Jewry." In effect, she led an organization which focused at the time exclusively on persecuted Christians in the Soviet Union.

In New York City, Rabbi Rudin challenged the mainline Protestant NCC's cooperation with the Russian Orthodox Church. Leaders of the NCC believed that working with Soviet Orthodox officials enabled them to influence and preserve the human rights of religious groups in the Soviet Union. Rabbi Rudin, however, argued that preserving ties with the state controlled Orthodox Church, led to the NCC's neglect of human rights issues involving Jews and Christians affiliated with unregistered churches. Importantly, Rabbi Rudin of the AJC and not Sister Gillen of the Task Force dealt with the mainline Protestant NCC on the matter of Soviet Jewry. Similarly, in many of the Task Force hearings and subsequent publications, AJC's IAD played the dominant role; Rabbi Mittleman, rather than Sister Gillen, explained Task Force policy on advocacy for Soviet Jewry and human rights.

NOTES

1. Professor Lynn Buzzard, former director of the Christian Legal Society (CLS) planned to go on the mission but dropped out before departure. SHCJ covered Mittleman's expenses (Letter, Rabbi Mittleman to Sr. Patricia Phillips, February 7, 1986, SHCJ archives, Ann Gillen papers). Sister Gillen's honoraria covered her expenses and the AJC covered the expenses of Professor Bird who was invited to participate because of his fluency in Russian. Rabbi Mittleman worked at the AJC until 1988 (Rabbi Alan Mittleman, interview by author, NYC, March 18, 2014).

2. On September 29 and 30, 1941, German soldiers killed 33,771 Jews at the Babi Yar ravine on the outskirts of Kiev (www.holocaustresearchproject.org/einsatz/babiyar.html, accessed August 11, 2016).

3. Within a month or two, his relatives left the country. The three-person Task Force delegation returned via Rome where they met with Vatican officials (Letter, Rabbi Mittleman to Rev. Msgr. William F. Murphy, Pontifical Commission for Justice and Peace, Vatican, December 17, 1985. Also, see Mittleman "Sabbath in Minsk" *AJC Journal*, Spring 1986, pp. 7,8, Spertus, box 48).

4. Jewish temples, Christian Churches, the NCCJ, B'nai B'rith Women, local chapters of Hadassah, Church Women United, Jewish federation, and the CRC sponsored the event titled: "A celebration of our American Human Rights and an appeal for Soviet Jews and Christians" (box 302, folder 2).

5. Hillel, Catholic Center, and others sponsored the program. The follow-up publicity mentioned only the plight of Soviet Jewry. In a talk at Temple Rodfei Zedek in Chicago on October 16, 1983 (box 175), Sister Gillen explained that Soviet Jewry was her full-time work. She focused almost entirely on Soviet Jewry and Israel. She hoped Christians would stand with Israel.

6. "The World Without War Council" in cooperation with the AJC, the ADL and others sponsored.

7. Sister Gloria Coleman was with the Office for Ecumenical and Interreligious Affairs of the Archdiocese of Philadelphia. Interfaith Women's Committee in cooperation with Church Women United sponsored the event (box 301).

8. She spoke on the future of Soviet Jewry and Gephardt reported on his recent visit to Moscow. Prior to the event, she spoke in Houston at an interfaith meeting, rally and march. She and Congressman Bill Archer (R-TX) spoke about the plight of Jews and Christians in the USSR (Flyer, "Human Rights Day Rally and March, December 4, 1983, box 301). In Houston, she also talked with Union of Council people and others about a possible local Task Force (Memo, Sister Gillen to Rabbis Rudin and Mittleman, December 3, 1984, box 301, folder 7).

9. In Toronto, she helped three ethnic groups co-sponsor a Tribute to the Prisoners of Conscience. With Maureen Giroux and Genya Intrator, she helped initiate a local Task Force in Ottawa—the Ottawa Helsinki Human Rights Meeting. A local Ukrainian group and the Toronto Task Force offered to share an office. Sister Gillen asked the AJC for funding for the Ottawa project.

10. She spoke on three separate radio programs and gave two newspaper interviews. Ray Sharfman had a reception at his home for her and Reverend Jim Lyons. Jim suggested they raise thirty thousand dollars for a national speaking tour for Ann and himself.

11. The Omaha Section of National Council of Jewish Women, Jewish Federation of Omaha, ADL/CRC, and the Union of Councils sponsored the event.

12. Organized in 1198 and again in the 14th century, the Order of the Most Holy Trinity and of Captives ransomed Christian captives. They held an interfaith protest-vigil in New Orleans in December where a rabbi spoke about Soviet Jewry ("Report NITFSJ"). In Toronto in 1985, Sister Gillen met with the Sisters of Sion. Originally organized to evangelize Jews, after the Second Vatican Council, they promoted dialogue and fought anti-Semitism through research and conferences.

13. Andrew Goodman, national Chair of the AJC Appeal for Human Relations, wrote Sister Gillen (May 28, 1985 (box 301, folder 8), "I understand that your eloquent remarks and your insights into our mutual concerns for human rights and civil liberties had a positive impact on a most attentive audience." She also participated in a symposium on Soviet Jewry in Stamford, CT (Flyer, "What Hope for Soviet Jews," May 14, 1985, box 301, folder 8). In addition to the local AJC chapter, the Catholic-Jewish relations Committee of Fairfield County, the local Soviet Jewry Task Force, and the CRC of Stamford co-sponsored. In May she participated in an additional AJC event and attended meetings of the Tananbaum Foundation in NYC.

14. In May 1983, she wrote ("Interreligious Concern for Soviet Jewry" in *Interfaith Perspectives*, IV, no.1) that the Philadelphia Task Force encouraged diverse religious and ethnic groups to cooperate, to forego discussions about the problems of the past, and to get on with the work of solving present problems.

15. Sister Gillen hoped that it might also lead to the creation of more local interreligious task forces to assist persecuted Jews and Christians in the Soviet Union. The Task Force hoped to expand the project in 1984 throughout the United States. In early 1984, the editor of the *Toronto Sun* contacted Sister Gillen about the project. She visited and helped organize an Interreligious Task Force for Human Rights and Religious Freedom, which later co-sponsored the Lifeline Letters on a continuing basis.

16. In a letter of December 15, 1983 Mr. Michael L. Richardson, Associate Editor of the *St. Petersburg Evening Independent*, to William S. Trosten (AJC) (Box 301, folder 1) thanked W. Gralnick for his inspiration leading to the paper's running the Lifeline Project for the month of December 1983.

17. The American representative from Keston College supplied her with the information about prisoners of conscience (Letter, Sister Gillen to David Ziomek, December 30, 1985, Spertus, box 111, folder 1, some corr.). The paper published the names, pictures, addresses, and a brief description of the "crimes" of Jewish and Christian prisoners of conscience.

18. A 1983 Task Force report noted that AJC's William Gralnick helped translate its Lifeline of Letters writing project into a wider program involving newspapers. Also see Memo, Gralnick to Gillen, January 5, 1984 (box 301, folder 3). The Task Force (Memo, NITFSJ, "Our View . . ." January 6, 1984, box 301, folder 3) reported stories about Lifeline that the Associated Press ran in papers around the country and United States Information Agency (USIA) published worldwide. Gralnick wrote Reverend Tom Trulson (January 13, 1984, box 301, folder 3) about adapting Lifeline Letters for the airways. A "Report of Task Force Activities," C 1984 (Spertus, box 48, folder Rudin) reported about a Lifeline Letter Project in Toronto with the *Sun* and the diocesan Catholic paper. Sister Gillen also worked to enroll the Catholic press in Austria (Letter, Sister Gillen to Mr. Erich Leitenberger, December 1, 1986, Spertus, box 32). The *Seattle Times* launched its Lifeline Letters project during Passover and Easter (April 7, 1985). It also carried an article by Helen M. Jackson about her late husband's concern about the UN Declaration of Human Rights and the right to emigrate and a short article about the persecution of Christian churches in the Soviet Union. Another article described the AJC's Seattle interreligious task force on religious freedom in the Soviet Union. Finally, it ran an article by Sister Gillen on "Christians and Jews in the USSR." It reissued the Lifeline Letters in April 1986 ("Issues Lifeline Letters." April 6, 1986, box 301, folder 8). It also printed articles by David Ziomek of Keston College USA, "Keep writing if there's no reply"; "Religious prisoners one year later: where and how are they now?" and a piece by Rabbi Alan Mittleman on religious survival in the USSR among Christians and Jews (Letter, Ann Gillen to NITFSJ friends, "Chicago Catholic's extension of our Life Line Projects," April 1986, box 300).

19. The Task Force planned an interreligious trip to the USSR by key Christian leaders. They also worked on a filmstrip about Soviet Jews, anti-Semitism, and human rights with a Teacher's Guide and audiotape to be used in church schools and youth groups.

20. The local AJC organized it and the Ecumenical Ministries of Oregon co-sponsored. Rogoway proposed having Senator Mark Hatfield (R-OR) speak regardless of his stand on Israel. She also proposed an evangelical activist Professor Kent Hill, who had helped the Siberian Seven at the American Embassy, and Reverend Douglas Huneke of San Francisco. Other participants included Sister Ann Gillen and Prof Fruim Yurevich, a Soviet Jewish émigré at the University of Oregon.

21. They submitted the findings to the CSCE meeting on Human Rights in Ottawa, Canada (May 7–June 17, 1985) which Sister Gillen attended. The NITFSJ urged the Ottawa Conference to bring relief to all who struggled in the USSR to retain or regain their cultural and religious rights. It called for the release of all prisoners of conscience of every religious and ethnic group. It urged respect for religious liberty and the right to emigration. The State Department invited Sister Gillen to a preparatory meeting for the Vienna Conference held in Chicago on June 11, 1986 (Letter, Amb. Warren Zimmermann to Ann Gillen, May 21, 1986, Spertus, box 32). The Task Force submitted the

testimony to delegations at the Vienna CSCE Review Conference, November 3, 1986 (Ibid.). The Canadian Inter-Religious Task Force for human rights and religious freedom in the Soviet Union and Soviet dominated areas representing Christians and Jews in Canada also submitted a report. Sister Gillen served on their board of directors (Ibid.). In an interview in June 3, 1991 (JCC Women's Auxiliary Oral History Project, Spertus, (box 1, folder 3) Sister Gillen commented "in all the Helsinki negotiations, the process became this: The State Department holds a meeting in advance and invites our non-governmental organization leaders to come and to strategize and make suggestions. It became kind of a working partnership as the result of Jimmy Carter's administration's introduction of a department on Human Rights in the State Department. . . . "

22. The event took place on Holocaust Memorial Day, April 25, 1985. The panel hearing testimony included Rev. Eugene Boutilier, the Southern California Ecumenical Council; Hon. Barvin Braude, member, Los Angeles City Council (LACC); Rabbi Paul Dubin, the Board of Rabbis of Southern California; Rev. Canon Harold G. Hultgren, Canon Missioner of Ecumenical and Interreligious Affairs, the Episcopal Diocese of Los Angeles; Rev. Truman Northrup, the Pacific Southwest Conference of Church of Brethren (retired); Hon. Edmund D. Edelman, Board of Supervisors, County of Los Angeles; Father James N. Loughran, SJ President of Loyola Marymount University; and Hon. Joy Picus, LACC. Later Edelman asked Sister Gillen (Letter, April 29, 1985, box 300) to change the name of Task Force to include "Christians in the title "since both Jews and Christians being persecuted . . . .this would allow you to broaden your base of support or alternatively set up a new organization to show that Christians and Jews are working together on religious freedom in the Soviet Union."

23. Exiled in 1980, he moved to the United States. In 1979 he conducted a study of a secret Soviet court system.

24. Mikhail Gorbachev became Secretary of the Communist Party on March 11, 1985 (Lazin 2005: 17, n.29).

25. She referred to priests sentenced to labor camps and exile. One received a ten-year sentence for organizing a Christmas party for parish youth and another three years for leading a procession to a cemetery. She also noted that Father Bronius Laurinayicius, who served on the local Helsinki Monitoring Commission, was "pushed to his death under an oncoming truck" in 1981. She added that the election of a Polish Pope had excited many Roman Catholics in the Soviet Union.

26. Born in the Soviet Union, she grew up in Shanghai. She edited the *Samizdat Bulletin*, which translated and distributed extracts from the *Free Press* in the USSR. Zev Kessler (Letter to Alan Mittleman, May 14, 1985, box 301, folder 9) reported that she said that there was only a slight difference between the USSR and Nazi Germany regarding the suppression of the Russian Orthodox Church. She displayed letters and pictures " . . . of mass murder of clergy and destruction of churches."

27. Sister Ann Gillen noted that the Reverend Georgi Vins reported on forty-seven Baptists in prison.

28. The Reverend Eugene Boutilier criticized Hill: "I do not agree at all: if the inference is that the Council does not consider religious oppression a serious concern . . . its slanderous to say so." Hill replied that the NCC "has failed to support effectively Christians behind the Iron Curtain." He said that while some registered Soviet clergy were "dedicated Christians who have made a tactical decision to accommodate" others were "in fact working for the KGB." Boutilier replied that he did not question that there "are severe . . . restrictive anti-religious activities" in the USSR but he was convinced that "an important, valid strategy is to develop a working relationship with the existing above-ground religious institutions, help them get concessions, help them grow and survive."

29. In a letter to Mittleman, (May 14, 1985, box 300) Kessler cited an article by Kit Glaser "Hearings show little hope for Soviet Jews" in *Heritage* which quoted Dr. Hill on Gorbachev: "the most dangerous because his urbanity and his attractive wife will impress the West." Vilis Varsbergs of the Latvian Evangelical Lutheran Church in America may have spoken on "Oppression of Churches in Soviet Occupied Latvia."

30. He referred to historic anti-Semitism, the absence of seminaries to train Rabbis, and the "accelerating" efforts to eradicate Jewish culture. Although Jews were considered a national group, the Soviets refused to recognize Hebrew as the Jewish language.

31. The panel hearing testimony included Pastor O.R. Harbuziuk, First Ukrainian Baptist Church and President, All Ukrainian Baptist Fellowship; Marcia Lazar, President of AJC Chicago; Dr. André LaCocque; Rev. Danile Montalbano, the Office of Human Relations and Ecumenicism, Archdiocese of Chicago; Rep. John Porter, (R-IL); and Sister Margaret Traxler. The program stated that "The NITFSJ unites men and women of many backgrounds for the rights of Jews and Christians in the USSR. . . . Founded in 1972, the Task Force monitors the condition of Soviet Prisoners of Conscience and builds interreligious support to press for the rights guaranteed by the Helsinki Accords."

32. There were five program coordinators, including Sister Ann Gillen; Midwest AJC director Jonathan Levine, Rabbi Alan Mittleman; Rabbi James Rudin; and Richard Zelin, Midwest AJC.

33. She mentioned the Task Force's multi-year campaign for the return of the Church in Klaipeda.

34. He had been denied permission to travel to Lithuania "for the jubilee of the nation's patron St. Casmir." She quoted Professor Albert Boiter, a Soviet law expert who argued that the Soviets progressively "eroded the substance of laws regarding religious "freedom, thus denying freedom of conscience."

35. Between 1929 and 1940, Soviet authorities arrested more than twenty-five thousand Evangelical Christian Baptist ministers. Twenty-two thousand died and almost all churches were either closed or destroyed. She called for protest as the Soviet Union was sensitive to Western voices. Other speakers included Professor Vasyl Markus of Loyola University Chicago on the status of Ukrainian Catholics; and Richard Rice of the Chicago Conference on Soviet Jewry on "The Struggle for Jewish Religion and Culture within the Soviet Union." Professor John Woods of the University of Chicago talked about "Muslims in the Soviet Union" and Vis Varsbergs, President of the Latvian Evangelical Lutheran Church in America spoke about "The Predicament of the Latvian Church in the Soviet Union."

36. Organized in 1984, it included the AJC, the ADL, the Roman Catholic Diocese, the Church Council of Greater Seattle; the CRC of the Jewish Federation, the International Christian Embassy of Israel, the NCCJ, the Seattle Action for Soviet Jewry, and the World Without War Council. A press release from the Greater Seattle AJC, April 12, 1986 (box 284) had the Task Force being set up in 1983 and included Bridges for Peace.

37. Rabbi Simon Benzaquen of Seattle; Reverend David C. Bloom, Church Council of Greater Seattle; Margaret Casey of the Washington State Catholic Conference; Priscilla Collins, King Broadcasting; State Senator Jim McDermott; Rosanne Royer of the Tashkent Seattle Sister City Committee; and Judge Charles Z Smith, University of Washington School of Law heard testimony. A lunchtime ceremony honored the *Seattle Times* on the first anniversary of its "Lifeline Letters" series. One hundred people attended the Seattle event. Organizers hoped to report testimony presented at human rights meetings in Bern, Switzerland. Sister Gillen had spent two weeks at the meetings in Bern ("Dear family and friends," C April 1986, SHJC archives). The Soviets refused to allow entry to observers, so Sister Gillen attended an alternative conference of the NGO International Resistance. Anatoly Shchaaransky, recently freed from a Soviet jail, and Yelena Bonner, wife of Sakharov, also attended (*The Economist*. "The long, slow, muddy road from Helsinki." May 31, 1986, box 283).

38. On her recent visit to the Soviet Union, she searched for Catholic churches. In Minsk, the Intourist guide pointed out a large cinnamon factory that had formerly been a Roman Catholic church. In Kiev, the large imposing planetarium was also a former Roman Catholic cathedral.

39. In 1974, 102 priests sent a protest petition to Constantine Tcherenko calling attention to injustices suffered by the faithful. Another petition in 1981 protested the slander in the *Soviet Encyclopedia* and pressure not to have children attend Christmas celebrations.

40. One hundred thousand Lithuanians signed a petition to have the church restored. Ukrainian Bishop Steven Sulick of Philadelphia called for "meaningful protests against the persecution of Catholics in the Soviet Union . . . urging Catholics to follow the example of world Jewish community leaders in developing such demonstrations and asking the synod to develop meaningful protests against the denial of religious freedom." Sister Gillen had written to all American Catholic Bishops about the Lithuanian church but received only one reply. Later, Cardinal Joseph Bernadin responded and wrote an article in *Chicago Catholic,* which was later published in *Catholic Digest.*

41. For example, authorities jailed a priest who organized an independent Christian Committee for Defense of Believers' rights in 1976.

42. Judy Balint, Chairwoman of the Seattle Action for Soviet Jewry, said that 400,000 of the two million Russian Jews had requested permits to leave. She pointed out that Jews were the only one of one hundred and nineteen ethnic minorities in the Soviet Union with no schools or museums.

43. The report included the testimony of Yuri Yarim-Agaev (on Helsinki monitoring groups), Richard Rice (Soviet Jewry), Judy Balint (Soviet Jewry), Sister Ann Gillen (Roman Catholics), Ginte Damusis (Roman Catholicism in Lithuania), Vasyl Markus (the Ukrainian situation), Irene Barinoff (Russian Orthodox Church), Kent Hill (Evangelicals), Natalia Vins ("Unregistered" Evangelical Christian Baptists), Vilis Varsbergs (Oppression of Churches in Soviet Occupied Latvia) and Henry L. Mason III (Muslims).

44. He argued that the Task Force set up by the AJC and the CCIRJ was the child of quiet revolutions that occurred after 1945. He cited the change in Christian-Jewish relations, from persecution and confrontation, to cooperation and respect. Under Sister Gillen, hundreds of thousands of people during the previous fourteen years "witnessed committed Christians working on behalf of persecuted Jews." In keeping with its ecumenical origins "it is natural for the Task Force to cooperate with other groups concerned for their communities in the Soviet Union." He cited Shcharansky's report on the solidarity of religious activists in labor and prison camps.

45. At a meeting on January 29, 1986, the two women discussed a possible panel of witnesses, including former prisoners of conscience from the Jewish, Protestant, and Ukrainian Catholic communities, a presentation by Morris Abram or Rabbi Marc Tanenbaum, and recruitment of local clergy for a steering committee. Lorraine Meyer commented that a significant goal for the AJC was to move the key players into a vehicle for other kinds of interreligious and intergroup activity in the city. She urged Rabbi Mittleman to join the steering committee.

46. Sister Gloria Coleman, Lorraine B. Meyer, and urban ministry representatives from the Ukrainian and Lithuanian communities invited various religious groups to co-sponsor. At the April 22, 1986 meeting they discussed inviting Representative Lawrence Coughlin (R-PA), Michael Bociurkiw, Peter Vins, and Professor Thomas Bird. Organizers wanted to attract teachers in religious schools, representatives of the various denominations, professional organizations, Congressional representatives, local academicians, seminarians, clergy, and ethnic leaders. They wanted to put the testimony into the *Congressional Record*. They wanted Congressman Bill Gray III (D-PA) to give brief remarks at lunch. First choice for keynote was Reverend Georgi Vins. Rabbi Marc Tanenbaum was a possible speaker on Soviet Jewry and Dr. Kent Hill on the Baptists.

47. Sponsors were the AJC Philadelphia Chapter, the Cardinal's Commission on Human Relations and Urban Ministry, the Lithuanian American Community of USA Inc. Philadelphia chapter, NITFSJ, and the Ukrainian Human Rights Committee Philadelphia.

48. Rabbi Mittleman wrote that it cost the AJC about $500 to secure Michael Novak as speaker and "co-sponsorship for the NITFSJ." Mayor Wilson Goode issued a proclamation declaring September 25 a day of awareness of religious persecution. Approximately one hundred and forty (mostly Christians) attended. Novak spoke too long and with a Question and Answer session allowed by Sister Coleman the program was off by fifty minutes. The Ukrainian speaker could not be understood (poor English) but was powerful as had been in the Gulag, while the Jewish speaker was poorly organized and failed to make points "about the distinctive nature of the Jewish situation." "Despite these shortcomings, I believe that the memory of this conference will last a long time in Philadelphia and nurture good relations between the Jewish community and ethnic groups involved in the conference." He thought it would have been a more rigorous program had Lorraine Meyer not moved to Cincinnati in the final weeks before the event.

49. He spoke at the Task Force hearings in Los Angeles in 1985 and in Seattle in 1986.

50. Sister Gillen informed Rabbi Mittleman that she would be attending the planning meeting for the May 1 demonstration. Sponsors included the National Association of Evangelicals (NAE), The Institute of Religion and Democracy (IRD), Christian Response International, Lithuanian Catholic Religious Aid, Keston College USA, the Christian Defense of Orthodox Prisoners, Prison Fellowship, the Ukrainian Congress, Freedom House, Inc., and "ourselves listed as National Interreligious Task Force."

51. The updated steering committee included the All-Ukrainian Evangelical Baptist Fellowship, the Christian Rescue Effort for the Emancipation of Dissidents (CREED) (Dr. Ernest Gordon), Christian Response International, the Committee for the Defense of Persecuted Orthodox Christians, Concerned Women for America, the Congressional Human Rights Caucus, Freedom House, Inc., The Institute for Religion and Democracy (Kent Hill), Lithuanian Catholic Religious Aid (Ginte Damusis), the NAE, the National Committee to Commemorate the Millennium of Christianity, the National Interreligious Task Force (Sister Ann Gillen), the Slavic Gopal Association, the Ukrainian Congress Committee of America, and a Research Consultant from Keston College USA (Mr. David Ziomek).

52. Former prisoner of conscience, Irina Ratushinskaya, a Russian Orthodox Christian and poet recently released from a Soviet prison, also spoke.

53. Press release, Coalition for Solidarity with Christians in the U.S.S.R., May 1, 1987 (Spertus, Ibid.). Dr. Robert Dugan led a prayer and response. Anita and Peter Deyneko of the Slavic Gospel Association presented representatives of Congress with petitions signed by over forty thousand American Christians requesting "the President and the Congress to take all action necessary to secure the release of all Christians imprisoned in Soviet labor camps." Hill recounted years later that both the Soviet Jewry movement and Sister Gillen inspired him; she often gave him advice as to how to organize and operate (Dr. Kent Hill, phone interview by author, October 30, 2014). *The Task* May 6, 1987 reprinted from *Catholic Review* of Baltimore, Spertus, box 80; *The Task* 1986, "Glasnost? Nyet, Christian groups rallies for religious freedom in USSR" by Liz Schevtchuk. *The Task* week ending December 18, 1987 (SHCJ archives) had a note on page one from Sister Gillen reporting that the Center for Democracy asked her to write to Soviets who were defending human rights activists and independent media and their staff to protect them from unlawful persecution. "Since the cause of Soviet Jewry and that of religious and cultural freedom are all part of human rights, I hope that you will join me in sending such letters to Gorbachev." It reprinted from the NITFSJ: "Rally for Soviet Christians set for May 1, 1987 in D.C. run by the Coalition of Solidarity with Christians in the USSR included both Christian ministries and human rights organizations."

54. The Society of St. Stephen and the Trinitarians joined the steering committee.

55. Bayer would brief him at the Louisville airport and then fly with him to New York. Rabbi Rudin ((Memo, to Rabbi Tanenbaum, December 3, 1982, box 301), who probably arranged the briefing, suggested to NJCRAC that they advise NCC officials

to raise the issue of Soviet Jewry with their hosts and with members of the Soviet government. He urged a meeting with Shcharansky's mother, Ida Milgrom, (and to urge Soviets to allow her to visit her son "a pastoral and humanitarian concern") and with the Christian Pentecostal families in the American Embassy in Moscow. He advised against meeting with other Soviet Jewish refuseniks.

56. Sister Gillen gave her the address and phone number of Ida Milgrom. Rabbi Tanenbaum also spoke with her before the flight.

57. Armstrong told Bayer that he would not be "manipulated by the Soviet authorities." During his May 1982 visit to the Soviet Union, Graham defended "the Soviet record on religious rights" and suggested "that the Russian Orthodox Church is freer under communism than the Church of England is under the Queen. . . . " See Jim Gallagher "How the Soviets duped Billy Graham" *Chicago Tribune* May 16, 1982 (archives.Chicagotribune.com/1982/05/16//page/23/article/how-the-soviet-duped-billy-graham, accessed August 10, 2016). Sister Gillen wrote Fred Smith (Montreal, July 19, 1983, Ibid.) that she sent Billy Graham briefing materials before the trip "Either he did not read these, or he opted for his 'diplomatic' approach in the hope that he would be able to return to preach the gospel to the millions—which is his life work. I believe he did a great disservice to the many martyrs who lived and are living by deep-rooted religious and holy, human values."

58. According to Dr. Randall, the new exchange aimed to reflect on "pressing theological and spiritual concerns, develop practical means to support each other's peacemaking efforts . . . and recommendations for the future." Due to strained relations between their countries, Dr. Randall noted that it was ". . . important for the churches to keep their contacts vital, for the church knows no boundaries" (*RNS*, "NCC plans joint us USSR peace effort," December 17, 1982, box 301).

59. The first visit to the USSR was scheduled for late 1984, with a reciprocal visit a year later. This would be the fourth in a series of exchanges started in 1956.

60. The NCC scheduled briefings for June 4–6 in NYC. They focused on the status of Soviet Jews and Christians, as well as on issues of human rights and religious liberty. The Task Force also provided background materials for all participants. Jerry Goodman of the NCSJ probably conducted the Task Force briefing.

61. The delegation broke into ten smaller groups to attend Russian Orthodox, Roman Catholic, Lutheran Pentecostal, and Baptist services. The previous month, nineteen religious leaders from the Soviet Union had visited eight American cities.

62. The Russian Orthodox Church had forty to fifty million adherents in a total population of 270 million.

63. The Soviet press quoted visitors supporting world peace and praising Soviet freedom of religion. One member, Alan Geyer, Director of the Center for Theology and Public Policy in Washington, D.C., blamed his own government for the failure to resume arms negotiations talks. The *Wall Street Journal*, ("Deferential Reverends," June 27, 1984, box 301, folder 10) reported that the delegation did not meet with the unofficial Soviet peace group whose leaders had been arrested. When a member of the tour asked about them, he was told "that the organization doesn't exist, and besides, its members are Jewish refuseniks seeking an emigration dodge."

64. Perry added: "I understand that the numbers of churches are very small."

65. During Reverend Billy Graham's last visit, a demonstrator was led away by security guards after he held up a banner referring to Baptists imprisoned for worshipping at unregistered churches. Graham said he "had not noticed the incident."

66. She had lived and taught English in the USSR on three separate occasions.

67. She felt that government restraints on attending a seminary were more severe on Catholics than on the Orthodox. She joined the trip because she had been unable to get a visa on her own. She had been blacklisted following a short visit in 1979. On this trip, she signed up to visit Lithuania. But when she arrived in the USSR, it was cancelled. She demanded that the head of the tour denounce what had happened with the protest by unrecognized Baptists. She believed that the NCC dragged its feet in order

not to rock the boat with Soviet authorities. She herself asked pointed questions of Soviet authorities (Ginte Damusis, phone interview by author, December 16, 2016).

68. "By distorting the actual condition of religious believers in the USSR, these statements threaten to undermine progress toward greater religious freedom in the Soviet Union sought by people of conscience in the West and in the USSR, itself."

69. He then gave examples of Pentecostals being sentenced to three and four years respectively for "infringing the person and rights of citizens under the guise of performing religious rituals" and a Baptist youth sentenced to three years in labor camps for distributing Christian literature. Finally, he noted the decline of Russian Orthodox churches from 54,000 in 1914 to 7,000 in 1984 and the absence of rabbinical seminaries in the USSR. Jews who studied Hebrew were subject to imprisonment.

70. In a note of praise to Rudin (June 24, 1984, box 301, folder 10) for his letter to the *NYT*, Sidney Hook suggested that they were wined and dined "having won Rev. Billy Graham over with a bowl of caviar, the Kremlin followed the same technique with others."

71. He held a prior press conference in Moscow on June 20. Six other tour leaders joined him at the NYC press conference: Rev. Julia Allen, Associate Pastor of First Presbyterian Church in Kirkwood MO; Helen Hamilton, Secretary of the National Executive Committee of United Presbyterian Women, Tacoma WA; Rev. John B Lindner who had been on loan from the Program Agency of the Presbyterian Church to the NCC to direct the tour project; Father Vladimir Berzonsky, Pastor of Holy Trinity Orthodox Church of Cleveland; and Rev. Robert White of the Social Witness Reformed Church.

72. In his view, some churches did not register because they claimed there was no basis for it in the New Testament. Others believed registration would compromise the church, and some saw non-registration as a protest against a socialist government.

73. Sakharov and his wife had been on a hunger strike since May 2, demanding that she be allowed to leave the country for medical treatment. Geyer had also raised this issue during a Soviet delegation visit to Washington, D.C. in May.

74. Rigdon cited visits to reopened and new churches, doubling the number of theological students in Zagorsk, Leningrad, and Odessa, and the return of the Danielovsky Monastery in Moscow to house the Russian Orthodox Church's HQ. He noted that the Leningrad seminar was moving to larger quarters and that the Odessa seminary was building a new dorm. Lindner had visited a synagogue in Georgia that was filled with people. He noted that the building was in good condition, but the prayer books from 1901 were in tatters.

75. Rigdon was upset that the demonstration disturbed the decorum of the religious service. In a June 26, 1984, editorial, the *Washington Post* stated that *NYT* reported that delegation leaders "voiced irritation that the harmony of their visit had been marred when two demonstrators, demanding religious freedom, held up banners. . . ." Some of Rigdon's group left the church to speak to them. A demonstrator, Vera Zinchenko, remained and talked about her husband in jail. The next morning Rigdon asked the church's pastor, Alexei Bichkov, to explain what happened. Rigdon understood that three or four demonstrators were allowed to leave and go home and were not arrested.

76. An article in the *IHT* (Ari L. Goldman. "U.S. Religious Leaders Assailed for Soviet Visit." *IHT*, June 27, 1984, box 301, folder 10) focused on Rabbi Rudin's assertion that the NCC tour leadership had ". . . missed an enormous opportunity for moral suasion and moral leadership." The author quoted Rigdon that progress on human rights was a secondary purpose of the visit. The primary purpose was "to demonstrate that the unity which God has given the church transcends all boundaries of ideology, nationality and social system and to contribute to the peacemaking programs." Rabbi Rudin felt that it was unacceptable "to contend that human rights were secondary to Christian unity."

77. A *Washington Post* editorial (June 26, 1984) argued: "Still, one could wish that the recent delegation had shown better judgment." It notes that its leaders at the Moscow press conference "ignored the voluminous record of the Soviet State's outlawing and persecution of all independent forms of religious activity."

NINE
Closing the Task Force

By fall 1986, the AJC had reservations about continuing to support the Task Force.[1] Rabbi Mittleman wrote of Sister Gillen and the Task Force:

> Its approach—linking the Jewish cause to general human rights problems and to the violation of religious rights suffered by Christian groups—has always been controversial. Minimally, this broadened concern facilitates a quid pro quo with Christian human rights and religious activists. Maximally, it expresses a commitment to work for fundamental change in the USSR, a commitment which surely goes beyond the agendas of the Soviet Jewish movement in the United States but not beyond the hopes of some Soviet Jewish activists, such as Anatoly Sharansky. This approach accounts for our unique role in the Soviet Jewry movement (Letter, Rabbi Alan Mittleman to Mimi Alperin, November 12, 1986, box 300).[2]

Over the past fifteen years, he continued, Sister Gillen had built up "an impressive number of contacts" in the American government, the world of NGOs, religious communities here and abroad, and in European diplomatic corps. She was "well known and highly respected.... Although the novelty of the Catholic sister working for Soviet Jews has worn off, her reputation has not." When he was with her in the USSR, he observed that she was warmly embraced by many refuseniks. Leading refuseniks, he said, including Alexander Lerner and Vladimir Slepak "... treated her as an old and trusted friend." At a rally in New York in May, Anatoly Sharansky shook her hand on the dais and told her that, although they had not previously met, her fame had preceded her and that he had known of her work for years. "I've always wanted to meet you," he said.[3]

By 1985, Sister Gillen and the Task Force had become less active. She remained an organization of one now focused, more and more, on human rights and persecuted Christians in the Soviet Union (Mittleman, email message to the author, November 29, 2016.)⁴ The cause of Soviet Jewry persisted, but had become less central (Father John Pawlikowski, interview by author, New York City, August 5, 2011).⁵

Rabbi Mittleman called for a major revitalization of the Task Force (Letter to Alperin, November 12, 1986). He wanted to transform the agenda and add personnel and sponsors.⁶ He believed that advocacy for Soviet Jewry was changing as Soviet Jews in America become "more proficient in advocating their own cause." He favored new leadership. He referred to ". . . all the people on the letterhead of the Task Force who no longer mean a thing."⁷ He suggested a possible reconstituted Task Force on the fifteenth anniversary of its founding.

It was not to be. Rather than rejuvenate the Task Force, within two years, in May 1988, the AJC would close it down. Several factors contributed to its closure. By this time, the situation of Jews in the USSR was undergoing vast and important positive change. The Gorbachev government allowed more Jews to emigrate, and those remaining enjoyed increased freedom to practice their religion and actively preserve their cultural heritage (Rabbi Rudin, interviews by the author, NYC, May 8, 2012 and July 30, 2015; and Rabbi Mittleman, interview by author, NYC, March 18, 2014).⁸ Advocacy for Soviet Jewry was becoming less of a priority for the American Jewish community and the AJC. In addition, the AJC would soon lose its major source of financial support for the Task Force. Finally, the response of Sister Gillen to the Israeli trial of John Demjanjuk, accused of being the notorious guard "Ivan the Terrible" at the Treblinka death camp, may have hurt her standing in the AJC and other major Jewish organizations.⁹

THE LEGAL TASK FORCE AND AMERICAN BAR ASSOCIATION (ABA) AGREEMENT WITH THE ASSOCIATION OF SOVIET LAWYERS (ASL)

In early 1982, Sister Gillen and the AJC in Chicago established the National Interreligious Task Force on Human Rights (NILTFHR/Legal Task Force) to support international human rights agreements, foster public awareness of these rights, and gather "and disseminate information about human rights violations." It hoped to redress these violations (AJC, Notes on meeting of Interreligious Attorney's Task Force on Human Rights in the Soviet Union, June 30, 1982, Spertus, box 86, folder 3). Sister Gillen served as director and Professor Ralph Ruebner and Reverend Keith Roderick were co-chairs (Minutes of meeting of NILTFHR, February 17, 1983, box 301; and Ruebner, phone interview by author, February 17, 2015).¹⁰

In May 1985, the leadership of the ABA "entered into the cooperative agreement with the" ASL. The agreement provided for ". . . exchange visits, . . . {joint} seminars . . . and exchange [of]their publications . . ." (E.R. Shipp, "A.B.A. Maintains an agreement with Soviet Lawyers' group," http://www.nytimes.com/1986/08/12us/aba-maintains-an-agreement-with-soviet-lawyers-group.html, accessed March 24, 2015).[11]

Proponents of the agreement argued that it enabled the ABA to influence their Soviet counterparts on human rights issues. They hoped that increased communication would lead to the Soviets learning more about the American position on human rights (Altshuler 2005, 84). Critics charged that "Contrary to the agreement's terms the Soviet group is known to be a KGB-dominated agency of propaganda and disinformation" (Press release of Independent Task Force on ABA Soviet Relations, Inc. January 29, 1988, SHCJ archive). The Union of Councils for Soviet Jewry (UCSJ), Professor Alan Dershowitz, and Natan Sharansky denounced the agreement as "legitimization of Soviet anti-Semitism" and as "total abrogation of ABA's commitment to human and legal rights" (Dershowitz, 1991, 264).

Patience Huntwork, a lawyer in Phoenix, Arizona, worked to repeal the agreement (Patience Huntwork, phone interview by author, January 7, 2015, and *NYT*, August 12, 1986).[12] She argued that the ASL was a tool of the Soviet Union that helped suppress human rights and persecute Jews. Sister Gillen and the Task Force joined her efforts. The controversy focused on the issues of the corruption of the Soviet legal profession and Soviet efforts to discredit entire communities of exiles, including Ukrainians and Lithuanians who criticized Soviet rule of their homelands. Patience Huntwork failed to have the ABA repeal the agreement (*NYT*, August 12, 1986 and Patience Huntwork, phone interview by author January 7, 2015).[13] In April 1988, the ABA let the agreement lapse. It was not renewed.

JOHN DEMJANJUK

John (Ivan) Demjanjuk was born in 1920 in Dubovi Makharyntsi in central west Ukraine. While he was a POW during World War II, the Germans recruited him to serve in the SS auxiliary force. He trained at the Trawniki Camp and then worked at the Sobibor, Majdanek, and Flossenburg camps. He entered the United States as a sponsored refugee in 1952. On becoming a citizen in 1958, he changed his name from Ivan to John (Douglas 2016, 26–30).[14]

During the 1970s, in response to American Jewish groups, representatives Joshua Eilberg (D-PA) and Elizabeth Holtzman (D-NY) influenced the Immigration and Naturalization Service (INS) to place, within its New York office, a Project Control Office responsible for investigating alleged Nazi collaborators who had become American citizens (Ibid., 39).[15] Known former Nazis and their collaborators residing in the United

States were only "handled as persons who had entered the country illegally or under false premise." Section 340(a) of the Immigration and Nationality Act of 1952 authorized denaturalization proceedings in cases where citizenship was "illegally procured or . . . procured by concealment of material fact or by willful misrepresentation" (Ibid., 9).

In October 1975, Senator Jacob Javits (R-NY) received a letter "purporting to list seventy Ukrainian war criminals residing in the United States" (Ibid., 30–33).[16] Javits forwarded the letter to the INS office in New York, which reduced the list to nine suspects, including John Demjanjuk "who allegedly had served at Sobibor."

The Office of Special Investigations (OSI) of the Department of Justice was reluctant to prosecute Demjanjuk but did so after receiving evidence supplied by Israeli investigators.[17] OSI hoped to "denaturalize . . . Demjanjuk for having lied on immigration forms and then to deport him to a country that could bring criminal charges" (Ibid., 2, 37–39). Federal authorities filed a complaint on August 25, 1977 seeking to strip Demjanjuk of his citizenship.

Demjanjuk was denaturalized after a judge found him guilty (Ibid., 25).[18] The Supreme Court rejected his petition for review. INS initiated deportation proceedings on December 6, 1982. A hearing was held in 1984 and the judge ordered his deportation to the USSR. Demjanjuk appealed. At the same time, on October 18, 1983, Israel issued an arrest warrant for Demjanjuk and petitioned the United States to extradite him. Following a judicial ruling in favor of the request from Israel, Demjanjuk flew to Israel on February 27, 1986 (Ibid., 60–67).[19]

His trial began on February 16, 1987. Demjanjuk's lawyers argued that the Israelis had the wrong man. They also portrayed the events as a show trial. They argued that the KGB had forged his SS-issued Trawniki ID card.[20] Eventually, the Soviets provided the original card, which was authenticated by American authorities (Ibid., 55, 92).[21]

Before the end of the trial, and four months after Mittleman's letter advocating reassessment of the Task Force, Sister Gillen, as director of the NITFSJ (which was funded and supervised by the AJC), wrote a letter to the Israeli ambassador in Washington, D.C. expressing her "grave concerns about the way the trial of John Demjanjuk is being conducted in Israel" (Letter, March 27, 1987, SHCJ archive, folder correspondence, business, personal).[22] She wrote that she "was amazed and very distressed to see the Prime Minister on TV" referring to the accused as "a Nazi." "He's a killer . . . such pre-trial condemnation by a head of state alarmed me." Her friends told her to trust "the integrity of Israeli judges." But the trial, she argued, took on the appearance of a Soviet show trial being used "mainly to educate the younger generation regarding the horrors of the Holocaust." The bitter memories she argued were "not very conducive to unbiased judgment regarding the innocence or guilt of one person." She doubted that Jewish judges could resist such pressures.

She emphasized that she had recently heard that the judges accepted evidence given by informers smuggled into an Israeli prison for this purpose. She argued that such techniques were "typical of Soviet procedures, not American Justice." Most importantly, it had been reported "that Soviet evidence has been accepted for use in the trial, evidence which the Foreign Minister refuses to allow the defense attorney to test" (see note 30).

She recounted her struggle for Soviet Jewry, which protested injustices against Anatoly Sharansky, Josef Begun, and countless others, including Sakharov. "I cannot remain silent when Soviet evidence and techniques are used by the American and/or the Israeli government in such court procedures." She argued that the Soviets had a long record "of giving disinformation" for their own purposes. "They seek to promote divisions among groups which criticize their system and their abuses of human rights and national self-determination." They had every reason to target émigrés in the United States and "to falsify evidence. . . . Such evidence must be rejected as tainted at the source by all who seek justice. . . . Anyone, Jew or non-Jew, who protested the injustice shown to Sharansky by Soviet courts and prisons surely cannot remain silent when Soviet evidence is used in the trials of any other human beings." If the Israeli judges found him not guilty "whether because of lack of evidence after forty years or some other reason, that will be possibly a miracle. I sincerely hope that *will* be the verdict for the sake of all concerned, Jews and non-Jews."

While some close to Sister Gillen within the AJC had trouble recalling the incident years later, her position at the time was known within the American Jewish community.[23] The AJC and IAD leadership had to be aware that the head of an AJC-sponsored organization had challenged the legitimacy of an Israeli trial of an alleged Holocaust war criminal. This had have to affected her standing and that of the Task Force.[24]

Her involvement in the controversy over the Demjanjuk trial prompted Sister Gillen to respond to a request by younger sisters in her order to explain her position on controversial issues (Sister Ann Gillen, "Note to Sisters," November 10, 1988, SHCJ archive). She explained that for the past sixteen years in her work for Soviet Jews and Christians she "witnessed great good accomplished by small groups working together to plan peace in the good earth of justice. Now much of this cooperation is threatened by a very divisive issue, the prosecution of alleged ex-Nazis." She had two specific problems with the Demjanjuk case: the way the case was tried in Israel and the way traditional due process procedures in the United States were not followed in these cases (Memo, Patience Huntwork to "Our friends in the human rights community," February 24, 1989, SHCJ archive).[25] The Demjanjuk trial showed, she argued, that justice was not done in Israel, nor in the USSR where the courts were not free of government control.[26]

Sister Gillen had previously written to Attorney General Edwin Meese "to appeal for some intervention in the case of Karl Linnas, alleged ex-Nazi war criminal" (Letter, Sister Ann Gillen to Attorney General Edward Meese, February 24, 1987, SHCJ archive, folder, personal correspondence).[27] She emphasized that, in her work for the cause of freedom for Soviet Jews and Christians, she had learned a great deal about the Soviet legal, judicial, and penal systems which led her to conclude that "any evidence from the Soviet sources is seriously suspect." She claimed that the same system that labeled Sharansky "a traitor for his human rights activity," and which "sent Sakharov into exile without due process, was quite capable of doctoring 'evidence' to drive a wedge between Jewish . . . and other ethnic and religious groups in the west." All of these groups suffered under the Soviets and had "good reason to make some kind of common cause in their quest for human rights." The Soviets were aware of this and had good reason "to try to prevent this development." They saw Baltic and Ukrainian nationals as "collective dissidents. . . . These alleged ex-Nazi trials give USSR officials a perfect opportunity to seek vengeance on these 'dissidents' for their opposition to the Soviet regime." Where Nazi war criminals existed, they should be given a jury trial and all evidence should be treated as "they would by United States standards, *not* Soviet usage." Linnas was being deported, she believed, because he had lied and since he had been sentenced to death, to deport him would be "a manifest injustice."

Several months after Sister Gillen's letter to the ambassador, attorney William Wolf made the issue public. In an op-ed, he charged that the Demjanjuk trial lacked justice. He described chants of death in the courtroom and the overall absence of due process (William Wolf, "Ivan did not get a fair trial," *Phoenix Gazette,* June 21, 1988).[28] He claimed that the United States Department of Justice withheld exonerating evidence from the defense and that fifty Treblinka survivors could not identify him.[29] The sole evidence, he argued, was the Trawniki ID card, which the defense believed had been tampered with by the Soviets.[30] He questioned why the Soviets would frame such a person and surmised that Demjanjuk and other refugees who fled the Soviet Union after WWII were "the last survivors of the crucible of Soviet terror. Their children and grandchildren are vicarious witnesses to Soviet crimes against humanity. The Soviets know that if the large and vocal Ukrainian communities in the United States can be stigmatized, discredited and drained of their financial resources through continuous litigation, their voice in revealing the past and cautioning future generations can be diminished."[31]

Sister Gillen joined the public debate about the Demjanjuk trial covered in the Phoenix press and elsewhere (Sister Ann Gillen, Letter to the editor, *Arizona Republic,* October 3, 1988, SHCJ archive).[32] She argued that the Israeli prosecution had pressured Treblinka survivor Richard Glazar not to testify. For her, this was the latest in a long series of warning signs about injustice in the trial.[33] She asked how there could be a fair trial if prior to the trial Prime Minister Peres had told CBS News that Demjanjuk was a Nazi and killer, and if the atmosphere in the courtroom was like a Soviet "show trial," with one-sided rulings and, above all, "acceptance of Soviet supplied (and likely, fabricated) evidence, and the final guilty verdict and courtroom cries for death. "Was this revenge or justice?" she wondered. Since a man's life was at stake she said, "I can no longer protest only in private." She argued that it was imperative to learn from this trial that accused ex-Nazis would receive justice only if they were granted "United States due process procedures, including presumption of innocence, right to counsel, and a jury trial." She prayed that "the Appeals Court will overturn the lower court's guilty verdict" (Letter to the editor, November 1, 1988 and November 14, 1988, *Arizona Republic*, SHCJ archive).

Her letters to the Jewish and non-Jewish media about the trial prompted a private response by Judith Herschlag Muffs, Director of Special Projects at the ADL (Letter, Judith Herschlag Muffs to Sister Ann Gillen, November 29, 1988, supplied by ADL to the author, October 28, 2016). The two knew each other but had had little contact in recent years. Judith Muffs wrote that she had attended the trial "and I must tell you that I was very moved by the concern of the judges to be fair. It was not a show trial." She sent along an ADL memo, which praised the fairness of the trial. Sister Gillen responded: "It grieves me to be at odds with friends, but I am sure that you must understand that I must follow my conscience where a human life is at stake" (Letter, Sister Gillen to Judith Muffs, January 11, 1989, supplied to author by ADL, October 28, 2016).[34]

Burt S. Levinson and Abraham H. Foxman of the ADL took "strong issue with her perception of the recent trial of Nazi war criminal John Demjanjuk in Israel . . . " (Burt S. Levinson and Abraham H. Foxman, "Letter to the editor," *Washington Jewish Week*, December 13, 1988, supplied by the ADL to author, October 28, 2016).[35] They argued as lawyers and as people who had attended parts of the trial "that the atmosphere was not a circus, but one of decorum. . . . The Israeli judicial system is known for its independence, its integrity and its competence, and all those qualities were on display in the Demjanjuk trial. . . . Hardly a 'show trial,' the Israeli proceedings bore all the hallmarks of fair and impartial justice." They also claimed that before his extradition to Israel, Demjanjuk "exercised every opportunity to prove his contention that he was not 'Ivan the Terrible' in American courts but was unable to do so." They found offensive her claim that no accused Nazi war criminal could be tried objectively in Israel because there were "so many memories traumatized by the Holocaust." Moreover, they felt that she misunderstood the Demjanjuk case. "The issue was not whether 'Ivan the Terrible' committed atrocities; it was whether Demjanjuk was Ivan. The evidence, objectively evaluated, provided a positive answer."

Sister Gillen wrote to friends and associates about the Demjanjuk trial. Max Kampelman replied, "I had not been too familiar with the issue you raised (Demjanjuk), but I want you to know that I consider your interest in it to be perfectly consistent with your activities on behalf of Soviet Jewry. Consistency is very important to maintain in issues of principle. There may be criticism, but there is also the issue of integrity so that we must be understanding and tolerant of whatever criticism might develop" (Letter, Max Kampelman to Sister Ann Gillen, July 26, 1989, SHCJ archive).[36]

In April 1988, the Israeli court found Demjanjuk guilty of being Ivan Grozny (Ivan the Terrible), the infamous guard at the Treblinka Death Camp. They sentenced him to death. He appealed to the Israeli Supreme Court. During the appeal process his lawyers found documents in the USSR showing he served at Sobibor, Majdanek, and Flossenburg. In July 1993, the Supreme Court of Israel "threw out Demjanjuk's conviction as erroneous" (Douglas 2016, 92–97). The judges confirmed that the accused was not Ivan Grozny (Ivan the Terrible) and that he had served as a guard in Sobibor and not in Treblinka. "In releasing him, the judges said it would be too difficult for Demjanjuk to defend himself, although the truth is that the lack of living witnesses would have made it impossible to bring such a case" (Gita Sereny, "John Demjanjuk is not innocent," the *Independent*, August 2, 1993 . . .).[37] After the trial, the Sixth Circuit Court of Appeals ordered his reentry to the United States (Douglas 2016, 110–111).

Prior to the decision by the Israeli Supreme Court, the Sixth Circuit Court of Appeals had opened Demjanjuk's *habeas* challenge to his extradition *sua sponte*. A study panel report to the Court claimed that the OSI had withheld evidence and engaged in "prosecutorial misconduct" (Douglas 2016, 114–115).[38] On February 20, 1988, a federal judge vacated the denaturalization order. On May 19, 1999, the OSI filed a new complaint against Demjanjuk.[39] In his second denaturalization trial the judge stripped Demjanjuk of his citizenship on February 21, 2002. Deportation proceedings followed in December 2004 and lasted until December 2005 when the court ordered him deported to the Ukraine, Poland, or Germany (Douglas 2016, 134). He arrived for trial in Munich, Germany, on May 12, 2009 (Ibid., 216–219). In May 2011, the court found John Demjanjuk guilty "of serving as an accessory to the murder of at least twenty-eight thousand and sixty Jews at the Sobibor death camp." He received a five-year jail sentence but was released on appeal. He died in Germany on March 17, 2012 (Douglas 2016, 3).

THE LARGEST DEMONSTRATION IN THE AMERICAN ADVOCACY MOVEMENT FOR SOVIET JEWRY

The largest demonstration of the American Soviet Jewry advocacy movement took place on December 6, 1987, in Washington, D.C. More than 250,000 people participated.[40] The demonstration was held one day before the Washington, D.C. summit of President Ronald Reagan and Secretary Mikhail Gorbachev. The NCSJ, in cooperation with eight other Soviet Jewry umbrella organizations, organized the demonstration (Lazin 2003, 224).[41] Rabbi James Rudin recruited Christian dignitaries to speak (Letter, Rabbi Rudin and David Harris to Archbishop John L. May, NCCB, November 7, 1987, box 300).[42] Sister Gillen attended but did not speak (Memo, Robert S. Brill, Milwaukee, December 6, 1987, box 300).[43]

The day began with a morning reception for speakers at B'nai B'rith International, followed by a gathering at the Ellipse at the far end of the Washington Mall to assemble for the early afternoon march along Constitutional Avenue, ending at the opposite end of the Mall across from the Capitol's reflecting pool. A ninety-minute program followed with short presentations by elected US officials, including Vice President George Bush and the Speaker of the House, leaders of Soviet Jewry advocacy, heads of major Protestant and Catholic church groups, Eli Wiesel, the ambassador of Israel, and a group of former Soviet refuseniks, including Natan Sharansky and Ida Nudel ("Freedom Sunday Program participants [draft], December 1987, Box 300; and December 1987 demonstration DC on CSPAN, (http://www.c-span.org/video/?454-1/freedom-rally-soviet-jews, last accessed August 29, 2016).[44]

The rally focused on Soviet Jews (Natan Sharansky, Form letter, November 30, 1986, box 300). Many of the speakers promoted the Israeli (Liaison Bureau) position, demanding free emigration for Soviet Jews and repatriation to their homeland of Israel. Some emphasized the more general right to emigrate and freedom of religion for those that remained.[45] While Sister Gillen was not on the program and no speaker mentioned the Task Force, their impact was evident. First, several speakers emphasized that the demonstration included Americans from every religion and race. Morris Abram described the crowd as comprising "every creed and color." Both Vice President Bush and Elie Wiesel emphasized that Christians and Jews were now both active on behalf of Soviet Jewry.[46] One of the former refuseniks and the Israeli Ambassador, Moshe Arad, reiterated that before them stood Christians and Jews, blacks and whites. Secondly, while the emphasis was specifically focused on Soviet Jewry, some speakers referred to the persecution of "others" in the Soviet Union. Mayor Ed Koch talked about all oppressed people and asked for the Soviet Union to open its gates for both Jews and Christians. Congressman Jack Kemp (R-NY) explicitly referred to both Jews and Christians in the Soviet Union, while Helen Jackson voiced concern for all humanity.

Peter Yarrow and Mary Travis (of the musical trio Peter, Paul and Mary) sang about the lighting of candles for oppressed Jews and all oppressed peoples.[47] Third, several speakers referred to the Holocaust when talking about the current situation of Soviet Jewry. Elie Wiesel suggested that if Jews and Christians had stood together and demonstrated then as they were now doing, many lives might have been saved. Finally, Vice President Bush emphasized that after Auschwitz and the Holocaust "Never again can we remain silent about the abuse of human rights."[48]

The two speakers representing the Christian faith remained on theme. Reverend Arie Brouwer of the NCC talked about the need for more synagogues in the Soviet Union, but he focused on freedom of religion: "I believe American Christians are duty bound to join with American Jews in demanding religious freedom in the Soviet Union" (The *Catholic Standard*, December 10, 1987, box 300).[49] Bishop William Keeler, NCCB, also focused on Soviet Jewry ("Let our people go"), but mentioned persecuted Catholics and Baptists: "whether we speak of Jew or Baptist or Roman Catholic . . . in the Soviet Union . . . our hearts must ache, our voices must rise because they are our brothers and sisters and because they suffer."[50]

In what was, perhaps, reminiscent of the keynote address given by Mayor Charles Evers at the 1972 founding of the NITFSJ, Representative John Lewis (D-GA) read a statement from Coretta Scott King (in her absence): "You were with us in Selma, you were with us on the Mall with Martin Luther King and we are *proud* to be with you today for the fight for freedom for Soviet Jewry."[51]

In the evening at an event following the rally, the AJC awarded Natan Sharansky its American Liberties Medallion. Sister Gillen, executive director of the NITFSJ, gave the benediction (AJC Freedom Sunday Dinner program, December 6, 1987, box 300).

FINANCIAL CHALLENGES

During the 1980s, the Task Force suffered from insufficient funding which reached a crisis level by 1985 (Memo, Sister Ann Gillen to Rabbi Jim Rudin, March 8, 1983, box 301). It operated on an annual grant from the Tananbaum Foundation, AJC subsidies, and honoraria for Sister Gillen's speaking engagements.[52] In addition, the AJC donated staff time and covered travel expenses for the national, Chicago, and other area offices involved in Task Force activities (Memo, Rita Blume to Sister Ann Gillen, November 26, 1984, box 301, folder 7).[53] In May/June, 1987, the AJC received a grant of $29,500 from the Tananbaum foundation. It then applied for a renewal for 1988 (Letter, Rabbi A. James Rudin to Arnold S. Alperstein, June 17, 1987, box 300).[54]

In February 1988, Arnold S. Alperstein of the Tananbaum Foundation informed the AJC (Letter to Rabbi Rudin, February 12, 1988, box 300) that, due to recent portfolio losses, the Foundation would be unable to make future grants to the Task Force.[55] He wrote Ann Gillen (April 6, 1988, box 300) ". . . our inability to continue with support in no way reflects on our sincere respect for the work that you have accomplished and does not in any way reflect on your you or the staff of the AJC."

Consequently, in early 1988, the major source of Task Force funding ended its support. Taken together with the decline in the Task Force's activity, and the expected positive change in the status of Soviet Jewry, the AJC decided to close the Task Force. Rabbi Rudin later reflected on the closing, saying that, at the time, the Soviet Jewry advocacy movement was winding down (Rabbi Rudin, interviews by the author, NYC, May 8, 2012 and July 30, 2015). Evidently, the success of the December 1987 rally in Washington, D.C. had influenced the White House, Congress, Jewish advocacy groups, the Liaison Bureau, and the Soviets. For example, the Coalition to Free Soviet Jewry, formerly the GNYCSJ, cancelled the spring 1988 national Solidarity Day demonstration in NYC, which had been held every year since 1972 (Lazin 2005, 240, n. 80).[56] Rabbi Rudin believed that, for the AJC, the status and importance of the Task Force had diminished. Other projects took precedence when the AJC allocated its limited resources.[57] After talking with AJC's executive vice president, Bert Gold, Rabbi Rudin confirmed that Sister Gillen would be closing the National Interreligious Task Force on Soviet Jewry effective May 31, 1988 (Memo, Rabbi Jim Rudin to Philip Shamis. April 28, 1988, box 300).[58]

In March 1988, aware of the closing down of the Task Force, Sister Gillen quoted *Ecclesiastes* in a letter to friends: "There is a time for planting and a time for uprooting what has been planted." It was time to "harvest and replant." She wrote that many of the honorary sponsors had died and that the AJC would continue its long dedication to this cause in a new form to be announced. She proudly stated that the Task Force had aided 275,000 Soviet Jews in emigrating, as well as in freeing many long-time prisoners. Unfortunately, she said, some remained in jail. She wrote that the Task Force had helped to spotlight the notorious Soviet abuse of psychiatry and the law and "awakened consciousness in many regarding their long repression of religious and cultural freedom." She thanked the recipients for their support and urged them to send Passover and Easter Greetings to Jews and Christians in the USSR who needed their support. She closed by saying that she would continue activities and speaking engagements, either as a consultant or with another group (Sister Ann Gillen, Letter to friends on NITFSJ stationery, March 1988, SHCJ archive).[59]

In an interview twenty-five years later, Rabbi Rudin said that the AJC had not given her a going away dinner or banquet, which she deserved (Rabbi Rudin, interview by author, NYC, May 8, 2012).[60] This may (or may not) indicate that there was tension between her and the leadership of the AJC.[61]

AJC held an event in her honor in Chicago on May 5, 1988. The national AJC expressed its good wishes and praised her " . . . extraordinary efforts in behalf of Soviet Jews and other oppressed peoples." Her name, they suggested is identified worldwide with "a strong commitment to human rights and religious liberty" (AJC memo to Ann Gillen from Jack Lippin, Chair National Interreligious Affairs Commission, Rabbi A. James Rudin, Judith Banki, Rabbi Alan Mittleman, Benita Gayle Almeleh, Florence Mordhort, and Celia Horowitz, May 5, 1988, box 300).

At the event someone read a statement recognizing Sister Gillen's contributions and achievements. It emphasized that of the three crowns mentioned by Rabbi Simon "the crown of a good name exceeds them all." For countless Jews and Christians in the Soviet Union her name stands for "hope, solidarity, friendship and a blessing." Her activism benefited thousands including Ida Nudel, Viktor Brailovsky, Alexander Lerner, and so many others that counted her "as their trusted friend." To the Jews trapped in the Soviet Union her name meant "that someone remembers them; someone cares; someone will not let the world forget their plight. . . ." For Americans, Sister Ann's name "is a call to conscience and an uncanny feat of interreligious cooperation." It praised her sixteen years of leading the nation's "model of interreligious cooperation in the cause of human rights." She exhibited "patience, dedication, perseverance and religious conviction" and taught that "for those who enjoy liberty and who often disagree with one another under liberty to unite to save those who are denied liberty. . . . Her work has daunted and troubled those who deny our brothers and sisters freedom. For this, she bears the crown of the good name. And we are honored by honoring her tonight" (Sister Ann Gillen Tribute, May 5, 1988, box 300).[62]

SISTER ANN GILLEN'S ACTIVISM AFTER THE TASK FORCE

Sister Gillen continued her efforts on behalf of Christians and Jews in the Soviet Union and elsewhere. She became executive director of the Society of St. Stephen (SSS), founded in 1982 and headed by Reverend Keith Roderick (Letter, Rabbi Rudin to Sister Ann Gillen, April 29, 1988, box 300). Named after the first deacon and first martyr of the Church, SSS provided "support to Christians who are being persecuted for their faith." Members prayed for the persecuted church and those in prison, wrote letters to prisoners and their families and provided them with material assistance. The Society urged interested groups and individuals to adopt a prisoner and his/her family (Brochure, "Society of St. Stephen," C1988 [SHCJ archive] and press release, SSS, December 1, 1988, box 300).[63] She remained active with the group for a year or two (SSS press release, December 1, 1988, box 300).[64] In this role she cooperated with the Union of Councils for Soviet Jewry (UCSJ).

While working for the SSS, Sister Gillen also served as director of the renamed National Interreligious Task Force.[65] Reverend Keith Roderick and Professor Ralph Ruebner of John Marshall Law School served as executive co-directors. The NITF hoped to organize local "citizen support groups across the United States for prisoners of conscience, urging various ethnic and religious groups to work together in their behalf" ("Statement of the NITF to the CCSE Meeting in Moscow concerning human rights," September 1991, SHCJ archive). They promoted full "realization of and respect for religious freedom" in the USSR hoping that Moscow and other republics would develop and respect religious pluralism, human rights, and religious liberty. They supported elimination of the Council of Religious Affairs in the USSR and asked for an inquiry into the disappearance of Raoul Wallenberg.[66]

In September 1989, Sister Gillen became involved in the controversy of the Carmelite convent located on the grounds of the Auschwitz concentration camp (Sister Ann Gillen, Letter to the Editor, *Chicago Sun Times*, September 1989, SHCJ archive).[67] In a letter to the editor, she referred to a comment by Steve Melech, editor of the newsletter of the World Union of Jewish Students that "The Carmelite nuns who occupy the convent, are praying to convert to Catholicism the souls of the Jews who perished in the Nazi gas chambers." She argued that this was not an accurate statement because "Catholics do not believe that conversion is possible *after* death." She also argued that Carmelite nuns gave their lives to the "prayer of expiation" defined as "the act of atoning for a crime; the act of making amends for wrong-doing or guilt; atonement. . . . This would *not* seem to be offensive to the Jewish community. . . . I sincerely doubt that the sisters are praying for the conversion of Jews at all for they must know the teaching of Vatican Council II. They seek to make atonement of the crimes committed at Auschwitz."

According to an archivist at SHCJ, Sister Gillen's intense service primarily to Jewish-Christian concerns came to an end in 1990 when she was asked to become Editor of the *SHCJ News*. She returned to work at the SHCJ Convent near Philadelphia. Around this time, she was diagnosed with cancer for which she had surgery in 1991.[68] She died on January 14, 1995 at the age of 76. She was buried wearing "two necklaces: a cross and a Star of David" (https://archive.jta.org/1995/01/18/archive/nun-who-embraced-cause-of-soviet-jews-dies-at-76).

The following is from a eulogy at her funeral given by Rabbi Rudin:

> "Someone said shame that she left no children. I got angry . . . she had six hundred thousand children . . . Jews who came out of the Soviet Union and found freedom in Israel . . . totally committed to bringing freedom to a people that suffered under an oppressive regime . . .

excited by the Second Vatican Council that advocated positive Catholic-Jewish relationships and human rights . . . most considered her "naïve, even foolish in her relentless quest to free Soviet Jews. She brought the message of Soviet Jews to tens of thousands in churches and synagogues. . . . She stalked the halls of the UN, the White House, the State Department, and the United States Congress to gain support for Soviet Jews . . . Picketed Soviet embassies in D.C. and the World Conferences at Brussels, Jerusalem, Belgrade, Madrid and personally visited "many Jews, her "family" in USSR . . . two central ideas. . . . She remained absolutely convinced that Soviet Jewry would eventually be freed . . . {and had faith so } she was never overawed by the vaunted power and prestige of the Soviet Union. {Second} that everyone, but everyone, was potentially redeemable. . . .

Everyone in the Soviet Jewry movement knew and respected Ann's indomitable spirit. She displayed enormous physical, emotional and spiritual strength in her meetings with United States Presidents, Senators and Representatives, Vatican and United States officials, Soviet authorities and members of the clergy and media. . . . She would conclude every meeting with friend and "temporary adversary" alike with the Biblical words "Let my people go."

Sister Ann Gillen is now with the God of freedom who endowed her with such extraordinary power and strength. Rest well, my dear friend. Your achievements and memory will always be an inspiration."

NOTES

1. (Rabbi James Rudin, interviews by author, NYC, May 8, 2012 and July 30, 2014). He argued that the best years for the Task Force were between 1972–1984 or 1985. Then it declined. After Gorbachev came to power in March 1985, it became harder to make a case for the persecution of Soviet Jews.

2. He copied Rabbi Rudin and Sister Gillen.

3. Sister Gillen was one of the first activists to take up his cause. After his arrest, the Liaison Bureau and mainstream advocacy groups initially did not support him because of his ties with dissidents (Lazin 2005, 234, n.23 and Pam Cohen, phone interview by author, March 25, 2018).

4. He remembered "There's no question that it was a one-person operation. There were no functioning committees. . . ."

5. Father Pawlikowski argued that her involvement with Catholics in the Soviet Union was legitimate but that later it was at the expense of Soviet Jewry. But Jonathan Levine (phone interview by author, May 15, 2013) who headed AJC's Midwest office in Chicago in the 1980s stated that she remained focused on Soviet Jewry despite her concern with Christians in Eastern Europe and the USSR. Dr. Kent Hill (phone interview by author, April 3, 2018) argued that her passion was "saving Jews." She saw it as a personal call from God "to be a Catholic witness on solidarity with Jews, this is her passion."

6. He wrote about a new project, a "Sabbath of Conscience" where Jews, Catholics, and Evangelicals would discuss persecution of co-religionists in USSR. He mentioned possible consultations with peace groups visiting the USSR; American church groups hosting religious delegations; and preparing background papers and briefings on human rights violations.

7. "I think here not of Sr. Ann and myself—who, God willing, have a few good years left to go." He discussed with Sister Gillen recruiting a Jewish and a Christian person from the USSR now living in the United States.

8. Rabbi Rudin (interview by author, NYC, August 26, 2011) suggested that after the December 1987 demonstration (see below) there was a feeling that the movement was over. He also thought it had become harder for Sister Gillen to travel and that she may have already been suffering from cancer. Rabbi Mittleman (interview by author, NYC, March 18, 2014) thought her age may have been a factor.

9. Rabbi Rudin (interview by author, July 30, 2015) mentioned that her involvement with the issue of churches in Lithuania was not appreciated by some in the Jewish world.

10. AJC's Chicago Office hosted the meetings and helped staff the Legal Task Force (see chapter 7). Professor Ralph Ruebner, an attorney, served on the human rights committee of the Decalogue Society. He spoke at the 10th anniversary meeting of the Task Force (Letter, Rabbi Rudin to Prof Ralph Ruebner, September 23, 1982, box 302, folder 3). He joined the faculty of John Marshall Law School in Chicago in 1981. After the Iranian revolution, he participated in a legal task force to aid Iranian students (Jewish and non-Jewish). He later assisted Russian immigrants at a Chicago JCC. At the local Jewish Federation, he was involved with international affairs and Soviet Jewry. Reverend Keith Roderick was an Anglican Minister in Illinois involved in issues of human rights and religious persecution. He directed the Society for St. Stephen (SSS) which sought to free imprisoned Christians (see below).

11. In June 1986, the parties modified the agreement to declare that "both organizations respect the rule of law."

12. Patience Huntwork organized the Independent Task Force on ABA-Soviet Relations, Inc. Her co-chairs were Orest A. Jejna , a Ukrainian American lawyer, and William Wolf , a Jewish American lawyer. The advisory board included Ginte Damusis, Douglas J. Feith, Sister Gillen, Dennis Prager, Glenn Richter (SSSJ), and Lynn Singer (UCSJ) (Press release, Independent Task Force . . . ., January 29, 1988, SHCJ archive). Former NCSJ chair and President of the Conference of Presidents of Major American Jewish Organizations, Morris Abram, viewed the agreement as a "tool to educate Americans and Soviets about human rights" and "provide a valuable opportunity for leverage" (see *Jewish World . . . of Palm Beach Co unty*, box 300). He favored continuation of the agreement on condition that ABA pressed Soviet attorneys on human rights and Jewish rights issues. The UCSJ, the ADL, and the CRCs of several Jewish Federations urged the ABA to abrogate the agreement (*JTA* of April 6, 1987 and "Position of the Union of Councils . . . on the ABA agreement with the ASL," December 1986, box 301).

13. The ABA policy making group voted against cancelling the agreement in August 1986.

14. Most of the information in this section is from the Douglas book.

15. This became a Special Litigation Unit (SLU) within INS to coordinate investigation of all cases involving alleged Nazi War Criminals. By July 1977, the INS had set up a Washington- based unit which, in 1979, moved out of INS into the Justice Department and became the Office of Special Investigations (OSI).

16. Michael Hanusiak, editor of *Ukrainian Daily News* wrote the letter. He was an American of Ukrainian decent and a loyal communist. He received an award from the Ukrainian SSR and visited Kiev often.

17. Several Treblinka survivors identified him as being Ivan Grozny ("Ivan the Terrible") the Ukrainian guard who operated the gas chamber at Treblinka. A unit of Israel Police notified OSI. OSI also had a deposition from former SS Sergeant Otto Horn who had served at Treblinka and identified Demjanjuk as Ivan Grozny. Later evidence suggests that his identification was "prompted" by OSI (Ibid., 91).

18. The judge ruled that he had trained at Trawniki and served at Treblinka.

19. The judge dismissed the defense claim that Demjanjuk was not Ivan Grozny.

20. At the 1986 meetings of the Board of Governors of the Arizona Bar in Tucson, Alexander Sakharov of the ASL remarked that the ABA-Soviet Agreement enabled the ABA to provide "the Trawniki ID card to the Justice Department for the Demjanjuk prosecution." Patience Huntwork also heard that ABA President "William Falstaff, Menachem Berger, Israel Bar President, and Alexander Sakharov arranged for the "transfer of Soviet evidence in the Demjanjuk case" (Memo, Patience Huntwork to Human Rights Activists . . . . re: "The Demjanjuk Case," February 21, 1989, SHCJ archive). She immediately brought this information to the attention of the Demjanjuk family. The Soviet supplied copy of "of an ID card issued at Trawniki . . ." accurately gave birthplace, date of birth and father's name and noted "scar on back." Later, "(as) a document discovered and reproduced by the Soviets, the card was treated by American investigators with due caution. . . ." It listed his eye color as grey and hair brown, but his eyes were blue, and his hair had been blond. The card had his height as 5' 8"; he stood 6' 1" (in metric 75 cm rather than actual 85cm, a possible typo) (Ibid., 52). Importantly, ID indicated that Ivan Demjanjuk served at Sobibor not Treblinka. Later, a denaturalization trial defense "stridently insist that nothing that came from Soviet sources could be trusted."

21. Shimon Peres spoke with Armand Hammer who contacted Leonid Brezhnev. He had the original flown to Israel.

22. She wrote the letter on plain paper, signed Sr. Ann Gillen, SHCJ.

23. In several conversations and email messages with the author Rabbi Rudin, Rabbi Allan Mittleman, Mimi Alperin, Eugene DuBow, Jerry Goodman, and Professor André LaCocque had no recollection of an incident involving Sister Gillen and the trial of John Demjanjuk. In contrast, Father John Pawlikowski (interview by author, NYC, August 5, 2011) claims that she argued that Demjanjuk was innocent and that her view was known publicly. Moreover, he argued (interview by author, NYC, September 21, 2014) that she became so involved with the Demjanjuk case that it almost consumed her. He added that no one affiliated with the Task Force followed her on this and that she alienated "all of us" on this issue. Finally, he noted (email message to author, July 18, 2011) that her defending some very questionable people such as Demjanjuk created "considerable tension between herself and the leadership of the Soviet Jewry movement." Sister Gloria Coleman (interview by author, Rosemont, PA, June 10, 2015) commenting on the Demjanjuk incident stated "Ann, when she believed in something, she was determined and did not pull back." Former AJC staff person Adam Simms (phone interview by author, September 22, 2014) said of her stand on Demjanjuk that if she had doubts about his guilt, then she was serious for she was "not frivolous-a serous person." Importantly, Sister Gillen expressed her criticism of the trial publicly in letters to the editor of several American Jewish newspapers (see below n.32).

24. Sister Gillen was sensitive to criticism about her stand on the issue. In a December 10, 1988 letter to Pat (handwritten note, SHCJ archive) she commented that she was invited to speak in Skokie to the "Women's Plea for Human Rights." The chair called and asked her what she would say "reminding one that little children will be part of the program. That seemed unusual to me but perhaps I am reading too much into the interchange. A note of questioning has entered into the dialogue as you will see when you receive the copy of Judith Muffs response to my letter about the trial" (see below).

25. Patience Huntwork summed up the position held by Sister Gillen, William Wolff, and herself. They favored "changes in the procedure by which the OSI . . . prosecutes alleged war criminals." They favored giving defendants the "full safeguards of US criminal law. . . . the accused's guilt should be demonstrated in American courts using American due process procedures, including the usual presumption of innocence, right to counsel, and jury trial." They wanted to end the deportation of defendants and, where relevant, to hold war crimes trials in the US ". . . based on the doctrine of *hostii Humani generis universality*" (Memo, Patience T. Huntwork, " re: "The Demjanjuk case." February 21, 1989, SHCJ archive).

26. She wrote her fellow Sisters that Patience Huntwork had asked her to join her on the Oprah Winfrey Show to talk about the appeal in the Demjanjuk death sentence. "If I go on this talk show, how should I be introduced if asked—simply as RC Sister or Sister of the H.C.? If you have strong feelings let me know" (Ann Gillen, "Note to Sisters," November 10, 1988, SHCJ archive).

27. She signed the letter without reference to the Task Force. A Soviet court sentenced Linnas to death in absentia in 1962 for commanding a Nazi concentration camp at Tartu, Estonia, from 1941–1943. He later fought with German forces (Andrew Rosenthal, "The U.S. Case Against the Estonian," April 24 1987, *The New York Times*). He entered the United States in 1951. In 1982 Federal District Court stripped him of his citizenship for having lied about his Nazi past upon entering the country. The judge said his crimes "were such as to offend the decency of any civilized society." A 1986 federal appeals court upheld the deportation order ruling that evidence against him was "overwhelming and largely uncontroverted." On April 20, 1987, the US Supreme Court refused to hear a final appeal. He was then flown to USSR and died three months later in a prison hospital on July 2, 1987.

28. He added that the deportation procedure lacked criminal procedure.

29. In response, a lawyer from the ADL argued that since only sixty persons survived Treblinka, she doubted the claim that fifty survivors had failed to recognize him (Ruti G. Teitel, "Reflections of an American Lawyer on the Holocaust Trial of John Demjanjuk, June-July 1988, published in *Phoenix Gazette* on June 21, 1988 (supplied to the author by the ADL).

30. Moreover, the defense was not allowed to remove the photo from the card to examine the reverse side. "The Soviet authorities had instructed the Israelis not to allow the photograph to be removed from the card for such an examination and the Israeli court complied."

31. Also see Patience T. Huntwork, "Nazi Hunt Must Reach New Level of Fairness." *National Conservative Weekly*. July 9, 1988, SHCJ archive. She suggests that Congress provide a statutory basis for war crimes trials in United States under criminal, rather than civil standards, of due process.

32. This also appeared again on November 14, 1988 and as letters to the editor in *Jewish Week* (Washington DC November 17, 1988, *Jewish Advocate* November 10, 1988, (title "Injustice in Demjanjuk Trial;" and in the *Jewish Exponent* November 11, 1988, title "Has Justice been done in Trial of Demjanjuk?"). She signed letters as Sister Ann Gillen. In some papers, they noted her work with Jews and Christians in the Soviet Union and in some to her having been director of the NITFSJ. At the time she no longer directed the NITFSJ.

33. Taped telephone conversation (September 27, 1988) between Attorney William Wolf and Mr. Richard Glazer of Switzerland (part of brief, SHCJ archive). Sister Gillen cited Richard Lessner's article "Evidence suggests prosecution misconduct in Demjanjuk trial (October 24, 1988, SHCJ archive).

34. She questioned how attending sessions could be an adequate means to assess due process. "For that purpose, it would be necessary to make an analysis of the trial court's evidentiary rulings, all the evidence presented, the conduct of the entire trial and the fairness of the verdict and sentence." Sister Gillen wrote on paper of the "National Interreligious Task Force" (NITF) (See below).

35. Levinson was National Chairman of the ADL and Foxman its National Director. They noted that she "has long been a friend of oppressed Jews in the Soviet Union and in Eastern Europe."

36. He replied to her letter of April 19, 1989. She signed it as executive director of the St. Stephen Society (see below).

37. http://www.independent.co.uk/voices/john-demjanjuk-is-not-innocent-gitta-sereny-has-been-close-to-the-ivan-the-terrible-case-since-it-started-in-the-us-15-years-ago-she-has-come-to-know-john-demjanjuks-family-who-always-thought-he-was-innocent-as-an-expert-on-treblinka-she-already-knew-the-survivors-who-were-

mortally-sure-he-was-guilty-last-thursday-she-saw-their-last-day-in-court-1458754.html, accessed January 16, 2015.

38. The three-judge panel report to Sixth Circuit, headed by Thomas Wiseman, (November 17, 1993) held that in failing ". . . to produce exculpatory materials" the " OSI attorneys acted with reckless disregard for the truth." Wiseman argued that OSI had proceeded with prosecution "to please and maintain very close relationships with various interest groups because their continued existence depended on it." Sereny ("John Demjanjuk is not innocent" *The* Independent, August 2, 1993) argued that Sobibor survivors could not recognize his photograph but survivors of Treblinka believed that he resembled Ivan the Terrible. She cited testimony of Ignat Danilchenko who served as SS auxiliary in Sobibor and told a Soviet prosecutor in 1949 that his best friend there was "Ivan Demjanjuk and that they were transferred together as guards to the concentration camps of Flossenburg . . . in Germany." The Danilchenko testimony, known by both the prosecution and the defense, was one of several documents held by OSI "that were never passed on to the Israelis, an appalling handicap to the proper conduct of the case."

39. OSI argued that evidence showed that he "served at Okzow, Majdanek, Sobibor and Flossenburg " and that he had "directly assisted the Nazi government of Germany in implementing its racial . . . policies. . . ." It claimed that thirty thousand Jews had been gassed during the five and one half months that he served at Sobibor (Douglas 2016, 131). "He participated in . . . persecution that should have barred him from acquiring American citizenship. . . ."

40. Morris Abram had used the police count of 200,000 taken at 2:00 pm. David Harris wrote him that many media outlets use 250,000 and that they should, too (Memo, David Harris to Morris Abram, April 4, 1988, box 300).

41. David Harris, the AJC Washington, D.C. director, headed the organizing committee. Over fifty national Jewish organizations and three hundred local federations and CRCs participated. The UCSJ participated fully. The NJCRAC played an active role.

42. They sent similar letters to Arie Brouwer, General Secretary of the NCC; The Most Reverend William Keeler, NCCB; Dr. Robert P. Dugan Jr. of the NAE; and to Dr. Ray H. Hughes, President of the NAE. Dr. Dugan and Dr. Hughes did not attend. Dr. Dugan dictated a phone statement of support (November 25, 1987, box 300), ". . . Evangelical Christians stand in solidarity with the Soviet Jews and with all who seek to remove Soviet barriers to Jewish emigration." Dr. Ray H. Hughes (Memo, Jim Rudin to David Harris. December 4, 1987) also supported the demonstration.

43. A separate ecumenical prayer vigil for persecuted Christians in the Soviet Union was held the same day in Washington, D.C. ("Press release" November 10, 1987, box 300; and *Washington Post* "Church leaders set . . . Vigil to Pray for Summit," November 25, 1987, box 300). Church leaders from the United States and the USSR held the vigil at 4:00 pm on December 6 and on each day of summit. Kent Hill's "Coalition for Solidarity with Christians in the USSR" held a press conference to coincide with the upcoming Gorbachev/Reagan summit at 11:00 am on December 7. The Congressional Human Rights Caucus co-sponsored. Three Congressional Representatives, Ginte Damusis, Ernest Gordon, and Kent Hill spoke (Memo, Kent Hill to Members of the coalition . . . ," November 19, 1987, Spertus, box 43, file DC correspondence; and Kent Hill, phone interview by author, April 3, 2018).

44. Speakers included Helen Jackson, founder of Congressional Wives for Soviet Jewry and wife of the late Senator Henry Jackson (D-WA); Vice President George Bush; Senator Robert Dole (R- KS); Moshe Arad, ambassador of Israel; Natan Sharansky; Morris Abram, president, NCSJ; house speaker, Jim Wright (R-TX); Reverend Arie Brouwer, NCC; Bishop William Keeler, NCCB; Pamela Cohen, chairwoman, UCSJ; Yosef Mendelovitch, former prisoner of Zion; Elie Wiesel; Representative John Lewis (D-GA); Representative Jack Kemp (R-NY); Vladimir and Masha Slepak; Mayor Ed Koch; Shoshanna Cardin, president, CJF; Marty Stein, United Jewish Appeal (UJA); Gordon Sacks, UJA: Robert Loup, UJA; Senator Daniel Inouye (D-HI); Governor

Thomas Kean (R-NJ); Jacqueline Levine, co-chair of the event; Yuli Edelstein, former prisoner of Zion; John Sweeney, AFL-CIO; and Ida Nudel.

45. Most public relations and press releases carried a quote "Our fight must go on . . . every Jew in the Soviet Union who wishes to leave must be given that right. Together we will do it." Vice President Bush, Rep. Jim Wright, Sen. Robert Dole, Morris Abram, and Elie Wiesel called for free Jewish emigration. Wiesel also urged religious and cultural freedom for those that remained. Morris Abram read a letter from President Reagan saying that he would press Gorbachev for full freedom of emigration and of religion.

46. Connie Smukler, (interview by the author, Philadelphia, March 6, 2014) an active leader of the advocacy for Soviet Jewry movement in Philadelphia, remembered that there were Christians among the fourteen thousand strong Philadelphia delegation. Similarly, Pam Cohen (phone interview by author, March 25, 2018) then head of the UCSJ argued that the organizers wanted a large Christian presence to impress both Reagan and Gorbachev. Former UCSJ president Morey Schapiro (phone interview by author, November 20, 2015, remembered groups of Christians in the crowd. Also, Christians were between five and ten percent of UCSJ members.

47. John Sweeney, International President of the Public Service Employee Union of the AFL-CIO called for the right of Jews to emigrate, the end of a forced labor system that denied unions, the end of discrimination against Jews, Ukrainian Catholics, and Baptists, closing of psychiatric hospitals, and freeing of all prisoners of conscience.

48. Governor Kean argued that if they had gathered fifty years ago, the St. Louis might have docked in an American port. Representative Kemp argued that had they not been indifferent, the Holocaust would not have happened.

49. He noted the importance of NCC ties to the Russian Orthodox Church in working together to prevent a nuclear Holocaust.

50. The bishop added that their common vision reflected the vision shared by Pope John Paul II and Jewish leaders who met him in Miami where Pope said, "Catholics and Jews must unite whenever human rights are threatened."

51. Coretta Scott King said that her husband had concerns about the spiritual genocide of Soviet Jews (Robert S. Brill, "Thoughts at Random on "Freedom Sunday" December 6, 1987, box 300). In the mid-1980s she served on the UCSJ National Advisory Board. Sister Gillen, Reverend Blahoslav Hruby, and Father Robert Drinan also served ("Coretta King named to Advisory Board of UCSJ" *Atlanta Daily World*, January 19, 1986; *ProQuest Historical Newspapers: Atlanta Daily World, 18)*. Later the entire demonstration sang "We shall overcome" with one verse being "We shall be free."

52. The 1983 Task Force budget was projected to be $61,000. Actual expenditures were $49,000 ("Report on the Activities of the Fiscal Year 1983" ND (Box 301). A second document ("NITFSJ Financial Statement 1983." September 1984, box 301)) listed income as $58,485, which included a Tananbaum grant of $29,500, $6,600 travel reimbursements and honoraria, $2,000 from contributions, and $20,060 from AJC appropriations.

53. The Tananbaum Foundation renewed its grant of $29,500 dollars for 1984. The 1985 budget (NITFSJ "1985 year," n.d., box 301, folder 8) listed overall expenses at about $52,000. In May 1986, the AJC ("Budget submission by AJC to Tananbaum Foundation." May 1986 (Box 300)) submitted a budget of $77,000. It listed the expected Task Force's income for 1986 as $60,000 including a grant of $29,500 from the Tananbaum Foundation and $24,000 from AJC, honorarium and contributions.

54. The request included a proposed budget of about $75,000 for 1988 (NITFSJ "Budget 1988," n.d., box 300). In a Task Force memo from Sister Ann Gillen, "1987–1988 Summary of expenditures," (n.d.) she listed a $70,000 budget for 1988.

55. He would send a check for $10,000 to be applied to the 1987 grant (Letter, Martin Alperstein to Rabbi Rudin, April 5, 1988, box 300).

56. The Liaison Bureau probably approved the cancellation. The NCSJ and the UCSJ supported the cancellation. The SSSJ called the decision an outrage.

216   Chapter 9

57. Bill Gralnick (phone interview by the author, November 4, 2014) described "territorial struggles" between programs within AJC which had competed with the Task Force.

58. Rabbi Rudin (interview by the author, May 8, 2012) recalls Bert Gold saying to him "Let's shut it down" (or words to that effect). The AJC gave Sister Ann Gillen $10,000 in severance pay and her secretary $4,400.

59. In March 1988, she joined an Institute of Religion and Democracy sixteen-day tour to the Soviet Union led by Dr. Kent Hill and his wife (Confidential Report, "Millennium Tour . . . , March 26 to April 11, 1988," SHCJ archive). The group comprised twenty-one religious leaders (seventeen Evangelicals, three Episcopalians, and Sister Gillen). They visited Moscow, Leningrad, Kiev, Tallinn, and Riga, as well as the church centers at Zagorsk and Suzdall. They met with church leaders, spokespeople for the Program to Promote Atheism, and Jewish activists and Christians in recognized and unrecognized churches (Document, April, May 1988, Spertus, box 48, Rudin folder). In visiting the Jewish activists, Sister Gillen noted their ties to UCSJ groups in Chicago and Florida.

60. In an interview by the author (July 30, 2015), Rabbi Rudin said that he pushed for a dinner or other event in New York, but he could not get support for the idea. Adam Simms (phone interview by the author, September 22, 2014) stated that she realized "she was being left out to dry."

61. Her friend and colleague Sister Gloria Coleman (phone interview by author, October 27, 2014) said that Sister Ann "was aware that they (AJC) did not have an event around her leaving or finishing almost twenty years of work." She added that "they did not thank her."

62. The comments may have been from Rabbi Rudin but read by someone else as he was not at the event. At the end of April, Rabbi Rudin wrote Sister Gillen (April 29, 1988, box 300) in the name of the AJC saluting her "magnificent leadership" as head of the Task Force for sixteen years. He praised her "extraordinary service" to the "cause of Soviet Jewry and other oppressed peoples in the USSR." Her strength, courage, and wisdom resulted in many men and women gaining their human rights and religious liberty. He confirmed the closing of the Task Force on May 31, 1988.

63. Located in Macomb IL, SSS opened a Chicago office in the former office of the Task Force at 1207 South Wabash, Suite 221. The Reverend Keith Roderick remained its general director.

64. SSS and the Chicago Conference on Soviet Jewry (CCSJ) held a public hearing on December 9, 1988 in Chicago about proposed changes in laws concerning religion in the USSR. Rev. Keith Roderick, Prof. Ralph Ruebner (delegate to CCSJ), Julian Kulas (Chicago Helsinki Committee), and Sr. Gillen, SHCJ (executive director NITF) heard testimony. In March 1989, Sister Gillen undertook an eighteen day fast of bread and water to protest the refusal of the Soviets to allow George Samoilovich, a Jewish man who suffered from lymphoma, to emigrate. She linked the event to other Jewish refuseniks and "the plight of Catholics in Czechoslovakia and Ukraine . . . still struggling for basic religious freedom {and} . . . unregistered churches . . ." (SSS Press release, March 14, 1989, SHCJ archive). In May 1989, Sister Gillen and Reverend Roderick attended a conference on "Free Movement" in Moscow sponsored by the International Foundation for Survival and Development of Humanity and sanctioned by the Soviet government ("Report of the SSS Delegation to the Int. Conf. . . ." May 17–20, 1989, SHCJ archive; and "Moscow Conference Opens on Freedom to Emigrate." May 17, 1989 AP www.apnesarchive/1989/moscow-conference-opens-on-freedom-to-emigrate/id-23f9422cc2ca405c8fe3a83aed37c524, accessed December 27, 2014). Both met with priests, ministers, refuseniks, former prisoners of conscience, and those fighting for religious freedom and liberty and the right to emigrate.

65. The new organization had dropped "on Soviet Jewry" from its name. On October 5, 1988, she testified before a Congressional committee on "The Slepak Principles" ("Testimony of Sr. Ann Gillen, SHCJ, SHCJ archive). She was listed as "Director of the National Interreligious Task Force." She wrote Rabbi Rudin (Letter, April 28, 1988,

(Spertus, box 48, Rudin folder) "I will also continue some work from the same office as consultant or director for the NITF." It is noteworthy that in a fax to Sister Gillen of May 18, 1992, Ralph Ruebner (SHCJ archive) wrote that the National Interreligious Task Force "was founded in Chicago in 1972 through the cooperation of the AJC and the NCCIJ. NITF has worked primarily for promoting emigration, religious freedom and related human rights in the USSR and Eastern Europe." In effect, the NITF replaced both the NITFSJ and the National Interreligious Legal Task Force on Human Rights (NITFHR). Ralph Ruebner (phone interview by the author, February 17, 2015) did not recall that the new organization replaced the old. After Sister Gillen left Chicago in 1990, it is likely that Ruebner ran the Task Force. In 1991, the NITF had meetings at John Marshall Law School.

66. This was signed by Sister Ann Gillen, SHCJ NITF; Rev. Keith Roderick, SSS; Prof. Ralph Ruebner, John Marshall Law School; and the Decalogue Society of Lawyers.

67. She wrote in response to Deena Metzger's "Vigil at Auschwitz" reprinted from *Chicago Sun Times* on September 10, 1989.

68. Letter, Dorothy Cropper, SHCJ Archivist to Norma, n.d. (1995) Spertus, box 10, folder correspondence/news and Spiegel 2008. According to "Necrology: Sister Ann Elizabeth Gillen, SHCJ" prepared by the SHCJ, she was diagnosed with cancer in 1989. It also has her moving from Chicago in 1989. In Philadelphia, she also worked on marketing a new biography of Cornelia Connelly who founded the Sisters of Holy Child Jesus (SHCJ).

TEN

Conclusion

The Contribution of Sister Ann Gillen and the Task Force to the American Advocacy Movement for Soviet Jewry

As originally envisioned by the AJC and the NCCIJ, the Task Force was to have an interfaith group of ten to twenty theologians who would deal with the issues relating to Soviet Jewry. Although the AJC prepared and later revised the list of participants, the "task force" of theologians never functioned. A similar fate befell the honorary sponsors and the honorary chair of the Task Force. AJC had appointed a group of well-known persons from government, the arts, and sports as honorary sponsors.[1] While a few attended formal events in the early years, most were inactive. If a sponsor died, neither the IAD nor the Task Force replaced them. The honorary chairman of the advisory board, Sargent Shriver, served in name only.[2] He rarely attended major Task Force activities. Some Task Force activists considered his sending a message or greetings for an event to be an important contribution. Nevertheless, as a member of the Kennedy family and vice presidential nominee in 1972, he brought prestige to the Task Force. Similarly, the public standing of many of the honorary sponsors enhanced the status and political clout of the Task Force.

Sister Margaret Traxler, Professor André LaCocque, Father John Pawlikowski, Sister Gloria Coleman, Professor Thomas Bird, Reverend John Steinbruck, Congressman Robert Drinan and a few others volunteered their services, speaking at events and conferences and attending meetings. But none participated in the Task Force on a regular or continuing basis.[3] In time, the Task Force became an organization of one, Sister Ann Gillen, assisted by a secretary.[4]

Sister Gillen ran the organization under the guidance of the IAD. Despite the need to clear many decisions with the IAD and her dependence on the AJC for funding and administrative support, she became an independent director and administrator of the Task Force. Her independence increased as she learned to navigate among the many organizations of the Soviet Jewry advocacy movement and American Jewish community.[5] She made contacts with activist advocates for Soviet Jewry in cities throughout the country. She worked well with the establishment National Conference on Soviet Jewry (NCSJ) and with the grass roots Union of Councils for Soviet Jewry (UCSJ).[6] Several AJC area (regional) directors, including Eugene DuBow, admired and respected her. She had a close professional and personal relationship with her IAD (AJC) supervisor Rabbi A. James Rudin, who advocated for her and the Task Force within the AJC.[7] She excelled in her personal relations with Jewish and Christian prisoners of conscience whom she met on her visits to the Soviet Union. Many of them were excited to meet an American Christian and a nun who cared so much about their plight. Her offer to Soviet authorities to finish the term of banishment for Ida Nudel moved the Soviet Jewish activist. Sister Gillen developed excellent ties with several Catholic and evangelical Protestant activists and groups advocating for Soviet Jews, their Christian brethren, and human rights in the Soviet Union.[8] Evangelical Protestant leaders turned to her for advice and guidance. In their eyes, she was a very persistent, committed, and dedicated advocate who often challenged mainline Protestant cooperation with the Russian Orthodox Church. She cultivated ties with members of Congress and the State Department.

For many, she became the Christian face of the Soviet Jewry advocacy movement in the United States. Importantly, in many of her activities, Sister Gillen attracted publicity. She was a novelty, a nun wearing a Star of David protesting the persecution of Soviet Jewry. In Rabbi Rudin's view (interview by author, NYC, September 17, 2009), "She was a woman you could not not pay attention to." Her aggressiveness, which included verbal attacks against visiting Soviet diplomats, officials and religious leaders, brought attention to herself and the cause she was fighting for. She sometimes alienated friends and allies, including the NCC. Once, she insulted visiting Russian Orthodox clergy in a reception in NYC, which Rabbi Rudin (interview by author, NYC, August 26, 2011) found to be "unpleasant for AJC and myself." She remained a valuable resource for the Soviet Jewry advocacy movement until the closing of the Task Force in 1988.

Sister Gillen was representative of many of the Catholic and Protestant clergy and lay persons affiliated with the Task Force. She had been influenced by Vatican II's call for Catholics to learn more about Jews and Judaism. She shifted her apostolate work to education, with a special emphasis on Jewish Christian concerns. She had an emotional tie to the

Holocaust believing that Christianity and the Church had not done enough to prevent the slaughter of the Jews. She wanted to rescue Soviet Jews from a possible religious and cultural genocide. It became her mission. She saw it as a personal call from God "to be a Catholic witness on solidarity with Jews, this is her passion" (Dr. Kent Hill, phone interview by the author, April 3, 2018).

CONCERN FOR CHRISTIANS AND A CHANGE IN TASK FORCE FOCUS

As Task Force director, Sister Ann Gillen took up the cause of persecuted Christians with the backing of Rabbis Marc Tanenbaum and James Rudin of the IAD, despite objections from some in the Task Force, the AJC, the wider American Jewish community, and the Israeli Liaison Bureau.[9] While she consistently emphasized that Soviet Jewry remained the main concern of the Task Force, by the mid-1980s the Task Force's involvement with persecuted Soviet Christians equaled its concerns for Soviet Jews. Several important decisions taken by Sister Gillen, as well as other independent events, had shifted the focus of the Task Force away from Soviet Jewry.

First, the Helsinki Final Act of April 1975 provided the justification and motivation for a more inclusive and universal human rights agenda for advocates for Soviet Jewry. It justified Sister Ann Gillen's concerns with persecuted Christians (and Jews), dissidents, and others in the Soviet Union.

Second, Sister Gillen's involvement with lawyers concerned about human rights violations in the Soviet Union in the 1980s contributed to a shift in Task Force priorities. Ironically, the Israeli Liaison Bureau and the NCSJ had urged the AJC to engage lawyers to provide legal assistance to Soviet Jews. The AJC, in turn, may have encouraged Sister Gillen to engage legal groups in her advocacy for Soviet Jewry. She and Professor Ralph Ruebner organized the Interreligious Legal Task Force for Human Rights in the early 1980s. While concerned with Soviet Jews, the Legal Task Force emphasized human rights violations that involved persons of any or no faith in the Soviet Union. Their first project involved filing a writ of *habeas corpus* on behalf of Andre Sakharov.

Third, the activism of American Christians on behalf of their coreligionists in the Soviet Union inadvertently moved the focus of the Task Force away from Soviet Jewry. The plight of the Pentecostal Siberian Seven who took refuge in the American Embassy in Moscow in 1978, contributed to a surge of interest among American Evangelicals in their coreligionists in the Soviet Union. On May 1, 1987, Kent Hill, an American evangelical Protestant activist and director of the Institute of Religion and Democracy (IRD), organized a demonstration on behalf of persecuted Christians in the Soviet Union in Washington, D.C. on May 1, 1987.[10] Sister Gillen had the Task Force co-sponsor the event. Symbolically, she dropped the reference to Soviet Jewry; the "National Interreligious Task Force" sponsored the event.

Fourth, by the early 1980s, Sister Gillen had increased her contact with captive nation groups and their affiliates about issues of discrimination in the Soviet Union that were mostly religious in nature. Later, with information sometimes supplied by the Soviet Union, several American citizens who came to the United States from Eastern Europe after WWII faced charges of having lied (decades before) on their US citizenship applications by failing to mention having served in the military forces of Nazi Germany. Many of those charged had served as guards in concentration camps. A conviction could result in loss of citizenship and deportation from the United States.

Sister Gillen opposed these hearings on grounds that questioned the veracity of evidence supplied by the Soviet Union, which had falsified evidence against Natan Sharansky, Ida Nudel, and many other Jewish refuseniks. She also charged that the legal proceedings lacked due process. Finally, she argued that the Soviets had supplied false information as part of an effort to drive a wedge between Jewish, Lithuanian, and Ukrainian activists in the United States who each wanted freedom for their respective brethren in the Soviet Union.

AN INTERFAITH ENDEAVOR

Around 1970, the American public and government officials perceived of the American Soviet Jewry advocacy movement as being exclusively Jewish. Sister Gillen and the Task Force efforts to foster interfaith cooperation in the Soviet Jewry advocacy movement helped to alter this perception.

The NITFSJ was a positive and productive example of interfaith cooperation in the United States during the 1970s and 1980s. It brought together Jewish, Catholic, and mainline and evangelical Protestant clergy, congregations, and lay persons to work on behalf of Jews in the Soviet Union.[11]

The Task Force influenced the American public, media, and elected officials to view the issue of Soviet Jewry as being a concern of all Americans and not an issue that mattered only to American Jews. Christian clergy, congregations, and lay persons from coast to coast and in almost every state supported the struggle for Soviet Jewry. Those who observed the protests and demonstrations came to realize that American Christians were protesting alongside American Jews. These cooperative efforts contributed to influencing the American government to pressure the Soviet Union to allow free emigration of Soviet Jews and cultural and religious freedom for those that remained. The publicity given to Sister

Gillen and the Task Force made it clear to the Soviet authorities, as well, that this was not an exclusively Jewish movement.

The December 6, 1987, Washington, D.C. demonstration of more than two hundred and fifty thousand people who rallied for Soviet Jewry prior to a Reagan-Gorbachev summit is a case in point. In spirit and words the speakers focused on Soviet Jewry with an Israeli Liaison Bureau emphasis of "let my people go" to Israel. From the dais, speaker after speaker noted that the demonstrators represented Jews and Christians, blacks and whites, young and old. Leaders of the Catholic Church, mainline Protestants (NCC), and civil rights activists spoke, while Evangelical leaders sent their blessings. Several of the speakers mentioned the plight of persecuted Christians in the Soviet Union. Representative John Lewis, an African American Congressman and hero of the civil rights movement, recalled Martin Luther King Jr. and Selma. According to David Harris (1989, 19), President Reagan said to Secretary Gorbachev: "You have seen on December the 6th the breadth and depth of American support-not American Jewish–American support for the issue. It won't go away." In addition, the Task Force and its supporters took up the struggle for other religious groups in the Soviet Union including Adventists, Baptists, and Roman Catholics. By 1987, the issue on the table between President Ronald Regan and Secretary Mikhail Gorbachev had become one of human rights, religious freedom, and emigration for all who wished to leave the Soviet Union.

The findings here support the argument made by Rachel Snyder on the influence of the domestic civil rights movement on later international human rights struggles (2018, 10). In her case study of American Jews and non-Jews advocating for Soviet Jewry, she notes a sign hung in D.C. in 1965 linking "Selma to Moscow." The study here confirms this connection in a vivid way. Sister Margaret Traxler, a key personality in initiating and operating the Task Force, marched in Selma. Significantly, at the founding Consultation of the Task Force, Charles Evers, the brother of the slain civil rights activist Medgar Evers, gave the keynote. He talked about how Jews were present in the civil rights struggle and how he, as an African American, was happy to be part of the struggle for the rights of Soviet Jews. Similar sentiments were expressed by Congressman Lewis at the Washington, D.C. December 1987 demonstration, who also participated in events at Selma (see chapter 9).

The findings here also have implications for one of the arguments presented in the recent book by James Loeffler (2018) on Jews and human rights. In the chapter on the Prisoners of Zion, he comments (2018, 290–291) that the 1975 Helsinki Accords which "contained a minor but important mention of human rights . . . would prove crucial for dissidents fighting for democratic freedom in the Soviet Union. . . ." In the case of Soviet Jews wanting to emigrate in 1968 and resettle in their own homeland of Israel, he argues that human rights had little to do with their demands. He writes ". . . While it seems like a victory for international human rights, in reality it had much more to do with Zionism and Cold War geopolitics" (2018, 290–291). He is correct in his assumption that, in the end, détente (geopolitics) between the US and USSR made possible the mass exodus of Soviet Jewry. There is a problem, however, with his focus on Zionism and his dismissal of human rights as a factor in the liberation of Soviet Jewry. The Helsinki Accords and human rights may have become much more relevant for Soviet Jewry in the late 1980s than Loeffler has perceived them to be.

In the late 1960s, the Israeli Liaison Bureau encouraged mainstream American Jewish organizations including the AJC to establish a united effort to advocate for the liberation of Soviet Jewry (Lazin 2005). They urged American Jews to support a Zionist solution which portrayed the issue as one of *Aliya (immigration to Israel)*. However, early on, the Liaison Bureau doubted that an exclusively Jewish advocacy effort would move Washington to pressure the Soviet Union to let Soviet Jews leave for Israel. They urged the involvement of American Christians in the advocacy effort. That led to establishment of the Task Force by the AJC and the National Catholic Conference for Interracial Justice (NCCIJ).

Task Force activists accepted the focus of the Liaison Bureau on the emigration of Soviet Jews and their resettlement in Israel, although many were motivated more by the spirit of tolerance toward Jews and Judaism of Vatican II; guilt related to the Holocaust; and the desire to prevent the cultural and religion genocide of Soviet Jewry. The emphasis of human rights in Basket III of the Helsinki Accords "that would prove crucial for dissidents fighting for democratic freedom in the Soviet Union" (Loeffler 2018, 291) would also become crucial for Sister Gillen, Robert Drinan, and the tens of thousands of Catholics and mainline Protestants that joined advocacy efforts. Moreover, many in the IAD, the AJC and the NCSJ put human rights before *aliya* (emigration and resettlement in Israel).[12] Later, Congress and President Carter worked for implementation of the human rights guaranteed in the Helsinki Accords (Loeffler 2018, 292). According to Secretary of State George Schultz (1993, 586, 602, 1101), who accompanied President Reagan to several summits with Secretary Gorbachev, the two leaders discussed human rights.

Without an advocacy effort in the United States based, increasingly, on demands for human rights for Soviet Jews, neither President Reagan nor Secretary Gorbachev may have every discussed the rights of Soviet Jews to emigrate or religious and cultural freedom for those that chose to remain. For many of the participants in the advocacy effort, the issue and motivation had become universal human rights.

Ironically, by the late 1980s the IAD had replaced the Task Force as AJC's interreligious advocate for Soviet Jewry. Prior to the establishment of the Task Force in 1972, the IAD had been very active in interfaith relations with Catholic, mainline, and evangelical Protestant and Greek

Orthodox Christians in matters of anti-Semitism, Jewish-Christian relations, and Soviet Jewry. The Task Force became another interreligious activity and program of the IAD, alongside its existing pursuits with various Christian institutions and organizations in the United States and overseas. In many cases, the IAD coordinated with the Task Force its interaction with Christians in matters concerning advocacy for Soviet Jewry. Yet at times, on matters of Soviet Jewry, it acted independently of Sister Gillen and the Task Force.

By the mid-1980s, however, with the Task Force in decline, the IAD became the major player for AJC in the interreligious advocacy effort on behalf of Soviet Jewry. In 1985–1986, for example, the IAD and local AJC personnel organized the public hearings on religious and cultural persecution in the Soviet Union in Chicago, Los Angeles, and Seattle. At the December 1987 rally in Washington, D.C., the IAD, and not the Task Force, invited Christian leaders to participate.

CLOSING THE TASK FORCE

The increased concern and activity by Sister Gillen and the Task Force on behalf of persecuted Christians and closed churches in the Soviet Union, as well as her criticism of the Israeli trial of an accused Nazi War criminal, cost her support among mainstream Jewish leaders and advocates for Soviet Jewry. The Demjanjuk incident probably influenced her standing at the AJC when its leaders decided about the future of the Task Force.

While her public criticism of the Israeli government for trying an alleged guard in a German death camp during WWII may have upset some in the AJC, it was not the main reason that the AJC decided to close the Task Force in May 1988. In December 1987, following the massive demonstration on behalf of Soviet Jewry in Washington, D.C., President Reagan and Secretary Gorbachev furthered détente between the two countries. There were soon indications that the gates of the Soviet Union would open for Jews wanting to leave and that those wanting to stay would enjoy greater cultural and religious freedom. For many American Jewish leaders there was no longer a need for advocacy for Soviet Jews. Also, the AJC's IAD, in cooperation with AJC offices throughout the United States, now handled most matters related to the persecution of Jews, Christians, and others in the Soviet Union.

Around this time, the Tananbaum Foundation, which had provided an annual grant for the Task Force since its founding, suffered losses in the financial markets. It informed the AJC that it could no longer provide funds for the Task Force. The AJC had other programs and activities that had more legitimate claims for resources and funding.

When Sister Ann Gillen passed away in 1995, Connie Smukler, an activist in the Soviet Jewry advocacy movement in Philadelphia wrote the following note (SHCJ archive, January 16, 1995):

> How much a part of that history you were! Our tears were your tears, and our joy was your joy. What a comfort it was to always see you in the marches, at the conferences . . . your strength and convictions were our comfort. When the history of American Jewish Advocacy movement for Soviet Jewry is written, your name will be most prominent. Hundreds of thousands of Soviet Jews owe their freedom to you. You made a difference.

NOTES

1. Rabbi Rudin (interview by the author, NYC, July 30, 2015) stated that in recruiting honorary sponsors, he and Gerald Strober told them that they would not have to do anything.

2. Rabbi Rudin (interview by the author, NYC, August 26, 2011) argues that when he met Shriver in 1973–1974, he was helpful and not just a figurehead.

3. A comment by the Rev. John Steinbruck is revealing. "I really had little contact with Gillen; only when she came to D.C." (John Steinbruck (phone interview by the author, December 12, 2013).

4. In the 1980s, Sister Anna Marie Erst, SHCJ, headed and prepared materials for the Task Force- affiliated Institute for Catholic Jewish Education in the Task Force office.

5. Over the years, key leaders in the interfaith world of Catholics and evangelical and mainline Protestants and advocates for Soviet Jewry affiliated with the NCSJ and UCSJ viewed Sister Gillen as the head of an independent Task Force.

6. She became an honorary board member of the UCSJ affiliated Chicago Action Committee for Soviet Jewry (Pam Cohen, phone interview by author, March 25, 2018).

7. He became IAD head in the early 1980s.

8. In time, she established a good working relationship with the NCCB in Washington, D.C.

9. At the founding Consultation in April 1972, the Statement of Conscience referred to the persecution of Jews and "other doomed groups and nationalities" (see chapter 3).

10. IRD, an advocacy group of mainstream Protestants and Catholics, opposed NCC policies of cooperating with the state sponsored Russian Orthodox Church.

11. The movement included Catholics, mainline Protestants, and Evangelicals along with feminists, civil rights activists, and some members of captive nations. After participating in the first Consultation, the Eastern Orthodox Church left the Task Force.

12. After March 1976, most Soviet Jews upon arrival in Vienna chose to go West and not to resettle in Israel. In the United States among advocates for Soviet Jewry, a growing majority came to favor "freedom of choice," allowing Soviet Jews to choose the country where they wanted to resettle. When the gates of the Soviet Union opened in 1988 and 1989, the overwhelming majority of Soviet Jews preferred not to resettle in Israel.

Appendix

The author conducted all the interviews. He conducted them face-to-face or on the phone. The author is most appreciative of those who were willing to discuss the subject of the research. The author took notes and they are stored in his personal archive.

Mimi Alperin, AJC layperson, former Chair of AJC Commission on Interreligious Affairs, NYC, December 5, 2013.
Paul Applebaum, activist in Soviet Jewry advocacy among medical personnel in Boston, MA, NYC, August 25, 2009.
Stanley Balzekas, Jr., active in Lithuanian community affairs in Chicago, phone interview, May 9, 2016.
Judith Banki, former member of Interreligious Affairs Department (IAD) of AJC, NYC, August 8, 2012.
Steve Bayme, National director of Communal Affairs, AJC, NYC, September 23, 2009.
Jacob Yaakov Birenbaum, founder of Student Struggle for Soviet Jewry (SSSJ), phone interview, January 8, 2010.
Prof. Thomas Bird, Task Force activist, authority on religion in the Soviet Union, lay participant in ecumenical affairs of Roman Catholic Church, NYC, February 11, 2011 and Queens, NY, February 26, 2013.
Ken Bresler, former staff member of Congressman Robert Drinan, phone interview, January 19, 2016.
Prof. Lynn Buzzard, former director of Christian Legal Society (CLS) and Professor of Law at Campbell University, NC, phone interview, March 25, 2015.
Pam Cohen, former President Union of Councils for Soviet Jewry (UCSJ), Soviet Jewry activist in Chicago, phone interview, March 25, 2018.
Sister Gloria Coleman, SHCJ, head of interreligious affairs in Cardinal's Commission on Human Rights (Philadelphia), friend of Sister Ann Gillen, Rosemont, March 12, 2012 and June 20, 2015, and phone interview October 27, 2014.
Ambassador Ginte Damusis, director, Lithuanian Information Center (NY) 1980–1991, activist for human rights and religious freedom in Lithuania, phone interview, December 16, 2016.
Eugene DuBow, director of AJC in Chicago, director of AJC Community Services Department, NYC, January 14, 2010.
Eugene Fisher, former associate director for Catholic-Jewish Relations at Secretariat for Ecumenical and Interreligious Affair at USCCB, phone interview, February 16, 2017.
David Geller, former AJC coordinator of Soviet Jewry policy, member of Foreign Affairs Department (AJC) and former director of Greater New York Conference on Soviet Jewry (GNYCSJ, phone interview, April 11, 2018.
Eugene Gold, former District Attorney of Bronx, NY and former head of GNYCSJ, NYC, May 28, 2008.
Jerry Goodman, former director of National Conference for Soviet Jewry, NYC, December 1, 2009, August 16, 2011, and December 19, 2013 and phone interviews, May 17, 2012 and January 31, 2017.

William Gralnick, former director, Southeast Region AJC, active in Task Force programs and outreach to Evangelicals, phone interview, November 4, 2014.

Kent Hill, a PhD in Russian and East European intellectual history, former director of the Institute of Religion and Democracy, phone interviews, October 30, 2014, February 13, 2017 and May 2018.

Patience Huntwork, attorney and human rights activist, located in Phoenix, AZ, phone interview, January 7, 2015.

James Huntwork, election monitor in Ukraine in 1991 with Sister Ann Gillen, phone interview, April 13, 2015.

Abe Karlikow, former director AJC European Office, Del Ray Beach, FL, March 14, 2011.

Ed Koch, former Congressman and mayor of NYC, activist on issues of Soviet Jewry, NYC, interview, November 18, 2009.

Prof. Andre LaCocque, Protestant theologian at Chicago Theological Seminary, Task Force activist, phone interview, December 17, 2013.

Jonathan Levine, director of AJC Chicago (1981-2002), phone interviews, May 15, 2013 and April 1, 2015.

Irv Levine, former director, AJC National Project on Ethnic America, Jupiter, FL, March 2, 2016.

Rabbi Alan Mittleman, worked at IAD (AJC) (1984-1988), supervised Sister Ann Gillen, NYC, March 18, 2015.

Father John Pawlikowski, Catholic theologian at Chicago Theological Union, Task Force activist, NYC, August 5, 2011 and September 21, 2014.

Dr. Martin Plax, former AJC employee in Cleveland, OH, outreach to Ukrainian community, phone interview, November 5, 2014.

Glen Richter, activist in SSSJ, phone interview, October 16, 2015.

Rabbi A. James Rudin, former director, IAD and supervisor of Ann Gillen, NYC, September 17, 2009, August 26 2011 and July 30, 2015, and phone interview, May 8, 2012.

Ralph Ruebner, Prof. (Emeritus) at John Marshall Law School and co-founder of National Interreligious Legal Task Force on Human Rights, phone interviews, February 17, 2015 and April 12, 2018.

Morey Schapiro, Soviet Jewry activist in Bay Area Council for Soviet Jewry and past President of UCSJ, phone interview, November 20 2015

Cz Schnur, former director of Greater New York Conference on Soviet Jewry, NYC, July 15, 2014.

Naomi Schwartz, former chair of Berkshire (MA) Council for Soviet Jewry, phone interview, December 26, 2014.

Amir Shavit, former representative of World Zionist Organization in Los Angeles, NYC, December 2009.

Adam Simms, former assistant area director of AJC in Chicago, phone interview, September 22, 2014.

Connie Smukler, activist and advocate for Soviet Jewry in Philadelphia, Philadelphia, March 6, 2014.

Rev John Steinbruck, senior pastor at Luther Place Memorial Church in Washington, D.C., activist for Soviet Jewry and Task Force, phone interview, December 12, 2013.

Fr Robert George Stephanopoulos, past director of Ecumenical Affairs of Greek Orthodox Diocese of America and active in early years of Task Force, phone interview, December 12, 2013.

Gerald S Strober, worked for IAD (AJC), supervisor of Sister Ann Gillen and Task Force, NYC, December 22, 2009.

List of Abbreviations

ABA	American Bar Association
ADL	Anti-Defamation League
AJC	American Jewish Committee
ASL	Association of Soviet Lawyers
BB	B'nai B'rith
CCAR	Central Conference of American Rabbis
CCSJ	Chicago Conference on Soviet Jewry
CIC	Catholic Interracial Council
CJF	Council of Jewish Federations and Welfare Funds
CLS	Christian Legal Society
CR	*Congressional Record*
CRC	Community Relations Council
CREED	Christian Rescue Efforts for the Emancipation of Dissidents
CRIA	Council of Religion and International Affairs
CSCE	Commission on Security and Cooperation in Europe
CTS	Chicago Theological Seminary
CTU	Chicago Theological Union
DES	Department of Educational Services (of the NCCIJ)
FAD	Foreign Affairs Department (of the AJC)
GNYCSJ	Greater New York Conference on Soviet Jewry
IAD	Interreligious Affairs Department (of the AJC)
IHT	*International Herald Tribune*
ILTFHR	Interreligious Legal Task Force on Human Rights
INS	Immigration and Naturalization Service
IRD	Institute on Religion and Democracy
JCC	Jewish Community Center
JCCMB	Jewish Community Council of Metropolitan Boston

JCRC	Jewish Community Relations Council
JTA	Jewish Telegraphic Agency
LACC	Los Angeles City Council
LCA	Lutheran Church in America
LCWR	Leadership Conference of Women Religious
MFN	Most Favored Nation
NAACP	National Association for the Advancement of Colored People
NAE	National Association of Evangelicals
NAWR	National Assembly of Women Religious
NCAN	National Coalition of American Nuns
NCC	National Council of Churches in Christ
NCCB	National Conference of Catholic Bishops
NCCIJ	National Catholic Conference on Interracial Justice
NCEA	National Catholic Education Association
NCCJ	National Conference of Christians and Jews
NCNS	National Catholic News Service
NCSJ	National Conference on Soviet Jewry
NEC	National Executive Council (of the AJC)
NICSJ	National Interreligious Consultation on Soviet Jewry (initial name of the NITFSJ)
NJCRAC	National Jewish Community Relations Advisory Council
NITFSJ	National Interreligious Task Force on Soviet Jewry
NILTFHR	National Interreligious Legal Task Force on Human Rights
NJCC	New Jersey Council of Churches
NOBC	National Office for Black Catholics
NYC	New York City
NYT	*The New York Times*
OSI	Office of Special Investigations
RNS	*Religious News Service*
SFC	Sister Formation Conferences
SHCJ	Society of the Holy Child Jesus
SLA	Soviet Lawyers Association

SSS	Society of St. Stephen
SSSJ	Student Struggle for Soviet Jewry
UAHC	Union of American Hebrew Congregations
UCSD	University of Chicago School of Divinity
UCSJ	Union of Councils for Soviet Jewry
UJA	United Jewish Appeal
USCCB	United States Conference of Catholic Bishops
VOA	Voice of America
WCC	World Council of Churches
WJC	World Jewish Congress

Bibliography

Abram, Morris. *Testimony*. New York: William E. Wiener Oral History Library of the American Jewish Committee, March 6, 1989.
Altshuler, Stuart. *From Exodus to Freedom: The History of the Soviet Jewry Movement*. Lanham MD: Roman and Littlefield, 2005.
Banki, Judith. *Testimony*. NY: William E. Wiener Oral History Library of the AJC, June 3, 1980.
———. "Religious Education Before and After Vatican II." In *Twenty Years of Jewish-Catholic Relations*, edited by Eugene J. Fisher, A. James Rudin, Marc H. Tanenbaum, 125–234.
Bayer, Abraham. "American Response to Soviet Anti-Jewish Policies. In *American Jewish Year Book 1973* (74), edited by Morris Fine and Milton Himmelfarb.
Philadelphia & NY: AJC & JPS, 1973, 210–225.
———. *Testimony*. NY: William E. Wiener Oral History Library of the AJC, May 4, 1989.
Beckerman, Gal. *When They Come for Us We'll Be Gone: The Epic Struggle to Save Soviet Jewry*. Boston, NY: Houghton Mifflin Harcourt, 2010.
Bishop, Clair Huchet. *How Catholics Look at Jews: Inquiries into Italian and French Teaching Materials*. Mahwah, N.J.: Paulist Press, 1974.
Bookbinder, Hyman. "The Jewish Role in the US in the U.S political Process—Strategies for Effective Impact." Address presented at 54th General Assembly of CJF, Washington DC, November 14, 1985.
———. *Testimony*. NY: William E. Wiener Oral History Library of the AJC, Jun 3–4, 1974.
Borromeo, C.S.C, Sister M. Charles, ed. *The New Nuns*. NY: Signet books, 1967.
Buwalda, Petrus. *They Did Not Dwell Alone: Jewish Emigration from the Soviet Union 1967–1990*. Washington D.C.: The Woodrow Wilson Center Press/Baltimore: The Johns Hopkins University Press, 1997.
Chernin, Albert D. "Making Soviet Jews an Issue: A History." In *A Second Exodus: The American Movement to Free Soviet Jews*, edited by Murray Friedman, and Albert Chernin. Hanover, NH and London: Brandeis University Press Published by University Press of New England, 1999, 15–69.
Cohen, Richard. "With One Voice: A Day-by-Day Report on The Brussels Conference." *Congress Bi-Weekly* March 19, 1971, 4–10.
Connelly, John. *From Enemy to Brother: The Revolution in Catholic Teaching on the Jews, 1933–1965*. Cambridge MA & London, England, Harvard University Press, 2012.
———. "Converts who changed the Church: Jewish-Born Clerics Helped Push Vatican II Reforms." Forward August 30, 2012 http://forward.com/articles/159955/converts-who-changed-the-church/ (accessed August 20, 2012).
Decter, Moshe. *Testimony*. NY: William E. Wiener Oral History Library of the AJC, February 22, 1990.
De Jonge, Alex. *Stalin and the Shaping of the Soviet Union*. Glasgow: Collins, 1986.
Dershowitz, Alan M. *Chutzpah*. Boston: Little, Brown and Company, 1991.
Dinstein, Yoram. *Testimony*. New York: William E. Wiener Oral History Library of the AJC, November 28, 1989.
———. "Soviet Jewry in Crisis." Address presented at 53rd General Assembly of CJF, Toronto, November 14–18, 1984.

Douglas, Lawrence. *The Right Wrong Man: John Demjanjuk and the Last Great Nazi War Criminal Trial*. Princeton: Princeton University Press, 2016.
DuBow, Eugene. *Testimony*. NY: William E. Wiener Oral History Library of the AJC, October 17, 1980.
Feingold, Henry. *"Silent No More": Saving the Jews of Russia, the American Jewish Effort, 1967–1989*. Syracuse: Syracuse University Press, 2006.
Feldman, Egal. *Dual Destinies: The Jewish Encounter with Protestant American*. Urbana and Chicago: University of Illinois Press, 1990.
———. *Catholics and Jews in Twentieth Century American*. Urbana and Chicago. University of Illinois Press, 2001.
Fisher, Eugene, Rudin, A. James and Tanenbaum, Marc, eds. *Twenty Years of Jewish-Catholic Relations*. Mahwah, NJ: Paulist Press, 1986.
———. "Introduction: Nostra Aetate, For our Times and for the Future." In *Twenty Years of Jewish-Catholic Relations*, edited by Eugene J. Fisher, A. James Rudin, Marc H. Tanenbaum, 1–5.
———. "The Roman Liturgy and Catholic-Jewish Relations Since the Second Vatican Council." In *Twenty Years of Jewish-Catholic Relations*, edited by Eugene J. Fisher, A. James Rudin, Marc H. Tanenbaum, 135–155. NY: Mahwah Paulist Press, 1986.
Foxman, Abraham. *Testimony*. NY: William E. Wiener Oral History Library of the AJC, November 9, 1989.
Friedman, Murray and Albert Chernin, eds. *A Second Exodus: The American Movement to Free Soviet Jews*. Hannover, NH: University Press of New England, 1999.
Geller, David. "Second World Conference on Soviet Jewry." In *AJYB, 1977 (77)*, edited by Morris Fine and Milton Himmelfarb, Philadelphia and NY: AJC and JPS, 1976, 153–156.
———. *Testimony*. NY: William E. Wiener Oral History Library of the AJC, April 30, 1990.
Gibel, Inga. *Testimony*. NY: William E. Wiener Oral History Library of the AJC, September 17, 1980.
Gold, Bertram. *Testimony*. NY: William E. Wiener Oral History Library of the AJC, October 30, 1980 and December 10, 1980.
Goldberg, Arthur J. *Testimony*. NY: William E. Wiener Oral History Library of the AJC, January 17 and May 23, 1979.
Goldberg, J.J. *Jewish Power: Inside the American Jewish Establishment*. Reading MA; Addison-Wesley, 1996.
Goodman, Jerry. "American Response to Soviet Anti-Jewish Policies." In *American Jewish Year Book (AJYB) 1965 (66)*, edited by Morris Fine and Milton Himmelfarb. Philadelphia: AJC and JPS, 1965, 312–319.
———. *Testimony*. NY: William E. Wiener Oral History Library of the AJC, September 18 and October 3, 1979.
Harris, David. *Testimony*. NY: William E. Wiener Oral History Library of the AJC, March 7 and October 2, 1989.
Higgins, Rev. Msgr. George. "Twenty Years of Catholic Jewish Relations: Nostra Aetate in Retrospect. In *Twenty Years of Jewish-Catholic Relations*, edited by Eugene J. Fisher, A. James Rudin, Marc H. Tanenbaum, 19–38.
Hennesey, James, S.J. *American Catholics: A History of the Roman Catholic Community in the United States*. NY: Oxford University Press, 1981.
Henold, Mary J. *Catholic and Feminist: The Surprising History of the American Catholic Feminist Movement*. Chapel Hill: University of North Carolina Press, 2008.
Hoenlein, Malcolm. *Testimony*. NY: William E. Wiener Oral History Library of the AJC, June 14, 1989.
Isaac, Jules. *Jesus and Israel*. NY: Holt, Rinehart and Winston, 1971.
———. *Has anti-Semitism Roots in Christianity?* NCCJ, 1961.
———, *The Teaching of Contempt: The Christian Roots of anti-Semitism*. NY: Holt, Rinehart and Winston, 1964.

Koehlinger, Amy L. *The New Nuns: Racial Justice and Religious Reform in the 1960s.* Cambridge, MA: Harvard University Press, 2007.
Lazin, Fred. " The Response of the American Jewish Committee to the Crisis of German Jewry, 1933–1939." *American Jewish History* 68 no. 3 (1979): 283–304.
———. *The Struggle for Soviet Jewry in American: Israel versus the American Jewish Establishment.* Lanham, MD: Lexington Books, 2005.
Levanon, Nehemia. *Testimony.* NY: William E. Wiener Oral History Library of the AJC, December 3, 1989.
———. *"Nativ" Was the Code Name.* Tel Aviv: Am Oved, 1995 (Hebrew).
———. "Israel's Role in the Campaign." In *A Second Exodus: The American Movement to Free Soviet Jews,* edited by Murray Friedman, and Albert Chernin. Hanover, NH and London: Brandeis University Press Published by University Press of New England, 1999, 70–89.
Levine, Jacqueline K. *Testimony.* NY: William E. Wiener Oral History Library of the AJC, June 19, 1989.
Lewy, Guenter. *The Catholic Church and Nazi Germany.* NY: McGraw Hill, 1964.
Loeffler. *Rooted Cosmopolitans: Jews and Human Rights in the Twentieth Century.* New Haven and London: Yale University Press, 2018.
Miller, Israel. *Testimony.* NY: William E. Wiener Oral History Library of the AJC, February 15, 1990.
Mittleman, Allan, Sarna, Jonathan D. Sarna and Licht, Robert, eds. *Jewish Polity and American Civil Society: Communal Agencies and Religious Movements in the American Public Sphere.* Lanham, Boulder, NY and Oxford: Rowman and Littlefield Publishers, Inc., 2002.
Morse, Arthur. *While Six Million Died.* New York: Random House, 1968.
Orbach, William. *The American Movement to Aid Soviet Jews.* Amherst, MA: University of Massachusetts Press, 1969.
Passelecq, Georges and Suchecky, Bernard. *The hidden Encyclical of Pius XI.* NY: Harcourt Brace, C1997 (English edition, translated from the French by Steven Rendall.
Pawlikowski, John T. "New Trends in Catholic Religious Thought." In *Twenty Years of Jewish-Catholic Relations,* edited by Eugene J. Fisher, A. James Rudin, Marc H. Tanenbaum, 169–190.
Pinkus, Benjamin. "Israel Activity on Behalf of Soviet Jewry." In *Organizing Rescue: Jewish National Solidarity in the Modern Period,* edited by Selwyn Ilan Troen and Benjamin Pinkus. London: Frank Cass, 1992), 373–402.
Pratt, Yehoshua. *Testimony.* NY: William E. Wiener Oral History Library of the AJC, November 19 and December 4, 1989.
Preston, Andrew. *Sword of the Spirit, Shield of Faith: Religion in American War and Diplomacy.* New York: Anchor Books, 2012.
Rager, Yitzhak. *Testimony.* NY: William E. Wiener Oral History Library of the AJC, June 8, 1990.
Rosenne, Meir. *Testimony.* NY: William E. Wiener Oral History Library of the AJC, November 10, 1989.
Rudin, James. *Testimony.* New York: William E. Wiener Oral History Library of the AJC, April 12, 1990.
———. *Cushing, Spellman, O'Connor: The Surprising Story of How Three American Cardinals transformed Catholic-Jewish Relations.* Grand Rapids, Michigan: William B. Eerdmans Publishing Company, 2012.
———. "The Dramatic Impact of Nostra Aetate." In *Twenty Years of Jewish-Catholic Relations,* edited by Eugene J. Fisher, A. James Rudin, Marc H. Tanenbaum, 9–18.
Salitan, Laurie P. *Politics and Nationality in Contemporary Soviet-Jewish Emigration, 1968–1989.* NY: St. Martin's Press, 1992.
Sanders, Ronald. *Shores of Refuge: A Hundred Years of Jewish Emigration.* NY: Henry Holt, 1988.
Sanua, Marianne R.. *Let Us Prove Strong: The American Jewish Committee, 1945–2006.* Waltham, MA: Brandeis University Press, 2007.

Schroeter, Leonard. *The Last Exodus*. Jerusalem: Weidenfeld and Nicolson, 1974.
Schroth Raymond A., S.J.. *Bob Drinan: The Controversial Life of the First Catholic Priest Elected to Congress*. NY: Fordham University Press, 2011.
Schultz, Kevin M.. *Tri-Faith America: How Catholics and Jews Held Postwar America to its Protestant Promise*. NY: Oxford University Press, 2011.
Schwartz, Solomon. *The Jews in the Soviet Union*. Syracuse: Syracuse University Press, 1951.
Shultz, George P. *Turmoil and Triumph: My Years as Secretary of State*. NY: Charles Scribner and Sons, 1993.
Simon, Rita. *In the Golden Land: A Century of Russian and Soviet Jewish Immigration in America*. Westport CT: Praeger, 1997.
Snyder, Sarah. *From Selma to Moscow: How Human Rights Activists Transformed U.S. Foreign Policy*. New York: Columbia University Press, 2018.
Spiegel, Philip. *Triumph Over Tyranny: The Heroic campaign that Saved 2,000 000 soviet Jews*. NY: Devora Publishing, 2008.
Stern, Paula. *Water's Edge: Domestic Politics and the Making of American Foreign Policy*. Westport, CT: Greenwood Press, 1979.
Stossel, Scott. *Sarge: The Life and Times of Sargent Shriver*. Washington DC: Smithsonian Books, 2004.
Strober, Gerald. *American Jews: Community in Crisis*. Garden City, NY: Doubleday & Company, 1974.
———. *Testimony*. New York: William E. Weiner Oral History Library of the AJC, January 19, 1989.
Tanenbaum, Marc. *Testimony*. New York: William E. Weiner Oral History Library of the AJC, October 7, 19 and November 13, 1980.
———. "A Jewish Viewpoint on Nostra Aetate." In *Twenty Years of Jewish-Catholic Relations*, edited by Eugene J. Fisher, A. James Rudin, Marc H. Tanenbaum, 39–60.
Taylor, Telford. *Courts of Terror: Soviet Criminal Justice and Jewish Emigration*. NY: Alfred Knopf, 1976.
Wiesel, Elie. *The Jews of Silence*. Philadelphia, JPS, 1967.
Yockey, Roger. *I Never Stopped Believing: the Life of Walter Hubbard*. Xlibris, 2017.

Index

ABA. *See* American Bar Association
Abernathy, Ralph D., 51n37
abortion, 30n45
Abram, Morris, 156, 205, 214n40
Abrams, Elliott, 134n29, 157
Ad Council, 25n6
aggiornamento (updating of the church), 12n8, 18, 22, 29n32, 30n40
Ahmann, Matthew, 12n7, 25n7
AJC. *See* American Jewish Committee
Akhimov, V. S., 62
Aleksandrovich, Rivka, 33
Aleksandrovich, Ruth, 33
aliya (immigration to Israel), 107n21, 151, 165n30, 224
Alperstein, Arnold S., 206
American Bar Association (ABA), 9, 198–199
American Jewish Committee (AJC), 2, 4, 5, 49n21, 49n27, 57, 71, 98, 135n35, 161n2; "Blue Book" and, 132n4, 162n7; CSCE and, 132n5; hearings, 133n7; Helsinki Accords and, 112–114; immigration and role of, 2; Khrushchev and, 47n3; *Project Lifeline*, 9; Soviet Jewry and, 31–32, 32–33; Task Force and, 125–128. *See also* Interreligious Affairs Department; National Interreligious Task Force on Soviet Jewry
Amias, Saul, 108n26
Amnesty International, 43, 150
Anderson, Wendell, 152
Anderson-Kemp bill, 152
Andropov, Yuri, 172
"Another forgotten dissident" (Makus), 141n83
Arad, Moshe, 205
Archer, Bill, 80, 188n8
Ariev, Yacov, 136n47

Armitage, John, 66
Armstrong, James, 182, 183
Asher, Dan, 88n58
Association of Soviet Lawyers (ASL), Legal Task Force with ABA agreement and, 198–199
Azbel, M., 168n68

Babi Yar, 141n83, 171, 187n2
Bacon, Jack, 51n37
Badillo, Herman, 51n37, 54n63
Bailar, Richard, 69, 119
Baker, Andrew, 157, 175
Bakis, Audrys, 148
Balint, Judy, 192n42
Balzekas, Stanley, Jr., 137n57, 138n58
Baptists, persecution of, 143n103, 177
Baptist Standard Weekly (newspaper), 136n42
Bar. *See* Israeli Liaison Bureau
Barinoff, Irene, 178
Barnes, Michael, 142n93
Barrett, Daniel, 39
Basket III, Helsinki Accords and, 111–112, 164n23
Bassiouni, Cherif, 155
Bayer, Abe, 129, 141n88, 182, 193n55, 194n57
Bayh, Birch, 134n24
Baylinson, David, 143n95
Bea, Augustin, 12n11, 17, 18, 19, 27n17–27n18
Becker, Levy, 108n26
Begun, Josef, 147
Belgrade Conference on Security and Cooperation in Europe, 146–149
Bellow, Saul, 12n4, 47n4
Bennett, Joan, 108n26
Bergman, Elihu, 66
Bernadin, Joseph L., 8, 134n26

Bernstein, Leonard, 51n37
Berzonsky, Vladimir, 185
Bichkov, Alexie, 90n89
Bikel, Theodore, 50n30
Bird, Thomas, 39–40, 71, 75, 106n16, 107n18, 107n23, 108n26, 118, 137n57, 147, 171; Belgrade Conference and, 147; biography of, 133n10; Brussels II Conference and, 99, 100, 127; Helsinki Accords and, 112, 113, 133n7; Philadelphia conference and, 179; Task Force and, 157, 219
Birnbaum, Yakov, 54n62
Blake, Eugene Carson, 33, 48n12
Blaustein, Joe, 139n74
"Blue Book," AJC and, 132n4, 162n7
Blume, Rita, 83n6
Bohlen, Charles, 50n33
Boiter, Albert, 191n34
Bond, Julian, 51n37
Bookbinder, Hyman, 50n33, 87n48, 156, 158
Bosco, Anthony, 48n15
Boutilier, Eugene, 190n28
Brailovsky, Irina, 171
Brailovsky, Viktor, 73, 171, 208
Brandt, Willy, 106n11
Brauer, Jerald, 137n57
Brauer, Jerome, 51n36
Braun, Roger, 108n26
Brennan, Margaret, 72
Brezhnev, Leonid, 76, 87n53, 212n21
Brooke, Edward, 50n33, 51n37
Brouwer, Arie, 206
Brown, William, 59
Brown v. Board of Education, 16
Brussels I Conference, 51n35, 97, 98, 99, 106n6, 107n20
Brussels II Conference: with "Call to Christian Conscience", 101, 102–103, 103, 104, 108n28; catalyst for, 97–98; "Declaration of Principles", 100, 101, 103–104; delegates, 99–100, 100–101; Helsinki Accords and, 98, 99, 101; Interfaith Commission at, 101–102; Meir and, 103, 160, 161; planning stages, 97, 98–100; recommendations from, 127; success of, 104–105

Brussels III Conference, 145–146, 159–161
Bruster, Bill, 135n38
Buchanan, John, 131, 142n94, 143n99
Buckley, William F., 51n37
Bush, George H. W., 168n57, 205, 206
Butman, Lilu, 90n81
Buzzard, Lynn, 154, 187n1
"A call from Jerusalem to all People of Conscience" (Rudin), 159–160
"Call to Christian Conscience," Brussels II Conference with, 101, 102–103, 103, 104, 108n28

Campbell, Thomas, 36, 49n24, 51n36
Canon Law, 28n29–28n31
captive nations, 8, 111, 121, 128, 145, 156, 226n11; defined, 5; representatives of, 11n2, 161n1; support for, 163n21; VOA and, 138n65
Carlebach, Shlomo, 60
Carmelite convent, 209
Carter, Jimmy: Madrid Conference and, 149; Moscow Olympics and, 152; role of, 119, 129, 136n45, 141n87, 146, 190n22, 224
Castel, Pol, 136n52
Catholic Interracial Council, 22
CCSJ. *See* Chicago Conference on Soviet Jewry
Cechinni, Michel, 147
Center for the Study of Religion and Communism, 131
Chafin, Ken, 135n39
Chavez, César, 54n63
Chernin, Al, 105n5
Chernyak, Irma, 77
Chicago Conference on Soviet Jewry (CCSJ), 216n64–216n65
Children of the Otkazniki program, 61, 63
China, 14n24
Chomsky, Noam, 47n4
Chrisman, Oswin, 118
Christian Rescue Efforts for the Emancipation of Dissidents (CREED), 131, 135n30, 182, 193n51

Christians: Brussels II Conference and, 101; Coalition for Solidarity with Christians, 181–182, 193n53; Task Force with dissidents and Soviet, 82; Task Force with focus shift and concern for, 221–222
Church, Frank, 105n3, 107n24
Church Peace Union, 25n3
civil rights movement, 3, 13n18, 16, 22, 23, 25n8, 30n40, 223
Clifford, Donald, 68
Clinchy, Everett R., 16, 25n6
Coalition for Solidarity with Christians, 181–182, 193n53
Cohen, Dick, 100
Coleman, Gloria: Philadelphia conference and, 179; role of, 54n65, 68, 118, 137n57, 158, 172, 175, 188n7, 192n46, 216n61; in Soviet Union, 151, 152; Task Force and, 219
Commager, Henry Steele, 47n4
Commission on Security and Cooperation in Europe (CSCE), 112, 132n5
Community Relations Board of City of Cleveland, 134n25
Community Relations Councils (CRCs), 5
Conference of Major Superiors of Women, 29n32, 29n34
Connelly, Cornelia, 211n8
Connelly, John, 18
Consultation. *See* National Interreligious Consultation on Soviet Jewry
Cooke, Terence, 8, 79, 93n123
Coopersmith, Brant, 47n8, 76, 108n26
Cornelson, Rufus, 107n25
Corti, Mario, 163n17
Cotler, Irwin, 168n68
Cranston, Alan, 65
CRCs. *See* Community Relations Councils
CREED. *See* Christian Rescue Efforts for the Emancipation of Dissidents
Croin, August H., 147
CSCE. *See* Commission on Security and Cooperation in Europe

CSCE conferences. *See* Security and Cooperation in Europe conferences
Cummins, John, 86n40
Cushing, Richard, 13n16, 19

Dallas Times Herald (newspaper), 136n42
Damusis, Ginte, 136n52, 176, 179, 181, 182
David, Jean Paul, 108n26
Davies, Richard T., 47n8
Davis, Angela, 33
Davis, Margy Ruth, 120
Davis, Moshe, 108n26
Day, Dorothy, 51n37
"Declaration of Principles," Brussels II Conference and, 100, 101, 103–104
Decter, Aaron, 70
Decter, Moshe, 1, 132n4
delegates, at Brussels II Conference, 99–100, 100–101
Demjanjuk, John, 9, 13n23, 167n51; with deportation, 200; Gillen on, 198, 200–201, 202, 204; Task Force and, 199–204
demonstrations: at International Women's Conference (1980), 153; Task Force with, 205–206
Department of Educational Services (DES), NCCIJ, 23, 30n41
deportation, from US, 155, 200, 204, 212n25, 213n27–213n28, 222
Dequeker, Luc, 107n25, 108n26
Derby, Matt, 135n38
Dershowitz, Alan, 199
DES. *See* Department of Educational Services, NCCIJ
Devlin, Charles, 107n25, 137n57
Dicharry, Warren, 88n58
Dickinson, William L., 143n95
Diefenbaker, John, 106n11
Dinenzon, Luboc, 85n26, 122, 132n4
Dinstein, Yoram, 132n4
dissidents, 141n83; CREED, 131, 135n30, 182, 193n51; Israeli Liaison Bureau with, 128, 129; Task Force with Soviet Christians and, 82
Dobczansky, George, 142n94
Dole, Robert, 148, 168n63

Donovan, Meg, 157, 164n24
Donovan, Victor, 135n34
Dorbiansky, Lev, 142n94
Dorfman, Joseph, 179
Douglas, William O., 1, 47n4
Dreyfuss, Jacques, 108n26
Drinan, Robert, 168n64; Brussels II Conference and, 101, 102; Brussels III Conference and, 160–161; with Consultation, second, 121; Consultation and, 40–41; role of, 9, 49n28, 52n42–52n43, 70, 107n24, 108n26, 138n59; Sakharov and, 129; Solidarity Sundays and, 78; in Soviet Union, 74–75; Task Force and, 72, 158; *The Task* newsletter and, 76, 77
DuBow, Eugene, 90n82, 108n26; Brussels II Conference and, 105; role of, 12n5–12n6, 38, 49n24, 50n31, 57, 71, 123, 137n57, 220; Task Force and, 127–128, 129, 157, 158; *The Task* newsletter and, 75
Dulzin, Arye, 98
Dunlop, John, 142n94
Dushnyck, Walter, 113–114
Dymshits, Mark, 142n91

Early, Tracey, 184
Eastern Orthodox Church, 226n11
Edinger, Judy, 124
Egan, Edward, 39, 50n34
Ehrenkranz, Joseph, 108n26
Eilberg, Joshua, 107n24, 199–200
Eker, Rita, 150
Eliav, Arie, 75
Elmer, Colin, 108n26
Emancipation Proclamation, 16
Encyclopedia of Lithuania, 177
Engel, Irving, 31, 55n72
England, visits to Ireland and, 150–151
Eppelman, Pauline, 73
Ericson, Phil, 135n38
Erst, Ann Marie, 99, 107n23, 107n25, 107n25–108n26, 108n26, 149, 167n53, 169n71, 226n4
evangelical advocates, Gillen and, 180–182
Evangelicals, 7, 13n22

Evers, Charles, 39, 51n37, 206, 223
Evers, Medgar, 39, 223

Fahy, Thomas G., 107n23, 107n25, 108n26
Fainsod, Merle, 47n4
Fascell, Dante, 112, 162n5, 163n19
Favre, Charles, 107n25, 108n26
Federal Council of Church of Christ, 15–16
Federov, Natasha, 73
Federov, Yuri, 61, 73, 79, 85n26, 119, 122
Fedotov, Ivan Tetrovich, 136n47
Feldman, Egal, 5, 13n16, 26n11, 27n17
feminism, influence of, 24
Fenwick, Millicent, 137n55, 148, 168n63
finances, of Task Force, 55n70, 55n74, 57–59, 83n3–83n10, 84n13–84n15, 139n71–139n72, 206–208, 215n53–215n55, 216n58
Fine, Morris, 132n4
Finkelstein, Louis, 27n18
Fish, Hamilton, 107n24
Fisher, Eugene, 12n11, 26n13, 28n26, 157
Flannery, Edward H., 26n12, 28n26, 49n24, 51n36, 92n116, 137n57
Fletcher, William, 113
Flood, Mary Frances, 184
Foote, Peter, 137n57
Ford, Betty, 30n45
Ford, Gerald, 51n37, 77, 106n9
Fournier, M. Helene, 107n25, 108n26
Foxman, Abraham H., 203
Frank, Ann, 134n23
Frank, Barney, 143n95, 168n62
Freedman, Robert O., 170n82
"freedom of choice," Jews with, 226n12
Friedan, Betty, 29n35
Friedland, Eric, 62
Friendly, Alfred, 123

Galperin, Anatoli, 73
Galperin, Tamara, 73
Garment, Leonard, 50n33
Gaster, Theodore, 44
Gaudium et Spes, 29n37
Gecys, Terese, 179

Geller, David: Brussels II Conference and, 100, 105; Moscow Olympics and, 152; role of, 37, 46, 50n31, 64, 69, 87n57, 108n26, 109n40, 132n6, 137n57; with Soviet dissidents and Christians, 82; Task Force and, 127, 128
Gemal, Rosalind, 166n40
Gephardt, Richard, 172
Gerber, Dan, 108n26
Gerhardt, Bernard, 107n23, 107n25, 108n26
Geyer, Alan, 185
Gibbons, Thomas H., 52n44
Gilbert, Martin, 160
Gilboa, Yehoshua, 75
Gillen, Anne, 30n43, 83n1–83n2, 108n26, 109n37, 109n40, 166n45, 188n5; activism and, 8–9, 10, 208–210; Basket II and, 112; Belgrade Conference and, 146, 146–147, 148; Brussels II Conference and, 97, 99, 99–100, 100, 101, 103, 104, 105, 127; Carmelite convent and, 209; with Consultation, second, 120–121, 124; on Demjanjuk, 198, 200–201, 202, 204; in England, 150; eulogy for, 209–210; with evangelical advocates in US, 180–182; Helsinki Accords and, 114, 117, 133n9; International Women's Conference (1980), 153; Interreligious Legal Task Force on Human Rights and, 154, 154–156; in Ireland, 150; Jackson-Vanik Amendment and, 80, 81; legacy of, 6, 7, 8, 24, 25, 138n64, 219–226; Legal Task Force and, 198; with local interreligious task forces, 66–69; Madrid Conference and, 149; Meir and, 8; obituary for, 55n69; role of, 86n39–86n40, 189n16; Sakharov and, 129; Siberian Seven and, 131; sisters religious and, 21; Solidarity Sundays and, 79, 84n22; Soviet Jewry and, 23–24; in Soviet Union, 25, 72, 73, 151–153, 171, 172; speaking engagements of, 59–64, 85n32, 88n62, 114–117, 133n15–133n16, 134n19–134n20, 135n31, 171–172, 177; with speaking fees, 83n4; Steinbruck on, 226n3; Task Force and, 3, 5, 44–46, 57–64, 125, 129–130, 157, 158, 197, 206, 207, 225, 226n5; with task forces, local, 117–120; *The Task* newsletter and, 75, 76
Ginzburg, Alexander, 142n91
Giroux, Maureen, 188n9
Gittelsohn, Roland, 69
Glaser, Kit, 190n29
Glazar, Richard, 202
GNYCSJ. *See* Greater New York Conference for Soviet Jewry
Godfrey, Arthur, 51n37
Golbert, Howard A., 137n57
Gold, Bertram, 35, 50n32, 82, 83n8, 105, 140n78–140n79, 141n88, 207
Gold, Eugene, 105n5
Goldberg, Arthur, 51n37, 146, 147
Goldstick, David T., 83n3
Goldstick, Maurice (Mrs.), 45
Goode, Wilson, 193n48
Goodman, Andrew, 188n13–188n14
Goodman, Jerry, 25, 66, 67, 70, 105n5, 106n9; Brussels II Conference and, 100; with conferences, local, 125; Madrid Conference and, 149; Task Force and, 129, 157; *The Task* newsletter and, 76
Gorbachev, Mikhail: Reagan and, 10, 180, 205, 215n46, 223, 224, 225; rise of, 190n24, 210n1
Gordon, Ernest, 131, 143n100, 182
Gorman, John, 49n24, 51n36, 137n57
Goshen-Gottstein, Moshe, 44
Graham, Billy, 8, 33, 50n29, 53n50, 126, 137n55, 182, 184, 194n57, 194n65, 195n70
Gralnick, William A., 119, 120, 127, 139n73, 158, 189n18, 216n57; Project Lifeline and, 174; on religion in Soviet Union, 128–129
Graubart, Judah, 12n5, 36, 49n22, 49n24, 49n28, 55n73, 58, 84n19
Grayzel, Solomon, 44
Greater New York Conference for Soviet Jewry (GNYCSJ), 70–71

Greek Orthodox Church, 5, 6, 13n19, 139n73
Greenberg, Irving, 54n56
Greenberg, Maxwell, 65
Grivans, Maksimilians, 142n94
Groner, Oscar, 108n26
Gronouski, John A., 51n37
Grover, Veronica, 158
Grozny, Ivan, 204, 211n17, 211n19
Gruenther, Alfred, 51n37
Gwertzman, Bernard, 40, 50n33

habeas corpus, 9, 154, 166n45, 167n47, 221
Hammer, Armand, 212n21
Hardman, L. H., 108n26
Hargrove, Katherine, 135n32
Harkin, Tom, 143n95
Harman, Abraham, 73
Harris, David, 214n41, 223
Harris, Fred, 51n37
Harris, La Donna, 51n37
Hart, Philip, 51n37
Harter, William H., 157
Hatfield, Mark, 189n20
Hauser, Rita, 39, 133n9, 167n55
hearings, Task Force with, 174–179
Hearst, W. Randolph, Jr., 51n37
Heath, Edward, 106n11
Hebert, Felix, 107n24
Heller, Milt, 53n50
Hellman, Yehuda, 105n5
Helsinki Accords, 106n7, 134n25; AJC and, 112–114; Basket III and, 111–112, 164n23; Bird and, 133n7; Brussels II Conference and, 98, 99, 101; influence of, 5, 8; with panelists and testimony, 133n9
Henold, Mary J., 22, 28n29, 29n35
Hertzberg, Arthur, 101–102, 107n22, 108n27
Hesburgh, Theodore M., 27n17, 27n18, 47n4, 51n37, 137n55
Heschel, Abraham, 16, 18–19, 50n30, 51n37
Hewka, Orsysia, 179
Hiatt, Philip, 25n7
Hill, Kent, 176, 178, 180–181, 181, 182, 187, 189n20, 216n59, 221

Hines, John, 51n37
Hitler, Adolf, 17, 36
Hoenlein, Malcolm, 70, 78
Hofstetter, Adrian Marie, 49n24, 51n36
Hohman, Margaret, 80
Holocaust, 5, 26n11, 27n20, 45, 75, 173, 190n22; Brussels II Conference and, 101, 102; Roman Catholic Church and, 17; Soviet Union and, 77; Wiesel on, 206
Holtzman, Elizabeth, 199–200
Hook, Sidney, 195n70
Horn, Otto, 211n17
Hruby, Blahoslav, 114, 131, 136n52, 143n95
Hubbard, Walter, T., 39, 52n41, 107n23, 107n25, 108n26, 157–158
Huddleston, Walter D., 142n94
Hughes, Harold, 51n37
Human Rights Day, 60, 76, 86n43, 134n22, 135n33, 188n8
Humphrey, Hubert, 100
Huneke, Douglas, 189n20
hunger strikes, 60, 61, 71, 77, 85n29, 195n73
Hunter, David, 106n16, 107n23, 107n25, 108n26, 133n9, 136n51
Huntwork, Patience, 199, 211n12, 212n20, 212n25–213n26
Hyatt, David, 106n16

IAD. *See* Interreligious Affairs Department
Iakovos (Bishop), 33, 41, 51n37
immigration: AJC and, 2; politics of and advocacy for, 1–2; US and, 1
Immigration and Naturalization Service (INS), 199–200
immigration to Israel (*aliya*), 107n21, 151, 165n30, 224
In Our Time. *See Nostra Aetate*
Inouye, Daniel, 51n37
INS. *See* Immigration and Naturalization Service
Institute of Religion and Democracy (IRD), 221, 226n10
Interfaith Appeal of Conscience Foundation, 131

Interfaith Commission, at Brussels II Conference, 101–102
International Sakharov Hearings, 149
International Women's Conference (1980), 153
Interreligious Affairs Department (IAD), 4, 8, 12n6, 46, 49n23; Gillen and, 115; Mittleman and, 171; role of, 8, 125–126; Rudin and, 171
Interreligious Legal Task Force on Human Rights, 154
Intrator, Genya, 188n9
IRD. *See* Institute of Religion and Democracy
Ireland, visits to England and, 150–151
Irish Commission for Justice and Peace, 150
Isaac, Jules, 12n9, 12n11, 17–18
Israeli Liaison Bureau (*Lishkat Hakesher*), 1, 31–32, 105n1, 128, 129, 132n3; role of, 1, 11n1–12n3, 35; Task Force, relations with, 64–65

Jackson, Helen, 189n18, 206
Jackson, Henry, 42, 66, 76, 78, 80, 92n112, 98
Jackson, Mahalia, 51n37
Jackson-Vanik Amendment, 8; support for, 62, 66, 73, 76; Task Force and, 80–82; in *The Task* newsletter, 75; *The Task* newsletter and, 76
Jacobi, D., 168n68
James, Fob, 143n95
Javits, Jacob, 98, 200
JCCs. *See* Jewish Community Centers
Jepsen, Roger, 135n30
Jesus, 3, 11, 13n14, 26n12, 27n20, 27n23
Jesus and Israel (Flannery), 26n12
Jewish Community Centers (JCCs), 7
Jews, 13n13–13n14; with "freedom of choice", 226n12; interfaith endeavour with, 222–225; Roman Catholic Church and, 2–3, 15; in Soviet Union, population, 1
Jews of Eastern Europe and The Jews of the Soviet Union (Schwartz), 47n1
The Jews of Silence (Wiesel), 160
Joel, George, 135n34
John Paul II (Pope), 215n50

John XXIII (Pope), 17, 18, 22, 26n13–26n15
Jones, Elois, 66

Kadar, Janos Petran, 148
Kahane, Meir, 107n19
Kampelman, Max, 149, 163n19, 164n25, 172, 204
Karlikow, Abe: AJC and, 98; Belgrade Conference and, 146; Brussels III Conference and, 159; role of, 86n42, 95n140, 98–99, 100, 106n9, 106n12, 107n21–107n22, 109n34
Katz, Will, 56n76–56n77
Kean, Thomas, 215n48
Keeler, William, 206
Kemp, Jack, 135n30, 152, 205, 215n48
Kennedy, Ethel, 36
Kennedy, John F., 16, 27n18, 134n23
Kennedy, Robert F., 134n23
Kennedy, Ted, 106n11
Kerr, Clark, 51n37
Kevkov, Ilya, 113
Khaled, Laila, 165n39
Khrushchev, Nikita, 1, 31, 40, 47n3
King, Coretta Scott, 36, 37, 38, 206, 215n51
King, Jonathan, 135n34
King, Martin Luther, Jr., 7, 32, 38, 48n13, 134n23, 206, 223; NCCIJ and, 22; on tri-faith nation, 17
Kirkpatrick, Jeanne, 160
Kiselev, Alexander, 142n94
Kissinger, Henry, 50n33, 86n37, 105n2
Klietz, Martin, 137n57, 139n70
Kling, August, 69
Klu Klux Klan, 25n2
Klutznick, Philip, 83n2, 83n8, 136n54
Koch, Ed, 205
Kochan, Lionel, 75
Koch bill, 40
Koehlinger, Amy L., 13n15, 28n30
Kopp, Audrey, 30n44
Korenblit, Mikhail, 135n40
Korey, William, 76, 149
Kovalyov, Sergei, 74
Krasne, Norman, 108n26
Krol, John, 54n64, 68

Kuehner, Ralph, 107n23, 107n25, 108n27
Kuropas, Myron, 49n28
Kuznetsov, Eduard, 47n9, 85n27, 124, 142n91, 147, 162n6

LaCocque, André, 107n23, 108n27; AJC and, 49n21; Belgrade Conference and, 147; Brussels II Conference and, 99; with conferences, local, 124–125; Helsinki Accords and, 114; Jackson-Vanik Amendment and, 80; role of, 36, 38, 40, 46, 49n25, 53n51, 107n18, 111, 137n57; Task Force and, 129, 158, 219
LaFarge John, 22
Lagergren, Nina, 164n27
Landry, Tom, 51n37, 135n40
Laurinayicius, Bronius, 190n25
Law, Bernard, 106n16
Lawrence, Guenter, 51n37
Lawyers Legal Project, NCSJ and, 153–156
Lazaron, Morris S., 16
Lazin, Fred A., 10
Lebanon, 9, 159
Lee, J. Oscar, 25n7
Legal Task Force. *See* National Interreligious Legal Task Force on Human Rights
Lehman, Herbert H., 12n4, 32
Lerner, Alexander, 171, 197, 208
Levanon, Nehemiah, 82, 109n34
Levin, Carl, 143n95
Levin, Dick, 50n30
Levin, Ina, 134n22
Levin, Richard, 49n24, 51n36, 137n57
Levine, Jonathan, 154, 210n5
Levine, Melvin, 65
Levinson, Burt S., 203
Lewis, Flora, 164n26
Lewis, John, 206, 223
Liaison Bureau. *See* Israeli Liaison Bureau
Lincoln, Abraham, 16
Lindner, John, 184, 185, 186
Linnas, Karl, 202
Lipshutz, Robert, 151

Lishkat Hakesher. *See* Israeli Liaison Bureau
Lithuania, 177–178, 192n40, 211n9
Loeffler, James, 13n21, 223
Long, Russell, 81, 94n134
Lookstein, Joseph, 27n18
Lorge, Ernst, 41
Lowell, Stanley, 105n5
Luboshitz, Emil, 73
Lukianenko, Lev, 166n43
Lunts, Alexander (Sasha), 73, 117
Lynch, Kevin, 143n95
Lyons, Jim, 188n10

Maas, Richard, 40, 76, 109n40
Macdonald, Dwight, 47n4
Madrid Conference, 149–150
Makeeva, Valeriya, 149
Makus, Vasyl, 141n83
"male monologue", 24
Manschreck, Clyde, 49n24, 51n36, 137n57
Markish, Irena, 54n56
Marmur, Dan, 108n27
Marshall, Robert J., 88n60
Marshall, Thurgood, 1
Martin, John, 83n8
Martin A. Tananbaum Foundation, 57, 58, 139n71, 206, 225
Martins, Tony, 118
Matos, Hubert, 136n52
Mays, Benjamin E., 26n9
Mays, Willie, 51n37
Meany, George, 77, 106n11
media, 51n37; criticism of US, 134n21; propaganda by, 175; on Task Force in Soviet Union, 184
Meese, Edwin, 202
Meir, Golda, 8, 98, 103, 107n19, 151, 160, 161
Mejía, Jorge, 148
Melady, Thomas P., 133n9, 149, 173
Melech, Steve, 209
Mendelovitch, Yosef, 119, 134n20, 160
Mendelsohn, Walter, 55n72
Mendes-France, Pierre, 106n11
Mescheloff, Moses, 39
Meyer, Albert Cardinal, 16
Meyers, Bert, 154

Mezvinsky, Ed, 151
MFN. *See* Most Favored Nation
Mikado, Ian, 106n11
Mikoyan, Anastas, 31
Milgrom, Ida, 194n56
Miller, Arthur, 12n4
Miller, Gareth, 136n52
Miller, Israel, 159, 168n69
Minda, Albert, 27n18
Mitchell, John, 52n42
Mittleman, Alan, 134n26, 171, 179; Task Force and, 175, 177, 178–179, 197, 198
Modras, Ronal, 28n27
Moeller, Charles, 148
Mohs, Mayo, 51n37
Mondale, Walter, 139n69
Monoghan, Patrick, 158
Moore, Paul, 139n72
Morgenthau, Hans J., 51n37
Moroz, Valentyn, 142n91
Moscow Olympics, 152–153, 165n37
Most Favored Nation (MFN), 8, 42, 54n59, 62, 80
Muffs, Judith Herschlag, 203
Mura, Claude, 108n27
Murphy, Rosalie, 80
Murphy, William, 150
Murzhenko, Aleksi, 79, 119, 159
Muslims, 126, 133n8, 137n56, 138n61, 139n73, 142n90, 162n10, 175
Mydans, Seth, 184

Nardmann, Jean, 108n27
Narrowe, Morton, 108n27
Nashpitz, Marc, 164n27
National Association of Evangelicals (NAE), 34, 193n50–193n51, 214n42
National Catholic Conference on Interracial Justice (NCCIJ), 22–23; role of, 3; Task Force and, 2, 4, 17, 57
National Catholic Education Association (NCEA), 3, 21
National Catholic Welfare Council, 16
National Coalition of American Nuns (NCAN), 24, 30n44–30n45, 55n68, 84n21
National Conference of Catholic Bishops (NCCB), 8, 19, 24
National Conference of Christians and Jews (NCCJ), role of, 16
National Conference of Jewish Charities, 16
National Conference on Religion and Race, 16
National Conference on Soviet Jewry (NCSJ), 5, 42, 132n5, 153–156
National Council of Churches in Christ (NCC), 25n4, 182–186, 226n10
National Interreligious Consultation on Soviet Jewry (Consultation): second, 65–66; Statement of Conscience, 7, 41–42, 53n48, 53n50, 81, 86n37, 92n107, 92n116, 226n9; Task Force and, 39–42
National Interreligious Legal Task Force on Human Rights (NILTFHR, Legal Task Force): with ABA agreement and ASL, 198–199; founding of, 9, 198
National Interreligious Task Force on Human Rights, 145
National Interreligious Task Force on Soviet Jewry (NITFSJ, Task Force): AJC and, 125–128; clash in New York City, 70–71; closing of, 197–198, 225–226; with conferences, local, 124–125; Consultation, second, 65–66, 120–124; Consultation and, 39–42; Demjanjuk and, 199–204; with demonstration, 205–206; finances of, 55n70, 55n74, 57–59, 83n3–83n10, 84n13–84n15, 139n71–139n72, 206–208, 215n53–215n55, 216n58; with focus shift and concern for Christians, 221–222; Gillen and, 3, 5, 44–46, 57–64, 125, 129–130, 197, 206, 207, 208–210, 225, 226n5; hearings, 174–179; in historical context, 3–5, 31–39; with interfaith endeavor, 222–225; Israeli Liaison Bureau, relations with, 64–65; Jackson-Vanik Amendment and, 80–82; Legal Task Force and ABA agreement with ASL, 198–199; at local levels, 66–69; with New York City, possible move to, 71–72; patriarchy and, 25; Pen

Pal program, 61, 63–64, 77, 85n26, 122; with persecuted groups in Soviet Union, 128–132; Philadelphia conference and, 179; programs, 59–64; Project Lifeline and, 174; role of, 133n13, 143n104–143n105; setting up, 43–44; sisters religious and, 21; with Solidarity Sundays, 78–79, 84n22; with Soviet Christians and dissidents, 82; Soviet Union, travel to, 72–75; supporters of, 2, 4, 17; *The Task* newsletter, 75–77; tenth anniversary of, 156–158; trends, 187
National Jewish Community Relations Advisory Council (NJCRAC), 5
Navon, Yitzhak, 160
Nazis, 26n10, 113, 155, 167n52, 190n26, 199–200, 211n17, 213n27, 214n39–214n40
NCAN. *See* National Coalition of American Nuns
NCC. *See* National Council of Churches in Christ
NCCB. *See* National Conference of Catholic Bishops
NCCIJ. *See* National Catholic Conference on Interracial Justice
NCCJ. *See* National Conference of Christians and Jews
NCEA. *See* National Catholic Education Association
NCSJ. *See* National Conference on Soviet Jewry
Netzer, Zvi, 86n42
Neuhaus, John, 186
New York City, Task Force and, 70–72
Niebuhr, Reinhold, 1, 40, 78, 161
Niebuhr, Ursula, 106n16
NILTFHR. *See* National Interreligious Legal Task Force on Human Rights
Nimetz, Matthew, 125, 139n69, 151
NITFSJ. *See* National Interreligious Task Force on Soviet Jewry
Nixon, Richard, 33, 47n11, 52n47, 53n50, 80, 95n138; Consultation and, 39, 40, 42; Israeli Liaison Bureau and, 64; Jackson-Vanik Amendment and, 76, 82

NJCRAC. *See* National Jewish Community Relations Advisory Council
Noffke, Suzanne, 49n24, 51n36, 92n113, 137n57
Nostra Aetate (In Our Time), 26n16, 27n21; drafting of, 17–18; implementation of, 19–20; sisters religious and, 3; Vatican II and, 2–3, 7, 17–18, 19–20
Novak, Michael, 179, 193n48–193n49
Nudel, Ida, 24, 134n23, 205, 226n11; Madrid Conference and, 149; support for, 150–151, 153, 208, 220
Nudelstejer, Sergio, 105n5, 109n40

O'Donnell, John, 76
Ogilvie, Richard, 51n37
Ohio Helsinki Accords Council, 134n25
Olson, Arnold, 53n50
"Operation Redemption" program, 61
"Operation Write On", 61, 85n28
Origins of Anti-Semitism (Flannery), 26n12
Orlev, Yuri, 141n83

Pannitch, Herbert, 108n27
Parker, Virgil J., 107n25, 108n27
"A Passover Seder for Women" (Gillen), 24
patriarchy: "male monologue" of, 24; Task Force and, 25
Paul VI (Pope), 20, 26n14, 27n18–27n19, 47n10, 103, 108n29
Pawlikowski, John, 27n21, 28n27, 49n24, 111, 123, 129, 137n57, 141n89, 157, 210n5, 219
Pax Christi, 150
Pell, Claiborne, 133n14, 148
Pen Pal program, 61, 63–64, 77, 85n26, 122
Perc, Serge, 108n27
Percy, Charles, 51n37, 117, 122–123, 137n55, 138n65
Peres, Shimon, 212n21
Perfectae Caritatis, 29n36
Perlmutter, Phil, 69
Perry, Charles, 183
Peyser, Peter, 107n24

Philadelphia conference, 179
Phillippe, William R., 147, 149
Pierce, Luther, 68, 69
Pike, James A., 12n4, 32
Pimen I (Patriarch), 183
Pioneer Women, 151
Pipes, Richard, 157
Pittell, Elaine, 108n27
Pius XI (Pope), 17, 26n10, 26n11, 29n38
Pius XII (Pope), 3, 17, 21, 22
Plax, Marty, 134n26
politics, of immigration, 1–2
Pratt, Yehoshua, 35
Prestin, Vladimir, 25n8, 134n22
Preston, Andrew, 25n1, 25n8, 28n28, 52n47, 143n95
Pretschener, Elizabeth, 85n25, 89n66, 122
Prinz, Joachim, 108n27
prisoners of conscience, defined, 13n20
programs, Task Force, 59–64
Project Co-Adoption, 61, 174
Project Lifeline, 174
Project Lifeline, 9
propaganda, by media, 175
Protestants, 7; interfaith endeavour with, 222–225; Solidarity Sundays and, 79
Pruitt, Robert T., 66, 99, 104, 107n23, 108n27, 121, 137n55, 137n57
Pugevicius, Casimir, 35, 115, 123–124, 133n17, 136n52, 140n82

Rabinov, Arkady, 73
Rabinov, Lena, 73
race, religion and, 22–23
racism: Klu Klux Klan and, 25n2; religion and, 25; Zionism as, 98, 100, 101, 107n21
Rackman, Emmanuel, 27n18
Radano, John A., 147, 148, 149
Rager, Izo, 65, 87n46
Ramselaar, A. C., 108n27
Randall, Claire, 93n122, 182, 194n58
Randolph, A. Philip, 47n4, 51n37
Rangel, Charles, 79
Ratner, Kissye, 157
Ratner-Byaly, Judith, 157
Ratushinskaya, Irina, 193n52

Reagan, Ronald: Gorbachev and, 10, 180, 205, 215n46, 223, 224, 225; Siberian Seven and, 143n95
refuseniks, 13n20, 61, 63, 73, 75, 152. *See also* specific refuseniks
Regelson, Lev, 133n12
Reich, Jon, 137n57
Reich, Seymour, 108n27
religion, 131; IRD, 222; race and, 22–23; racism and, 25; in Soviet Union, 128–129; tolerance and Vatican II, 22
RESCUE, 136n46
Research Center for Religion and Human Rights in Closed Societies, 131
Reuther, Walter, 12n4, 47n4
Ribicoff, Abraham, 98
Rice, Madeleine, 136n52
Riegner, G. N., 108n27
Rigdon, Bruce, 182, 183, 184, 185, 186, 195n74–195n75
Rigney, James, 79, 90n81
Riquet, Michel, 102, 107n25, 108n27
Roberti, David A., 86n37
Roberts, Oral, 54n56
Robin, Ed, 176–177
Robinson, Jackie, 51n37
Roderick, Keith, 198, 208, 209, 216n63
Roger, Jewan, 108n27
Rohlfs, Ruth, 34
Roman Catholic Church: Hitler and, 17; Holocaust and, 17; interfaith endeavour with, 222–225; Jews and, 2–3, 15; in Soviet Union, 177–178; Vatican II and, 2–3, 5, 7, 17–20; women in, 3, 21–25, 30n46. *See also* sisters religious
Roncalli, Angelo, 26n13
Roosevelt, Eleanor, 1
Roosevelt, Franklin Delano, 25n5
Rosenthal, Edward, 136n48
Ross, John Elliot, 16
Roth, David, 137n57
Rothstein, Raphael, 51n37
Rowland, Joyce, 135n32
Rubin, Ronald, 75
Rudin, James, 107n20, 162n12; Belgrade Conference and, 146; Brussels II Conference and, 99–100,

101, 104, 105, 127; Brussels III Conference and, 159–160; with conferences, local, 125; with Gillen, eulogy for, 209–210; Helsinki Accords and, 112–113; IAD and, 171, 182; on King, M. L., Jr., 48n13; on Lithuania, 211n9; Madrid Conference and, 149; Moscow Olympics and, 152; on NCC, 184, 186; role of, 13n16, 33, 35, 36, 48n18–48n20, 63, 65, 111, 137n57, 205, 226n1; on Shriver, 226n2; Solidarity Sundays and, 79; speaking engagements of, 115; Task Force and, 126, 129, 157, 158, 207, 220, 221; with task forces, local, 118, 120

Ruebner, Ralph, 155, 198, 209, 211n10, 221

Russian Orthodox Church, 138n60, 163n17, 171, 182, 183–184, 194n62, 195n69

Rustin, Bayard, 47n4, 51n37, 107n24, 108n27, 125, 133n9

Rylaarsdam, J. Coert, 51n36, 137n57

Sadunaite, Nijole, 24, 30n47, 85n26, 122, 124, 147, 162n6

The St. Petersburg Evening Independent (newspaper), 174

Sainz-Munox, Fausino, 147

Sakalauskas, Kajatona, 179

Sakharov, Andrei, 8, 63, 74, 86n35, 115, 161, 195n73; *habeas corpus* and, 9, 154, 166n45, 167n47, 221; Israeli Liaison Bureau and, 129; Madrid Conference and, 149; support for, 82, 111, 149, 155, 185, 221; *The Task* newsletter and, 76

Sandberg, Neil, 84n19, 118

Sanua, Marianne R., 20

Schmidt, Stanley A., 68, 99, 107n17, 107n23, 108n27, 137n57, 142n94

Schneier, Arthur, 131

Schonberg, J., 108n27

Schroeter, Leonard, 86n45

Schroth, Raymond A., 29n38

Schultz, George, 224

Schultz, Kevin, 25n8

Schwaat, Rona, 108n27

Schwartz, Solomon, 47n1

SCLC. *See* Southern Christian Leadership Conference

Scott, Hugh, 50n33, 51n37

Second Brussels Conference, 8

secret police, in Soviet Union, 177, 184

Security and Cooperation in Europe (CSCE) conferences, 5

SFC. *See* Sister Formation Conferences

Shambour, Mary Catherine, 184

Shapiro, Murray, 53n50

Sharansky, Anatoly. *See* Sharansky, Natan

Sharansky, Natan, 9, 91n102, 124, 134n23, 142n92, 147, 149, 160, 162n6, 191n37, 197, 199, 201, 202, 205, 206, 214n44, 222

Sharfman, Ray, 188n10

Shcharansky, Anatoly. *See* Sharansky, Natan

Shcharansky, Avital, 164n27

SHCJ. *See* The Society of the Holy Child Jesus

Sheen, Fulton J., 41, 52n47

Sheheglov, Vadim, 179

Shelby, Richard, 143n95

Shelkov, Vladimir, 141n83

Shepshalovich, Misha, 87n50

Sheridan, George, 136n52

Sherman, Jonathan, 106n16

Shestack, Jerome, 150, 164n24

Shkolnik, Feiga, 164n27

Shoop, Simon, 135n34

Shriver, Sargent, Jr., 16, 30n42, 38, 50n29, 54n53, 84n15, 134n29, 142n90; NITFSJ and, 17; role of, 7, 37, 50n31, 51n38, 137n57, 163n20; Rudin on, 226n2; Soviet Jewry and, 23; Task Force and, 65, 158, 219; *The Task* newsletter and, 76

Siberian Seven, 130, 143n95, 145, 154, 189n20, 221

Siconolfi, Constantin V., 135n34

Silver, Bert, 142n94

Silvestrini, Achille, 148

Simms, Adam, 116, 129, 163n20, 212n23, 216n60

Simon, Mary, 55n66

Simpson, David E., 158
Singer, Lynn, 157
Sister Formation Conferences (SFC), 21, 22
Sisters of Sion, 91n96, 188n12
sisters religious: civil rights movement and, 22; evolution of, 21–25; *Nostra Aetate* and, 3; with religion and race, 22–23; role of, 3, 6, 7
Sittler, Joseph, 49n24, 51n36, 137n57
Six Day War (1967), 20, 45
Skuodis, Vytautas, 136n47, 142n94
SLA. *See* Soviet Lawyers Association
Slepak, Maria, 24, 30n47, 73, 85n26
Slepak, Vladimir, 30n47, 77, 85n26, 132n1, 197
Smith, Charles Z., 147, 149
Smukler, Connie, 215n46, 226
Snyder, Rachel, 223
Social Gospel Movement, 15–16
Social Security, 83n5–83n6
The Society of the Holy Child Jesus (SHCJ), 3, 11
Solidarity Sundays, 78–79, 84n22
Soloveitchik, Joseph B., 27n18
Soper, Donald, 107n25, 108n27
Southern Christian Leadership Conference (SCLC), 32
Soviet Cage (Korey), 76
Soviet Lawyers Association (SLA), 9
Soviet Union, 108n30–108n31; with Christians and dissidents, 82; Drinan in, 74–75; Gillen in, 25, 72, 73, 151–153, 171, 172; Holocaust and, 77; MFN and, 8; NCC and, 182–186; persecuted groups in, 128–132; population of Jews in, 1; religion in, 128–129; Roman Catholic Church in, 177–178; secret police in, 177, 184; Task Force and travel to, 72–75
Spellman, Francis, 13n16
Spertus Institute, 11
Sprayregen, Joel J., 136n54
SSSJ. *See* Student Struggle for Soviet Jewry
Stacevich, Olga, 176
Stagg, Paul, 107n23, 108n27, 136n51, 137n57

Stalin, Joseph, 1, 40
Starr, Joyce, 151
Statement of Conscience, 7, 53n48, 92n107, 226n9; Nixon and, 53n50; purpose of, 41–42; support for, 81, 86n37, 92n116. *See also* National Interreligious Consultation on Soviet Jewry
Steif, William, 104
Steinbruck, John, 32, 59, 76, 88n59, 107n23, 108n27, 137n57; Brussels II Conference and, 99, 104; on Gillen, 226n3; with local interreligious task forces, 66; Madrid Conference and, 149; Task Force and, 158, 219
Stephanopoulos, Robert G., 38, 50n34, 55n75, 92n108
Stevenson, Adlai, 51n37
Stevenson Packwood bill, 91n103
strip searched, 25, 152
Strober, Gerald, 51n36, 53n51, 54n55, 83n8, 90n89; AJC and, 49n27; IAD and, 49n23; role of, 12n7, 36, 37, 38, 47n8, 49n24, 50n31–50n33, 58, 67, 81, 84n11, 226n1; Task Force and, 58–59
Strokata-Karavansky, Nina, 179
The Struggle for Soviet Jewry in American Politics (Lazin), 10
Student Struggle for Soviet Jewry (SSSJ), 43
Sullivan, Ed, 51n37
Summerscales, Peter, 147
Susskind, David, 105n5
Sussman, Eileen, 135n37
Sutton, Percy, 79, 108n27
Sweeney, John, 215n47
Swidler, Leonard, 28n27
Swings, Maria, 108n27

Tanenbaum, Marc, 107n20; with Consultation, second, 120; Consultation and, 38, 41, 42; *Gaudium et Spes* and, 29n37; Helsinki Accords and, 114, 133n9; Israeli Liaison Bureau and, 64, 65; Jackson-Vanik Amendment and, 80; role of, 20, 33, 35, 36, 45–46, 51n39, 70, 111, 137n57; Solidarity Sundays and, 78, 79; with Soviet dissidents

and Christians, 82; Task Force and, 58, 71, 72, 158, 221
Task Force. *See* National Interreligious Task Force on Soviet Jewry
The Task newsletter, 75–77
Taylor, Telford, 166n41
Tcherenko, Constantine, 192n39
The Teaching of Contempt (Flannery), 26n12
Texas Jewish Post (newspaper), 136n42
Thatcher, Margaret, 160
"theology of contempt", 12n10
Thering, Rose, 136n51, 137n57
Third Brussels Conference, 9
Thomas, Norman, 12n4, 32
Thompson, Llewellyn, 50n33
Thorne, Ludmilla, 185
Toaff, Elio, 107n22
torture, 92n113, 132n1, 176, 177
Townsend, Dorothy, 63
Trans-Sister newsletter (NCAN), 30n44–30n45
Traxler, Margaret Ellen, 95n135, 107n23, 108n27, 168n60; Brussels II Conference and, 99, 102; civil rights movement and, 223; with Consultation, second, 121; Consultation and, 41, 42; DES and, 23, 30n41; Helsinki Accords and, 114; International Women's Conference (1980), 153; Jackson-Vanik Amendment and, 80, 80–81; NCAN and, 24, 30n44; NCCIJ and, 3; role of, 2, 6, 11, 12n5, 29n39, 36, 51n37, 62, 63, 136n53, 137n57, 141n89; sisters religious and, 23–24; Task Force and, 71, 129, 219
Treblinka, 9
trends, Task Force and, 187
tri-faith nation, 7, 15, 16, 17
Trulson, Tom, 189n18
Tschoepe (Bishop), 118
Tsongas, Paul, 135n30
Turkow, Marc, 105n5
Turner, Charlotte, 108n27

UCSJ. *See* Union of Councils for Soviet Jewry
Ukraine, 13n21, 177
Ukrainian Catholic Church, 171
Ukrainian Evangelical Reformed Church, 133n11
Ukrainian Lutheran Church, 133n11
Unger, Leopold, 162n4
Union of Councils for Soviet Jewry (UCSJ), 5, 115
United States (US): criticism of media in, 134n21; deportation from, 155, 200, 204, 212n25, 213n27–213n28, 222; Gillen with evangelical advocates in, 180–182; immigration and influence of, 1
updating of the church (*aggiornamento*), 12n8, 18, 22, 29n32, 30n40
Urban, R., 108n27
US. *See* United States

Vance, Cyrus, 151
VanderWerf, Nathan H., 140n75
Vanik, Charles, 66, 76. *See also* Jackson-Vanik Amendment
Varnovitsky, 73
Vatican II: in historical context, 17–20; influence of, 2–3, 5, 7; *Nostra Aetate* and, 2–3, 7, 17–18, 19–20; religious tolerance and, 22
Veil, Simone, 160
Veinbergs, A., 113
Vergis, Emanuel, 41
Vins, Georgi, 61, 85n30, 124–125, 131, 135n40, 142n91, 143n101, 147, 162n6, 190n27
Vins, Natasha, 177
Voice of America (VOA), 52n45, 122, 138n65
Voinovich, George V., 116

Waldheim, Kurt, 42
Wallenberg, Raoul, 150, 164n27, 209
Ware, Ann Patrick, 137n57
Warren, Robert Penn, 12n4, 47n4
Washington Post (newspaper), 195n75, 196n77
Watson, Tommy, 168n59
WCC. *See* World Council of Churches
Wedel, Cynthia C., 41, 47n10, 52n47, 106n16, 121, 137n55
Weigel, George, Jr., 172

Weiler, William, 106n16, 107n25, 108n27, 137n57
White, Robert, 185
White, Theodor, 51n37
Whited, Charles, 136n45
Wiesel, Elie, 50n30, 100, 160, 205, 206
Wiesenthal, Simon, 149
Wildenthal, John, 66, 80
Wilkins, Roy, 51n37
Willebrand, Johannes, 20
Williamson, Cecil, 143n95
Wilson, M. L., 53n50, 78
Wilson, Pete, 181
Wilson, W. L., 41, 52n47
Winter, Elmer, 50n30, 51n37, 109n40, 137n57
Wiseman, Thomas, 214n38
Wishner, Maynard I., 126
Wistrich, Robert, 26n11
Wolf, Alfred, 140n76
Wolf, Frank, 181
Wolf, William, 202
women: in civil rights movement, 22, 223; Conference of Major Superiors of Women, 29n32, 29n34; feminism and, 24; International Women's Conference (1980), 153; *Pioneer Women*, 151; in Roman Catholic Church, 3, 21–25, 30n46. *See also* sisters religious
Working for Peace, 150
World Council of Churches (WCC), 8, 26n9
World Union of Jewish Students, 31
Wortman, David, 179

Yakunin, Gleb, 133n12
Yankelevich, Tatyana, 141n86
Yarim-Agaev, Yuri, 175–176
Yarmon, Mort, 42, 50n33
Yaroslavsky, Zev, 63
Yates, Sidney, 158
Ylius, Antana, 177
Young, Andrew, 32, 72

Zackian, Myrtle, 108n27
Zalmanson, Sylva, 47n9, 60, 61, 71, 77, 84n23, 122, 142n91
Zand, Mikhail, 37, 49n24
Zimmerman, Warren, 150, 154
Zinchenko, Vera, 195n75
Zionism, as racism, 98, 100, 101, 107n21

About the Author

Fred A. Lazin is professor emeritus at Ben Gurion University of the Negev in Israel and a resident of New York City. He earned an MA and PhD in political science from the University of Chicago. He has taught at American University, New York University, the University of California, Los Angeles (UCLA), George Washington University, Cornell, Tufts, and the City University of New York (John Jay College and Hunter College). Dr. Lazin has been a visiting scholar at universities in France, Australia, China, Croatia, Sweden, Canada, and the Czech Republic. He has authored more than eighty scholarly articles and chapters in books. He has written and edited eleven books dealing with comparative public policy, Israeli politics and society, and Jews in American politics. Prof. Lazin's pioneering research on the response of American Jewish organizations to German Jewish refugees in the 1930s opened a new field in Holocaust Studies. His previous work on Soviet Jewry, *The Struggle for Soviet Jewry in American Politics: Israel versus the American Jewish Establishment*, was published by Lexington Books (2005). In 2014, The Commercial Press in Beijing, China published a Chinese language edition of the book.

www.ingramcontent.com/pod-product-compliance
Lightning Source LLC
Chambersburg PA
CBHW032035300426
44117CB00009B/1072